The Book of Steps
THE SYRIAC *LIBER GRADUUM*

Translated,
with an Introduction
and Notes by

ROBERT A. KITCHEN
and
MARTIEN F. G. PARMENTIER

❖

cistercian publications
KALAMAZOO, MICHIGAN

Cistercian Publications
Editorial Offices and Customer Service
Institute of Cistercian Studies
Western Michigan University
Kalamazoo, MI 49008

British and European Customer Service
Alban Books Ltd
14 Belford Road
Edinburgh EH4 3BL [UK]

http://www.spencerabbey.org/cistpub/

The work of
cistercian publications
is made possible in part
by support from
WESTERN MICHIGAN UNIVERSITY
to The Institute of Cistercian Studies

ISBN 0-87907-696-8 (pb)

Cover design by Elizabeth King

Typography by Gale Akins at
Humble Hills Press, Kalamazoo, Michigan

Text type is *FF Scala* by Martin Majoor of The Netherlands,
issued by FontShop International, Berlin, Germany, 1999
with supplemental accents from *UBS Graeca*
from Linguist's Software, Edmonds, WA
at www.linguistsoftware.com
Display type is *Delphin 1* by Georg Trump, 1953, for C. E. Weber, Stuttgart

PRINTED IN THE UNITED STATES OF AMERICA

CISTERCIAN STUDIES SERIES: NUMBER ONE HUNDRED NINETY-SIX

The Book of Steps:
THE SYRIAC *LIBER GRADUUM*

❈

Table of Contents

v

Preface

In a variety of ways the syriac work entitled *Liber Graduum* by modern scholars is an anomaly. Intentionally anonymous and lacking in concrete details of historical and cultural setting—and saddled for many years with the aspersions of the messalian heresy—this long collection of thirty *mēmrē*, or discourses/sermons, has been long recognized as an important, yet understudied, work of the fourth-century Syriac Church. Since few people could give more than a summary outline of the work, its place in the history of the syriac church has remained enigmatic.

While the original manuscripts do not provide a proper title, a consensus on an appropriate name has existed for over a century. William Wright, in his 1871 *Catalogue of Syriac Manuscripts in the British Museum*, referred to the work in several manuscripts as the 'Book of Steps'.[1] When Michael Kmosko edited the text for the series *Patrologia Syriaca* in 1926,[2] he utilized a syriac title '*ktaba dmasqata*' and rendered the latin translation '*Liber Graduum*', by which it has become generally known.

Modern scholars have translated the syriac term with various shades—'Book of Grades/Degrees/Ascents'—and then back to 'The Book of Steps'. The key word '*masqātā*'—from the root '*s-l-q*': to rise up, ascend—is found in only two *mēmrē*: Nineteen ('On the Discernment of the Way of Perfection') and Twenty ('On the Difficult Steps that are on the Road of the City of our Lord'), referring to the succeeding levels that a Christian attains on the climb toward the heavenly city of the kingdom.

1. *Catalogue of the Syriac Manuscripts in the British Museum* Part II, by W. Wright (London, 1871) 989.
2. M. Kmosko, ed., *Liber Graduum, Patrologia Syriaca* 3 (Paris, 1926); henceforth, *LG*.

Systematic theology the *Liber Graduum* is not. Syriac writers do not follow the western pattern of cumulatively building an argument toward a conclusion. Instead, the conclusion is typically stated very early and then returned to frequently with embellishments and nuances. The author of the *Liber Graduum* describes the steps of Uprightness and Perfection in a loosely systematic fashion in the first nine *Mēmrē*, but then meanders through a variety of other themes, regularly returning to the issues of the Upright and Perfect.

Many have noted that this description of the spiritual life of these two steps provides the primary theme of the *Liber Graduum*. Yet, as will be demonstrated, this collection of thirty *mēmrē* is not a pure 'rule'. The pastoral concerns of the anonymous author, who has seen the once proud standards of Uprightness and Perfection gradually erode and now desires to revive the integrity of the tradition, provides the guiding motif. Persistently, the reader is enabled to listen in on the author's observations and groaning about the conflict and difficulties of the christian community under his care.

Is the *Liber Graduum* 'the key to early Syriac Christianity'? The *Liber Graduum* does not provide us with comprehensive solutions, but it does permit us to look in on the life of a faith community in the mid-to-late fourth-century Syriac Church, which does not exhibit the hyperbolic tendencies to asceticism usually associated with the Syriac Church. The *Liber Graduum* is for us a 'living document', recording the ups and downs of a real community, not merely a theoretical description of an idealized society.

For over twenty years I have read and lived with the *Liber Graduum*, and even now I am just beginning to know the author and his magnificent work. I am certain that I will spend the rest of my life poring over its many nooks and crannies and finding many treats for the mind and spirit.

Its length alone guarantees this seemingly infinite resource, but it is primarily the creativity and deep spirituality of this anonymous author that provides so much pleasure and insight to the reader.

I first read the *Liber Graduum* at the suggestion of Fr Alexander DiLella OFM at the Catholic University of America, Washington, DC; eventually I wrote an MA dissertation on Philoxenus of Mabbug and the *Liber Graduum*, assigning the *Liber Graduum* secondary importance in my mind. That did not last for long as I kept going back to the book for conference papers and, frankly, for inspiration.

The idea of translating the *Liber Graduum* into English came from a suggestion by Peter Brown, the scholar of Late Antiquity. But by then I was a local parish minister and the fulfillment of that idea seemed out of reach. Then, in September 1984, I met Dr Martien Parmentier at the IV Symposium Syriacum in Oosterhesselen, The Netherlands, where I gave a paper on the *Liber Graduum*. Dr Parmentier had begun an english translation a few years earlier and had recently published the Preface and first six *mēmrē*. He introduced me to Dr Sebastian P. Brock of the Oriental Institute, Oxford, his doctoral advisor, who agreed to continue supervising our work. Together we planned to divide up the remaining *mēmrē*.

Things moved slowly for both of us. Other academic projects and the continuing duties of pastoral ministry kept us both from making rapid progress. Eventually, Dr Parmentier gave me the green light to finish the project and slowly I was able to pick up speed. Accepted to read for the D. Phil. at Oxford under Sebastian Brock, I did not take long to revise my initial drafts and complete the assignments. Dr Brock's generosity of spirit and acuity of mind mark all that has been done by both Martien Parmentier and myself, but certainly any mistakes or errors of judgment belong on my side of the ledger.

I must offer gratitude to all who have led and accompanied me on my pilgrimage in Syriac: Dr Victor Gold

of Pacific Lutheran Seminary, Berkeley; Dr Ariel A. Bloch
of the University of California at Berkeley; Fr Michael
Guinan of Franciscan School of Theology, Berkeley; Fr
Alexander DiLella, Msgr Patrick Skehan, Fr Sidney H.
Griffith of Catholic University of America; and Dr Sebastian
P. Brock of Oxford. Hieromonk Alexander Golitzin of
Marquette University, Milwaukee, and Dr Jeffrey Childers
of Abilene Christian University have read the translation
and contributed important suggestions.

My wife, Molly, knows almost as much as I about
the *Liber Graduum* from her patient listening, reading, and
suggestions throughout the years. Our children, Winifred
and Sidney, have absorbed the same through osmosis, and
while they may not want to do so, I hope someday that they
will be able to quote long sections by heart.

Martien Parmentier has translated the Preface,
Mēmrē 1-6 and 28, while I have translated the rest and
prepared the introduction.

There are innumerable translation decisions in a
work this size and inevitably better suggestions will be made
by others and—on reflection—by me. There are two that I
want to mention briefly here.

I have simply transliterated the title *'mēmrā'* for each
of the literary sections since 'sermon', 'homily', and 'discourse'
all have their shortcomings. The syriac genre of *'mēmrā'* is
widely used and does not neatly fit any one western literary genre. Ephrem's poetic hymns have the title, as
do Jacob of Serug's long biblical poems. The *Liber Graduum's*
material ranges from biblical exegesis, exposition of the two
steps, several exhortatory sermons, and a section previously
mistaken for and strongly reminiscent of the work of Evagrius
Ponticus—all are *mēmrā*. To try to squeeze these thirty sections into the straitjacket of sermons or homilies did not seem
appropriate, so why not call them what they are and enable
readers in some small way to recognize and appreciate this
syriac contribution to literary form.

The other decision was to use 'the Upright' and

'Uprightness' instead of 'the Just' and 'Justice' for the syriac terms *'kēnē'* and *'kēnūtā'*. The traditional terms 'Just/Justice' have so many problems in english usage that an alternative has long seemed necessary. Some have used 'the righteous/righteousness' and, while these often seemed appropriate, confusion with the syriac terms *'zadīqē/zadīqūtā'* rendered this unsatisfactory over the long haul. Dr Brock made the suggestion of 'Upright/Uprightness' and it made immediate sense to me. Again, I realize that others will make equally compelling suggestions.

In the numerical references in the translation and introduction I am following the edition of Michael Kmosko, including the enumeration of the *mēmrē* and the division of sections within the individual *mēmrē*. The numbers in parentheses in the translation refer to the column numbers of Kmosko's syriac text for those who wish to consult the original (Kmosko included a latin translation in the facing columns, accounting for the missing column numbers). Likewise, the references in the introduction are to the column and line numbers of the syriac text.

Introduction

THE SPIRIT *of* SYRIAC CHRISTIANITY

Few western Christians are aware that there was and is a great tradition situated just to the east of the centers of Latin and Greek Christianity. The Syriac Church, literature, and tradition are worthy counterparts to its western contemporaries, but for most readers a little introduction is necessary.[1]

Even the name of the language is geographically confusing for moderns. Arguably the most historically significant of the aramaic dialects, Syriac was spoken over wide areas of both the Roman and Persian Empires. Its center, however, was not in modern-day Syria, but in Edessa (*'Urhāy*) now Urfa in southeastern Turkey. In fact, it was the edessene dialect that was gradually adopted as the stan-

---

1. There are a number of excellent short introductions to Syriac Christianity emphasizing different aspects. Sebastian P. Brock, 'Early Syrian Asceticism,' *Numen* 20 (1973) 1-19; idem., 'Oriental Christianity' in S. P. Brock, *The Syriac Fathers on Prayer and the Spiritual Life*, Cistercian Studies 101 (Kalamazoo, MI: Cistercian Publications, 1986) x-xli; Robert Murray, 'The Features of the Earliest Christian Asceticism' in *Christian Spirituality: Essays in Honor of Gordon Rupp*, ed. Peter Brooks (London: SCM Press, 1975) 65-77; idem., 'The Characteristics of the Earliest Syriac Christianity' in *East of Byzantium: Syria and Armenia in the Formative Period*, ed. Nina G. Garsoian, Thomas. F. Mathews, Robert W. Thomson (Washington, DC: Dumbarton Oaks, 1982) 3-16; Roberta C. Bondi, 'The Spirituality of Syriac-speaking Christians,' *Christian Spirituality I* (New York, 1986) 152-161; O. C. Edwards, Jr, 'Extreme Asceticism in Early Syriac Christianity' in *Worship Points the Way: A Celebration of the Life & Work of Massey Hamilton Shepherd, Jr.*, ed. Malcolm C. Burson (New York: The Seabury Press, 1981) 200-213; Susan Ashbrook, 'Creation and Asceticism: Syriac Christian Thought' in *Christian Thought: A Brief History*, ed. Adrain Hastings, Alistair Mason, and Hugh Pyper (Oxford: Oxford University Press, 2002) 33-37.

dard form of the language from the Levant to Iraq and
Iran and south to Qatar.

The origin and early development of syriac Christianity are shrouded in obscurity, for syriac literature did not really blossom until the fourth century. There are several early works of note: the second century *Odes of Solomon*[2] and Bardaisan's *The Book of the Law of the Countries*.[3]

Nevertheless, the literature and the distinctive spirituality of the Syriac Church begin in this obscure period with the translation of the Bible into the language. The *Peshitta*, or 'simple version/Vulgate', exerted a formative influence on virtually all syriac writers and is considered one of the most important early witnesses to the text of the greek New Testament.

Yet, even more influential in the earliest era of syriac culture, which includes the period of the writing of the *Liber Graduum*, is the *Diatessaron* of Tatian, composed in the last quarter of the second century. The original language of this harmony of the Gospels, whose complete text has been lost, is now thought to have been Syriac with a translation into Greek following not far behind. Tatian's strong leanings to an encratic or severely ascetical interpretation of the christian life colored what he retained and omitted from the canonical Gospels. The *Diatessaron* became the Bible for the infant Syriac Church until the first third of the fifth century.[4] Ephrem, the greatest syriac spiritual writer and biblical exegete alive in the mid-fourth century, wrote a commentary on the *Diatessaron* that has survived in an armenian translation and in an only recently

2. *The Odes of Solomon*, translated & edited James H. Charlesworth (Oxford, 1978).
3. Cf. H. J. W. Drijvers, *Bardaisan of Edessa* (Assen, 1966).
4. Cf. William L. Petersen, *Tatian's Diatessaron: Its Creation, Dissemination, Significance, and History in Scholarship* (Leiden: E.J. Brill, 1994) 35-83.

discovered partial syriac original.[5]

When the syriac writer wrote, his words were those of the Bible and, at least in the third-fifth centuries, those biblical words possessed an undeniable flavor of asceticism—the rigorous discipline of the body for the sake of one's soul. Aphrahat, Ephrem, the author of the *Liber Graduum*, John the Solitary, and Philoxenus of Mabbug, all weave Scripture seamlessly into their poetry and discourses on the spiritual life. The characters of the Old and New Testament were considered part of the contemporary christian playing field.[6] Syriac spirituality was relatively untouched by greek philosophical ideas in its early period, the latter certainly not providing the basis of syriac theological language.

From its beginning, therefore, Syriac Christianity was an ascetically-motivated faith and it is in this mode that it is most frequently perceived and remembered. Marcionitism, Manichaeism, and other dualistic sects which emphasized radical separation between body and spirit were active in early syriac christianity. Encratism rejected marriage and sexuality, eating meat and drinking wine, and owning property. It also advocated homelessness and the renunciation of stability. This is clearly evident in the *Acts of Judas Thomas*,[7] the Apostle to India. The *Odes of Solomon* and the *Pseudo-Clementines* (originally Greek but extant only in syriac translation) also speak of the prevalent institutions of virginity (*btūlūtā*) and holiness (*qaddīšūtā*), the latter being the euphemism for sexual continence after marriage. Prior to the fourth century, celibacy was a requirement·for

5. *Commentaire de l'Évangile Concordant: Texte syriaque (Chester Beatty Manuscrit 709a)*, ed. and trans. Louis Leloir, Chester Beatty Monographs 8 (Dublin, 1963); idem., *Folios Additionnels (Chester Beatty Manuscrit 709b)* (1990).
6. Cf. Elizabeth A. Clark, 'Reading Asceticism: Exegetical Strategies in the Early Christian Rhetoric of Renunciaton,' *Biblical Interpretation* 5 (1997) 82-105.
7. A. F. G. Klijn, *The Acts of Thomas*, Supplements to Novum Testamentum 5 (Leiden: E.J. Brill, 1962).

baptism in the Syriac Church.[8] Such an extreme requirement had passed out of favor and practice by the time of
Ephrem and Aphrahat—both of whom cautiously praised
marriage—in the first part of the fourth century. Yet, the
ideal of celibacy as a necessary step on the road to perfection for the elite among the spiritual pilgrims continued as
a fundamental tenet of syriac spirituality.

'Holiness' or celibacy was aimed at allowing the
Christian to replicate the life of the angels, as was implied
by Jesus in Luke 20:35-36. ' . . . but those who are considered worthy of a place in that age and in the resurrection
from the dead neither marry nor are given in marriage.
Indeed they cannot die any more, because they are like
angels and are children of God, being children of the resurrection' (NRSV translation). For Ephrem and the author
of the *Liber Graduum*, the quest for the angelic life is found
in a kind of reverse eschaton: the recovery of the life in
Eden 'while Adam had not yet sinned'. In a number of
works, including the *Acts of Judas Thomas*, we find the
theme of the Christian as a 'stranger' or 'foreigner', a person who does not belong to this corruptible world.[9]

By the early fourth century, these ideals were insti-
tutionalized in a group called the Sons/Daughters of the
Covenant (*bnay/bnāt qyāmā*), most fully described by
Aphrahat in his Sixth Demonstration.[10] These initially celibate ascetics lived alone or with one another or their parents in or near a village. Monasticism, in the commonly
understood sense of a group of ascetics living spiritually
and geographically apart from the rest of society under the
direction of a spiritual father, would not appear until the
end of the fourth century. As monasticism began to estab-

8. Arthur Vööbus, *Celibacy: A Requirement for Admission to Baptism in the
Early Syrian Church*, Papers of the Estonian Theological Society in Exile 1
(Stockholm, 1951).
9. S. P. Brock, 'Early Syrian Asceticism,' 8-9.
10. Aphrahat, *Demonstrationes*, ed. I. Parisot, *Patrologia Syriaca* 1/2 (Paris,
1894, 1907) Demonstration 6: 'On the Bnay Qyama', columns 239-312.

lish itself, the *bnay/bnāt qyāmā* remained within the communities and increasingly assumed the role of diaconal ministers to the physical needs of their contemporaries, relinquishing their contemplative role to the monastics.

Those who committed themselves to the pilgrimage toward perfection were given a general title whose ambiguous meaning has engendered considerable debate and speculation. They were the *īḥīdaye*, 'the solitary ones'. The term in the singular is also the syriac translation for '[Christ,] "the only-begotten one"' (*monogenēs*—see John 1:18. Therefore, the *īḥīdaye* are those who have a special relationship to Christ the only Son of God.[11]

It is the solitary, individualistic character of the famous syriac saints that indelibly marks the spirituality of the Syriac Church in the memory of the wider church. Nowhere is this seen with more startling clarity than in the *Historia Religiosa* (or *History of the Monks in Syria*) of Theodoret of Cyrrhus.[12] Writing in Greek, Theodoret relates the biographies of a number of syrian holy men whose ascetical feats tend toward eccentricity. The syrian ascetics renounce all aspects of civilized life— fire, clothing, dwellings—as well as devise their own mortifications by chaining themselves to rocks and heavy weights, immuring themselves in caves or cells.

The exemplar of syriac ascetics is one of Theodoret's subjects, Simeon Stylites, who lived nearly forty years atop a pillar.[13] Not only did he practice a very athletic form of asceticism—spectators who counted the number of full-length prostrations he performed during his prayers

11. R. Murray, 'The Characteristics of the Earliest Syriac Christianity,' 8. Sidney H. Griffith, 'Singles in God's Service: Thoughts on the *īḥīdaye*, in the Works of Aphrahat and Ephraem the Syrian,' *The Harp* 4 (1991) 145-159.
12. *Theodoret of Cyrrhus: A History of the Monks in Syria*, translated R. M. Price, Cistercian Studies 88 (Kalamazoo, MI: Cistercian Publications, 1985).
13. *The Lives of Simeon Stylites*, trans. and ed. Robert Doran, Cistercian Studies 112 (Kalamazoo, MI: Cistercian Publications, 1990).

testified to well into the hundreds—but he was able to exert considerable influence by means of the counseling and mediation he doled out to the supplicants at the base of his pillar.

Not all of syriac spirituality was so extreme, and as we shall see, the *Liber Graduum* portrays a prime example of a community that summoned Christians to a higher way, but still viewed this life, body, and Church as part of God's world.

Syriac spirituality is marked by profoundly symbolic vision through which its writers perceive the natural world as windows onto the mysteries of God. The language of Aphrahat, Ephrem, the *Liber Graduum*, Philoxenus of Mabbug, Jacob of Serug, and many others abounds in vivid images and typologies, largely biblical.[14] An example is the symbol of the Tree of Life, which is found in both Aphrahat and Ephrem and is the theme of *Mēmrā* Twenty-One in the *Liber Graduum*.

A singular feature of syriac spirituality in the context of the early Church lies in its frequent use of feminine imagery for God. *The Odes of Solomon*, for instance, speaks of the milk of the breasts of the Father.[15] Mary has a particularly high profile in a number of authors.[16]

To mention the *Liber Graduum* to an earlier genera-

14. See Robert Murray, *Symbols of Church and Kingdom: A Study in Early Syriac Tradition* (Cambridge, 1975) for a masterful treatment of the range of these literary symbols and metaphors.

15. *The Odes of Solomon*, ed. J. H. Charlesworth, 8:14; 14:2; 19:1-4. 'The Holy Spirit opened Her bosom, and mixed the milk of the two breasts of the Father' (19:4).

16. Sebastian P. Brock, 'Mary and the Eucharist: An Oriental Perspective,' *Sobornost* 1/2 (1980) 50-59; Robert Murray, 'Mary, the Second Eve in the Early syriac Fathers,' *Eastern Churches Review* 3/3 (1971) 371-384. Other studies and collections of texts dealing with the function of women in syriac literature include: Sebastian P. Brock and Susan Ashbrook Harvey, *Holy Women of the Syrian Orient* (Berkeley: University of California Press, 1987); Susan Ashbrook Harvey, 'Sacred Bonding: Mothers and Daughters in Early Syriac Hagiography,' *Journal of Early Christian Studies* 4 (1996) 27-56.

tion of scholars is to conjure up its alleged role in one of
the on-going controversies of the late-fourth to early-fifth
centuries—the messalian controversy.[17]
The Messalians emerge dimly out of the reports
and condemnations of fourth- and fifth-century synods and
councils. Their name is Syriac, meaning 'those who pray'
(*mṣallyānē*), leading scholars to assume a mesopotamian
origin. Yet, while Nilus of Ancyra identified Adelphius of
Mesopotamia and Alexander the Sleepless as messalian
leaders,[18] there are no self-proclaimed documents that give
any direct evidence of historically verifiable personalities
or factions within this movement. Columba Stewart points
out that one can speak historically only in terms of the
messalian controversy, not the messalian movement.[19]
This historical vagueness is easier to understand
once one has read the nebulous surviving descriptions of
their doctrines and practices. The basic concept was that all
one has to do to reach perfection and salvation is to pray
unceasingly—indeed to pray is the only effective thing one
can do to reach the goal. Fasting is forsworn. The Church
and its sacraments are considered useless in both the long
and the short run. Such views did not endear Messalians
to the ecclesiastical authorities; it was not their theology
however, but the manner in which they thumbed their
noses at the conventions of society and the Church that
elicited their condemnation.
Since their goal was unceasing prayer, some groups

17. The best treatment of the whole subject is Columba Stewart, osb,
'*Working the Earth of the Heart': The Messalian Controversy in History, Texts,
and Language to AD 431* (Oxford: Clarendon Press, 1991). Other earlier
studies include: Jean Gribomont, 'Le Dossier des origines du
Messalianisme,' in *Epektasis: Mélanges J. Danielou*, ed. J. Fontaine and C.
Kannengiesser (Paris, 1972) 611-625; R. Staats, 'Beobachtungen zur
Definition und zur Chronologie des Messalianismus,' *Jahrbuch der
österreichischen Byzantinistik* 32.4 (1982) 235-244.
18. Stewart, *Working the Earth*, 45-46.
19. Stewart, *Working the Earth*, 5.

determined that dreams were a form of prayer. One can only dream while asleep, so excessive sleep was considered a spiritual discipline and this 'discipline' was conducted anywhere at any time, even in the open streets of Antioch. Still, other conduct garnered comment. As the messalian bands included both men and women, outsiders assumed controls on sexual behavior had been shamelessly relaxed. They abjured possessions, undertook no responsibilities and no means of livelihood, and so survived by begging. Work, after all, would be inimical to the spiritual quest. Moreover, when questions were put to them, their answers seldom made any sense or appeared to be outright lies or fabrications. Antoine Guillaumont, in recounting a contemporary description of such carefree bands in the Antioch of the 370s, reveals a prejudice of the 1970s in labeling these Messalians as a 'kind of hippies'. [20]

Stewart has sorted the various accusations against the Messalians into ten themes, half of which are the social behaviors mentioned above. Several doctrinal ideas were associated with the heresy; the principal one was that a demon indwelt every human soul. Baptism was ineffective in expelling the demon; only prayer could affect its expulsion. Upon reaching spiritual perfection one receives the Holy Spirit and attains liberation from the passions or *apatheia*.

The Messalians were condemned by the Third Ecumenical Council at Ephesus in 431, but by that time there were probably no Messalians available to condemn. As Robert Murray has observed, Messalianism never really existed as a self-conscious sect, but was a 'movement' that found a place in a variety of groups, in a way similar to that by which the contemporary charismatic movement exists in a number of different denominations.[21]

Messalianism had already become a theologically

---

20. Antoine Guillaumont, 'Un mouvement de "Spirituels" dans l'Orient chrétien,' *Revue de l'Histoire des Religions* 189 (1975) 126.
21. Robert Murray, *Symbols of Church and Kingdom*, 35.

and socially pejorative label with which to attack dissenting groups. Those who would place emphasis upon the experiential aspects of prayer were particularly susceptible to the messalian label, as happened again with the fourteenth-century hesychast movement.

The author of the *Liber Graduum* wrote about the indwelling of 'something of Satan' and 'something of the Spirit' in the soul of the Christian. Through spiritual development the soul will eventually become completely filled by the Spirit, who is the Paraclete.[22] While this is not the same as the messalian concept, the *Liber Graduum* does echo what had developed into a messalian theme. Yet it is only an echo. The author of the *Liber Graduum* professes too much allegiance to the necessity and validity of the visible Church and its sacraments for salvation to come anywhere close to the messalian camp. Prayer, while fundamental to the christian life, is never singled out in the *Liber Graduum* as the only way to Perfection and salvation.

THE SYRIAC *LIBER GRADUUM*

Introduction and Scholarship

In 1926, Michael Kmosko published a critical edition of a collection of thirty syriac homilies (*mēmrē*[23]) on the spiritual life to which he gave the latin title *Liber Graduum*[24] or 'the Book of Steps'. The history of scholarship on this lengthy work has been one of successive steps—indeed degrees—in understanding its message and historical function.

22. See below, section on 'The Pledge of the Spirit'.
23. Instead of homily or sermon, the original terms *mēmrā* (singular) *mēmrē* (plural) will be used to identify the literary form of the author's work. See the Preface for an explanation.
24. M. Kmosko, ed., *Liber Graduum*, Patrologia Syriaca 3 (Paris, 1926). [References to the text of *LG* are that of the column and line numbers in Kmosko's edition.]

Kmosko set the scholarly agenda for a generation by the sources he included in his introduction. Perceiving the *Liber Graduum* as a key witness to the messalian movement that swept northern Mesopotamia and Asia Minor in the late fourth and early fifth centuries, Kmosko performed a great service to scholars by collecting in one place all the principal greek texts regarding the messalian controversy.[25] As a result, however, the *Liber Graduum* was identified in early christian history as the syriac messalian book. The *Liber Graduum* and the Pseudo-Macarian *Homilies*[26] were identified as the sources of the messalian heresy, indeed as the lost *Asceticon* purportedly displayed and then condemned at the Council of Ephesus.

Key themes and vocabulary characteristic of Messalianism, Syriac for 'pray-ers', which had been identified by the councils at Gangra and Ephesus were shown to lurk menacingly in the *Liber Graduum*. Irénée Hausherr inaugurated the first issue of the journal *Orientalia Christiana Periodica* with two articles on the *Liber Graduum*, both affirming its messalian character.[27]

Others soon accepted the heretical affiliation of the *Liber Graduum*.[28] In reviewing a new french translation of

25. M. Kmosko, ed., *Liber Graduum*, Patrologia Syriaca 3 (Paris, 1926), *Praefatio*.

26. *Intoxicated With God: The Fifty Spiritual Homilies of Macarius*, translated George Maloney (Denville, NJ, 1978). The syriac version is found in *Die Syrische Überliererung der Schriften des Makarios*, vol. 1 (syriac text), vol. 2 (translation and introduction), ed. Werner Strothmann (Wiesbaden: Otto Harrasowitz, 1981). Cf. George L. Marriott, 'The Messalians and the Discovery of their Ascetic Book,' *Harvard Theological Review* 19 (1926) 191-198.

27. I. Hausherr, 'L'erreur fondamentale et la logique du Messalianisme,' *Orientalia Christiana Periodica* 1 (1935) 328-360; see also 'Quanam aetate prodierit *LG*,' 495-502.

28. A. Rücker, 'Die Zitate aus dem Matthäusevangelium im syrischen Buche der Stufen,' *Biblische Zeitschrift* 20 (1932) 342-354; I. Hausherr, 'Spiritualité Syrienne: Philoxène de Mabboug en version française,' *Orientalia Christiana Periodica* 23 (1957) 181-182; J. Gribomont, 'Les Homélies de Philoxène de Mabboug et l'écho du Messalianisme,' *L'Orient Syrien* 2 (1957) 422, note 8.

Philoxenus' *Homélies* by Eugène Lemoine,[29] Hausherr—noting that the principal codex employed by Kmosko in preparing his edition of *Liber Graduum* also contained Philoxenus' *Homelies*[30]—felt compelled to defend the doctrinal purity of Philoxenus despite the company kept by his works. Arthur Vööbus, who challenged this view both in a 1954 article[31] and in a section in the first volume of his *History of Asceticism in the Syrian Orient*,[32] directed scholars to the positive content of the *Liber Graduum*: its remarkable witness to early syriac spirituality and asceticism. Soon, now that the messalian matter had been de-clawed, others began to investigate other themes. Paul Bäss,[33] A. J. M. Davids,[34] Antoine Guillaumont,[35] and Robert Murray[36] focused on issues of authorship, pneumatology, and ecclesiology. More recent studies have examined the theological anthropology of the *Liber Graduum*,[37] its rhetorical method,[38] prayer,[39] and its function within a christian community.[40] Vincent Desprez, who sees the itinerant missionary work of the Perfect ones prefiguring the messalian communities through their austerity, refusal to work, humility, poverty, and prayer, has posited a 'neo-messalian' interpretation of the *Liber Graduum*. Lack of historical evidence one way or the other, however, renders this theory tentative.[41]

29. *Philoxène de Mabboug: Homélies*, ed. E. Lemoine, Sources Chrétiennes 44 (Paris: Cerf, 1956).
30. Hausherr, 'Spiritualité Syrienne'—Ms α: Codex Bibliothèque Nationale de Paris Syrus 201 (12th century). Philoxenus folios 1-172; *Liber Graduum* folios 172b-281a.
31. A. Vööbus, '*Liber Graduum*: Some Aspects of its significance for the History of Early Syrian Asceticism,' *Papers of the Estonian Theological Society in Exile* 7 (Stockholm, 1954) 108-128.
32. A. Vööbus, *History of Asceticism in the Syrian Orient*, I, Corpus Scriptorum Christianorum Orientalium 184/Subsidia 14 (Louvain, 1958) 178-184.
33. Paul Bäss, 'Der *Liber Graduum*, ein messalianisches Buch?' *VII Deutscher Orientalistentag II* (Wiesbaden, 1969) 368-374. ▼

Nevertheless, a number of passages demonstrate an attempt by the author to denounce and reform certain negative patterns of behavior that could be interpreted as Messalian or the forerunner of messalian practices.[42]

Research on all aspects of *Liber Graduum* has increased in recent years. Two scholars have taken Robert Murray's lead in identifying recurrent literary themes and terms of biblical, jewish, and christian origin that enrich and underlie early Syriac literature. John Corbett has demonstrated how the Deuteronomic 'Call to Holy War' (Deuteronomy 20: 1-20) provides the structure for the ascetic endeavors of the Perfect ones in *Liber Graduum*.[43] Alexander Golitzin traced the recurrence of the concepts of 'the Glory of Adam' and 'divine light' in the Dead Sea Scrolls, Aphrahat, Ephrem, Pseudo-Macarius, and *Liber Graduum*.[44]

Robert Doran focused on an *agraphon* (unknown saying) of Jesus: 'As you will be found, so you will be taken

34. A. J. M. Davids, 'Von Anonymität zur Pseudononymität: Der *Liber Graduum* und das Corpus Macarianum,' *VII Deutscher Orientalistentag* (Wiesbaden, 1969) 375-379.

35. A. Guillaumont, 'Les "arrhes de l'Esprit" dans le Livre des degrés,' *Mémorial Msg. Gabriel Khouri-Sarkis* (Louvain, 1969) 107-113; 'Situation et signification du *Liber Graduum* dans le spiritualité syriaque,' *Orientalia Christiana Analecta* 197 (1974) 311-322.

36. R. Murray, *Symbols of Church and Kingdom* (Cambridge, 1975) 34-36, 263-269.

37. A. Kowalski, *Perfezione e giustizia di Adamo nel Liber Graduum, Orientalia Christiana Analecta* 232 (Rome, 1989).

38. A. Böhlig, 'Zur Rhetorik im *Liber Graduum*,' *Orientalia Christiana Analecta* 229 (1987) 297-305.

39. A. Kowalski, 'Die Gebete im *Liber Graduum*,' *Orientalia Christiana Periodica* 55 (1989) 273-282.

40. R. A. Kitchen, 'The Gattung of the *Liber Graduum*: Implications for a Sociology of Asceticism,' *Orientalia Christiana Analecta* 229 (1987) 173-182.

41. Vincent Desprez, 'L'ascétisme mésopotamien au IVe siècle: III. Le "Livre des degrees",' *La Lettre de Ligugé* 262 (1992) 16-29.

42. See below, 'The Decline of Perfection and Messalian behavior'.

43. John Corbett, 'They Do Not Take Wives or Build, or Work the Ground: Ascetic Life in the Early Syriac Christian Tradition.' Paper presented at Canadian Society for Syriac Studies public lecture series, University of Toronto, January 22, 2003.

44. Alexander Golitzin, 'Recovering the "Glory of Adam": "Divine Light"

away' (columns 3.3, 49:26-27; 15.4, 344:15-16). Doran observed that the author expanded and interpreted the canonical gospel sayings in a free and creative manner.[45] Shafiq Abouzayd analyzed the numerous references to the dark side of *Liber Graduum*, the violent, sometimes murderous conflict, internal and external, that characterized the *Liber Graduum* community as well other early christian communities.[46] Peter Nagel also examined the conflict involved in the appearance of the martyrs of faith and martyrs of love in *Mēmrā* Thirty, 'On the Commandments of Faith and the Love of the Solitaries'. Nagel identifies the principal theme of *Liber Graduum* to be the recovery of the divine glory that Adam had lost and humanity's return to the paradise of Eden.[47]

Daniel Caner, in his monograph on wandering and begging monks in the fourth and fifth centuries, treated the *Liber Graduum* as one of the main literary sources for these distinctive ascetic lifestyles that challenged institutional church authority all over the Roman Empire. The author of the *Liber Graduum's* proscription against work for the Perfect ones is the attribute Caner considers to be critical to understanding the conflict and phenomenon.[48]

Traditions in the Dead Sea Scrolls and the Christian Ascetical Literature of the Fourth-Century Syro-Mesopotamia.' International Conference on the Dead Sea Scrolls, St. Andrews, Scotland. June 28, 2001. Cf. R. A. Kitchen, 'Syriac Additions to Anderson: The Garden of Eden in the Book of Steps and Philoxenus of Mabbug,' *Hugoye: Journal of Syriac Studies* 6.1 (2003).

45. Robert Doran, 'The Agraphon at *Liber Graduum* 3.3,' *Catholic Biblical Quarterly* 63 (2001) 298-303.

46. Cf. below, section titled, 'Conflict and Transition'; Shafiq Abouzayd, "Violence and Killing in the *Liber Graduum*," *Aram* 11-12 (1999-2000) 451-465.

47. Peter Nagel, 'Die "Märtyer des Glaubens" und die "Märtyrer der Liebe" im syrischen *Liber Graduum*,' *Religion und Wahrheit. Religiongeschichtliche Studien. Festschrift für Gernot Wiessner*, ed. B. Kohler (Wiesbaden, 1998) 127-142.

48. Daniel Caner, *Wandering, Begging Monks: Spiritual Authority and the Promotion of Monasticism in Late Antiquity* The Transformation of the Classical Heritage 33 (Berkeley: University of California Press, 2002).

David Lane has presented a concise, well-balanced overview of *Liber Graduum*. He perceived the critical tension to be between the contradictory commandments of the Bible and how these have been played out in the different levels of the christian life. In Lane's evaluation *Mēmrā* Nineteen, 'On the Discernment of the Way of Perfection', and *Mēmrā* Eighteen, 'On the Tears of Prayer', are the most important sections in the work.[49]

Renato Roux approaches the *Liber Graduum* from a different angle. He argued that the 'imitation of Christ' is the main christological theme in the work. *Mēmra* Seventeen, 'On the Sufferings of Our Lord who became through them an Example for Us', provides the most significant ideas for this aspect.[50]

Paolo Bettiolo adopted yet another approach. He argued that the correct discernment of the divine and biblical commandments is a central theme and dynamic of the *Liber Graduum*. Distinguishing the major from the minor commandments results in the development of the two primary levels of Christians, the Perfect who fulfill the major commandments, and the Upright who need only heed the minor ones.[51]

Manuscripts

The principal manuscript for the edition—Ms *a*: Codex Bibliothèque Nationale de Paris Syrus 201 from the twelfth century—is one of the latest among the fifteen manuscripts available to Kmosko, but the only complete one. Its folio-mate, the *Discourses (Mēmrā)* of Philoxenus of Mabbug, shows remarkable parallels with the *Liber*

---

49. D. J. Lane, 'The Book of Grades, or Steps,' *The Harp* 14 (2001) 81-88.
50. Renato Roux, 'The doctrine of the imitation of Christ in the *Liber Graduum*: Between Exegetical Theory and Soteriology,' *Studia Patristica* 30 (1997) 259-264.
51. Paolo Bettiolo, 'Confessare Dio in perfetta spogliazione. La via del discernimento dei commandamenti nel *Liber Graduum*,' *Cristianesimo nella Storia* 19 (1998) 631-651.

Graduum regarding the institution of the Upright and Perfect. In fact, Philoxenus is the only syriac author who exhibits the apparent influence of the *Liber Graduum*. While the fact that the two works found their way into the same manuscript should not lead to facile conclusions, the scribe and/or sponsor of the manuscript obviously recognized some affinity between the texts. At the very least, Hausherr's fear that Philoxenus would be contaminated by the heretical *Liber Graduum* was not shared by the scribe.

Kmosko had basically completed his critical edition on the basis of fourteen manuscripts when a fifteenth was made available to him—Ms R: Saint Mark's Jerusalem Syrus 180, dating to the seventh or eighth century.[52] Although the first twenty-one folios have been mutilated, Ms R clearly belongs to a different textual tradition. Nevertheless, Ms R's colophon, just like the one in the printed edition, claims not to know the name of the author, even though the scribe adds in the margin: 'Father Philo is his name. . . . Just as I thought, my brothers, Philo is his name, one of the seventy evangelists'.[53] The scribe apparently could not stand the thought of anonymity and while Kmosko made a tentative suggestion about Philo's identity, he did not seem all that convinced himself.

A later manuscript—British Library Add. 17193 (AD 874) folios 3a-3b—includes an extract from the 'Book of Steps' and ascribes the work to a certain 'Eusebius the Solitary'.[54] Recently, Brian Colless has conjectured that Adelphius, the original messalian heretic banished by Flavian of Antioch, was the author—or at least a reader—of the *Liber Graduum*.[55] Again, the identification lacks any

52. Cf. Mar Filoksinos Yohanna Dolabany, *Catalogue of Syriac Manuscripts in St. Mark's Monastery (Dairo DMor Marqos)* (Sidawi Printing House: Damascus, 1994) 377-380, for a list of *mēmrā* titles.
53. Kmosko, *Praefatio*, ccxcv.
54. *Catalogue of the Syriac Manuscripts in the British Museum* Part II, by W. Wright (London, 1871) 989.
55. Brian Colless, 'The Book of Degrees and Adelphios of Edessa'. Paper presented at VIII Symposium Syriacum, Sydney, Australia, August 2000.

discernible basis. The problem is not one of pseudonymity, but of intentional anonymity, not an unusual strategy in texts of late antiquity. 'The blessed one who did not make known his name' is his full title given by the editor/scribe. It reflects his desire and that of his community to keep his identity obscure.

The other thirteen manuscripts (ten of them found in the British Library) contain only one significant witness: Ms β: BL Add. 14613 includes eighteen *mēmrē* plus the Preface. Ms γ (BL Add. 17178) contains five *mēmrē*, and Ms E (BL Add. 14621) four. The eight remaining manuscripts contain only one *mēmrā* each.

A case could be built cautiously around the importance of the *mēmrā* that occur most frequently. *Mēmrē* Fourteen, 'On the Upright and the Perfect', once thought to have been written by Evagrius Ponticus,[56] occurs in seven manuscripts and most succinctly outlines the duties and the contrast between these two levels, though the distinctions become more nuanced in later *mēmrē*.

Mēmrā Nineteen, 'On the Explanation of the Way of Perfection', the longest *mēmrē*, is found in six manuscripts, as is *mēmrā* Twenty, 'On the Difficult Steps that are on the Road of the City of Our Lord'. *Mēmrā* Nineteen presents twenty-five pairs of scriptural texts: the first text describes the 'difficult road' to the heavenly city and Perfection; the second text, the needs of those who require a less rigorous 'path' of Uprightness veering to the side of the road. *Mēmrā* Twenty intensifies the examination of the three most difficult steps, focusing on the affliction of prayer required for Perfection. *Mēmrē* Nineteen and Twenty are the only two that refer to the concept of *masqātā* or 'steps'. Together these three *mēmrē* could readily have served as a

---

56. J. Muyldermans, ed., *Evagriana Syriaca*, Bibliothèque du Muséon 31 (Louvain, 1952). BL Add. 14578, in which this *mēmrā* is embedded (fol. 102a ff.), is devoted entirely to various short and long works of Evagrius.

digest of the themes of the *Liber Graduum*—as was probably the intention of some of the scribes—for in the majority of cases these were included as sole representatives of the *Liber Graduum* in a larger manuscript.

The order of the *Mēmrē* is problematic since only three manuscripts approach completeness (α, β, R). Only Mss α and R contain the *mēmrē* 6, 7, 9, 18, 22, 23, 25. Kmosko's edition takes its order from Ms α—the same as R—making Ms β the interesting one to examine for its order.

Ms β (BL Add. 14613) opens with the *Liber Graduum*. The first *mēmrā* is number 21, followed by 26, 15, 10, 3, 4, 5, 8, 11, 12, 13, 18, 19, 16, 24, 28, 29, and 30. There seems to be no reason for placing the first three at the front except the preference of Ms β's scribe since none of these command the central arguments of the work.

Structure

The *Liber Graduum* provides no apparent schema for the layout of his work's *mēmrē*. Although the *Liber Graduum mēmrē* present no systematic theology, there is a consistency to the fabric, particularly noteworthy as no compelling reason can be found to assign any part of the work to more than one author.

A basic assumption about such a huge work is that it was written, not at one time, but over a period of years in which the circumstances in the community and, correspondingly, the perspective of the author changed. Diverse materials and genres are utilized in the *mēmrē*, again without any apparent system, yet not without benefit.

BASIC COMMANDMENTS: *Mēmrē* 1-9

Three broad sections appear to divide up the *mēmrē*. The first nine *mēmrē* set out the core exposition of the doctrine and purpose of the *Liber Graduum*: the basic commandments of the Upright and the Perfect. Lionel Wickham sees these nine as essentially one single treatise in their original writing and posits that the editor would later have divided this treatise into separate *mēmrē*, marked by connecting words.[57] This may be too speculative to be proven conclusively as none of the available manuscripts preserve any 'combined' *mēmrē*.

The Preface (1-9), a *mamllā* ('explanation'), written by a syriac editor at an early stage, is concerned with giving an introduction to the author rather than the content of the work. The editor does not know who the author is, but appeals to the tradition that he is one of the last of the apostles and one of the first to write in Syriac. The editor makes it clear that the author is a Perfect one (*gmīrā*), having received the spirit of the Paraclete.

To demonstrate the virtuosity of the author, the editor inserts what is purportedly the last section of the last *mēmrā* at this juncture. This 'last section' does not appear again in *Mēmrā* Thirty, although in Ms R it is *found* in its 'proper' place.

Mēmrā One, untitled (columns 12-24), is the author's own introduction, serving as an overture to most of the themes he will develop.

Mēmrā Two, 'About Those Who Want to Become Perfect' (columns 25-44), begins the explanation of the great or major commandments directed to the Perfect. At the end, the notion of the small or minor commandments is brought forward, the so-called milk and vegetables reserved for the Upright and for those in the spiritual infancy of their pilgrimage.

Mēmrā Three, 'The Physical and Spiritual Ministry' (columns 45-81), slides into the comparison of the Perfect and their religious inferiors, the Upright. The responsibilities of the Upright lie in performing the physical ministry to the needy on earth, while the Perfect pointedly do not work physically, but act as spiritual guides and teachers.

57. Lionel Wickham, 'The "Liber Graduum" Revisited,' *Orientalia Christiana Analecta* 247 (1994) 181-182.

Mēmrā Four, 'On the Vegetables for the Sick' (columns 84-97), and *Mēmrā* Five, 'On the Milk of the Children' (columns 100-137), describe the small/minor commandments for those aspiring at the lowest levels to the way of the Perfect. The 'Sick' are morally rigid, anxious to judge others, while the 'Children' or 'Infants' are the inexperienced and immature who are easily influenced away from faith. A concluding section describes the process of one receiving the full Spirit—the Paraclete—and becoming Perfect.

Mēmrā Six, 'On Those Who are Made Perfect and Continue to Grow' (columns 140-144), is the shortest in the work, utilizing a non-biblical analogy of a royal treasure chest in which jewels are placed just as a Perfect one accumulates virtues until he attains angelic status and becomes perfect or complete.

Mēmrā Seven, 'On the Commandments of the Upright' (columns 145-188), focuses on those who choose not to travel the hard road of Perfection. The way of Uprightness is, nevertheless, inferior to that of Perfection.

Mēmrā Eight, 'On One Who Gives All He Has to Feed the Poor' (columns 189-200), continues the good, though inferior, path of the Upright.

Mēmrā Nine, 'On Uprightness and the Love of the Upright and the Prophets' (columns 201-248), is the final chapter in this initial section of the *Liber Graduum*. It is an extended biblical exegesis explaining the violence of the Old Testament prophets—most of whom violated the principles of Uprightness—and then placing them in the salvation history that culminates in Jesus and the Apostles.

This last *mēmrā* appears driven by two motives. First, the need of a 'systematic' thinker to tie up loose ends regarding the standards of Uprightness/Perfection, and, to discuss what to do about biblical heroes who do not make even the minimum grade. Second, to illustrate that while the Old Testament is Scripture, the New Testament has superseded it.

ADVANCED PERFECTION: *Mēmrē* 10-24

The second section of the *Liber Graduum* begins with *Mēmrā* Ten and extends through *Mēmrā* Twenty-Four. These *mēmrē* adopt a variety of literary forms, but generally pursue the themes of 'advanced Perfection'.

Mēmrā Ten, 'On Fasting and the Humility of Body and Soul' (columns 249-269), provides a break both in form and content. It is a straightforward sermon, an exhortation with barely a trace of the exposition found in the previous nine *mēmrē*. The Upright and the Perfect are, in fact, mentioned only twice. The purpose of the sermon is to argue against a spiritualizing or quietistic approach to asceticism in which physical fasting, for example, is disdained by disciples who believe they have become superior to anything physical or bodily. This concern will be reiterated on several other occasions.

Why a sermon was included among a series of expositions on essentially a 'rule' of the ascetical life is not immediately evident, but there are at least two other 'sermons' (*Mēmrē* 25 and 29), as well as extended biblical-theological exegeses of fundamental issues (*Mēmrē* 9, 21, and 23). A simple suggestion would be that these *mēmrē* were all written 'by this same holy person' (column 248:2-3), to cite the extended title of *Mēmrā* Ten. The *Liber Graduum*, we conclude, was therefore perceived not as a neat systematic treatise, but as the 'collected works' of the author. The sermon itself is not incongruous with the rest of the *Liber Graduum*, but provides a bit of pastoral leaven and caution to enthusiasts on the road to Perfection.

Mēmrā Eleven, 'On the Hearing of Scripture When the Law is Read Before Us' (columns 272-284), is the first full-fledged example of 'advanced Perfection', discussing the need to be able to discern the major from the minor commandments, a discussion proceeding from *Mēmrā* Two. This requirement is apparently set against the background of criticism of the author, claiming that Scripture is intended for only one audience rather than two or more levels.

Mēmrā Twelve, 'On the Hidden and Public Ministry of the Church' (columns 285-304), has drawn the most
attention from scholars, but is included in only the three
complete or near complete manuscripts (*a*, *β*, R). It provides a rationale for *Mēmrā* Ten in combating the spiritualizing factions in the church/community. Describing the
three levels of the Church—Visible, of the Heart, and Hidden—the author emphatically declares that the visible
Church is the true Church through which one must travel
to the Church in the heart as well as to the hidden or higher
Church. Robert Murray's comment that the author of the
Liber Graduum 'perhaps protests too much fidelity to the
public church'[58] assumes that the *Liber Graduum* was primarily addressed to outsiders rather than, as is the case in
this particular *mēmrā* at least, to the members of the author's
community.

Mēmrā Thirteen, 'By the Same Author on the Ways
of the Upright' (columns 305-321), is the most detailed description of the activities of the Upright, particularly within
the community and the Church, and goes beyond *Mēmrē*
Seven and Eight. In a rhetorical twist, Uprightness is
personified throughout the *mēmrā*, resulting in the gram-
matical feminization of the concept.

Mēmrā Fourteen, 'On the Upright and the Perfect'
(columns 324-333), presents another literary form, a comparison of the characteristics of the Upright and Perfect in
evagrian-style couplets. The Upright are described in more
concrete terms as avoiding evil actions and emotions; the
Perfect are always perceived as transcending these worldly
conflicts.

Mēmrā Fifteen, 'On Adam's Marital Desire' (columns
336-385), initially appears discordant, but as an extended
discourse on the origins and consequences of the human
sexual drive it deals with the issue of celibacy, one of the
main requisites for Perfection. The author uses the *mēmrā*

---

58. Robert Murray, *Symbols of Church and Kingdom* (Cambridge, 1975) 35.

to prove that sexual lust is not innate in human beings, but derives from the temptations of Satan. Marriage, as a result, is provisionally blessed.

Mēmrē Sixteen, Seventeen, and Eighteen constitute 'graduate studies' in the ascetical methodology of Perfection. 'On How a Person May Surpass the Major Commandments' (columns 388-413) looks at the next level up for the one already perfected. This is accomplished by going beyond any quantifiable definition of Perfection. As an ideal of the Perfect life, the model of the holy fool is given.

'On the Sufferings of our Lord Who Became Through Them an Example for Us' (columns 416-429) moves into the methods of asceticism. The author proposes the imitation of the sufferings of Jesus as the way for those who believe, and contrasts it with the use of signs for those who do not believe in God.

'On the Tears of Prayer' (columns 432-444) urges the necessity of agony and struggle in prayer, the mournful weeping and prayerful tears that eliminate sin from within and enable one to be perfected.

Mēmrā Nineteen, 'On the Discernment of the Way of Perfection' (columns 445-525), the longest *mēmrā*, offers the most nuanced perspective on the distinction between the Upright and the Perfect. The core of the *mēmrā* consists of twenty-five pairs of biblical citations: the first depicting the difficult road to the heavenly city of the Perfect; the second the path along the side of the road intended for the 'Sick' and 'Children' who are diverted until they gain enough strength to resume traveling on the steep and narrow road. The recurring theme is the universal vision of the Perfect contrasted with the parochial perspective of the Upright.

Mēmrā Twenty, 'On the Difficult Steps that are on the Road of the City of Our Lord' (columns 528-581), continues the same imagery as the previous *mēmrā*, but intensifies the pilgrimage by describing the three most difficult steps. The final step is the uprooting of the very root of the sin that Adam experienced in Eden. Emphasis is also applied to the affliction of prayer, as in *Mēmrā* Eighteen.

Mēmrā Twenty-One, 'On the Tree of Adam' (columns 584-632), develops the biblical-theological picture of how Jesus, the Tree of Life, is the actualization of what Adam was meant to be in the Garden. Perfection as the recapturing of the state of Adam and Eve before the Fall is the fundamental motif of the entire *Liber Graduum*, but it is in this *mēmrā* that the case is most explicitly made.

Mēmrā Twenty-Two, 'On the Judgments that Do Not Save Those Who Observe Them' (columns 633-689), returns to the concerns of Uprightness, at first to clarify that Uprightness is not simply the application of the *lex talionis*, 'an eye for an eye'. God appointed evil judges and kings to treat people harshly, but, nevertheless, restrains their evil tendencies. Even in these most harsh conditions, the Ten Commandments along with the Gospel are sufficient for salvation.

Mēmrā Twenty-Three, 'On Satan and Pharaoh and the Israelites' (columns 692-712), is another extended biblical-theological treatise on whether God grants free will to evil persons, in particular here, the Pharaoh. God does not predestine the 'hardness of heart' of the Pharaoh; the evil derives from Satan. In this *mēmrā*, the author demonstrates how God's kindness actually brings about the rebellion of evil, just as Jesus' humility brought out resistance among the jewish leaders. This *mēmrā* has close parallels with *Mēmrā* Nine; both try to explain the problematic Old Testament question of free will.

Mēmrā Twenty-Four, 'On Repentance' (columns 713-732), deals with the need that all below the level of the Upright have for repentance and redemption. The theme is God's mercy, which against reason created Uprightness as a way to escape the taste of death. As is the case throughout the *Liber Graduum*, the possibility of reaching Perfection is tendered to the Upright. The Perfect are beyond the need for repentance and mercy, having no enemies in their heart upon whom to be merciful.

LATER PERIOD AND REDEMPTION
OF THE UPRIGHT: Mēmrē 25-30

The third section of the Liber Graduum completes
the text in Mēmrē Twenty-Five through Thirty. These reflect
a later period in the author's/community's life, during
which the author meditates upon the decline in standards
while reaffirming and validating the status of the Upright
in salvation history.

Mēmrā Twenty-Five, 'On the Voice of God and of
Satan' (columns 733-756), is another sermon, calling upon
both the Upright and the Perfect to discern properly the
divine or satanic motives behind their manner of life. Caution is recommended first to the Perfect not to be seduced
into adopting the worldly ways of the Upright and thereby
abandoning Perfection. Then the Upright are exhorted not
to terminate their own journey upward to Perfection. A
different tone appears in the author's voice, a sense of frustration, even disappointment, in the progress of those under his pastoral care. As with Mēmrā Ten, a sermon is used
to make a break with a previous series and this makes it
appear to be the methodology.

Mēmrā Twenty-Six, 'On the Second Law that the
Lord Established for Adam' (columns 757-765), is a short
mēmrā on the law of Uprightness that God gave to Adam
after he transgressed the first law. The author points out
that the Gospel of Jesus is the same as the law that Adam
transgressed, so there is still hope for the Upright to be
able to reach Perfection.

Mēmrā Twenty-Seven (columns 768-784) bears the
nonsensical title 'About the History of the Robbers' in
Kmosko's edition. But Ms R records the title 'About the
History of the Thief Who is Saved'.[59] Neither title seems to
have a basis in the content of the Mēmrā, though the latter

59. Mar Filoksinos Yohanna Dolabany, Catalogue of Syriac Manuscripts in St.
Mark's Monastery (Dairo DMor Marqos) (Sidawi Printing House: Damascus,
1994) 379.

title appears a little more plausible. Possibly it is an allusion to Luke 23:39-43, yet, even so, it is nowhere to be found in the actual body of the *Mēmrā*.

There is a sermonic tone to much of this discourse. Its theme centers on one's readiness to suffer like Jesus on the way to Perfection. The author's concern again turns to the immature, lest they stray unaware into idolatry or paganism, especially if they have had a negligent teacher. They are cautioned not to leave home on the christian journey until they are mature enough to withstand the sufferings, lies, slanders, and injustices that are typically incurred.

Mēmrā Twenty-Eight, 'On the Fact that the Human Soul Is Not Identical With the Blood' (columns 785-805), is a theological exposition of the inbreathing of the Holy Spirit, the Paraclete, in the Perfect and the lesser gift of the Holy Spirit to the Upright. The approach to this topic produces perhaps the least characteristic writing in the *Liber Graduum* in its initial section. The final sections return to the theme of *Mēmrā* Twelve on the visible Church as the image of the heavenly Church, and provide the example of the salvation of Abraham who while married and with many possessions did what God told him to do.

Mēmrā Twenty-Nine, 'On the Discipline of the Body' (columns 808-857), is a longer sermon directed to all those in the Church, exhorting them to perform their ministry with passion and enthusiasm and not go mechanically through the motions 'by rote'. The author expresses painful frustration brought on by a religious movement that has lost its charisma. The Upright who are good to other people and follow their own rule are preferable to false or failed Perfect.

Mēmrā Thirty, 'On the Commandments of Faith and the Love of the Solitaries' (columns 860-932), the second longest *mēmrā*, concludes the *Liber Graduum*. It begins by distinguishing between the commandments of faith and the commandments of love—the latter being an intermediary level of discipleship between the Upright and the Perfect. The author seems to be aware that this is the last *mēmrā*, for he summarizes the standards of Perfection, mirroring the opening *mēmrā* in its attempt at overview. The final four and a half sections, however, are concerned not with the Perfect, typically the focus of the *Liber Graduum*, but with establishing conclusively the validity and salvation of the Upright.

While not fitting any overarching pattern, the *Liber Graduum* clearly forms a single unit. The themes of the *mēmrē* weave in and out through most of the text. The original order of the *mēmrē* is open to conjecture, but that there are three broad divisions in the material is evident from the diverse content. I doubt, however, that the author intentionally planned these divisions.

THE UPRIGHT AND THE PERFECT

While the overall purpose of the *Liber Graduum* is to elaborate a picture of the spiritual life, the thread running through it is the description of the two principal groups of Christians—the Upright (*kēnē*) and the Perfect (*gmīrē*) —their duties and pilgrimage toward heaven and salvation, as well as their relationship with one another and the wider Church.

There are, in fact, six levels of discipleship in the *Liber Graduum* and the first task is to sift out the characteristics, duties and responsibilities at each level. The author uses three means of distinguishing between the ways of life (*dūbbārē*) of the Upright and the Perfect. The first is a general condition: the Upright are assigned the small or minor commandments to fulfill, while the Perfect are to follow the great or major commandments (column 12:1-5). God recognizes that all persons are not capable of the same standards and so provides a means of salvation for all (column 188:8-12). Indeed, '[the scriptures] were not addressed to [only] one [type of] person' (column 273:27).

The second means of distinction is achieved by placing the tasks of and commandments to the Upright and

Perfect in virtually adversarial dichotomy. This is particularly evident in *Mēmrā* Fourteen. The third means involves another set of dichotomies, the 'roads' of Perfection and the 'paths' of Uprightness. These will be treated below. Here let us summarize the fundamental expectations of persons at each level.

UPRIGHTNESS

The Upright one is expected to carry out the active ministry of the Christian: feed the hungry, clothe the naked, and visit the sick (columns 48:21-49:21). Pointing out that wealth is allowable to the Upright only if he uses it for the welfare of others, the author insists on the responsibility the Upright has to care for the social needs of the world. 'The Upright feed the hungry and clothe the naked and rescue the afflicted by their possessions and wealth' (column 328:2-5). Naturally, this social service extends to the welfare of the poor in the Church. 'On Sunday [Uprightness] places in the Lord's house some of [the fruit of] its labors for the needy because [the latter] visit the house of our Lord' (column 309:3-5).

Involvement in worldly business, without being 'of the world,' sets the Upright apart from others.

> [Uprightness] claims what belongs to it according to its [fair] measure, but does not get involved in usury or come near a bribe. [Uprightness] possesses wealth righteously, buying and selling as is appropriate before God. [Uprightness] neither deceives nor borrows something it lacks, but claims only the thing that it has loaned without interest, even if it will be one hundred years [before it is repaid] (column 305:2-7).

The Upright are to avoid traditional vices: no adultery, stealing, or cheating; they are not to swear oaths, but simply reply 'yes' or 'no' to a question (column 324:1-9). Moreover, the Upright are not allowed to judge, curse, or take revenge on anyone. When someone who has stolen something from an Upright One is caught, the Upright One takes back only what belongs to him and does not despise the thief (column 313:10-14).

> [Uprightness] is not permitted to call a person by another name and to grieve him or [to call him] fool or contemptible or stupid or spiteful, for if it is able to give him honorable names [it does so]; yet if not, [Uprightness] does not give him insulting names, but calls a person simply by his [regular] name (column 308:14-19).

In terms of religious duties, the Upright must fast twice a week, pray three times a day in the morning, in the evening, and in the middle of the night (column 312:22-26), keep the law of God, give alms, and pray for others (columns 184:24-25,26-185:2,4-6).

THE SICK AND THE CHILDREN

Two sub-levels of aspiring solitaries on the road to Perfection are best located here: the Sick[60] and the Children.[61] Whether these two groups are considered part of the Upright level or fledgling Perfect ones is unclear. Both groups have not attained the maturity required for a serious pursuit of Perfection and must be fed the minor commandments of Uprightness until they gain the strength and health to commence travel on the difficult, steep, and narrow road of Perfection.

The problem for both the Sick and the Children lies in their relationship with evil people. The Sick desire to

60. Cf. *Mēmrā* 4: 'On the Vegetables for the Sick'.
61. Cf. *Mēmrā* 5: 'On the Milk of the Children'.

judge, condemn,. and at times harm their enemies. 'Just as a sick person rejects all food, so he who suffers from moral rigidity can never cope with anything in which he discovers some imperfection, however small' (column 84:5-8).

'As a sick person rejects good food, so the one whose soul is diseased grumbles against gentle moral attitudes, for he does not observe the beam in his own eye, but condemns the person who is, in fact, just like himself. Instead of correcting and admonishing him in love, he drags him into court' (column 84:8-14). The 'medicine' prescribed for the Sick person is to channel his judgmental anger through the 'conflict management' procedures outlined in Matthew 18:15-17, in which one brings the recalcitrant offender before increasingly greater numbers of people in the Church for persuasion.

The Children, because they are young in the faith— even portrayed as infants still at the breast—are easily distracted and seduced away from the true faith by idolaters, pagans, and heretics. Consequently, they are strongly advised to stay away from all manner of sinners lest they be influenced to follow their evil ways.

> As an infant, he is required not to eat bread with [heretics], nor to mix with them, being still a child, whom they easily persuade to agree with their way of thinking, because he is inexperienced and can easily be seduced like all children. The commandment orders him not to dwell with them until he knows himself and has grown up. Only at that point is he commissioned to go and teach them to be a lamb amongst them and to make these wolves into innocent lambs (column 100:4-13).

The author understands that this principle is not permanent and that one needs to be able eventually to leave it behind. 'Note that the Apostle only said "Do not eat with them", and did not say that one should become their enemy or expose them. So whoever makes peace with them while being on his guard is more virtuous than he who does not eat bread with them, but exposes them' (column 101:8-10).

The way of Uprightness seems solid and secure, but the author observes that it is a tenuous existence with regard to final salvation. 'Uprightness is below on the earth, standing on the boundary of evil. The Upright are being battered by it at all times because they are the children of [evil's] boundary and [the Evil One is] the resident of these cursed frontiers' (column 753:10-13).

PERFECTION

The boundary line between Uprightness and Perfection is the renunciation of the world and the requisite celibacy. Incompleteness, not error, limits the spiritual advance of the Upright, yet they are still promised a real reward: 'Therefore, although the Upright, the doers of good deeds, do not inherit the particular portion of the Perfect since they have not abandoned their riches and their wives, they will inherit the lower portion, which is smaller' (column 52:9-13).

The Perfect, on the other hand, 'go all the way' in renouncing the world and its possession, beginning with material property, but also involving virginity and continence. 'The Upright are not able to do all the will of our Lord unless they come to holiness [=celibacy] and empty themselves' (column 328:20-329:2).

The Perfect must fulfill the major commandments, the language of which typically reflects that complementary to or opposes that describing the Upright. The Perfect turn the other cheek (column 28:14-15), do not vent anger against one another (column 32:5-10), and do not judge (column 120:24-121:2). In religious activities, they need to go further in degree than the Upright. The Perfect must fast everyday and pray all day (columns 184:24-185:8).

Following the model of Jesus, the Perfect abstain as completely as possible from the world. 'The Perfect do not take wives, nor do they work on the land, nor acquire possessions, nor have a place to lay their heads on earth like their teacher' (columns 365:26-368:2). Their greatest call is to possess unlimited love for their sin-ridden companions. 'Because greater is the love of Perfection than that of Uprightness, the Perfect wish to die [so that] sinners may live' (columns 317:26-320:3).

The foundation of the Perfect one's spiritual being is his humility or sense of lowliness.

> So it is also with a person once he has humbled himself more than everything on earth, has broken his mind night and day, who counts everyone else better than himself, has emptied himself of all he possessed and kisses the feet of his enemies: our Lord will look upon this person's humility and send him the Spirit, the Paraclete, and he shall know the whole truth (column 141:7-14).

The Perfect thus become 'strangers', even 'dead', to the world, avoiding involvement with commerce and worldly pursuits. They must 'become attached to our Lord in heaven and become dead from the use of the world' (column 316:2-5). In fact, 'The Perfect are like angels, as our Lord said' (column 752:1-2).

The primary function of the Perfect is to teach, or more precisely, to direct spiritually those below them (column 893:7-13).

> For he who takes up the Cross with regard to visible things receives the burden of having to pray for all people, and humbly to give counsel and to teach them all.

> He does this hoping that they will listen
> to him, but whether they do listen to him
> or not, he is bound to continue humbly
> to teach all people, whether they are wor-
> thy or not, because our Lord wanted it this
> way: he should even teach murderers, and
> pray alike for all who do evil to him and
> for all who love him (column 61:10-14).

Apparently, however, some members of the *Liber Graduum* community had attempted to reform society more directly; the author advises against this. 'If they are in leadership positions and pursue Perfection, they should leave these positions. Then they can be perfected because the Perfect teach every one with humility and are not able to coerce a person as the rulers [do]' (column 493:10-15).

DISCIPLES OF LOVE AND FAITH

The *Mēmrā* Thirty closes the collection with a dichotomy only hinted at previously—the disciples of love (Perfect) and the disciples of faith (Upright).

The description of the disciples of faith is virtually synonymous with the Upright, while the disciples of love are on an intermediary level between Uprightness and Perfection.

> As a person ascends from love to Perfection,
> in order that they may not be troubled and
> perish, [faith] establishes for them a tempo-
> rary law until they have strength and are filled
> with knowledge; and then [faith] will commit
> them to love in order to instruct them [in] Per-
> fection, and make them acquire that great,
> acceptable, and perfect mind of Christ (col-
> umn 861:24-864:4).

The behavior of the disciples of love is barely distinguishable from that of the Perfect, though the author sees a clear distinction. At the very least, the two levels are compatible and generous in spirit with one another. 'Between the disciples of love and these disciples who minister in Perfection there is peace. When they speak with one another they do not contend about anything, because love does not contend with its teachers, but they speak their words persuasively' (columns 877:19-880:2).

Perhaps playing the role of front-line troops of the Perfect, the disciples of love are sent out into the world to encounter evil.

> Love teaches its disciples since it knows they have the strength, 'I am sending you as lambs among wolves so that you might be good ones among evil ones in order to convert them. Be innocent like doves and cunning like snakes, so that you may be all [things] with all [people] and know how to speak with everyone in order to give vegetables to the sick and milk to the infants, and [the minor] commandments to the Upright and solid food to the Perfect and the strong, so that you may take on the illness of the sick' (column 864:13-23).

The author recognizes that the disciples of faith have a different kind of problem. 'But the commandments of faith are harder than those of love: they flee from being with evil ones' (column 864:7-8). It is easier to live chastely among sinners, the author believes, than to have to expend the energy always avoiding them.

While many of the usual themes regarding the superiority of the way of love/Perfection are repeated, the author does not lay down his pen before making clear that the disciples of faith/Uprightness deserve a higher life.

> Listen to me, O members of the house-
> hold of faith, and I will instruct you how
> you can grow great pleasantly until [you
> attain] the peace and the bread, the water
> and the garment and the washing of feet
> (column 885:3-6).

The closing section of the entire work, in fact, has not the Perfect but the Upright as its concern.

> You see that whoever wishes to imitate
> the example and hope of Abraham will
> be called by the righteousness of Abra-
> ham. For it is written in this way in [the
> Psalms of] David about people who love
> visible gain and property and marriage
> and children, and wish to become Up-
> right ones while keeping their posses-
> sions and to be saved on the day of our
> Lord [for] eternal life (column 928:15-21).

THE ROAD AND PATHS

The third means of distinguishing the Upright and the Perfect is found in the longest *mēmrā*, Nineteen, 'On the Explanation of the Way of Perfection' (columns 445-525). Most of the *Mēmrā* is formulaic, beginning, 'The Perfect way is this....', typically with a Gospel quotation; followed by the phrase 'But the path that leads you away from it is this...', generally with a Pauline or Old Testament quotation. Twenty-five such dichotomies are given, illustrating more clearly the superior compassion required to journey on the Perfect road. It would not be far off track to perceive most of the Perfect roads following the spirit of Jesus' Beatitudes.

GRADUATION FROM UPRIGHTNESS TO PERFECTION

An important issue for the two levels is how one is able to advance from Uprightness to Perfection. The answer remains consistent throughout the work: an Upright one must renounce his possessions and become celibate. In the first two sections of the *Liber Graduum*, the author looks pessimistically at the prospects of the Upright ever changing; the gap is too big and their involvement in the world too deep. But in the last section, a more mellow and encouraging perspective emerges. The Upright still have to renounce the world, but they are almost there. 'If they desire to leave behind the earth, as our Lord commanded, and journey in the footsteps of his humility, they will quickly ascend to Perfection, for they are not very far from it' (columns 749:23-752:1).

THE PLEDGE OF THE SPIRIT

Marking the progress of the spiritual journey of the Upright toward Perfection is a unique interpretation of 'the pledge of the Spirit', a phrase adapted from Paul in 2 Corinthians 1:22 and 5:5.[62]

At the heart of the matter is the enigmatic word; *ūrbānā*, commonly drawn from the root *ʿ r b* ,'to mix, mingle'. Antoine Guillaumont, however, opts for the meaning 'to pledge, guarantee', which fits the usage in 2 Corinthians (*arrabōn*) and in its corresponding rendering in the *Peshitta* (*rahbōnā*).

The basic condition of the Upright Christian is an inner coexistence of 'pledges of the Spirit' and 'pledges of Satan'. The proportion of these deposits of good and evil depends upon the spiritual progress of the Upright one. Increasingly, the Upright is able to reduce the proportion of the pledges of Satan as he moves toward Perfection, until

62. Cf. Antoine Guillaumont, 'Les "arrhes de l'Esprit" dans le Livre des degrés,' *Mémorial Mgr Gabriel Khouri-Sarkis*, (Louvain, 1969) 107-113.

finally these are eliminated and the pledges of the Spirit completely occupy the individual. At that point, one receives the fullness of the Holy Spirit—the Paraclete—and is perfected.

Mēmrā Three has an extended section that deals with the pledges and their spiritual process.

> There is another category of people in whom there is 'something of God' and 'something of Satan'. They do good works because of the pledge of the Holy Spirit that is in them, and they sin and do evil works because of the pledge of sin that is in them. The pledge of the Holy Spirit admonishes them constantly to quit evil, to do good works and to crucify themselves with the evil one in order to conquer him. If they conquer him, they become Upright, and if they are prepared to raise themselves further, they will become Perfect; whereas if they remain as they were,[63] then on the Day of Judgment they will receive the reward of their bad and good works, or they will receive mercy, be delivered and saved (columns 68:18-69:4).

It is this idea of 'something of Satan' dwelling within the Upright one that raised suspicions of a messalianizing tendency to declare that a demon inhabits the person from birth and is removable only through prayer. The author, however, never claims that Satan substantively dwells in a person and then advocates a holistic approach to spiritual development, involving participation in the Church, its sacraments, and prayer.

The gradual triumph of the pledges of the Spirit in the Upright and the reception of the Paraclete in the Per-

63. That is, Upright.

fect parallel inwardly or spiritually the external decision noted in the previous section to renounce possessions and become celibate. The abiding concern of generations of spiritual leaders is that aspirants for the religious heights will only mimic the outer customs and practices of the saints without possessing a genuine inner spirit. The author does not yet perceive an incongruity between the inner spirit and public practice, for progress or decline in one is mirrored in the other.

The Social Situation of the Liber Graduum

TIME AND PLACE

The real significance of the *Liber Graduum* is not, ultimately, in its biblical and extra-biblical witnesses, nor in its messalian connections. Its importance lies in the historical role it played during the late fourth-century transition from the 'pre-monastic' period of early syriac asceticism to the subsequent era when the image of egyptian monasticism colored the lenses through which we are allowed to perceive syrian monasticism.[64] To understand this picture, we must grapple with the social structure and setting of the *Liber Graduum*, its community, and its author—of which there have been few attempts at a synthesis.[65]

What do we know about the time and place of the *Liber Graduum?* Several oblique references to persecutions by idolaters and pagans have been aligned with persecution of Christians by the persian Shapur II from 340-372. The syriac editor praises the mettle of the author as being

64. Sebastian P. Brock, *The Luminous Eye: The Spiritual World Vision of Saint Ephrem the Syrian* (Kalamazoo: Cistercian Publications, 1992) 131-141; Sidney H. Griffith, 'Asceticism in the Church of Syria: The Hermeneutics of Early Syrian Monasticism,' *Asceticism,* Vincent Wimbush and Richard Valantasis, eds. (Oxford, 1995) 221-222.
65. The best is a short section by Peter Brown in his *The Body and Society: Men, Women, and Sexual Renunciation in Early Christianity* (New York: Columbia University Press, 1988) 334-337.

equal to the likes of Gregory Nazianzen, Basil of Caesarea, and Evagrius Ponticus (column 5:18). Since all three gained renown in the late fourth century, the editor could not have done his work before that period. The upper limit for the writing of the *Liber Graduum* may then be placed at the late fourth century to the early fifth century.

The author refers metaphorically to the inability of a young student to swim across the Lesser Zab River (column 896:2), a branch of the Tigris, located in present-day northeastern Iraq between Mosul and Kirkuk in the region known classically as the Adiabene. Of course, this does not pinpoint a location for the *Liber Graduum* community, but the humorous nature of the author's reference indicates that the Lesser Zab was familiar to his readers and so not that far away. Nevertheless, without any other historical or geographical details regarding the author and the *Liber Graduum* community, we can only say that the *Liber Graduum* was probably written in the mid-to-late fourth century in a region within the Persian Empire.

The *Liber Graduum* exudes the rich aroma of being written in the midst of a living community of faith with ample human conflict and weakness, to which the author addresses his pastoral care and calls the Upright (*kēnē*) and the Perfect (*gmīrē*)—the two 'steps' (*masqātā*)—to a higher standard. This is not a monastery, however, the author is not an abbot, and there is none of the characteristic vocabulary of later syriac monasticism.[66] In this pre-monastic era of syrian asceticism, the author appears to be the spiritual father of the wider community,[67] dealing with those outside the Church as well as with those who have consecrated themselves to a special calling. He is the pastor and

66. The popular conception of a monolithic rise of monastic communities divorced socially and geographically from village and town society is challenged by James E. Goehring, 'Withdrawing from the Desert: Pachomius and the Development of Village Monasticism in Upper Egypt,' *Harvard Theological Review* 89 (1996) 267-285.
67. I will utilize the term '*LG* community' to refer to the religious community of faith ('Church') out of which the author of the *LG* functions.

teacher of a church who must tend to all of his flock, the ninety-nine and the one.

One is struck by the interdependence of the various levels of the *Liber Graduum* community: the ordinary laity, wealthy sponsors (column 57:9-12) and non-Christians. The Upright ones are ordinarily depicted as worldly merchants (column 305:2-7), providing for the physical needs of the poor and the 'professional' religious leaders of the community (columns 308:22-309:5; 328:2-5). The remarkable aspect of the Upright is that living in the midst of the work-a-day world they are a consecrated laity with their own rule and discipline to follow. Continually reminded of the possibility of rising to the level of Perfection, the Upright are working to create an ascetic life-style in the midst of a non-ascetic society—to a degree still the challenge of the Church today.

The Perfect ones are the 'mature' Christians who no longer struggle in the contest against evil. They have, to turn Athanasius' phrase around, made the city into a desert by living in the realized *eschaton* of the original Eden, while Adam 'had not yet sinned'.

Distinct from the image of the cloistered monk or even the solitary hermit, the Perfect did not take a vow of stability. Wandering in the region with no permanent domicile (columns 365:26-368:2; 505:16-19), they taught all manner of people (columns 61:10-14; 893:7-13), begged (column 529:10-12), and mediated disputes in other churches and communities (columns 37:9-14; 93:24-96:2). While the Perfect ones' intention was to transcend this worldly existence, their teaching and mediation brought them into continual contact with its conflict and weaknesses.

CONFLICT AND TRANSITION

Regrettably, the best source for information about the character of a society derives from its witness to conflict and transition. The author has revealed a rather substantial corpus of information on such matters; in fact, in a work of this length it would have been impossible for him to conceal his concerns and observations, some of which must have provided motivation for his writing in the first place.

There are three arenas in which these concerns and observations play: conflict and violence among several groups in the *Liber Graduum* community and from outside sources; a spiritualizing or quietistic tendency within the Church; and a perception of a spiritual malaise and loss of higher standards within the *Liber Graduum* elite.

Internal Conflict

On a quick survey, the main personages of the *Liber Graduum* appear to live a tranquil, uncomplicated life, fighting the internal battles of asceticism against evil, to be sure. In reality, there is considerable evidence of misunderstanding of the actions, functions, and purposes of Uprightness and Perfection among the wider community and within the ranks of the Upright and the Perfect themselves.

The author notes that many of those who are helped—'the needy'—will grumble at the Perfect one, claiming that he has money, food, etc., but 'he will not give', in an attempt to distract him (column 60:7-17). 'There will be controversy against him [Perfect one], yet he will neither judge nor demand [anything from] anyone, but will love everyone as a saint of our Lord...' (column 765:7-10). The author bemoans the fact that some of the *Liber Graduum* community still say that Uprightness is simply 'not doing evil to anyone' (column 636:3-10). All three statements point to a gap that has developed between the various constituencies in the wider community. Because their life-style is not simply defined and does not involve physical labor, the the Perfect are open to all sorts of fantasies and projections by the populace. So the hungry perceive the Perfect as well-fed, and the poor see them as comfortable and wealthy, which in turn makes them game for all sorts of accusations, perhaps similar to the celebrated case of Macarius the Egyptian, falsely accused of making a young woman pregnant.[68]

The Upright likewise have had their basic principles twisted by popular thinking, namely that since the higher standards of Perfection are not expected of them, they are free to live in the world just like anyone else—no better and no worse (column 636:3-10).

Tension also existed between the Upright and the priests to whom the former brought food and offerings from their business profits 'without being envious of the tranquil life of the priests' (columns 308:22-309:3). Among the several constituencies, therefore, there was suspicion and rivalry based on how each saw the other contributing to or abusing the economic system.

Religious Conflict

Conflict arose in many arenas, one being theological on the surface. 'Therefore, those who argue that our Lord has only one place of Life and a single Gehenna, where do they place these people who are a little unjust and a little righteous' (column 361:24-27)? The author seems to be confronting a conservative or fundamentalist faction in the *Liber Graduum* community whose moral rigidity caused it to see issues in black and white.

Conflict also arose when some families did not respond well to their children accepting the covenant of Uprightness or Perfection. The author observes that 'the world condemns Christianity', for parents found their children to be distressingly stubborn and disrespectful (column 772:11-25). The author admits that some young, immature Christians are arrogant about their faith and they should be humble and accept their family's criticism as long as they can. A Christian must be prepared anyway to accept lies and slander from many sides of society (column 773:2-

---

68. *Apophthegmata Patrum: The Sayings of the Desert Fathers, The Alphabetical Collection*, Cistercian Studies 59, trans. Benedicta Ward SLG (Kalamazoo: Cistercian Publications,1975) 105-106.

13). Almost paradoxically, the neophyte Christian is encouraged to stay at home as long as he can—the journey truly does begin at home (columns 773:14-776:7)—in order that he may be able to endure the persecution he will have to face once he begins his transient ministry of Perfection.

History has sadly shown on many occasions that the most violent conflict can occur between religious factions and that appears to be the case with three remaining segments of the *Liber Graduum* community. The disciples of faith and the disciples of love—intermediate 'steps' between the Upright and the Perfect—both experience violent and sometimes fatal persecution. The problem is that the disciples of love are persecuted by the disciples of faith (column 869:10-14)—a situation that previews the crisis of the deterioration of the Church. No explanation is given, but one can assume the forces of jealousy and desire for power as motivations for violence.

The disciples of faith, however, are, in turn, persecuted by idolaters and pagans (column 869:14-18)—possibly the Persians during one of Shapur II's persecutions—but there is too little evidence to be able to pinpoint the identity of any perpetrator. The author calls them the 'martyrs of faith' for they are also being killed by the idolaters. The disciples resolutely confront the idolaters and tear down their altars (column 869:18-25)—a popular and volatile practice in several regions of the Christian East in the fourth century—on account of the latter's evil doctrine.

The 'martyrs of love' are persecuted by yet another insider group, the 'members of the household of faith' (*bnay baytā dhaymānūtā*); they are essentially the local church members, the laity in traditional terms of the Church (column 872:15-17). The author sees the conflict originating in the arrogance of the members of the household of faith who, believing they possess the whole truth through faith, are enraged when the disciples of love speak about some 'hidden thing'—perhaps a more theological and theoretical perspective of the Perfect (column 872:19-25).

Importance of the Visible Church

The author assures the reader that those who kill do not become disciples of faith, but are *de facto* disciples of Satan (column 873:9-13). Nevertheless, these murderers are initially identified as the disciples of faith, which indicates that either admission controls to the discipleship were failing or that a strong-willed faction had broken away from the tradition of the fellowship.

The members of the household of faith appear several more times and the unfolding picture of the local church adherents is generally not positive. In an allusion to the Parable of the Prodigal Son in *Mēmrā* Ten, the author mentions 'the sons of the household of the father' (*bnay bēt abā*) (column 260:10-11, 17-18). These are local residents of the town who belong to the patriarchal establishment, a segment of society very similar to the members of the household of faith. They are the church members who 'have been here forever'. The author calls upon the faithful Christian to be hospitable to strangers, in apparent opposition to the less than welcoming behavior demonstrated by 'the sons of the household of the father' to strangers and sojourners in town.

Elsewhere, the author raises a problem familiar to modern churches when he blames Satan for convincing those in the Church that their profit margins are falling, and as a consequence these businessmen do not attend worship on Sundays—and presumably work (column 185:8-12).

Two messages are pointedly given to the members of the household of faith. Until one's knowledge and education is complete and mature, do not declare that the ideas of two teachers are the same. Examine many teachings first, for not all sons of the Church teach equally, says the author, or according to the will of the Lord (column 885:10-16).

As befits the Children or the immature Christians, the members of the household of faith are cautioned that while greeting evil people not to get involved with them

and absorb their ideas. Do not, on the other hand, persecute them and become their enemies, and therefore become evil oneself—both situations that the author had un-
doubtedly observed happening (column 889:12-25).

Robert Murray interpreted *Mēmrā* Twelve—with its
strident affirmation of physical prayer, baptism, sacraments,
and Church—as the over-stated apology of a sectarian group
trying to prove its orthodoxy.[69] But the issue is: which audience is the author addressing? Consistently, his audience
has primarily been his own community, not the wider
Church from which he might attempt to gain legitimacy.
When he declares that the visible church is the true Church,
the mother of all baptized, and the only way to the Church
of the heart and the hidden Church (column 292:21-25),
the author is counterattacking the inroads of a spiritualizing movement within the *Liber Graduum* community, which
sees the physical Church and its ministry as the impure
shadow of the Church in heaven.

The author later evokes an even stronger declaration of the integrity of the worldly Church. 'No one should
doubt the church or its priests, [for] from the catholic
Church all truth shall be known. Let us love even idolaters
and infidels, while the catholic Church is great in our eyes'
(column 780:1-5).

The Decline of Perfection and Messalian Behavior
There is no theoretical knowledge apart from the
practical, as the author points out in *Mēmrā* Twenty-Nine,
when he chastises the present generation, which ignores
the ascetical standards of past generations, preferring, if
not luxury, then at least a less severe life-style (columns
820:5-821:11)—a certain sign that the author considers himself to be in a deteriorating, spiritually declining church.

69. R. Murray, *Symbols of Church and Kingdom* (Cambridge, 1975) 35. 'There is
something "sectarian", something isolated and defensive, about the *LG*, with its
elaborate account of the Church "in the heart" and its relationship to the public
Church, to which the author perhaps protests too much fidelity.'

This painful assessment is a main theme of the penultimate twenty-ninth *Mēmrā*, but hints are given from the beginning of the work that vigilance to the standards of Uprightness and Perfection must be maintained. In the opening *mēmrā*, the complaint is more than rhetorical, 'But we have fallen even from Uprightness, doing to others what we do not like to have done to ourselves' (columns 17:27-20:2).

In *Mēmrā* Eleven, he warns those on the road to Perfection never to break a minor commandment while residing in the major commandments (281:10-13). No libertarian license is given here. Moreover, at the conclusion of *Mēmrā* Nineteen, he disdains the contentment of some to walk on the easier paths, which run beside the steep road to the heavenly city and Perfection, in order not to undergo as much discomfort in their asceticism. He reminds them that no one reaches Perfection that way (column 524:10-20).

While the author knows that most people know the commandments, he also knows that rationalizations for not following them are the first tactic of Satan, and the author has heard them all. When we want to eat lustfully, 'It is not what enters a belly which is harmful, but what comes out' (column 261:10-14; Matthew 15:11). When we do not want to pray, 'In our heart let us praise the Lord' (column 261:14-15). When we do not want to be diligent and work hard for the church, 'Our heart is a church' (column 261:15-17). If we want to put on luxurious clothing, 'Inwardly we mourn, for God does not care for visible things' (column 261;17-19). If we do not want to be bothered comforting the naked or poor, 'In our soul we are justified and shall hear our own illnesses (first)' (column 261:19-22).

The author is not fooled, for he declares that evil teaches us all these things and makes us believe we work in the heart, while in fact we work neither in the heart nor in the body. No one accomplishes righteousness with his heart and does not also accomplish righteousness with his body (columns 263:23-264:3).

This spiritualizing of physical asceticism qualifies as alleged faults of the messalian movement—an unhinged discipline that convinces its practitioners that they are spiritually advanced beyond the need to fulfill the law within the physical world. Physical fasting, prayer, simple clothing, helping the needy do not matter anymore, if they can accomplish all these disciplines 'in their hearts'. The author of the *Liber Graduum* recognizes the bankruptcy of this attitude, calls it by name, and summons the Perfect, in particular, to repentance.

The author has come to realize the practical consequences of such a misinterpretation and mispractice of the ideal of Perfection. It takes quite a while for ascetics to callous their bodies and spirits to the demands of physical asceticism. In the same way, little by little one can undo all the progress made in the pursuit of Perfection through an imbalanced spiritualizing (columns 265:23-268:2). One becomes fat and petulant like the Israelites, the author complains, and after a while may even forget that he is a Covenanter (*barqyāmā*) and forget to serve God, just as the Israelites forgot God who had saved them (column 265:15-22).

Mēmrā Twenty-Five, 'On the Voice of God and the Voice of Satan' (columns 733-753), is another sermon in which the author approaches the same problem of relaxed discipline from a different angle. The author observes that the Perfect, being childlike and not really mature, are susceptible to the scheming of the Evil One since they do not know how to discern the voice of God from the voice of Satan.

The Evil One is crafty, changing his snares everyday, so the Perfect cannot easily figure him out by means of a routine. Indeed, 'because [the Perfect one] does not understand the truth in any way, the Evil One makes [him] stray and binds him onto the earth, yet that person is convinced that, in fact, he is bound in heaven' (column 733:1-15).

The results of the Evil One's activities, however, are discernible to the author. Under the pretext of providing comfort for the afflicted, Satan convinces the Perfect that acquiring a little wealth through occupations allowable in Uprightness and building a little dwelling adequate for hospitality to strangers is a virtuous initiative (column 741:21-26). Cultivating a little garden to grow vegetables for the sick and healthy certainly cannot be a bad idea, even though laboring is usually not a prerogative of the Perfect (columns 741:26-744:2). Gradually, Satan has made the Perfect abandon their perfect road and return unwittingly to Uprightness. The Evil One has beguiled the Perfect back down to earth, just as he did to Adam (column 744:19-21).

Then before long, the Evil One will pull them down as well from Uprightness. Satan sends messengers to them telling them that 'people are plundering your house'; 'others are picking through your garden'; still others are stealing and killing your flock of sheep. All this starts with the Evil One advising a heavenly one to own property and build a house upon it (column 748:1-19).

It is in this sermon that the author begins to laud the Upright ones whom he perceives to be more serious and often more mature in their asceticism. Nevertheless, it all begins with the witness and example of Jesus, for the ascetical, celibate life is deemed the original shape of existence. '[Jesus] demonstrated clearly through his person Perfection and the holiness (*qaddīšūtā*) of the first creation of Adam' (column 736:15-17).

Perfection is still the goal of fallen humanity. The author muses that if all people had reached Perfection, God would have rained food and clothing upon them without them having to work for it (column 737:18-23). Moreover, if all people had earnestly desired holiness/celibacy, God would have created children for them just as God had made a daughter (Eve) for Adam without marriage or lust (columns 737:26-740:2).

But after God saw that Adam loved earthly things,

God allowed him to be married and to become an Upright one in this world, and therefore to be saved and not utterly perish (column 736:23-26). Whoever works the earth in Uprightness will inherit eternal life, but will not become a Perfect one (column 740:4-7). Our Lord commanded the Upright to feed and clothe the Perfect, and they will then be able to live the life of the new world as a reward (column 737:13-18).

The author remonstrates against a pattern of behavior, perhaps recently begun, that works to undermine the basic mission of the Perfect. God commanded these 'heavenly ones' to treat every person well. Evidently, among the Perfect some exceptions had arisen.

'Where did you get the idea that no one should speak with a worthless or deceptive [person], because it may be [the case] that he will become a Perfect or an Upright one?' The author refers to the incident of Jesus speaking to Ananais regarding the notorious Saul (Acts 9:11-15). Ananais recoils at the thought of dealing with such an evil man, but Jesus tells him that Saul is his chosen instrument, a fact that he may not yet understand (column 745:13-23).

The Perfect appear unable to comprehend the mature nature of their calling and are easily manipulated to live a distorted version of the way of Perfection. The author perceives that they have lost their bearings on the nature of truth—hearing voices of Satan rather than voices of God. As such, these failings of the Perfect do not appear to be messalianistic—in some instances, a well-meaning intent to use their financial resources and property for the good of the needy. Yet, without a clear understanding of how the rigors of Perfection intersect daily living, they appear susceptible to a variety of libertarian and insideous misinterpretations of the christian way of life. Certainly, one cannot make Messalians out of them at this point, but the litany of their misunderstandings of Perfection does till fertile soil for the excesses of Messalianism.

The author continues to challenge the luxurious

life-style the Perfect have adopted, denigrating the memory and reputation of the ascetical saints who have gone before them. 'We teach others, but do not teach ourselves' (column 820:13-14). They eat meat and drink wine improperly, dress in lavish clothes, possess wealth and are lords of the domain, and keep a suspicious eye on strangers (columns 820:14-821:3).

The author never mentions Messalians and may well have had no idea of their existence in his frame of reference. He does not like the shift he has seen develop among his charges of undisciplined and luxurious living, boredom with aspects of the spiritual life, and a prideful elitism separating themselves from their inferiors. The author roundly condemns this behavior, which has fallen from Perfection to a state below even that of Uprightness, as illegitimate.

The author perceives his lapsed Perfect ones as betrayers of the Christian ascetical ideal, and in numerous sections, the *Liber Graduum* assumes an anti-messalian agenda. So here is a book that provides both an unwitting source for the messalian trajectory, while at the same time rejecting vehemently the legitimacy of any such distorted practices.

Purpose for Writing of Liber Graduum

It is the persistent witness of conflict that makes the greatest impression. Violence at the hands of non-Christians and jealous fellow Christians, internal struggles for social status and honor, the battle to negate the influence of magical practices (columns 152:7-156:7), the controversies involving heretical teachings and idolatry (columns 769:9-13; 776:26-777:7; 781:26-784:2), as well as a quietiestic tendency among some in the church to do away with physical attributes of the ascetic and religious life, and a perceived slackening of spiritual standards and fervor in the Church; all this is fairly normal for any town in the mid-fourth century and cannot be suppressed by a spiritual father presenting a rule for religious life.

It was on account of this conflict and deterioration
that the author of the *Liber Graduum* determined to set pen
to parchment. The vision of the Church as the road to Perfection and the heavenly city was unraveling in the pas-
sionless conduct of the Upright and the Perfect, the desire
for comfort and property among the Perfect, and the pen-
chant for bitter rivalry and violence among the members
of the household of faith. While it is not spelled out, the
author appears to be particularly frustrated with the cur-
rent generation of the Perfect. He is more impressed by
the sincerity and diligence of the Upright and so spends
the last six *Mēmrā* focusing on their nurture and encour-
agement. If these worthy Upright ones can eventually
graduate to Perfection, a change of guard will have been
effected.

To address this situation, the author sets out in great
detail the ideals, duties, and theology of Uprightness and
Perfection—the way things should be. These formal discourses are mixed with a variety of other literary forms
through which we can see the existence of the less than
ideal. The *Liber Graduum* is, therefore, not a mere tranquil
treatise on the structures of the spiritual life, but a book set
in the midst of controversy and conflict, designed to ignite
a spiritual reformation.

The issue of anonymity still blocks us from seeing
further, especially in the interest of knowing whether the
author succeeded or failed. Intentional anonymity is not
the usual route for ancient documents; pseudonymity is
the more typical course.[70]

My conjecture is that anonymity was more in touch
with the spirit of Perfection in humility and self-effacement.

---

70. A. J. M. Davids suggested that the title 'blessed one' (*tūbānā*) given to
the author by the editor is intended to be the syriac rendering of the greek
'Makarios', perhaps the author of the *Fifty Spiritual Homilies*, which have a
literary affinity to the *LG*. Few have adopted the suggestion.

The *Liber Graduum* community, the Church, was the living Body of Christ that would survive, not the name of a writer. The community of the *Liber Graduum,* therefore, was not destined to survive in a public way, for its strong group identity was built apparently around an individual who in turn felt the group was more important than the individual. As we have seen, even his standards, the status of Perfection, while strong at times, slid toward weakness in the *Liber Graduum* community at the end of the book (his life?). At his death, his insistence on anonymity further weakened the group. What remained were his writings, his description, and his aspiration for the Perfect life. These survived silently in his followers and those who followed them.

The Use of the Bible by the Author of the Liber Graduum

As is the case generally with fourth-century syriac writers, the author lives in a thought-world saturated by the Bible.[71] Virtually all his illustrations and allusions are biblical—with the exception of *Mēmrā* Six, 'On Those Who are Made Perfect and Continue to Grow' (columns 140-144), which gives the analogy of a king having a chest made for his jewels.

The author's use of Scripture does not dwell upon the exegesis of words or 'proof texts', though certain texts reappear as frequent themes, nor he is shy in relying upon the words of Jesus and Paul. His primary focus, however, is on narrative units, extended exegeses being numerous on these passages.

Predictably, the author's free retelling of a biblical story has the not-too-veiled purpose of interpreting and

71. Cf. Hughes Oliphant Old, *The Reading and Preaching of the Scriptures in the Worship of the Christian Church, volume 2: The Patristic Age* (Grand Rapids, Michigan: William B. Eerdmans, 1998). Old includes Chapter IV: "The Syriac Church" (247-295) examining the preaching and Biblical scholarship of Ephrem of Nisibis, Narsai, Philoxenus of Mabbug, and the Syriac Lectionaries of Mosul and Athanasius V.

justifying the institutions of the Upright and the Perfect. *Eisegesis*—reading *into* the text the meaning one desires—is the author's most delightful foible, for this practice elicits a creativity that presumes that the patriarchs and apostles are still contemporary models and companions for the faithful journey.

There are also a good handful of references to non-canonical works, some of which are debatable whether they are direct quotations or merely dips into the same common reservoir of thought from the period. *Sirach*,[72] the *Acts of Paul and Thecla*,[73] the *Didache*,[74] the *Shepherd of Hermas*,[75] and the *Gospel of Thomas*[76] have each been hinted at, at least, in the writings of the author. The most fruitful path will be to examine briefly several approaches the author utilizes in his biblical *eisegeses* of the origins and behavior of the Upright and Perfect.

Mēmrā Nine, 'On Uprightness and the Love of the Upright and the Perfect' (columns 201-248), is an extended exegesis or, perhaps better, a catena or chain of exegeses on a peculiar theological problem raised by the status of the Upright and the Perfect. If these two 'steps' mirror the exploits of biblical predecessors, how do we interpret the status of the Old Testament prophets? These were the spiritual heroes of yore about whom no one doubted their impassioned devotion and relationship with God. Yet their violence against the foes of God and Israel—even murder—not only violated the principles of Perfection, but dragged them far below the standards of Uprightness as well. The Author details the sins and virtues of Jeremiah, Moses, David, Abraham, and Elisha.

72. Werner Strothmann, 'Jesus-Sirach-Zitate bei Afrahat, Ephraem und in *Liber Graduum*,' in *A Tribute to Arthur Vööbus*, ed. R. Fischer, (Chicago, 1977) 153-158.
73. Cf. column 772.
74. Cf. columns 145, 184, 185, 253, 308, 317, 320, 672, 921.
75. Cf. columns 193, 257, 525, 837.
76. Cf. columns 373, 485, 541, 605, 660, 825, 828, 856.

The strange case of Elisha and the children who teased him provides a striking example.

> But in another place [in the Scriptures], the Lord brought [Elisha] down from Uprightness and from love, when [Elisha] did to these children the thing that he would have hated that someone should do to him if he transgressed. To those who sought to kill him he did good things instead of bad, as is appropriate for one who seeks Perfection. [But on the other hand,] to those children who laughed and said, 'Go up, baldhead!', he did the thing that love and Uprightness do not do. But it had been the will of Elisha when he fed his enemies. Yet, when he killed the children, it was the will of God (columns 225:21-228:6; see also, 2 Kings 2:23-24).

Whether this was an issue that came to the mind of the author, or whether it was an astute objection to the Upright and Perfect from a dissident within or outside the Church, is not determinable. While not denying that the prophets committed some terrible deeds for which they were denied even the status of Uprightness, the author works hard to show that the violent prophets had many redeeming qualities and for the most part pursued Perfection. In the end, however, they were eventually admitted to the kingdom following the admittance of the disciples of Christ, the author explains, because they did what they did at God's command, not by their own will.

> Then there is a place [in the Scriptures] in which the Lord brought the prophets down from Uprightness and from love, while the rest pursued Perfection. If they were over-

> come [by temptations] here and there, and
> transgressed Uprightness without a com-
> mandment, the Lord reproved them, and it
> was obvious that they had acted foolishly.
> They [then] washed away their offenses and
> ascended to love and were confirmed (col-
> umn 228:6-12).

This divinely sanctioned exemption, however, was closed
with the canon; no one can commit such travesties today
against humanity and God and secure salvation in the end.

Mēmrā Nineteen, 'On the Discernment on the Way
of Perfection' (columns 445-525), the longest of the work,
adopts the typology of a road[77] winding a steep and peril-
ous climb to the heavenly city—the road of Perfection, a
'stairway to heaven' (a term actually never used). Veering
off the road are numerous paths[78] that are admittedly easier
to travel, either as alternatives or respites. These paths are
intended for the Upright, the Sick, and the Children, and
while they are virtuous, they will never reach the top.

The author presents twenty-five dichotomies of
roads and paths that offer the most nuanced distinction between Uprightness and Perfection in the *Liber Graduum*.
The roads and paths are scriptural verses that characterize
the two steps by adopting the formulaic pattern of 'the road
of Perfection is this...', and then, 'but the path that leads
you away from it is this...'. While the scriptures are fairly
well divided between Gospel and Epistle, with a couple of
Old Testament readings, the predilection is a Gospel for
the 'road' and an Epistle for the 'path'.

A couple of examples will give the flavor.

> This is the Perfect road, 'I am sending you
> as lambs among wolves' (Matthew 10:16).

77. ᶜūrhā
78. šbīlē

But the path that will lead away from it is this, 'Do not enter the villages of the Samaritans' (Matthew 10:5). This is addressed to the imperfect ones lest they enter with just anyone, until they receive the power from on high. When they are perfected in Christ, they will be able to be with any person and with whomever they wish to travel (columns 504:11-18).

Just to show that rules always have exceptions, an earlier dichotomy features a pauline scripture for the Perfect and a Gospel saying of Jesus for the Upright.

The Perfect road is this, 'Do not allow a spiteful word to come out of your mouth' (Ephesians 4:29). But the path that will make you turn back without coming near to the road is this, namely, when you seek to imitate our Lord and call the people, 'Brood of vipers, how can you do what is beautiful, being evil ones and sons of the Evil One?'(Matthew 12:34); or [if] you imitate the Spirit that spoke through Paul and you call people, 'Fools and those lacking in intelligence' (1 Corinthians 15:36). This power was not given to you (column 488:10-19).

A more decentralized, yet fundamental theme to the theology of the *Liber Graduum* is the description of the events in the Garden of Eden, including the Fall of Adam and Eve. In common with Ephrem and Aphrahat, the author idealizes the condition of the original human beings 'while Adam had not yet sinned'. In fact, the status of Perfection is perceived as a return to the angelic life before the Fall. Uprightness, by implication, is post-Fall—a virtuous, yet limited life-style.[79]

79. Cf. *Mēmrā* 21: 'On the Tree of Adam' (584-632); A. Kowalski's, *Perfezione e giustizia di Adamo nel Liber Graduum*, Orientalia Christiana Analecta 232 (1989), deals with this subject at length.

A problem the author apparently had to counter was why there had to be more than one status in the christian life. Responding to charges of elitism, the author interpreted the story of Simon Peter and Tabitha (Acts 9:36ff) as the model of differentiated ministry.

> When Simon had raised her and saw then that she could not bear the intensity of the higher ministry, he took her by her hand and gave the needy who had to be fed and clothed over to her, so that she could belong to the kingdom. But she would still remain inferior to the Perfect (column 81:6-11).

Later on, however, the author found it necessary to challenge the internal development of such elitism targeted against the Upright, along with pagans and foreigners. His biblical model of tolerance and openness is the familiar story of Paul and Ananias.

> Where did you get the idea that no one should speak with a worthless or deceptive [person]? Because it just may be [the case] that he will become a Perfect or an Upright one. As our Lord said to Ananias, 'Go, speak with Paul'.[80] And Ananias said to our Lord, 'My Lord, he is an evil man, and I have heard of the affliction he has laid upon the saints who are in Jerusalem'. Our Lord replied to him, 'Go speak with him, because he is my chosen instrument, for you do not understand' (column 745:14-23).

---

80. Ac 9:11-15

Perhaps the most compelling characteristic of the Upright and the Perfect is the sense of lowliness and humility that one must exhibit to all, especially to one's enemies. 'Consider others better than yourself' (Philippians 2:3), is cited numerous times, and is modeled by the relationship of Jesus to Judas Iscariot.

> [Here is] another [form of] suffering: when our Lord submitted himself and washed the feet of the person who was going to sell and deliver him to death, becoming a neighbor to his murderers. Our Lord made him sit and [then] stood before him like a servant and washed the feet of the one who hated him before he washed [the feet of] his friends. [For example, here was, on one hand,] the dreg of the disciples, that is, [Judas] Iscariot the thief; and [on the other], Simeon the chief [disciple]; but he began with Iscariot and finished with Simeon. Therefore, if you know who are your betrayers and the ones who will sell you out and the companions of your murderers, control your tendency [to strike out] and make them sit down and wipe their feet before [going on to] the feet of your loved ones, and do not make [it] known that they are your enemies, just as our Lord did not expose Iscariot (columns 420:14-421:1).

In the last few *mēmrē* the author becomes increasingly defensive of the worthiness of the Upright status, virtually not mentioning the Perfect. The biblical model for the Upright is taken to be Zacchaeus (Luke 19:8-9), with whose story the author performs a creative *eisegesis* to show that it is not necessary to renounce all one's wealth in order to be saved.

Understand from this that people are saved
if they do as they were commanded: [fol-
lowing] that precept, which is lower than
that perfect and superior precept, [even]
while they are married and possessing
wealth. [This is clear] by that demonstration
when our Lord entered the house of
Zacchaeus, a sinner and an extortioner and
doer of evil things, and admonishing him
made him a disciple with these commandments that are inferior to Perfection. [Jesus]
did not say to him, 'Unless you leave your
wife and your house and your children and
empty yourself from everything you own,
you will not be saved'. Look, the response
of Zacchaeus makes it clear that our Lord
admonished him in such a way that he need
not empty himself, because he knew that
he could not reach the power of that great
portion. Zacchaeus said, 'Everyone whom
I have cheated I will repay four-fold, and
half of my wealth only I will give to the
poor'. See, while he did not say to our Lord,
'I will abandon everything I have,' our Lord
did say the following to him, 'Today salvation has come into this house'. Zacchaeus
shall be called a son of Abraham, he who
when he promised to repay their lords what
he had extorted had said, 'half of my wealth
only I will give' (columns 924:13-925:9).

The Pastoral Sense of the Author of the Liber Graduum

There is no absolute certainty that the author of the
Liber Graduum was ever the pastor of the spiritual community of which he was a member. Nevertheless, it is obvious
that he wrote with deep pastoral concern for his audience,

and in the long run this concern provides the motivation for the writing of the work.

In detailing the characteristics and responsibilities of the Upright and Perfect, the author's primary focus is to ensure the salvation of his spiritual children at a time when maintaining the standards of old is more difficult. Witnessing the foibles of his protégés, the author has felt called to summon them back to a standard that will liberate rather than inhibit them.

As any pastor knows, however, the first steps on the path to freedom are not that free. Rigorous discipline is necessary for beginners and the immature, whom the author has frequently dubbed the 'Children' and the 'Sick'. A frequent prohibition directed to the Children is that they should avoid eating with sinners lest they be lured into evil ways. The author, nevertheless, understands that among the immature the prohibition to avoid sinners leads frequently to a hatred of the latter. While understandable, this enmity continues to inhibit the spiritual progress of the Children.

Instead, the author advises his students:

> If this child wants to be the most virtuous of all children, if he wants to mature quickly and reach perfect stature, and if he does not want evil to take root in him, nor to strike him down with children's complaints, he should take care not to be taken in by means of food or to be allured to a wrong way of thinking. Nor should he become anyone's enemy or expose sinners, but he should make peace with them, without eating bread with them (columns 100:14-101:7).

Yet to be a child, physically and spiritually, has its benefits for the pilgrim as he matures. The author must have had Jesus' words, 'Whoever does not receive the kingdom of God like a child shall not enter it' (Luke 18:17), in mind when he advises the solitaries who are encountering various dens of iniquity. The author shows as well that the psychology of children is not unfamiliar to him.

> Our Lord told us to become humble like that infant who suckles milk or [who] is being weaned. Where will you find a child who judges in the village or who knows who are adulterers or thieves in it? So not even the adulterers really hide from the children of whom our Lord said, 'become like them', because they do not know how to put them to shame, nor even is uncleanness revealed to their intelligence. But bring the child to the house in which there are adulterers and thieves and say to him, 'Enter and see what is inside', and notice that he does not perceive them as evil, nor whether they are naked, nor whether they are adulterers. We also should become infants with regard to these evil things and become Perfect ones in knowledge, in love, and in lowliness (column 400:2-19).

Demonstrating his balanced view of asceticism and the spiritual life, the author is emphatic in *Mēmrā* Ten that there is no authentic spirituality apart from the body and the physical realm, countering the tendency among many ascetics to consider the body evil and irrelevant to the spiritual journey.

> Gluttony harms bodies [even] when they are healthy, and hateful words and everything evil harm the soul. In other words, if the soul is harmed, the body is harmed; and if the body is harmed, the soul is harmed. For there is no inner person without an outer

[person], and there is no outer [person] without an inner (column 253:19-25).

Apparently responding to a disavowal of physical fasting by some of the Perfect, the author underlines the fundamental model of Jesus and his disciples.

When our Lord and the apostles emptied themselves, they emptied themselves completely and fasted fully with [both] their bodies and their souls. For they never said, 'We fast', while they lived luxuriously, enjoying delicacies. Nor [did they say], 'We renounce', while possessing. Nor, 'We build as if we do not build'. May no one turn us away from the ascetic discipline of our Lord and his apostles, not even from the fast that the prophets fasted, while they lay upon each side three hundred and sixty days (column 268:3-13).[81]

The test of a capable pastor is how well he is able to discern what is appropriate for individual pilgrims. The author knows not only what to do in the obvious situations, but also has had experience with individuals whom did not fit the usual categories. His solution is useful as well as compassionate.

He sends all the sick to the strong and the strong to the sick, as it befits the strong to bear the sickness of the sick. To the person who is not able to teach, not even himself, he says, 'Do not go to the sick, but to the healthy', lest [the sick] go to one another

81. Ezk 4:9

and die because there is no one who will
heal them (columns 280:24-281:2).

The fourth century was a time of tremendous
change and transition in the still young christian world,
conditions that typically engender conflict, inwardly- and
outwardly-directed. No christian community was immune
to conflict, so it is not surprising that the author frequently
must mention the occasions of conflict as well as offer counsel on how to resolve them.

Witnessing to the tension existing between the Perfect and the poor of the community arising over the perceived economic situation of the Perfect, the author offers
a concrete strategy.

> In case the rich do not see where the
> afflicted are, the person who wants to be
> Perfect should just show them where they
> are, and not himself take them into his
> house, thus involving himself in a great deal
> of distraction. Many will grumble at him,
> aggravate his spirit, and not allow him to
> become Perfect. For this is what happens:
> the person who has been helped grumbles
> and complains, 'You have got it, but you
> will not give it to us', and then they inflict
> harm on him who came too close to visible
> things (column 60:7-17).

Jesus' call to bear one's cross in following him extends also to enduring the pain of spiteful words and public reprobation. The author calls upon his disciples to transform evil into good.

> When [the Perfect] try to reconcile enemies
> who speak ill of each other because of their
> mutual hate, we must transform this speech

and instead speak good of them in this way: 'What if I tell you that the person you hate is very sorry he is not on good terms with you, and he wants to make it up with you'. He says, 'I am unhappy about this animosity; Satan has tempted me to abuse my brother who is a member of me'.[82] Even if he, whoever he is, has not said it this way, it will create a pause until the anger of those who are so far apart has cooled down, and they come to greet each other with a holy kiss.[83] If we do not transform their harmful words into harmless ones, as a result of all the spiteful remarks they make about each other, what a fine mediator you will make if you go and retail each side's exact words to the other! You will just stir up more trouble and they will not even be reconciled (column 96:2-18).

One of the most difficult and subtle tasks for any pastor, ancient or modern, is knowing when and how to advise separation from unrepentant sinners. Doing so without becoming an enemy of the sinner is a recurring concern of the author. He begins with the contrast between the disciples' angry inclination and Jesus' injunction.

This is the Perfect road, 'In every house you enter, proclaim peace over it and pray for its residents'.[84] But the path that leads you away from it is this, 'If they do not receive you, shake off your dust against them in anger,[85]

82. Rm 12:4
83. 1 Co 16:20
84. Mt 10:12
85. Mt 10:14

and ask who [else] is worthy? Enter and proclaim peace there'.[86] If this is the way it is,
we will love only whomever loves us and
we will fall short of that fast pursuit of Perfection. This is addressed to the disciples
who are young, lest they get into a quarrel
or get injured with words, as these disciples
who were still too young for Perfection said
there, 'Our Lord, do you wish that we
should call out and have fire descend and
burn up these who did not receive us?' But
our Lord rebuked them,[87] 'Do not talk like
this. Instead, love your enemies and those
who hate you and your murderers'. Because
of this he permitted them to shake off the
dust and leave (columns 500:6-501:1).

Moreover, there is a practical wisdom in separation
that works to the benefit of both sides.

This is the Perfect road, 'Forgive the
offender four hundred and ninety faults,
[even] if he offends you during a single
day'.[88] But the path that leads you away from
it is this, 'If he is not obedient to you, in the
presence of the church let him be separated
from you so that you do not associate with
him'.[89] This was spoken on account of the
wrathful and the dissolute, lest the wrathful destroy through their rage and the dissolute be encouraged in [their] sin, because
no one rebukes them and [so] they become
corrupted. But once they have separated

86. Mt 10:11
87. Lk 9:54-55
88. Mt 18:22
89. Mt 18:16; 1 Co 5:9; 2 Th 3:14

themselves there will be peace on both sides: on one side, in that they will not cause harm in their anger seeing the indignation of the offenders; and on the other side, in that they will not be harmed through their indolence because they see that no one rebukes, chastises, or warns them lest they come to these (column 492:8-22).

Our Lord allows the injured and the leader of the church, 'when you have censured the oppressor and the offender personally, or before one, two, or three, or before the whole church and he does not pay any heed, that person is a rebel'.[90] Get rid of that matter and forgive that offense and you will not ruin yourself nor be impoverished, because you will have brought to an end that matter. It will be an advantage for you to no longer demand requital for that fault. Our Lord will judge your judgment. Evict [the offender] lest another like him will be daring and become an oppressor and an offender like him.[91] From then on, distance [yourself] from whoever does not fear our Lord, from his sins and his destructiveness; even excommunicate him from your community without blows and without chains and our Lord will take vengeance from him if he does not repent and become ashamed, and being regretful, turn away from his evil deeds (column 497:1-18).

Most conflict, fortunately, assumes the quieter form of personal obligations and debts. One must not be casual

90. Mt 18:17
91. 1 Co 5:13

and cavalier about these seemingly minor situations, for they can lead to much more profound controversies.

> We ought to love everyone as the apostle said, 'Do not owe anything, except to love one another'.[92] We should know what we owe every person:[93] to whoever [requires] honor, [let us give him] honor; to whoever [requires] fear, [give him] fear; to whoever [needs] a greeting, a greeting; to whoever [wants] love, love; to whoever [needs] a visit, [pay him] a visit; to whoever [requires] knowledge, [give him] knowledge. But [if] the one to whom we owe honor is greater than us, let us not give him teaching so that he might find fault and say, 'Are you teaching me?' And to whomever we owe fear, let us not show him a naive love [lest] he should abuse us. And to whomever we owe an ordinary love, let us not show him sadness and distress him. To whomever we owe a visit, let us not greet him from afar [lest] he complain about us. And to whomever we owe a greeting, let us not linger with him lest he burden us with his stories and fables. To whomever we owe knowledge, let us not stop being with him until he is assured [of the truth], lest he be scandalized and perish (columns 780:20-781:16).

These insights witness to the fact that the author has not been isolated from mature relationships with people within the community.

Let your lowliness be evident to everyone

92. Rm 13:8
93. Rm 13:7

by its right measure, so that you will know
to which one you should owe each one of
these acts of lowliness and to whom [is owed]
two of them and to whom three and four,
and to whom you should owe all of them,
to him who brings you to Perfection and to
perfect food, as it is written, 'Let your lowliness be evident to all people.[94] And know
what you owe every person':[95] to whom a
greeting, to whom love and compassion,
and to whom fear and honor. Do not owe a
person anything except to love one another
(column 837:1-12).

The pastoral instinct of the author becomes clearest
in the last six *mēmrē* in which he moves from idealization
of the Perfect to justification and approval of the Upright.
He no longer focuses on the inferior achievement and spirituality of the Upright; he encourages them to keep all the
commandments and to renounce the world, so that they
too will reach Perfection. 'If they [the Upright] desire to
leave behind the earth, as our Lord commanded, and journey in the footsteps of his humility, they will quickly ascend to Perfection, for they are not very far from it' (columns 749:23-752:1). In any event, if they are faithful to
their calling as the Upright, they will be saved.

Not surprisingly, the author decides to throw his
lot increasingly with the Upright rather than the Perfect.
Rejecting the 'false fasters', those who make a great show
of their holiness, but without genuineness, he implies that
it is better to be a good Upright one than a failed or false
Perfect.

Therefore, the Lord reviled these false
people who fraudulently fasted and lowered

94. Ph 4:5
95. Rm 13:7

themselves falsely, and said, 'I will not accept a deceitful lowliness and a false fast. It
would be better for a person to eat and drink
and wear white [clothes] than to do evil
things while fasting and wearing sackcloth
and causing everyone to wail through the
evil things he does' (column 844:11-17).

The dichotomy by which the author portrays the
spiritual dilemma of his community and Church in the later
period is 'with passion/by rote'. Instead of throwing our
souls wholeheartedly into the ministry of the Church, we
prefer to go through the motions and do everything by
rote (column 816:17-820:5). The time had arrived for a reform of the hearts of the *Liber Graduum* community.

Most interpretations of the *Liber Graduum* have oper-
ated with the implicit assumption that the author was primarily a practical theologian, describing the aims and duties of
the Upright and Perfect within the ecclesiology of the mid-to-
late fourth-century Syriac Church. The starting point of the
Liber Graduum, however, was the pastoral response of the
author to the situation of his faith community. Along the way
he inevitably became a theologian in order to correct the abuses
and deterioration of the two steps. Aside from all his other
skills and gifts as a biblical exegete, elegant writer, and theore-
tician of the ascetic life, it is the concern of the author as a
pastor for his spiritual flock that motivates and directs the course
of the *Liber Graduum*.

The Value of the Liber Graduum *for Reader and Scholar*

For the reader who wishes to appreciate the *Liber
Graduum* for its spiritual message, there is an abundance
of material here by one of the great, though unsung, spiritual masters of the early Church. While there are count-
less insights to be culled from a work of this scope, three
general features of the *Liber Graduum's* spiritual journey
bear mentioning.

First, the author appropriately depicted the struggle for Perfection as a steep, narrow, and treacherous road. The Perfect may indeed be saints and 'like angels', but they did not float on clouds unencumbered by worldly problems on their way to the kingdom. Uprightness is a way of doing; Perfection is beyond doing—it is a way of being. It never is an easy road and the author does not present the reader with hagiography, but describes the difficulties and pitfalls that the Perfect encounter. As a result, Perfection actually becomes more attainable, for it is a road traveled by authentic and finite human beings, not floated over by angels.

Second, the author's impassioned preaching returns again and again to themes of a theology of the cross. Basic is the call to renounce the world, empty oneself and become celibate, take up the cross and follow Christ. Even more fundamental for the author is the reminder to consider others better than yourself (Philippians 2:3), in particular, those who are your enemies and sinners. This worldview reaches a climax with the plea to follow the example of Jesus in washing the feet of Judas Iscariot, his betrayer, before he washed the feet of Simon Peter, his greatest disciple.

Add this continual emphasis on humility, lowliness, and self-emptying to the anonymity of this author 'who did not make his name known', and one can see a very different model of the christian Church. Particularly, in contrast to the public relations-conscious contemporary church intent upon 'church growth', the faith community of the *Liber Graduum*, living in the midst of a not-too-friendly Persian Empire, offers a vision of simple reliance upon God's power and grace. What could be more beguiling in today's atmosphere than to see that the Perfect of the *Liber Graduum*—who have spiritually re-entered the Garden of Eden 'while Adam had not yet sinned'—do no work because that is the way God would have had it if Adam had not sinned and wanted to be like God? (columns 605:1-4; 612:3-4)

Third, the spiritual reader will take much gratification in the author's justification of the Upright in the last six *mēmrē*. Much of eastern christian writing on the spiritual life and asceticism leaves little room for a reader who does not personally embark on the monastic and/or celibate life. Gradually, the author comes to the realization that the persistent faithfulness of the Upright—'worldly Christians'—is to be preferred over a false Perfection and to be celebrated, not denigrated as inadequate. Once again, we are being permitted to look in on the triumphs and struggles of a real, living community of faith, not just listen to a theoretical idealization of the ascetical life.

Scholars, in turn, may reap analogous rewards as they are able to capture a picture of the Syriac Church during the so-called 'pre-monastic period'. The *Liber Graduum* is not written out of a monastery in any traditional sense, but in the midst of a secular community that copes with commerce and the poor, marriage and celibacy, the punishment of the courts and wanton violence. This 'pre-monastic' picture illustrates that the extreme asceticism for which the Syriac Church has become famous through such works as the *Historia Religiosa* of Theodoret of Cyrrhus[96] was not universal. Nor does syriac asceticism owe its entire heritage to the star of egyptian monasticism, as the *Liber Graduum* demonstrates a significant portion of the indigenous syriac tradition.

A major problem for the study of the *Liber Graduum* is that its theology of asceticism apparently disappears from the chronicles and literature of the Syriac Church. Its singularity works to further isolate the *Liber Graduum* from the historical record, making it appear as an exception rather than part of the rule. This is not, however, completely the case, for the trajectory on which the *Liber Graduum* rides touches down in the ascetical writings of Philoxenus of

---

96. *Theodoret of Cyrrhus: A History of the Monks of Syria*, trans. R. M. Price (Kalamazoo: Cistercian Publications,1985).

Mabbug in the early sixth century.

Philoxenus carries on the tradition and theme of the *Liber Graduum* in his even longer collection of *Ascetical Homilies or Discourses*.[97] No christological controversies concern this intersection of Philoxenus and the *Liber Graduum*, but it is the shape and social structure of asceticism and the spiritual life on which they agree.[98]

Not the exact same institution, of course, for the 'changed situation' of the late fourth century has become a new situation. Philoxenus, the monophysite bishop of Mabbug (485-519), is seen here addressing some of the monks (*dayrāyē*) on the spiritual life.[99] We are no longer in the pre-monastic era; monasticism in the traditional sense is the reality.

Therefore, when Philoxenus no longer describes the Upright and the Perfect in adversarial terms, but as a continuity, it is because the issue of renunciation of the world is no longer an issue for his audience. Not that every monk is a Perfect one. Indeed, Philoxenus adapts the Upright/Perfect dichotomy of the *Liber Graduum* to provide a progressive 'stairway to heaven' for his charges. 'The spirituality in which the Perfect exist is the reward of the righteous and the Upright' (column 350:8-10).

The *Liber Graduum*'s link between the pre-monastic period and traditional monasticism is beyond our scope and concern for now. Yet the question raises the potential for study that will enable us to locate the contribution and enduring legacy of the *Liber Graduum* to the life of the early Syriac Church.

97. *The Discourses of Philoxenus, Bishop of Mabbôgh*, I-II, ed. E. A. W. Budge (London, 1894-1895); *Philoxène de Mabboug: Homélies*, Sources Chrétiennes 44, ed. E. Lemoine, Paris: Cerf, 1956).
98. Jean Gribomont, 'Les homélies ascétiques de Philoxène de Mabboug et l'écho du messalianisme,' *Orient Syrien* 2 (1957) 419-432.
99. André de Halleux suggested that they might be the monks of Senoun, to whom Philoxenus had written several other important letters. André de Halleux, *Philoxène de Mabboug. Sa Vie, Ses Ecrits, Sa Théologie* (Louvain, 1963) 286.

The Book of Steps:
THE SYRIAC *LIBER GRADUUM*

Syriac Editor's Preface

Summary: While desiring anonymity, the author is recognized as one of the last disciples of the Apostles—a spiritual, not scholarly writer. The editor illustrates the author's approach by inserting here the last (and lost) section of the Liber Graduum. (c.1)

On that blessed one who published this simple doctrine of his, which is a wealth of mysteries, while desiring to remain anonymous.

Since this blessed one desired to remain anonymous, and no other author tells us anything about him, and since we do not know precisely when he lived, we can only accept the tradition that he was one of the last disciples of the Apostles. And we gather from his words that he was one of the first teachers who wrote in Syriac. We can also conclude from his teaching that he was not an ordinary person.

In order that the greatness and power of this person of God's spiritual understanding might be clear and manifest to the reader, we have taken care to quote the very last section of his work first, and then to give a list of the titles of his sermons. This we have done (c.4) in order that the reader of this section might plainly understand from it that he was a prophet, that he had received the Spirit, the Paraclete, that he was found worthy to speak about God, that through the Holy Spirit he has revealed and interpreted all these mysteries, and that he was a great and perfect man

3

who ranks with the apostles and prophets, like Agabus and his companions who are mentioned in Acts.[1]

He did not receive this powerful and spiritual teaching, which he left to us, from the thoughts of people or from the teaching of the wise, for the simplicity of his speech shows that he was not a scholarly writer.

From the simplicity of his style and the vigorousness of this particular section, we gather and deduce that his style is that of the ancient syriac language, and we are fully convinced that he has accomplished this work through the power of the Holy Spirit alone. He does in fact say himself that he was a prophet, 'If anyone (c.5) asks "from where does he get these things", then he should realize that it has been written, "The spirit of the prophets is subject to the prophets"[2] and "I will pour out my Spirit on all flesh",[3] namely on those who keep the commandments of our Lord and who imitate his humility.'

By this the author shows that he himself kept the commandments of our Lord and imitated his humility. Once again, he clearly speaks about himself also when he says, 'Do not suppose that in our time there are no people who prophesy and discourse about God', and other similar sayings that come out clearly in the first *mēmrā*, and also in this particular section.

Now let the quotation that we give here serve the same purpose to the reader as an account of his great achievements of the kind that we find in the biographies of fathers like Gregory the Great,[4] blessed Basil the Great,[5] and blessed Evagrius,[6] for our author is their peer in the things of God.

1. Ac 11:28
2. 1 Co 14:32
3. Jl 2:28; Ac 2:17
4. Gregory of Nazianzus
5. Basil of Caesarea
6. Evagrius Ponticus

Here then follows the last section of the last *mēmrā* of his work:[7]

If anyone rejects the testimonies of the Scriptures—of the prophets, of our Lord and of the Apostles—by saying, 'Who knows whether this is true?' or by saying, 'The prophets and the Apostles knew that it was true then, but who today knows that these things are true?' then he should remember (c.8) that it has been written, 'The spirit of the prophets is subject to the prophets.'[8] He should also remember the prophet through whom the Lord said, 'In the last days I will pour out my Spirit on all flesh, and your sons and your daughters shall prophesy.'[9] Again he should remember another prophet who said, 'My heart overflows with good words; I shall proclaim the works of the King. My tongue is like the pen of a skillful scribe, who is fairer in countenance than anyone.'[10] You see how the Lord poured out his Spirit at certain times and how sons and daughters prophesy, namely, those who keep the commandments of our Lord and who imitate his humility. See how their tongue is 'the pen of a skillful scribe,' that is of our Lord, who is fair and beautiful in countenance (this is something that is beyond comprehension), and their tongue is

7. A portion of a *mēmrā* that is lost at the end of the most complete MSS of the *Liber Graduum* (It is placed here in Ms α, but does appear in its correct place at the end of *Mēmrā* Thirty in Ms R.).
8. 1 Co 14:32
9. Jl 2:28; Ac 2:17
10. Ps 45:1

a pen to him, with which he writes wonder-
ful rules concerning himself, which tell
humanity to get to know him and to keep
all his commandments. So do not have
doubts and say, 'There are no people who
prophesy or discourse about God in our
time.' Perhaps you might say, 'I accept the
ancient prophets and the Apostles, because
they are proved true to me by the signs that
God, who spoke through them, has done
through them.' If the prophets of our time
do not perform any signs, it is because our
Lord does not (c.9) want to perform signs
through them, seeing that in our time
everybody believes in him, and whoever
does not believe in the ancient signs will not
believe in recent ones either. But as far as
we are concerned, through whom no signs
happen, let our preaching be accepted on
the basis of the testimony of the books of
holy people who did perform powerful
signs. If the prophets and the Apostles and
our Lord, whom we adore, are trustworhty
to you, then let them witness with their
words, that these are true and conform to
theirs.

End of the last section of the work of this holy person.[11]

---

11. Now, in Ms α, follows a (partly illegible) list of the titles of the *mēmrē*.

Mēmrā One

Summary: Humbling one's mind and submitting to the Holy Spirit are necessary in examining the Scriptures. Those living in the world operate by the minor commandments. After Adam fell from Perfection, he remained in the state of Uprightness, from which we, having broken the Golden Rule, have fallen.

(c.12) In which can be found an exposition of the commandments, showing for what purpose each single one has been given and to whom, why our Lord Jesus Christ gave major and minor commandments, and how one can distinguish Perfection from Uprightness, and that through the major commandments one becomes Perfect and through the minor ones Upright.

1. You brothers and fathers, who are our 'brothers and sisters' in Christ,[1] we must inquire into the words of our Lord one by one, as the Apostle said, 'Inquire into these words today, tomorrow, and unto the ages of ages'.[2]

Again he said, 'Exhort one another every day, until the day that is called "today"',[3] that is until death, in order that you may be built up by these words and build up your brothers. And again he said, 'Prove and see what is the will

1. Cf. 1 Tm 5:1-2
2. Apocryphal
3. Heb 3:13

7

of God, what is acceptable and perfect'.[4] He also said, 'Prove and know whatever is honorable and humble and beautiful, and penetrate into that'.[5] Again he said, 'When the Scriptures are read, two or three or more, (c.13) then let the interpreter (that is, he who participates in the Spirit) interpret it'.[6] And he said, 'the fruits of the Spirit can be summed up as: goodness, lowliness, self-control, patience, gentleness and kindness, joy and peace with all people, and love for all people'.[7]

2. Therefore we must seek the truth, for as our Lord said, the truth will set us free.[8] That implies, however, that we must humble ourselves and subdue our mind,[9] for these are sacrifices to God;[10] this is [God's] will, and to such people he manifests his truth. But there are people who lower themselves to a certain degree only; they do not do it in front of everybody, and they do not subdue their mind. For this reason, they do not know what the truth is. There are others who do subdue their mind, but who do not lower themselves in front of everybody on earth. For this reason, they too are ignorant of the truth.

Indeed, pride is an obstacle preventing knowledge of the truth, and sluggishness is an obstacle to perceiving what lowliness really is. None can know the will of God from ink,[11] but only when he partakes of Him in the Spirit,[12] that is to say, unless he is the gentlest and humblest of all people, in accordance with the passage of Scripture that says: 'To whom shall I look and in whom shall I dwell except in a gentle and humble spirit who keeps my word'.[13] Therefore

4. Rm 12:2
5. Ph 4:8
6. 1 Co 14:27, 28
7. Ga 5:22
8. Jn 8:32; Mt 18:4
9. Literally, 'break our mind'.
10. Ps 51:17
11. That is, by simply reading the Scriptures.
12. Cf. Heb 6:4
13. Is 66:2

only the person who partakes of God in the Spirit can understand Scripture and distinguish the commandments. (c.16)

However, all of us labor for the physical ministry and not for the spiritual ministry.[14] Not one of us hates himself and takes up his cross while lowering himself (which implies that on earth he will not have a support for his head).[15] The diligent among us merely give alms from their possessions; this is a proper thing to do—in order to get saved thereby—for worldly people. But we really should leave everything,[16] enter into the lowliness of our Lord and into his self-emptying.[17] These things belong to the major commandments; we shall show in more detail what they consist of. Yet as it is, we are living by the minor commandments only, the 'vegetables' and the 'milk',[18] and not by the major ones, the true 'solid food'.[19]

Therefore, we do not know how to distinguish the major commandments from the minor ones, nor the higher ministry from the lower ministry. And we do not understand what the significance is of the 'food of the sick', which consists of 'vegetables', or of the 'milk of the children'. Equally, we do not know why forgiveness is given to one person only, and not to the other.[20] In the same way, we do not know which commandments must be kept in order to receive the Paraclete, or which ones must be kept by a 'sick' person in order to be healed, or which ones a person must keep to 'grow like a child'. Also, we do not know which are the commandments that have been given to everyone, by which one becomes a 'blessed one of the Father',[21] through the pledge of the Spirit.[22] (c.17)

---

14. Cf. *Mēmrā* 3
15. Mt 8:20
16. Mk 10:28; cf. Mt 25:21
17. Ph 2:7
18. Rm 14:2

19. 1 Co 3:2
20. Lk 23:43; cf. 7 below
21. Mt 25:34
22. 2 Co 1:22, 5:5

3.   There is however a difference between the gift of the
Spirit and the blessing of a 'limited pledge'. We do not understand why some commandments have been given to
one individual only, and cannot be used by anybody else.
Nor do we know what are those laws by which, if a person
keeps them, he is not saved, even though his punishment
may be less as a result—laws that do not apply to the Perfect or the Upright.

We also do not understand how, by the Paraclete, one
person 'grows' more than another, nor why by 'eating vegetables' one 'sick' person is healed more effectively than
another, nor why by 'milk' one 'child' becomes more beautiful than another, nor why one person is blessed more
than another when keeping the commandments that have
been given to everyone. And we do not know how to serve
our Lord physically, nor how we must serve him spiritually, nor why the torment of one person is more tolerable
than that of his fellow on the basis of the judgment that
has been passed on all. After all, it was the consequence of
one's own decision and of his own hardness of heart that
he fell from Perfection and even from Uprightness, which
is inferior to Perfection.

4.   Once our father Adam had fallen from the state of
Perfection, he remained in the state of Uprightness. This
state is characterized by the fact that one does not do to
anyone else what is hateful to oneself, and what one wishes
others to do to himself, one does to the other people he
meets.[23]

We, however, have fallen (c.20) even from this state.
We now do to others what is hateful to ourselves, and whatever we do not want others to do to us, we do to our fellow
human being; and as we want to be treated ourselves, we
treat nobody else. I personally, and indeed every one of us,

23. The Golden Rule: Mt 7:12; Lk 6:31.

want others to treat us well. But because we do not treat
anybody well, least of all the people who treat us badly, we
have abandoned Uprightness. I personally, and indeed all
of us, hate to be wronged by someone, even if we have
wronged him first. When, therefore, we do wrong to somebody, or when we do wrong to someone in revenge, we
have effectively fallen from Uprightness. For we do to others what we hate others to do to us, and we do not want to
do to others what we want others to do to us.

We shall explain further about Uprightness in the
appropriate place; for the moment, we shall try and define
the commandments. We must admit, however, that we do
not know for certain what each state comprises with regard
to the precise 'nourishments' and 'ministries', nor how
much higher the superior state is than the inferior state.
Also, we do not understand what our Lord meant when he
said, 'In my Father's house there are many places'.[24]

5.   Let us begin then to explain what we said above by
commenting on each commandment in turn, following the
instructions of our Lord.

Now the commandments that have been given to individual people only are the following. To Abraham alone
God said, (c.21) 'Sacrifice to me your son whom you love
so much'.[25] No one else can fulfill this command today, or
else he would be put to death. But one should take this
command as an example that one must love God more than
one's own son and that one must not put one's son above
the teaching of God.

6.   Furthermore, the Lord said to Hosea, 'Go, take yourself a harlot as your wife'.[26] But no one else could follow
this command today and take a wife who daily commits
adultery with other men. If anyone does marry such a wife,

24. Jn 14:2
25. Gn 22:2
26. Ho 1:2

he must do that after she has left the marketplace.²⁷ The Lord, however, allowed Hosea to take this woman as his wife while she was still standing in the marketplace. This he did in order to admonish, by means of her, the Israelites, who lived in fornication themselves.

So, when they came to judge him for taking a harlot as his wife, he then judged them and condemned them to death, 'If you judge me because I have taken a harlot as my wife at the command of the Lord, then how much sooner will the Lord condemn you to death, because you have fornicated and committed adultery with idols, having abandoned the commandments of the Lord your God'.

7.   There is a kind of forgiveness that is given to one individual only, such as to the robber who alone was forgiven without having any works to his credit.²⁸ Other people are not forgiven when they have no works to refer to, only when they have done penance.

We shall speak about the other commandments elsewhere. (c.24) If you want to understand why this robber was forgiven: in his case the king came to his door while he was not aware of it.²⁹ He granted him his petition and forgave him. Our Lord disposes of the things that are his own. To you he says, 'Repent and I will forgive you'. So he showed the richness of his mercy by the example of this one person, in order to encourage the penitent, who keep his commandments in their penance: how great are his mercies that he even had pity on someone who had no works to offer, and yet forgave him!

The end of the first *mēmrā* which is about the discernment of the commandments.

---

27. That is, after having given up her profession.
28. Lk 23:42-43
29. Cf. Heb 13:2; Mt 25:40

Mēmrā Two

ABOUT THOSE WHO WANT
TO BECOME PERFECT

Summary: Perfection is attained through the major commandments, by which one becomes humble and sees the Lord in the Spirit during this life. Those who keep the major commandments eat from the trees of the spiritual paradise, while the minor commandments are like milk and honey for those pursuing the lesser path. The Evil One tries to trick some not to go beyond the minor commandments, yet through the Paraclete one can surpass even the major. (c.25)

1. Now let us expound the major commandments, through which a person is made Perfect; that is to say, those commandments that were given by our Lord and his apostles to the Perfect, and distinguish them from the 'vegetables and milk'. Our Lord did not dictate them one by one, and it is not because we are more perfect than him and his apostles that we write them down one by one, but because today there are hardly any people who expound them. So it was necessary to write them down, so that even simple people may attain insight, and everyone may struggle to enter by the narrow gate[1] (c.28) of Perfection, or inherit the place[2] of Uprightness below it.

---

1. Mt 7:13   2. Jn 14:2, cf. *Mēmrā* 1.4

If someone does not make a sufficient effort, so that he does not even inherit the place below Perfection, he should undergo proper treatment in the quarters of the 'sick' or he should be fattened with the 'milk of the children'. By keeping those commandments that have been given to all people let him become a 'blessed one',[3] in other words, an Upright one. In the case of someone who has fallen from Uprightness, it is necessary for his good works to exceed his evil works in number if he wants to be rescued from hell and be saved, instead of slipping down and sinking into torment. If he does sink into torment after all, at least his agony will be a little more endurable.

2.   To those who want to become Perfect, our Lord has said the following:

□ To him who strikes you on the cheek, offer the other also; pray for him and be Perfect.[4]

□ If anyone forces you to go one mile, go with him two miles.[5]

□ If anyone takes your coat by force let him have your cloak as well.[6]

□ Love him who hates you, bless him who curses you, pray for the one who harms you and persecutes you.[7]

□ Say: 'Our Father (c.29) in heaven, forgive us as we have forgiven'.[8] This is because Jesus said, 'When you are

3. Mt 25:34
4. Lk 6:29; Mt 5:39
5. Mt 5:41
6. Mt 5:40
7. Lk 6:27
8. Mt 6:9,12; Lk 11:2,4

offering your confession to God, forgive your brother, be reconciled to him and then offer your gift'.[9]

□ Judge not, and you will not be judged; condemn not and you will not be condemned.[10]

□ And who made me a chief or a judge over you?[11]

□ Yet if I do judge, my judgment is true.[12]

□ I have not come to judge the world, but to teach them in lowliness, to save them, and to be an example to my disciples, that they should do as I do.[13]

3. To those who want to become Perfect, I teach this:

□ A good tree bears good fruit.[14]

□ Overcome evil by doing all kinds of good to everyone.[15]

□ I have no support for my head on earth.[16]

□ Imitate me and abide in my love, just as I have kept my Father's commandments and abide in his love.[17]

□ By this all people will know that you are my disciples, that you love one another.[18]

(c.32)
□ A new commandment I give to you, that you love one another, even as I have loved you.[19]

9. Mt 5:23ff
10. Lk 6:37
11. Lk 12:14
12. Jn 8:16
13. Jn 3:17, 9:39
14. Mt 7:17

15. Rm 12:21
16. Mt 8:20
17. Jn 15:10
18. Jn 13:35
19. Jn 13:34

☐ Bless and do not curse.[20]

☐ Do not call one another fool, or empty-head, or idiot, or odious fellow.[21] For if you do that, you will not attain Perfection.

4.   Whoever curses, gets angry, or finds a fault in himself but does not eradicate it, will not attain Perfection.

☐ Whoever does not leave everything, take up his cross and follow me (that is, my way of life), is not worthy of me.[22] That means, he will not inherit the kingdom of heaven together with those who do take up their cross.

☐ Whoever looks back is of no use to me.[23] That means, whoever abandons these major, gentle, and renunciatory commandments, descends to the minor ones.

☐ Whoever hates his life, loves me.[24] This refers to whoever does not love the life of this transient world.[25]

☐ Everyone who finds his life will lose it.[26] That is, he who weans it, but lets it fast from the world.

(c.33)
☐ Whoever does not forgive seventy times seven is not worthy of me.[27] That means that whoever demands reparation for even small injuries will not become Perfect.[28]

☐ Whoever does not wash the feet of his enemies—as I did to Iscariot—because he knows that they will hand him over to death is not worthy of me.[29] That means that he will not

20. Rm 12:24
21. Mt 5:22
22. Mt 10:37ff; Luke 14:26ff
23. Lk 9:62.
24. Jn 12:25; literally, 'he who hates his soul (=himself)'.

25. 1 Jn 2:15; 'life' also in Syriac.
26. Mt 10:39
27. Mt 18:21
28. Mk 6:15
29. Jn 13:3-15

become Perfect and become my brother, my mother, my sons, and my sisters.[30]

☐ Whoever does not go to whoever needs him, as I went to John (the Baptist) who needed me, will be no disciple of mine.[31] That means, he will not be great.[32]

☐ Everyone who humbles himself will be exalted, but everyone who exalts himself will be humbled.[33] That is so because (to exalt oneself) is an abomination before God.[34]

☐ Give to him who begs from you. That is to say, whatever you possess.[35] If you possess earthly goods, give from out of them. And if you possess heavenly goods, then give from out of those to him who asks for it. Otherwise there will be material envy in the case of someone who holds back material goods, and spiritual envy in the case of someone who holds back the Word from a person who is capable of it.[36]

5.   Pray and do not lose heart, that you may not enter into temptations and afflictions.[37] (c.36)

☐ [Saint Paul said:] To keep me from boasting of the abundance of revelations, a thorn was given me in the flesh, a messenger of Satan, to afflict me, to keep me from saying 'I have been highly exalted' or 'I have achieved very much'.[38]

☐ Do not be anxious about what you shall eat or what you shall drink.[39] That means: do not work for the sake of your own belly.[40]

☐ Those who keep these commandments and who are born

30. Mt 12:49; 2 Co 6:18
31. Mt 3:14
32. Mt 20:26
33. Lk 18:14
34. Lk 16:15
35. Lk 12:33-34; Mt 6:19-21
36. Cf. 1 P 3:15
37. Lk 18:1, 22:40
38. 2 Co 12:7; Jr 9:24
39. Mt 6:25; Lk 12:22
40. Rm 16:18

again, are like the wind that blows where it wills.⁴¹ That is, they are in heaven with our Lord, and there is no power that can overcome them, because they have conquered in the fighting without, in that they have no strife or battle with humanity; and they have discarded the fear within⁴² in that they only fight against sin and not against their brothers, the sons of Adam, even if the latter kill them. Therefore, they have delivered their will and liberty from him who wants to subject them to slavery;⁴³ they see the Lord himself in the Spirit, in this world as in a mirror, and when they have departed from their bodies, they will see him face to face,⁴⁴ as from glory to glory.⁴⁵ For they closed their eyes and shut their ears to wickedness, seeing the King in his beauty in distant lands.⁴⁶ (c.37)

6.   Count everyone better than yourself and become all things to all people.⁴⁷

□ Everyone who does not follow in my footsteps,⁴⁸ and does not enter into the house of tax collectors and prostitutes to teach them, as I have done to set you an example,⁴⁹ will not become Perfect.

□ Let all people know your forbearance; greet everyone with a holy and pure kiss.⁵⁰

□ Blessed are the pure in heart, blessed are those who make peace with everyone.⁵¹ They are the ones who not only reconcile their own enemies, but also help to settle the disputes of other people with their enemies. Thus they obtain the trees of the paradise above the heavens. Adam was al-

41. Jn 3:8
42. 2 Co 7:5
43. Ga 5:1; Col 3:5; Rm 8:21
44. 1 Co 13:12
45. 2 Co 3:18
46. Is 33:17

47. Ph 2:3; 1 Co 9:22
48. 1 P 2:21
49. Mt 9:10; Lk 15:1
50. Ph 4:5; Rm 16:16
51. Mt 5:8ff

lowed to eat of these trees[52] and enjoy them, before he obeyed the Evil One, and so was thrown out of paradise; its gates were shut in his face, not to reopen until Jesus decided to do so. For he broke down the wall of hostility,[53] and reconciled himself to the creation, making peace between what is on earth and what is in heaven by the blood of his Cross.[54]

7. Now the large trees of the spiritual paradise, of which those who keep the major commandments eat, are the following: faithfulness, abstinence, (c.40) lowliness, love, hope, truthfulness, and holiness in our Lord.[55] These are the things they eat and enjoy with our Lord.

Finally, I must say that no one should call any food common or unclean, as Simon (Peter) did.[56] These commandments, and other similar ones elsewhere in the New Testament, have been given to the one who wants to become Perfect. This person must use these commandments,[57] and abandon the others that are 'vegetables and milk',[58] in the same way as a child gives up [sucking] the milk of his mother as it gradually grows stronger. Then, instead of 'accuse your brother in court' and 'consider him as a Gentile',[59] the opposite is valid: 'judge not',[60] and 'forgive him whenever he sins against you'.[61]

The minor commandments, and other similar ones that have been given, are like the milk of the children and the vegetables of the weak; their effect is that a person does not grow up and is never healed. For this reason, I have taken special care to expound them, because there are people who want to become Perfect, but find themselves surrounded by the Evil One who out-maneuvers them with

52. Gn 2:16
53. Ep 2:14
54. Col 1:20
55. Ga 5:23; Ep 2:22
56. Ac 10:14; cf. Mk 7:14-19, Ga 2:12
57. That is, the major commandments.
58. That is, the minor commandments.
59. Mt 18:17; cf. Ga 2:14
60. Mt 7:1
61. Lk 17:4

the minor commandments. He prevents them becoming Perfect by making them believe that they would be sinning if they went beyond the minor commandments, but what they do not (c.41) realize is that it would in fact be very good for them to go beyond even the major commandments, provided they do it for the sake of love.

8.   If one is prepared to try, it will prove possible not only to surpass the minor commandments for the sake of love, but even the major ones. Our Lord said: To him who strikes you on the cheek, offer the other also.[62] Let such a person yield his back too, and then he will be greater than him who only presents his cheek. Let such a one never seek any revenge at all, and then he will be greater than him who only forgives seventy times seven.[63] Let him go more than [just] a [few] mile[s],[64] and then he will have humbled himself more than Jesus commanded. For he said: If anyone presses you with force to go one mile, go two more with him.[65]

In so treating the minor commandments, he will become ready for the major ones. Then he will teach the adulterers in peace,[66] and be greater than him who does not eat bread with them, who does not mix with them at all. So he teaches his brother in private not to sin. Such a person will also be greater than those who condemn him and dishonor him. Thus he will outgrow the minor commandments, stand fast in the major ones and become Perfect.

And he who stands fast (c.44) in the major commandments, which are gentle, will [go on to] lower himself more than is prescribed by the major commandments. Then he is glorified with our Lord[67] and has become greater than others who are standing fast in them. For it is possible to

---

62. Lk 6:29
63. Mt 18:21
64. Corrected. This whole passage is not very clear. Cf. section 4 above.
65. Mt 18:22, elsewhere in the *LG* simply: 'two miles' without 'more'.
66. Cf. Mt 9:11; Mk 2:16; Lk 5:30
67. Rm 8:17

become greater than other people through the Spirit, the Paraclete, when one lowers oneself more than is required by the commandments. Likewise, our Lord said: If I then, your Lord and teacher, who have not sinned or erred, have lowered myself so much, how much more ought not you, who are servants and sinners, to lower yourselves.[68] For since I have lowered myself before evildoers, how much more ought not you to lower yourselves before evil people! The end of the second *Mēmrā.*

68. Jn 13:14

Mēmrā Tḥree

THE PHYSICAL AND
THE SPIRITUAL MINISTRY

Summary: The Upright receive a lesser portion of the kingdom than the Perfect, engaging in ministry to the physical needs of others while not giving up possessions and wives. The Perfect perform the spiritual ministry of prayer, counseling, and teaching, while not being involved in commerce and worldly problems. God desired that no one would have to work, but Adam's sin prevented that from being realized. (c.45)

1. When two children eat the same vegetables and drink the same milk, one can still grow taller than another. In the same way, although the commandments have been given to all, one person still grows more than another: whoever lowers himself most grows best through the spiritual ministry, which consists in keeping the major and gentle commandments. Then there is also the physical ministry that is practiced by the person who simply gives to the needy in the manner of Abraham, without inquiring who deserves it and who does not, but who receives everyone as righteous people and as prophets,[1] though they may well be neither of the two. Our Lord gave his word that 'truly,

---

1. Mt 10:41

23

this person shall not lose his reward'.[2]

This also applies to him who makes his love shine on the good and the evil, as the Father's 'sun shines on all the good and evil',[3] but especially on those who build up and manifest the truth, who belong to the 'household of faith'. Scripture says, 'Do good to all people, and especially to those who are of the household of faith'.[4] So if (c.48) you give to the evil ones, you should give all the more to the good ones. If you are required to receive and refresh those who do have possessions and a profession, when they are staying or traveling in a country that is foreign to them, you should do that all the more to those who have no possessions or a profession, who apply themselves wholly to the teaching of our Lord, since 'no soldier on service, who gets entangled in civilian pursuits, can satisfy him who has enlisted him'.[5] For the servant of our Lord is continually in his presence, in accordance with what he said: 'Where I am, there shall my servant be also—with me and in my presence'.[6]

2.   One ministry is more excellent than another, just as one portion is greater than another; the portion of the Perfect is greater than the portion that is inherited by the Upright, who come second to the Perfect. The Upright are those who have various shortcomings, because they have not arrived at keeping all the commandments of our Lord. They do not do the whole of the 'great, acceptable and perfect will of God',[7] because they have not emptied themselves nor sought sanctification.

It was to these Upright ones that our Lord said, 'If you are not pursuing Perfection, then satisfy the hungry, clothe the naked, visit the sick, give relief to the oppressed, visit those in prison and supply their needs, welcome strangers, and whatever you do to those', thus our Lord says (c.49)

2. Mt 10:42	4. Ga 6:10	6. Jn 12:26
3. Mt 5:45	5. 2 Tm 2:4	7. Rm 12:2

to these, 'you do to me'.[8] 'Because of this,' he also said, 'Come, inherit the kingdom'.[9] Is this then a way for those who stand in the care and trouble of this world to become Perfect? No. Those who receive our Lord hungry and naked are always handicapped by various shortcomings due to the fact that they labor in earthly spheres and consequently cannot follow the whole truth, toiling as they are in [worldly] anxiety. Has he whom they have welcomed then deceived them when he said to them, 'Come, inherit the kingdom'? No, because our Lord never said that anyone who is not Perfect will not be saved. What he did say was that 'the disciple who cannot be of such a Perfection as I have demonstrated will not be able to attain to that portion from which Adam of old has fallen'.[10]

3.   But there remains a bequest even after the major portion; if someone acts justly in earthly matters in doing many good works and in not wronging anyone, he will thereby become an Upright one. Even people who occasionally commit transgressions or act in the wrong way, providing their good works are more numerous than their evil works, will still find mercy, be delivered, and saved. But they will not attain that major portion, which Jesus prepares for the Perfect, who will be allowed to dwell with him in eternal glory, unless they perfect themselves so that they are without faults when they depart from this world, in accordance with what has been written, 'As you shall be found, so you shall be taken'.

Such (c.52) people are contesting and wrestling like athletes; they 'strike and receive blows'. Our Lord said to them: 'If after having struck and after having received blows, you have won and come up from the contest, received the wreath and with it departed from this world, then your faults will not be remembered: as you are found in victory, so you will be taken, wearing your wreath'.[11]

8. Mt 25:40   10. Apocryphal, cf. Lk   11. Apocryphal, cf.
9. Mt 25:34   14:26, 27, 33   *Mēmrā* 15.4

Therefore, although the Upright, the doers of good works, do not inherit the particular portion of the Perfect, since they have not abandoned their riches and their wives, they will still inherit the lower portion, which is smaller than the first one.

4.   Our Lord said: 'I was hungry and you gave me food, I was thirsty and you gave me [something] to drink, I was a stranger and you welcomed me, I was sick, I was in prison and you came to me. Therefore, come, inherit the kingdom prepared for you'.[12]

The Perfect eradicate all their faults by the power of our Lord, while patiently praying to him. He then quickly grants them their petitions and vindicates them, for our Lord promised, 'I will vindicate them speedily'.[13] Behold, they are petitioning all the days of their lives, keeping (c.53) the commandments of our Lord and conquering their evil thoughts with which they fight continually within and without.[14] They patiently persist in petitioning until they have won, are crowned and receive the wreath of victory. Then they depart from this world and come with our Lord into that portion that he has prepared for them, that is to say, the highest level. This level is being prepared for those who through the Spirit have a spiritual ministry, which consists of keeping the major commandments. In this spiritual ministry and in this Perfection, they eradicate all their faults by the power of our Lord, as has been described above.[15]

To those, however, whose works are evil, the Apostle says the following, 'There is no inheritance in the kingdom of God for those who perform the works of the flesh: fornication, carousing, murder, drunkenness, adultery, and stealing'.[16] Because they never do an honest deed it is evident that they neither inherit the kingdom, nor receive salvation.

12. Mt 25:34, now ap-   13. Lk 18:7-8   15. Cf. 3.3 above
plied to the Perfect; cf.   14. Cf. 2 Co 7:5 and   16. Ga 5:19, 21
3.10 below.   *Mēmrā* 2.3

5.   About someone who every now and then does a few good deeds, and performs some occasional good works, the Apostle has this to say: 'On the day of judgment He will reward every person according to his works, whether good or evil'.[17] And as to the fact that I said that one portion is higher than another, our Lord refers to these two portions when he says: 'Whoever does not renounce all that he has, (c.56) takes up his cross, follows me and imitates me, is not worthy of me'.[18]

6.   Here he referred to the great and exalted mansion.[19] But when he said: 'Come, blessed ones of my Father, inherit the kingdom prepared for you',[20] he refers to a portion inferior to the first one, namely when he says, 'I was a stranger and you welcomed me'.[21] But who can receive strangers if he has no house, in accordance with the text 'I shall abandon my house and my goods'?[22] 'I was hungry and you gave me food'.[23] But who can satisfy the hungry if he has emptied himself and no longer possesses anything, in accordance with what our Lord said, 'Whoever possesses anything is not worthy of me'?[24] Is it not clear that this refers to the inheritance that is smaller than the one mentioned first? 'I was naked', He said, 'and you clothed me.' Who can clothe the naked if he has totally emptied himself and does not possess anything?

Well, a provisioner of the poor is such a man who in our Lord takes care of all sorts of miserable people, such as the sick, the naked and the foreigners, receiving from those who have and giving to those who have not. This is a good and honorable thing to do, and yet someone who does this does not empty himself in accordance with what the word of our Lord says, 'Do not be anxious in any way for your life in minding about food and clothing, but give away all you have to the poor, in a day or in a (c.57) month, and

---

17. 2 Cor 5:10   20. Mt 25:34   23. Mt 25:40˙
18. Lk 14:32; Mt 10:38   21. Mt 25:35   24. Apocryphal
19. Cf. Jn 14:2   22. Cf. Lk 14:33

then take up your cross and follow me.'[25] No, someone who does not possess anything himself, but receives from one person and gives to another, still stands in a relation of taking and giving, of accepting and providing with this world, and still does not empty himself in accordance with what our Lord said, 'Raise yourselves up from the earth and do not be anxious',[26] and in accordance with what the Apostle said, 'Seek the things that are above and set your mind on them'.[27]

7. It is better if such a person teaches his wealthy sponsors to become doers of good works personally and to give away out of their riches with their own hands to all the needy and afflicted, as the Apostle said, 'As for the rich who are in this world, teach them to be ready for good works and to store up treasures in heaven, and not to put their trust in transient riches'.[28]

So the person who has been put in charge of taking and giving should act as follows: he should teach the wealthy to give from their possessions to the poor with their own hands. He himself should be constant in prayer and intercession, in ministering and studying, in applying himself to the word of God's truth and to have it interpreted, in conformity with what our Lord himself and his apostles practiced when they appointed deacons for the sick, the naked, the strangers, the captives, (c.60) and all others in need, while they themselves attended to the word of God and prayer.[29]

Similarly, the person who takes up the Cross receives the Paraclete and becomes Perfect has no business whatsoever with things visible. However, if he does love those things, he is only an Upright person and not a Perfect one, because he has not severed himself from visible things.

---

25. Cf. Mt 6:25   28. 1 Tm 6:17-19; Mt 6:19-20
26. Apocryphal   29. Ac 6:4
27. Col 3:1

In case the rich do not see where the afflicted are, the person who wants to be Perfect should just show them where they are, and not take them himself into his house, thus involving himself in a great deal of distraction. Many will grumble at him, aggravate his spirit, and not allow him to become Perfect. For this is what happens: the person who has been helped grumbles and complains, 'You have got it, but you will not give it to us', and then they inflict harm on him who came too close to things visible.[30]

No, the perfect giver is whoever has renounced all his wealth and attends to those who are free for the knowledge of our Lord and to the salvation and perfection of all people. He is constant in prayer and supplication and in administering God's word on behalf of all people and of himself. Thus he is a benefactor to all people and to himself also, in prayer and in counseling concerning the new life. (c.61)

8.   Whoever takes up the Cross and teaches the Word can neither receive from one and give to another, nor buy and sell, nor take care of himself, unless the matter is very urgent. For our Lord said, 'Do not be anxious for your body, what you shall put on, nor about your own person, how to cover yourself'.[31] How can he who takes up his cross and who is required not to be anxious care for others with regard to these visible things? For he who takes up the Cross with regard to visible things receives the burden of having to pray for all people, and humbly to give counsel and to teach them all. He does this hoping that they will listen to him, but whether they do listen to him or not, he is bound to continue humbly to teach all people, whether they are worthy or not, because our Lord wanted it this

---

30. A similar warning against dealings with money intended for the poor is found in Basil of Caesarea, *The Letters*, vol. 1, Letter 42 *The Loeb Classical Library* (Cambridge, MA: Harvard University Press, 1961) 252-253.
31. Mt 6:25; Lk 12:22

way. He should even teach murderers and pray alike for
all who do evil to him and for all who love him.

9. There are people who hunger for visible bread and
there are people who hunger for righteousness and salvation.[32] Besides the physically naked there are those who
are devoid of the invisible garment, devoid of the light, the
life, and the kingdom. So they who possess visible wealth
clothe the visibly naked (c.64) and satisfy the visibly hungry, while they who are in the Spirit, who possess something that is invisible to carnal eyes, clothe those who are
devoid of the garment that is not transient, devoid of the
light and the life, with their wholesome teaching. They sow
into ears that hear clearly, according to what has been written, 'Rivers of living water shall issue from the bellies of
those who believe in Jesus, who keep all his commandments and do his entire will'.[33] Therefore, they satisfy those
who hunger for righteousness and for the solid food and
they make all people perfect in Christ. Our Lord himself
demonstrated to us what Perfection is and had these lines
as his record, 'You must be perfect, as your Father in heaven
is perfect'.[34] And the Apostle wrote, 'This is my struggle
and my toil, to make all people perfect in Christ by the
energy which works in me through the power of our
Lord'.[35]

10. This word of our Lord, 'I was hungry and you gave
me food, I was naked and you clothed me', must be given
a double meaning. First, that there are people who thirst
for the living waters about which our Lord said, 'Whoever
drinks from them will not thirst'.[36] Second, that there are
people who are infirm in body or in mind. So also there

32. Mt 5:6; righteousness = *kēnūtā* (uprightness)
33. Jn 7:38
34. Mt 5:48
35. Col 1:29, 28
36. Jn 4:14

are those whose body is being held captive by people, and those whose spirit is being held captive by Satan, (c.65) who do not receive the Spirit of the Lord, as Scripture says.[37] There are people as well who are alien to the human race as well as people who are alien to God. Now in the same way there are people who minister to those with spiritual needs. But those who minister to the spirit are of a much greater stature. For those who care for the needy are only opening a door for others, in that they receive from those who have and give to those who have not. The same goes for those who do good from their own wealth. If both of these categories of people keep themselves from all evil and do not do to others what is hateful to themselves, but treat other people as they would like others to treat them, then they are the 'blessed ones of the Father', to whom the Son said, 'Come, inherit the kingdom, which has been prepared for you'.[38]

But this is inferior to the good portion, which our Lord has prepared for those who have taken up their crosses, renounced everything visible, and followed after and imitated our Lord and his apostles. But all those 'blessed ones of the Father', who could not take up their crosses, are handicapped because they did not renounce everything they possessed, but are engrossed in this world through taking (c.68) and giving, and have not been able to receive the Spirit, the Paraclete, or to follow the whole truth, and become Perfect.

On the other hand, whoever takes up the Cross is exalted above what is visible. For just as when our Lord took up his visible cross, he was exalted above the earth and all that therein is, so whoever takes up his own concealed cross, separates himself from the earth, from its business, from all its work and from all its concern. Just as someone is bound alive to a visible cross, so a person is bound in the

37. 1 Co 12:14
38. Mt 25:34

spirit to this concealed cross while still alive and walking
on this earth.

11. There is a category of people who are devoid of the
pledge of the Spirit. They are rejected because they do not
have the Spirit of God at all. The Apostle said this, '. . . if the
Spirit of God is in you. And if not, you are rejected'.³⁹

There is another category of people in whom there is
something from God and something from Satan. They do
good works because of the pledge of the Holy Spirit that is
in them, and they sin and do evil works because of the
pledge of sin that is in them. The pledge of the Holy Spirit
admonishes them constantly to quit the evil and to do good
works and to crucify themselves for the Evil One in order
to conquer him. If they conquer him, they become Upright, and if they are prepared to raise themselves further,
they will become (c.69) Perfect; whereas if they remain as
they were,⁴⁰ then on the Day of Judgment they will receive
the reward of their bad and good works, or they will receive mercy, be delivered, and saved.

There is yet another category of people who have
cleansed themselves from the pledge of Satan and are full
of the Spirit of God every moment of their entire lifetime.
Our Lord said this to him who takes up his cross in imitation of himself, 'See I send you the Paraclete to be with you
until the end of the world'.⁴¹ The people of this category
belong to our Lord continually, and our Lord is in them.
But the person who does not even do one good work, neither in his body nor in his heart, and who never meditates
on honorable things, that person is devoid of God and his
grace.

12. As evil thoughts exist in the heart through the mediation of Satan, in the same way good thoughts exist in it

39. Rm 8:9
40. That is, Upright.
41. Jn 14:16; Mt 28:20

through the mediation of God, and whoever does both bad and good works has something from God and something from Satan inside himself. But whoever only does good works, empties himself, sanctifies himself, and loves all people—even those who are out to kill him—and he will not fail. He is made perfect by our Lord and filled with his Spirit, and whoever is full of the Spirit of Christ does all sorts of good works and thinks only good of all people, whether they are good (c.72) or evil; in him there is not a single fault. But if he should find some fault in himself, he will fight it, eradicate it, and so rise above what is hateful, even though he is still in this world. When he departs this life as a Perfect one, he goes to live with our Lord and will see him face to face.

There are also people in whom is only a little of our Lord; it is the so-called 'minor blessing', the minor portion which is called 'the pledge of God'. This category of people is to be distinguished from the people who have received the greatest of all gifts, which is called the Spirit, the Paraclete. They are fulfilled and replenished with this gift by God, so that Christ dwells in them completely.[42] A Spirit-filled person is recognized by the following characteristics: he is obviously instructed by that Spirit, he loves all people— even his enemies and those who are out to kill him—and he prays for them diligently.

13.   We must distinguish the greater gifts from the lesser ones, and the pledge from the full blessing. The Lord said this in connection with Miriam and Aaron—their gifts were smaller than those of Moses.[43] Also the seventy men who had received from the gift of Moses were inferior to him.[44]

In the same way, the portion of Martha was smaller than (c.73) that of Mary.[45] Although the Lord has commu-

42. Rm 8:11
43. Nb 12:2,7
44. Nb 11:16
45. Lk 10:38-42

nicated with all of them, only his pledge was in Miriam and Aaron, the seventy men and Martha. In this respect they were different from Moses and Mary the sister of Lazarus. But the person who does not do one single good work has nothing of the spirit of the Lord inside himself— he is rejected. Yet if we take up His cross in lowliness and holiness, we shall be exalted after our submission, just as he himself was exalted after he voluntarily submitted himself in order to become a model for us, as the Apostle said, 'Imitate me, brothers, as I imitate Christ'.[46] This is how Mary's portion came to be larger than Martha's, as our Lord testified about her, 'Mary has chosen the good portion'.[47] It was Mary who took up the Cross, which consists in practicing lowliness, the major commandments: she died to the world and its business and spiritually lived in our Lord; served him in the Spirit, was bound to him and glorified him all day (as the Spirit says about spiritual things, 'All day have we glorified God'[48]); and she instructed and taught women and made them disciples for our Lord, who worshipped and served together with those disciples who had received the Paraclete, serving our Lord in Perfection.[49]

At the same time, Martha served our Lord with clothing and food, for himself and for the crowd (c.76) that was with him, as she had a house and possessions, like Abraham, and she led an Upright life. But she did not go so far as to take up the Cross.

14.   So no one receives the Paraclete as long as his ministry is physically orientated, [if] he engages in taking and giving and his mind is tethered to the earth. No, he must shut his eyes to the evils of the earth and all its charm, which are the opposite of Perfection. The Perfect one is a stranger to the luxuries of royalty and court. This is the

46. 1 Co 11:1; Ph 3:17; cf. 1 Co 4:16
47. Lk 10:42
48. Ps 44:8
49. Mt 27:55, or after Pentecost?

reason why whoever is not Perfect is so much inferior to him who has been nailed to the Cross, who cannot move hands or feet, not being able to conduct business with the earth, but who contemplates, searches, and meditates on what is above, where Christ is seated on high at the right hand of God, and who has died to this world while he is still alive. On the other hand, those who do conduct business with this world and who use it to take care of the hungry and the naked, while doing evil to no one, will be saved; although they cannot receive the Paraclete, yet the pledge of the Holy Spirit will grow in them.

Those, however, who are in the Spirit are required by our Lord to be bound to him continually in thought in the sacrifice of the mind, in thanksgiving, in prayer and in lowliness,[50] and once (c.77) they have thus been polished while being set apart, to teach all people. The Spirit teaches them to instruct people in lowliness and to make all people ministers of God according to their abilities; whoever can serve in the spirit must be made a spiritual minister, and whoever can serve in the body must be taught how to serve our Lord physically. Ministers of the body are those who minister to the needy with food and clothing. Ministers of the spirit, however, are those who are able to distinguish the commandments and preach the true Word and show all people how to be saved and how to grow.

15. So no one should blame those who do not possess anything for not giving material alms, for this is not their ministry, nor does our Lord demand this of them. They are ministers of word and prayer. In the same way the apostles appointed seven deacons to take care of food and supplies, while they occupied themselves with teaching the word of God.[51] But even from these stewards, whoever wants to make the effort and empty himself, will reach the major

50. Ps 51:17; Is 57:15
51. Ac 6:4

commandments and stand fast in Perfection, as for example Stephen did, who was one of them. He emptied himself and received the Paraclete. He was killed while teaching the word and not while giving material alms. (c.80)

If many ministers are made who give material alms, but only one with a spiritual ministry who teaches people the truth and empties himself from the world, such a person, by means of many labors and keeping the major commandments and by teaching people to do the same, with difficulty will become a great teacher. And if he does more than he has been commanded to do, he will be praised highly by our Lord. It is such people that He wants as spiritual ministers.

To the ministers of the body our Lord has given the means of salvation for He who provides everything can provide for all in need, as He does provide for those higher worlds that do not labor or work for clothing and food, but continually give praise to the splendor of his majesty and do his will.

God in fact wanted these things to be this way; [God] wanted all humanity to praise him without having to work. It would have been so if Adam had only remained straight. But he did not, and neither did his sons; and we too exacerbate our Creator continually—our wickedness goes on increasing.

16. A spiritual ministry is greater than a physical ministry. Thus Simon [Peter]'s ministry was greater than Tabitha's: the latter was a minister of our Lord in physical things, but while she belonged to the kingdom, she was inferior to Simon and his inheritance, as he indicated when he prayed (c.81) for her to rise again.[52] Rather, Tabitha had the same ministry as Martha, and Simon the same ministry as Mary. Simon and Mary served our Lord spiritually, and Martha

52. Ac 9:36ff

and Tabitha served our Lord physically. When Simon had raised her and saw then that she could not bear the intensity of the higher ministry, he took her by her hand and gave the needy who had to be fed and clothed over to her, so that she could belong to the kingdom. But she would still remain inferior to the Perfect.

For Spirit-filled people treat all people with discernment. They show him who makes the effort to reach Perfection how to get there; and they make him into a spiritual minister in the ministry wherein the Spirit and salvation are found. They make the person who does not strive and seek this portion into a minister of physical things, that is, of what is visible, performing a visible service. Whoever is in the Spirit, however, ministers to what is invisible for corporeal eyes, namely to the soul, which is visible in the Spirit for the spiritual eye. Really, it is an easy enterprise for everybody; the only thing necessary is a deliberate effort of the will to empty and lower oneself, and then one can reach the highest level of Perfection. Then one will lower oneself even more and share in the glory of our Lord.

Here ends the third *Mēmrā* on the physical and the spiritual ministry.

Mēmrā Four

ON THE VEGETABLES
FOR THE SICK[1]

Summary: The diet of vegetables for the sick, designed for those still weak in the faith, is detailed. Procedures are outlined for those who feel the need to admonish others in order to maintain lowliness. Better yet, do not judge lest you be judged. Transform the hostile words of enemies into harmless ones and you will frustrate the Evil One by your gentleness to the good and bad alike.
(c.84)

1. Now, therefore, having shown what the commandments are that lead to Perfection, as well as what the ministry is that is inferior to Perfection, we shall give details about the diet of 'vegetables' for the healing of the 'sick'. Just as a sick person rejects all food, so he who suffers from moral rigidity can never cope with anything in which he discovers some imperfection, however small. As a sick person rejects good food, so the one whose soul is diseased grumbles against gentle moral attitudes, for he does not observe the beam in his own eye, but condemns the person who is, in fact, just like himself. Instead of correcting and admonishing him in love, he drags him into court.

This is why our Lord, who knows that the person given

1. Rm 14:2

to judging is at a loss with himself and does not take any notice of his own soul, nor has any mercy on (c.85) his brother, said to him, 'When you see your brother go astray, admonish him in love. If he does not listen, and you cannot shut your eyes from judging, nor close your ears from hearing evil about your brother, then go to him and rebuke him in private.'[2] For love covers very many offenses, but hatred incites judgment.[3] If he listens to you, you have gained your brother. But if he does not listen to you, and you feel you cannot leave your brother alone, then go to him with one other person. If he cannot be persuaded and you still do not feel easy about it, then go to him with two other persons. If he does not give in and you cannot keep silent and refrain from censuring him, then accuse him once more for the third time.[4] If you are not concerned about yourself and he is still unrepentant, then put him to shame before the whole church.

If he does not listen to the church either, then give up accusing him and leave him alone. This is enough; consider him as the rest of the pagans who are rebels.[5] You cannot rebuke such people, nor cause them to give up their fancies. Just as when you meet a pagan, and urge him to become a Christian, so you should urge your brother. (c.88) You must not regard him as an enemy, so that Satan may not devour him.[6]

Just as on 'solid food' one person grows more than another, namely the one who empties himself most, so also through this medicine for the 'sick' one person grows stronger than another.

2.   Therefore, whoever admonishes his brother in private instructs him if he listens, but if he does not listen he must leave him alone. It is better to do this than to expose him in front of another person. Yet whoever exposes him

2. Mt 18:15   4. Mt 18:16   6. 2 Th 3:15; 1 P 5:8
3. Pr 10:12; 1 P 4:8   5. Mt 5:17

in front of someone else has gained him if he listens. But if
he does not he should be left alone. It is again better to do
this than to expose him in front of two people. On the other
hand, whoever admonishes him and exposes him before
three people is a more tolerable person than the one who
judges and exposes him in front of the whole church. But
if evil does not allow to leave him alone, and he strikes or
expels him, then such a person has fallen from Uprightness because he hates the fact that nobody strikes the sinner, and therefore he strikes at [the sinner] himself.

So much for the discussion about those who should
eat 'vegetables' . . . If these people are willing to give admonition according to the manner that I have described for
them, they must admonish only in private. If they are being heard, they will have won their brothers, and if not,
the exhortations and judging should be dropped. They will
then quickly ascend to the 'solid food', and be healed and
made Perfect; they (c.89) will take care not to sin. For what
makes anyone fit to pass judgment on servants who are
not their own? If they fall or stand, they fall or stand before
their own master. Thus they can stand firm[7]—it is in the
power of Jesus to raise these people, as he raised Paul. For
how do you know whether the person you want to persecute and judge is not another Paul?

3.   Listen further to me, brother. Even in this admonition in private you must not be harsh on anyone, in order
not to do great harm to yourself. Rather, admonish humbly, calmly, and gently. For whoever wants to become Perfect must act according to what is written, 'Admonish him
who is affected by transgression with a humble spirit',[8] and
'Those who are strong must bear the failings of the weak
and be patient with everyone'.[9]

4.   Listen to me, brother. The advice I give to you and to
myself alike will be useful to you. When we meet an un-

7. Rm 14:4   8. Ga 6:1   9. Rm 15:1

clean person, we say only this to him, 'Brother, blessed are those who are holy and pure, for they shall see Jesus our Lord[10] and need not be ashamed in his presence; they are free from all evil and fast from the world and its pleasures'.

When you meet a stubborn person, speak to him as follows, (c.92) 'Brother, blessed are the meek, for they shall inherit the land of salvation'.[11] And then continue, 'Brother, if there is stubbornness in us, we must humble ourselves, sanctify ourselves, and through the greater and milder commandments we must strive to understand and know what is the height and depth and length and breadth with all the saints'.[12]

When you meet someone who has no mercy on his fellow human beings, then say to him, 'Brother, blessed are the merciful, for they shall obtain mercy,[13] even if they have committed manifold sins, because they forgive those who offend against them or rob them or do them great injury'. As they forgive, so they are forgiven by the just judge, and as they demand repayment, so God will require this at their hands. Ten thousand talents of transgression were remitted to the debtor, because he begged his master for it, although it was the rule that he, his wife, and his children should be sold. But then he went and demanded repayment from the man who owed to him;[14] 'So also my Father in heaven will act, unless each of you from the heart forgives his brother his sins,[15] even if they are four hundred ninety in one day'.[16] Let us realize that we too are all guilty before God. But if we forgive others, our Lord forgives us. (c.93)

5.   When you meet gluttons and thieves who hunger through greed, say: 'Brothers, blessed are those who hunger and thirst for righteousness,[17] and not for spoil, avarice, and greed, which is a kind of idolatry'.[18]

10. Mt 5:8	13. Mt 5:7	16. Mt 18:22
11. Mt 5:5	14. Mt 18:23-35	17. Mt 5:6
12. Ep 3:18	15. Mt 8:35	18. Ep 5:5

The whole sickness of morally rigid people basically consists in that they are convinced they get contaminated by the sins of their neighbor, even though they do not sin along with him. They think to themselves that if they see somebody sin and trespass and do not condemn or repel him—so they think—they get contaminated just like him. For this reason he whose spirit is diseased seeks to deal blows to him who transgresses, thinking that by putting such a person to death, or persecuting, or condemning him, he himself will come out justified and innocent and be safe from the other person's sins, which he imagines are gratuitously clinging to himself. This is why our Lord said: 'If your brother refuses to listen to you, consider him as the rest of the pagans who are rebels and are disobedient'.[19] Just as you do not judge outsiders, so you should not judge this brother of yours who has rebelled.[20]

6. When you meet people who are at enmity with each other, say, 'Brothers, blessed are the peacemakers, for they shall be called sons of God'.[21] Now peacemakers are those who reconcile enemies who belong to other churches, away from their own.[22] They make peace in the land of their Father, and are mediators (c.96) who reconcile people by imploring them, demonstrating lowliness to them, and admonishing them. When they try to reconcile enemies who speak ill of each other because of their mutual hate, we must transform this speech and instead speak good of them in this way: 'What if I tell you that the person you hate is very sorry he is not on good terms with you, and he wants to make it up with you'. He says, 'I am unhappy about this animosity; Satan has tempted me to abuse my brother, who is a member of me'.[23] Even if he, whoever

19. Mt 18:17
20. Cf. 1 Co 5:12
21. Mt 5:9
22. That is, they act as outside arbitrators, able to act because they do not represent any local interests.
23. Rm 12:4

he is, has not said it this way, it will create a pause until the anger of those who are so far apart has cooled down, and they come to greet each other with a holy kiss.[24] If we do not transform their harmful words into harmless ones, as a result of all the spiteful remarks they make about each other, what a fine mediator you will make if you go and retell each side's exact words to the other! You will just stir up more trouble and they will not even be reconciled.

7.   When you meet people who are inwardly entrenched in grievances toward each other, say, 'Brother, blessed are the pure in heart, for they shall see God'.[25] You should treat all people in such a discreet and humble way, advising them, from whichever point of access you may discover (c.97) to them. When the Evil One sees you being so gentle to both the good and the bad, it will howl:

> What shall I do? I have shown him impure and evil people, but he looks upon them as upon saints, and admonishes them as brothers! Alas, what shall I do? I now have nowhere to attack him, for my whole strategy is based on people hating each other, if only because of their sins! But this person loves sinners like our Lord! Alas, this person condemns me and destroys me just as He does! I had better quit and leave, rather than let him destroy me by a lowliness that resembles that of his teacher, Jesus!

Here ends the fourth *Mēmrā* on the vegetables for the sick.

24. 1 Co 16:20
25. Mt 5:8

Mēmrā Five

ON THE MILK
OF THE CHILDREN

Summary: The diet of milk is intended for the spiritually immature who avoid associating with sinners. Gradually, one may mix with sinners without imitating, exposing or condemning them. Jesus educated disciples to lead others to Perfection, as with Simon Peter regarding unclean food. The Paraclete comes only to those who are strangers to the world; reception of the Paraclete is the beginning of the way to complete Perfection, for one keeps growing until death.
(c.100)

1.   Now let us speak of those whose diet consists of milk. The command, 'Do not eat bread with adulterers, with violent people, with gluttons, with covetous people, or with people who swear'[1] concerns this person. As an infant, he is required not to eat bread with them, nor to mix with them. He is still a child whom they can easily persuade to agree with their way of thinking, because he is inexperienced and can easily be seduced like all children. The commandment orders him not to dwell with them until he knows himself and has grown up. Only at that point is he commissioned to go and teach them, to be a lamb amongst them, and to make these wolves into innocent lambs.

1. I Co 5:11

For this is what it says to him: if this child wants to be
the most virtuous of all children, if he wants to mature
quickly and reach (c.101) perfect stature, and if he does not
want evil to take root in him nor to strike him down with
children's complaints, he should take care not to be taken
in by means of food or to be allured to a wrong way of
thinking. Nor should he become anyone's enemy or expose sinners, but he should make peace with them, without eating bread with them. Note that the Apostle only said
'Do not eat with them', and did not say that one should
become their enemy or expose them. So whoever makes
peace with them while being on his guard is more virtuous
than he who does not eat bread with them, but exposes
them.

2.   Now someone could say, 'The fact that I do not eat
with so and so does effectively expose him, because those
who hear about it realize that there must be something
objectionable about him that makes me avoid him'. Indeed,
if one watches oneself, one will not have to be afraid of
eating bread with sinners. This in itself is not committing a
sin, not even when they are pagans. The Apostle merely
gave this command to prevent someone from being won
over to their wrong way of thinking, not because it would
be committing a sin.
     From this insight one quickly arrives at the command-
ment: 'Count everyone else better than yourself'.[2] Whoever has grown strong and arrives at this commandment is
engaged in loving all people, both fellow-countrymen and
foreigners, and suffers no harm in doing so. On the contrary, he honors them and regards them as better than
himself. Thus, whoever eats bread with them (c.104) while
being on the alert is better than he who does not eat with
them and exposes them with his lips. If the latter thinks
that on account of the other people's sins he is justified to

2. Ph 2:3

transgress and beat, curse or detest them, or to be their enemy in any other way, he falls from Uprightness. No, we should be at peace with them, just as with everyone else. We should admonish them; if they cannot be convinced, they fall into the hands of the malignant judges of this malignant world who will punish them. Yet, who knows whether our Lord will not deal with them as with Paul or the publican or the woman taken in sin?

3. For how do you know, you who are angry with a wrongdoer, if he is not another Paul, or one of the publicans, a Zacchaeus or a Matthew, or a Rahab the harlot, or someone like that samaritan woman who committed adultery with many men, about whom our Lord testified that she had had five husbands besides the one she had at the time he met her? All these people repented and were saved. Should we then exalt ourselves above sinners, without knowing ourselves whether we will end up as Solomon or as Iscariot, or like the others who were good to begin with but sinned in the end?

Scripture says, 'Do not rejoice at the destruction of your enemy',³ lest God brings his destruction on you and has no mercy on you as (c.105) you had no mercy on your brother. 'Whoever rejoices at misfortune will be his own ruin.'⁴ Is it right that our Lord should die for sinners, but that we should hate them? Even if we are merciful with them, we are still very much falling short of the kind of love our Lord had. But if we hate them, we shall see him in eternity.

4. There are still other commandments that come under the heading 'milk of the children', which our Lord gave to little ones. These are: 'Neither go on the way of pagans, nor inside the town of the Samaritans; instead, go to the sheep who have wandered from the house of Israel'.⁵ That

3. Pr 24:17   4. Pr 17:5   5. Mt 10:5

means, go to the sons of your own people and preach to them. Again: 'When you enter a village, ask who is worthy in it, and stay with him'.[6] 'Do not greet anyone on the way.'[7] 'When anyone does not receive you, shake off the dust from your feet as you are leaving, and it will be easier for Sodom on the Day of Judgment than for that town.'[8]

Are not these things, which our Lord said, contrary to the major commandments? After all, he himself said, 'Count everyone else better than yourself',[9] and 'Whenever you visit pagans at home, eat what they put before you'.[10] These two phrases seem to contradict each other: 'Visit pagans at home' and 'Do not go on the way of pagans'. (c.108) Our Lord really gave both these commandments. But he himself did not even ask first who was worthy before coming to stay. No, he stayed with bad people, so that the Pharisees murmured against him, because he always ate and drank with sinners, publicans, and prostitutes. 'Those who are healthy do not need a healer,' he said, 'only those who are entrenched in doing evil.'[11] Those words go further than the saying: 'Enter with him who is righteous and worthy'.

5.   The Apostle also, while being 'all things to all people'[12] himself in order to be able to counsel all people, commanded others not to mix with sinners in the way he himself did. For what would have happened if people who could not tell good people apart from bad had mixed with bad people? For this reason our Lord and the Apostle gave their disciples those commandments because of their weakness, which was the result of their immaturity. Just as when one who gives bread to a baby and seeing that he cannot eat it and is tormented by hunger, immediately gives him milk, which his physical capacity allows, with the result that he can now suck happily—thus did our Lord and the Apostle.

6. Mt 10:11   9. Ph 2:3   12. 1 Co 9:22
7. Lk 10:4   10. Lk 10:8
8. Mt 10:14   11. Mt 9:11ff

Because the disciples were truly children and had not yet grown into the knowledge of perfect disciples and were outwitted by clever speakers, they were afraid to visit pagans at home. In those days there were very many pagans. The Jews who feared (c.109) the Lord avoided the pagans as much as they could. For the Lord slew those sinners among them who visited pagans at home and who imitated them, forsaking Him and adoring idols. Because they had no power to resist, evil drove them to its way of thinking as soon as they looked to the pagans.

6. Seeing this, the Lord commanded the disciples, as children, not to visit pagans at home. For they thought, because they did not yet know the truth at this time, that whoever went off to teach the pagans was committing a sin, and that the Lord would slay him just like those who had exchanged the Good One who had fed them for Satan who was out to kill them; those who exchanged the living image for the dead calf. These people were bound with strong ropes, like slaves who had rebelled against their masters. Scripture says, 'Woe to those who call evil good and good evil'.[13] Just so the Israelites called the evil one who seduced them in the desert good, 'This is the Good One who brought you out of Egypt',[14] and they gave the impure one the holy name, 'The Mighty One of Jacob'.[15] So it is not the person who loves sinners, admonishes them and holds them to be good people—better (c.112) than himself—who incurs the wrath of God, but rather whoever distorts God's truth and whose love for evil people stems from the fact that he acts like them.

7. Thus [God] made them grow into knowledge step by step and he kept them from stumbling blocks until they were full grown and filled with the Spirit and would stumble

13. Is 5:20
14. Ex 3:24
15. Is 49:26

no more. For, 'Everyone who cannot retain solid food must feed on milk until he knows the truth'.[16] And 'Do not greet anyone on the way';[17] that means, do not speak with anyone until you have arrived at the place to which I have sent you. Our Lord told them this so that they should not, for the sake of a greeting, be caused to stumble or quarrel or strive if they happened to fall in with some argumentative person on the road.

Yes, our Lord gave them these commandments because they were children. But as they grew strong and big, they were allowed to become all things to all people, to help all people, and to counsel all people according to the example that our Lord gave speaking to all people in such a way as they could understand. For no one is punished for the sins of others and no one is rendered impure by contact with sinners, provided he does not imitate their works. The Apostle[18] expressed this when he said that not only those who commit sins are sinners, but also those who associate themselves with what they do; this is the case (c.113) with someone who turns a blind eye on thieves, adulterers, and murderers and so becomes their associate in murdering or stealing or adultery, or who shares in their spoil, or who is bribed to keep the secret. Because of any of these things, he places his portion with them.[19]

8.   Now if someone admonishes them in private and does not expose them seeing that they are his fellow human beings and because he would hate anyone to expose him if he had gone astray—with the result that he would have to beg everyone who saw him, 'Do not reveal me, or else I shall die'—such a person is not committing a sin. This is what one should say to a person who has gone astray, when observing him or hearing about him: 'My son, a bribe I shall not accept, but because love covers sins[20] and because

16. Heb 5:13-14   18. 1 Co 5:9f   20. Pr 10:12
17. Lk 10:4   19. Ps 50:18

I hate the disgrace of being exposed just as much myself, even if I had committed a murder, for this reason I shall do nothing that would make me fall from Uprightness. If I myself would hate to be exposed, how could I expose others and so become unjust instead of righteous? Therefore, no evil will come upon you through me.' It is written (c.116) thus, 'Evil comes, but woe to him through whom it comes'.[21] Let us understand that evil does not come upon people by itself. Someone either brings it on himself, or a neighbor brings it on him. Or it is brought on someone if God wants to test him or glorify him by means of Satan, like Job.

9.   It is evident then, that, in general, evil comes on someone through evil people—either through himself or through his neighbor. My son, evil will not come on you through me who just happened to see you, but if it has come through someone else who has seen you sin, or if it is through you yourself because you have committed this crime, then you must beseech God and make a covenant with him that you will not do this again and he will have mercy on you. But if you do not do this, then, even if you manage to escape the hands of people who know clemency, God will bring his wrath upon you. For you have hurt the heart of a person who is of your kin from Adam.

Far be it from me that evil comes through me and that I should do evil to anyone. In this way a person should correct his neighbor in private when he sees him commit a sin. In this way, he does not place his portion with adulterers and murderers, nor does he associate with them, but he is holy and fulfills the law of Christ. For whoever exposes the sinner does that which he hates other people (c.117) to do to him and he becomes unjust instead of righteous. If evil comes through him, he receives woe; yes, 'Woe to him through whom evil comes'.

---

21. 1 P 4:8

10. Then see how you are in fact running with thieves and how you put your portion with adulterers when you censure your brother or expose or scold him. Therefore, my brothers, let us admonish everyone in love: the sinner in a humble spirit, in order that he does not sin again; and he who stands upright, in order that he may stand firmer and firmer, continue to grow and not fall. Let us not judge or expose any person, lest evil comes through us. For it is written, 'Let us not judge, that we be not judged'²² and 'Be like your Father who is in heaven, who is kind to the good and the evil, who sends down his rain on the just and the unjust'.²³

Perhaps you will say to me, 'These words were written for the Perfect and I do not want to become Perfect, but only Upright'. Then do not get angry about what I am going to say to you. Let us assume for the moment that these words 'Do not judge' and 'Let evil not come through you' are addressed specifically to the Perfect. Then you will still have to admit that the opposite: 'Judge' and 'Expose' cannot have been addressed to the good, but merely to the weak, namely to those whom evil has conquered, who hate to the point of murder. Jesus said, 'After you have reprimanded a person, if he does not obey you, (c.120) consider him as a publican and a pagan'.²⁴ In other words, do not become so evil that you kill him or uproot him like a weed,²⁵ without perceiving whether or not he is perhaps really wheat.

11. There are people, like Paul, those publicans and those harlots, who were weeds in the beginning, but became good wheat in the end. Why should the Judge excuse you from the things he has commanded you, such as, 'Do not uproot the weeds',²⁶ or 'Whatever you hate that people should do to you, do not do that to others',²⁷ or 'Overcome evil with good',²⁸ or 'Judge not that you be not judged',²⁹ or

---

23. Mt 5:45
24. Mt 18:17

25. Mt 13:29
26. Mt 13:29
27. Mt 7:12

28. Rm 12:21
29. Mt 7:1

'Regard your neighbor as better than yourself',[30] or 'Forgive him who offends you seventy times seven',[31] or 'Yield your cheek and do not resist one who is evil',[32] or 'Woe to him through whom evil comes'[33]? What more should I write about your transgressing the whole law of the Lord, when you do evil to him who has offended you? And so, if you do evil to him who has not offended you, how very guilty and degraded you are before God, transgressing his law and not doing his will! He will certainly inflict severe punishment on you on the Day of Judgment. For you will not only not come to Perfection if you are judging and doing evil to someone, you will also fall from Uprightness.

But you (c.121) who seek to become either Perfect or Upright, give up judging. God will do the judging. Whoever is evil will fall into the hands of the evil judges of this evil world, and they will inflict punishment on him. If he escapes their punishment and does not repent, God will punish him, and from Him there is no escape. 'It is a fearful thing to fall into the hands of the living God', Scripture says,[34] for he will not be lenient on the Day of Judgment, as he still is here and now.

12. So, my brothers, in order that we be not judged while we are engaged in judging, or be hated while we hate, or vengeance be taken on us while we are avenging ourselves, or accused when we accuse and judged by the judgment that we apply ourselves, I advise that we leave off judging altogether and instead counsel all people in love. Scripture says, 'If you do not judge yourself, I will judge you, says God'.[35] However, if you blame or curse or beat someone, not controlling your anger and calming down, God will not judge you impartially. But if you want to be Perfect, then pray that our Lord will forgive the other person and that you will not be at enmity with him. For even Upright-

30. Ph 2:3; cf. *Mēmrā* 5.2, 6.1
31. Mt 18:22
32. Mt 5:39
33. Mt 18:7
34. Heb 10:31
35. Rm 12:19

ness, which is below Perfection, may not pray and beseech God that evil comes on him who does wrong to her. No, this is what Uprightness says: May our Lord act as he knows best. (c.124) If it is right that vengeance is taken, let him see to it; if it is right to forgive, let him forgive. Perfection, however, prays with her whole heart that God may forgive the person who has offended against her. God then does not avenge the person against whom the offense had been committed but only requires penance, because the Perfect pray for the offender to be forgiven.

13. There is no way in which anyone can resist the truth, do harm and distress to him who belongs to our Lord, and yet escape our Lord's chastisement. Only if he repents first, makes his supplication and prays for this transgression to be forgiven, will our Lord have mercy on him and forgive him. But if after our Lord's forgiving him, he goes off to demand satisfaction from someone who has transgressed against him, our Lord will change his mind and demand satisfaction from him. In the case of that debtor who had repented before our Lord, the Lord of the debt forgave him his debts.[36] He forgave him, although it had already been decided that he, his wife, and his children should be sold. But because this man in his turn indicted and sued a fellow-servant of his who was in debt to him (which means, he had transgressed against him) and did not want to forgive him, God retracted and required satisfaction for his former transgressions and did not spare him, as he had not spared his fellow-servant.[37]

So I advise that, as we have transgressed so much ourselves, we do not require satisfaction from anyone else for any transgression against us, but admonish both ourselves and him who transgresses, that until we are beyond transgressing, until we have done away with this ourselves, we should show mercy to our fellow-servants. For if we de-

36. Literally, 'sins'.
37. Mt 18:23-35

mand satisfaction, (c.125) God will certainly retract and demand satisfaction for the transgression for which we have done penance and which he has forgiven us initially, just as in the case of the debtor.

14. For there is no one among the sons of Adam, who has not in the first place sinned and subsequently been justified. This inclination was implanted in Adam on the day he transgressed the command. From then on it was implanted in all of his offspring from their mother's womb. As soon as they had come to know themselves, they struggled to overcome it and be justified, or they were overcome and defeated by it and started acting impiously. 'You wicked servant', it is written, 'should you not have spared your fellow-servant as I had mercy on you?'[38] 'So', it is written also, 'my father in heaven will do to anyone of you who does not from this heart forgive his brother his transgressions.'[39]

15. But let us return to the matter that was raised by us above, concerning the immaturity of the disciples, of whom God took good care. As a child, which is physically young, is educated by his physical mother with all the care and protection he needs, in order that he can grow fast and without infirmities and his growth may not be impaired, that his appearance may be handsome and beautiful, even so our Lord educated his disciples cautiously in the Spirit. [Our Lord did so] that they might quickly become spiritual and perfect people who would make many Perfect ones and turn again the captivity (c.128) of people out of the hands of Satan the corrupter, and prepare for the Lord a perfect people,[40] zealous for good works and loving its God with all its strength and all its heart and everyone else as itself—as it has been written in both Testaments,[41] a people

38. Mt 18:32   40. Lk 1:17   41. Dt 6:5; Mt 22:37;
39. Mt 18:35   Mk 12:30; Lk 10:27

proclaiming the one God and Lord of all, who is the Creator and Sustainer of everything to whom everything belongs.

16. Because of this he says to those who are immature: 'Ask who is outstanding and worthy and stay with him',[42] so that their mind is not impaired and harmed or ransacked and vilified by the evil one or by people through deliberate deception. If our Lord had not arranged it in this way of gradually tutoring them like children, we know they would have been caused to stumble. After they had received the Paraclete and our Lord had been taken up and the disciples learned the truth, they only spoke the word of God to Jews, and did not instruct the pagans and the sinners, in order not to be seized by evil people or by servants of the evil one, until our Lord moved them to do this. This was after they had received power and when he had sent a revelation to Simon, in which this one saw a picture of unclean animals. He said to him, 'Kill and eat'. But Simon rejected it with loathing and said, (c.129) 'Far be it from me'. But our Lord rebuked him three times, 'What God has cleansed, you must not call common'.[43]

17. Someone might object that he was speaking to him about real animals and meat, but this cannot be so since the apostles ate no meat at all; they fasted until the ninth hour and then they consumed just bread, salt, herbs, and olives. Rather, the explanation of 'Kill and eat' is: Seek the company of pagans and unclean people and teach·them—this is what God wants, so none of you will be defiled.

> And while Simon was perplexed about the vision, behold pagans entered and came toward him. The Spirit said to him, 'Rise, go with them without hesitation. For these are

42. Mt 10:11   43. Ac 10:13-15

the animals about whom the Lord has said
to you, "Kill and eat". What the Lord has
cleansed, none of you should call common
from this time onward.'[44]

Then Simon remembered that our Lord, before he
was taken up, had said, 'Go to all nations and make them
my disciples in the name of the Father and of the Son and
of the Holy Spirit'.[45]

Then everything became clear to Simon; he felt heartened, went out and began to make (c.132) the pagans disciples by teaching them what they had to do in order to be
saved. 'So, when he entered Jerusalem, the circumcision
party criticized him: "Why do you go to uncircumcised and
unclean people, and eat and drink with them, although
this is unlawful?"'[46]

But they criticized him on the basis of the minor commandments, 'You should not mix with sinners'. Thereupon,
he drew them on toward the major commandments, that
is, toward the solid food, saying, 'God has given me the
command that I should not call any person pagan or unclean'.[47] Thus God himself showed patience until the 'children' should grow strong. Then, once they had become
'adults', he gave them the 'solid food' through the Paraclete
and disclosed to them the whole truth. So they could now
build up each other, because they had come to know the
commandments that are superior to the others.

18.   So the Paraclete has come, whom the world cannot
contain, and whom no one can receive who has not become a stranger to the world, as our Lord said, 'The world
cannot contain the Paraclete, the righteous sons of this world

44. Ac 10:13-15, 17
45. Mt 28:19
46. Ac 11:2-3
47. Ac 10:28

can only contain the gift of the pledge'.[48] Now when the twelve apostles had received this Paraclete on that day at the same place, 'fear fell on them'.[49] For the Paraclete does not (c.133) make a person perfect straight away when he comes. He who has received the Paraclete has the knowledge of the whole truth so that he is saved, but he only stands at the beginning of the way to complete Perfection [for] right up to the day that he departs out of the world he keeps on growing. This is illustrated by what we discussed above, that when the apostles had received the Paraclete they were afraid to seek the company of pagans until our Lord reprimanded Simon, and Simon his comrades, 'for our Lord has sent us among wolves, not to righteous lambs'.[50] Paul, also, when he saw that his correspondents through fear were not straightforward about the Gospel after having received the Paraclete, corrected them, as is described in the Letter to the Galatians.[51]

19. Nonetheless, I am not saying that they were not in the process of being made Perfect. I am only saying that it never happens on one and the same day that someone receives the Paraclete, is made fully Perfect, and that fear is taken from him. However, whoever receives the Paraclete does receive knowledge of the whole truth. On the other hand, if someone does not know the truth, he has not received the Paraclete. The apostles, therefore, did know the truth after receiving the gift of the Paraclete, but on some occasions they were afraid and did not preach as they should have done. Therefore, Paul said to them, (c.136) 'You did not receive the spirit of fear',[52] and then they were heartened and, while accepting that they would be killed, they

48. Apocryphal. For 'the gift of the pledge', cf. 2 Co 1:22, 5:5; *Mēmrā* 1.2; 3.11-14; 15.16, 19.
49. Cf. Ac 2:2; *Mēmrā* 20.10
50. Cf. *Acts of John* (ed. Zahn) 4ff.
51. Ga 2:14
52. Rm 8:15; 2 Tm 1:7

now preached resolutely. Thereupon the Holy Spirit made them correct each other until they were Perfect. When the Paraclete comes, a person learns the whole truth. Once he has learned the whole truth, fear is gradually taken completely away from him; thus he is set free. And once he is free, he is made Perfect. When his vessel is perfect and he has fashioned its shape,[53] he grows day by day in love until the day that our Lord wants to take him off to himself. Then his dwelling is with him who is our God. He is everlasting and unchangeable, he remains forever as he is. He is glorified by his beloved and rejoices with them unto the ages of ages.

20. Concerning the saying 'Shake off the dust from your feet',[54] consider the following: When the apostles had entered somewhere and the inhabitants did not want to receive them, the apostles were angry with them and hard on them since they were still children in the truth. The apostles wanted to do the same as they had wanted to do when our Lord was still with them, namely call down fire from heaven on the village that did not receive them; this, in fact, meant that they reacted just like harsh people still react today. But our Lord reproved such an attitude firmly: 'Think no more of such a thing!'[55] He refuted them because, like children, they were still removed from the truth in this matter. He wanted them not to be so harsh, but to shake off the dust and leave (c.137) in peace. But from the person who did not receive them, not even when they prayed for him, our Lord will require satisfaction unless he repents. So whoever shakes off the dust and yet quarrels with the person who does not receive him is not an Upright person.

Finally, when they were Perfect in the Spirit, they heard from our Lord that they should pray for anyone striking them;[56] how much more should they pray for someone

53. Cf. *Mēmrā* 24.2   55. Cf. Lk 9:53-56
54. Mt 10:14   56. Mt 5:44

who does not actually strike them! Yet, woe on the Day of Judgment to him who has not received them.[57] After having become Perfect, they were indeed struck and dragged and thrown out through one gate, yet they returned through the other one, begging on behalf of their persecutors that they might live and not be burned, although they once begged just this about those who did not receive them.

Here ends the fifth *Mēmrā* on the 'milk of the children'.

57. Cf. Mt 10:15

Mēmrā Six

ON THOSE WHO ARE MADE PERFECT
AND CONTINUE TO GROW

Summary: Metaphors of the crafting of royal jewel chests and gold vessels parallel the preparation of a person for Perfection. Receiving the Paraclete, the Perfect one defeats Satan, dwells in the spiritual Eden, and grows to the level of angels. (c.140)

1. Let us now explain how one becomes Perfect, and how one can grow after he has become Perfect. Just as when builders and workers want to build a house or manufacture a chest for the king's precious possessions, they say to the king after they have built the house out of squared stones, and it has taken its shape, its construction is ready and its windows and doors have been decorated, 'See, the house has been completed,[1] you can now fill it with whatever you like'. Then the king begins to fill it day after day with all sorts of goods.

2. Goldsmiths also, when they cast a golden or a silver vessel make an opening in it with a lid on it, (c.141) provide a fastening with a catch in case a stranger wants to steal something out of it when the owner is not there. Then

1. Literally, 'made perfect'.

61

the goldsmiths say to the king, 'See, your chest is ready,[2] gather all your precious belongings into it; you can rely on it'. Then the king begins to store all sorts of merchandise in it day after day.

So it is also with a person once he has lowered himself from all things that are on earth, has subdued[3] his mind night and day, who counts everyone else better than himself, has emptied himself of all he possessed, and kisses the feet of his enemies. Our Lord will look upon this person's lowliness and send him the Spirit, the Paraclete, and he shall know the whole truth. Once he knows the truth, he will be able to distinguish truth from falsehood and wrestle with Satan and overthrow him as our Lord has overthrown him; and he will be free from evil thoughts. When he has conquered his enemy, he will be able to rest from this enemy's burning arrows—his painful sores will tighten into scars; his bruises caused by blows will heal, he will be his own guard of all his limbs. Then the king, Christ, will say, 'Behold, this person is now as perfect as on the day I fashioned him'. Then our Lord will open (c.144) the gates of heaven to him, and he will enter and enjoy the riches of its mysteries.

As the king we spoke of is daily putting precious objects into that treasury which the builder has built for him or the goldsmith has forged for him, so it is with this person: while living in the flesh on earth, his mind daily dwells in Eden in the Spirit, that is, in the heavenly Jerusalem. Thus he grows daily and is fattened, delighting and rejoicing in the Spirit, until he arrives at the measure of the spiritual angels. Then our Lord will come and take him away completely from this world, as he already took away his mind and introduced it into Paradise, and there, in the heavenly Jerusalem will be his dwelling place.

But first he will have kept the major commandments about which I have written above, and he will have be-

2. Literally, 'is perfect'.
3. Literally, 'has broken his mind'.

come Perfect. After having become Perfect and having lowered himself more than others, he will have mounted to that great glory—there is his dwelling place. Such is the dwelling with our Lord, which has been ordained for the humble and meek and holy, who are the inhabitants of the City of Life, who perform the good, acceptable and perfect will of our Lord,[4] while praying that the will of God be done by those on earth as it is done by those in heaven.[5]

The end of the sixth *Mēmrā* about the one who becomes Perfect and continues to grow.

4. Rm 12:2
5. Mt 6:10

Mēmrā Seven

ON THE COMMANDMENTS
OF THE UPRIGHT

Summary: Discourse on the way of Uprightness for those who choose not to take the hard road of Perfection. One needs to follow the Ten Commandments and the Golden Rule. The Upright must avoid dealing with any kind of magic or magicians. A person dies or lives according to God's decision, not Satan's. The Upright are given a medical ministry to those who need to be physically healed.
(c.145)

1. [This is] about the commandments addressed to the whole world on how to become Upright ones. Since not everyone drives himself to ascend to Perfection, these are the commandments for the Upright: 'Do not kill; do not commit adultery; do not steal;[1] honor your father and your mother;[2] have mercy upon the afflicted; do not fornicate; do not bear false witness;[3] do not plunder or defraud;[4] do not covet your neighbor's bull, nor his ass, his house, his wife, his field, nor his vineyard;[5] do not pull up his boundaries.[6] Whatever you hate, do not do [it] to your neighbor,[7] for as you wish people to do to you, so you should do to them.'[8]

1. Ex 20:13-16; Mt 19: 18
2. Ex 20:12; Mt 19:19
3. Ex 20:14, 16
4. Lv 19:13
5. Ex 20:17
6. Dt 19:14
7. Tb 4:5; Didache 1:2
8. Mt 7:12; Lk 6:31

However, by these commandments a person [only] becomes an Upright one, subordinate to the Perfect ones. For, just as one does not want someone (c.148) to kill him or steal from him or harm his animal or trespass on his field or vineyard or approach his wife or anything he owns on his land, if he himself does not do what he hates to his neighbor, he will then become an Upright one, passing through the property of his neighbor without causing grief to the latter, thereby becoming an Upright one before God.

Moreover, just as he does not want a person to curse him, not even when he makes a mistake, if he turns away from hating the one who shows him up, he would like them to forgive him when he is caught in transgression whether in adultery or in stealing. Even if he should go as far as to kill someone, he wants people to forgive him when he asks this from them. He should act similarly to whomever injures him with wrongs such as these, and [thereby] become an Upright one. Just as he would like someone to feed him when hungry and to refresh him when thirsty, and when he travels in a foreign country [to have someone] bring him into a shelter in winter and into the shade in the summer and give him what he needs, and just as he would like someone to clothe him when naked and give him shoes when barefoot, so should he do to others, his fellow human beings.

2.   For everyone is 'a son of Adam', indeed, our neighbor and our fellow human being. If it is difficult for a single individual to clothe a naked person on account of his poverty, five or ten should join together and clothe the flesh of their neighbors. But whoever does (c.149) this is inferior to the Perfect because he has not renounced the world and become sanctified and taken up his Cross, gazing upon heaven and understanding the truth that is the perfect Cross of our Lord.

Just as when he is ill in a foreign land he wishes that strangers would pick him up and heal his diseases and his trials, so also he shall do to the foreigners who meet him. In the same way he comes to these great commandments in the Torah, upon which depend the whole power of the Law and the prophets[9] and by which a person fulfills the whole Law and the prophets, [namely] 'You shall love the Lord your God with all your heart and your strength and with everything you have';[10] and the one after it is similar to it, 'You shall love your neighbor as yourself',[11] which means all people. You should take care of them just as you would for yourself, in as much as you are able to assist them.

For every person whom you meet is your neighbor, whether you treat him well or badly. A person does not treat someone well or badly who is distant from him, but rather hates the one who is beside him and loves the one who is with him. If a person has mercy on the one who meets him, he becomes his neighbor; yet if he treats him badly, he becomes his murderer. But if he neither treats him well nor mistreats him, he becomes his stranger, as was the case with the fellow citizens of the one who had gone down from (c.152) Jerusalem to Jericho. These fellow citizens became his strangers and the Samaritan foreigner who had compassion upon him became his neighbor.[12]

3.   Likewise, everyone is commanded to abstain from fornication and avoid [contamination] of the dead; and whatever is left, living or torn, do not eat as the pagans [do].[13] One should not consult oracles nor use magic arts, nor mutter incantations, which are whispered in the name of idols. One should not consult users of incantations, nor magicians, nor makers of amulets, because all these lead to idolatry.[14]

For it is said in the Holy Law, 'an oracle or a magician

9. Mt 22:40
10. Mt 22:37
11. Mt 22:39
12. Lk 10:29-37
13. Ex 22:31
14. Lv 20:6

or an amulet maker must not enter your land'.[15] Therefore, we must not do these things, not even if—may our
Lord never bring this about—we become completely insane or suffer some illness until our death, or if all we
possess perishes, or if our women become sterile for many
years like Sarah and Rebecca. On account of these things,
we go to imposters and depart from Uprightness. We do
not notice how much the ancients endured their temptation until the Lord saved them. On account of our
sufferings, we summon magicians and do not imitate Job
who endured (c.153) his temptation.

So on account of bearing children—and other problems—we make amulets and do not imitate Abraham and
Isaac who prayed to the Lord and he gave them sons.

On account of insanity, we make an incantation and
sprinkle water upon the one who goes insane, corrupting
him, and the Lord demands his blood at our hands. We do
not obey and neither are we able to be reformed. Not even
regarding the one in whom there was a legion of devils
and who dwelt among the tombs until our Lord healed
him[16] do we resemble his parents who did not sprinkle the
waters of incantation upon him and thereby corrupt him.

If the charmer desires to sprinkle water upon one who
is sound in body and harms him, [is it] not just like when a
person harms his companion using iron or a stick or a
stone? For [the charmers] are able to harm as our Lord
wishes to allow until the judgment day. It is easy for them
to harm because they hire evil spirits with their own souls.
They pay them soul for soul and then they cause harm. On
the day of judgment, God will demand from their hands
whatever [the evil spirits] have harmed and the return of
the souls that they had agreed upon as a reward for their
labor. For in this way, [the charmers] settle [the price] before they send them out to cause harm. (c.156) 'We will
give on that day a soul for the soul that you are going to kill

15. Dt 18:11   16. Mt 8:28-34

by our word and our hands.' Thus the charmers seize hold
of the spirits as [they do] swords and kill people. But for
every soul they corrupt they give their soul in return, loving the honor of the world and hating their soul.

4. Praise be to you, our Lord! How patient you are because you watch and do nothing, so that perhaps they might
repent and not go to the unquenchable fire. But I say to
you, upon whom there has come a testing and a temptation from God—whether on account of your sins or so that
you might repent, or because you do not pray—our Lord
allows you to enter into temptation from the evil one.

5. They can also be tempted by people who do harm to
their neighbors, or by Satan because they obey him. But
from God comes a testing upon people because he wishes
to examine whether they are true in faith, or because in
this way it is helpful to that person to become ill physically.
But from some people comes a temptation when they harm
their neighbors on account of their enmity, exchanging evils
with each other. Because of their evilness they heap evil
recompense upon (c.157) one another.

Neither a human being nor Satan is capable of making the soul depart from the body unless God wishes to
affect its departure through their agency. For [God] commanded them neither to commit evil nor to kill, lest 'You
will be avenged seven-fold on the day of judgment'.[17]

But God wishes to affect the departure of people, some
through illness and some through fire, or some by falling
into a pit or into a well. There are some who [die] through
an unclean spirit and some through evil people. God judges
those people who murder because he has established for
them a law that they must not murder, but he gave them
the freedom to do their [own] will.

17. Gn 4:15

6. [God] will say to them the following on that judgment day, 'On that same spot where you have killed, I have allowed the departure of those people you have killed. But as for you, how did you dare stretch out your hands upon your fellow human being and not fear me, since I have commanded you not to strike your fellow human beings, but to love and honor them deeply?' So when someone's soul ascends, whether the murderer makes his [victim's] blood pour out or batters him, he is condemned for the blood he has shed.

These other kinds of death happened according to the will of God, the souls of people departing by means of them. God himself may desire that [a person die] by means of a river or in a pit or in a well or from a high or small rooftop. How many times does [it happen that] one stumbles against a stone and dies? Even for an unclean spirit (c.160) it is not lawful to kill a person, unless God desires that the death of that person be through Satan. For if Satan had this power to separate the souls from the bodies of people, and especially if he had seen a person who sought to repent and escape from him, wherever [Satan] had an opportunity over him, he would have killed him. Moreover, if a sinful person has fled and transgressed against the law after he has converted, [Satan] has corrupted him. As long as a person keeps the commandments and takes refuge in God, [Satan] is afraid to come near to him.

But these evil spirits who kill, kill by means of a human being, through an enchanter or a magician. If not, therefore, can an enchanter or magician do anything else? Moreover, whoever uses water, and whatever they incant with it, in order to sprinkle upon someone and kill him, or when he buries the incantations in a place in order to harm him, does he not have fellowship with them?

Notice that the unclean spirit does not kill him unless God wishes to take his soul and send it wherever he desires, through whom he desires. That is, according to the level of his deeds, [God] will then prepare a prison for [the soul] until the judgment day when [the soul] will again take up its body and be resurrected with its deeds. (c.161)

7. Satan is guilty of [being] a rebel, teaching people evil deeds and contending with them so they might commit [evil deeds]. He teaches them to renounce God by the will of his soul. For just as people forge a sword and teach one another [how] to hold [it] in their hands, so unclean spirits teach people [how] to hold them in their hands and kill one another secretly with a hidden sword just as with a visible sword.[18] As [with] an iron sword, unless a person holds it with his hands and kills with it, it does not kill anyone; so also the unclean spirits are hidden swords that do not kill anyone unless a person takes them in his hands and secretly kills with them. People take hold of these spirits in their hands because they know [how] to make [the spirits] murderers, sons of Gehenna, denying God and acknowledging them and becoming for them ministers of evil deeds and of the detestable will of Satan who blinds the minds of people so they cannot see the truth.

8. These unclean spirits completely take over people of their own accord because they are obedient to these [spirits] and become their slaves. They violate the law of God and do not keep his commandments; their limbs are contorted (c.164) and the spirits torment them, sometimes openly and sometimes secretly. They have authority, however, only over those who listen to them, as Paul said, 'You are the slaves of whomever you obey'.[19]

9. Therefore, if you wish to defeat these unclean spirits, as well as these people who learn from them and distort their fellow beings through [these spirits], keep the commandments of the Lord and seek refuge in him until you

18. 1 Enoch 7:1, 8:1-2
19. Rm 6:16

depart from this world and you will be victorious in both worlds. But if not, watch out, the evil people will tear you to pieces in a single day. But whoever cannot endure this affliction in the short time of human existence, how indeed will he endure Gehenna? Are not my illnesses and my brief affliction worth it to me [for] the Lord will redeem me and I will go to his rest, rather than I should break his commandments on account of health that does not last, but then go to that eternal torment? The sons of Adam are convicted because they learn from Satan their murderer and treat with contempt God their savior.

10. Therefore, if our Lord does not desire that someone's life work be finished, he does not die, neither by means of Satan nor by people. Even if they mutilate (c.165) his body in some way, a person is saved and does not die if there is a single hour or day left for him. If this were not so, consider how people beat their neighbors until they maim them, and yet they do not die.

11. Consider how brigands fall upon people. Sometimes, a hundred people are killed by ten or twenty men. But there are situations in which a hundred brigands are not able to kill ten men because God does not wish to bring about their deaths on that day. These are murderers, guilty of spilled blood, from whom, despite their [the murderers'] will, [people] have escaped.

12. [In the same way], God does not allow evil beasts to kill people, unless [he] wishes to bring about their death through beasts, because it is written, 'I will cast fear and dread of you upon rapacious beasts'.[20] But wherever he wishes to take away the fear from evil animals, they will kill and tear people apart. Anyone who wishes to do evil to someone, but does not have an opportunity, sins greatly in

20. Gn 9:2

his heart, because as far as he is concerned the evil has already been done. Whoever by his desire refrains from evil and does good, praying to our Lord and shedding tears before him, turning away from (c.168) evil and doing good, our Lord will receive him and rejoice especially in the sinner who does good, as it is written, 'There shall be joy in heaven concerning a sinner who repents'.[21]

13. Consider again how people fall into wells and pits and streams and from precipices and from a rooftop; how many times are they beaten with iron and rods and stones and yet do not die, because God did not want their death to happen on that day they were beaten? [On the other hand,] how many times is one struck on the cheek or with a stick and his soul departs? Look, is it not evident that [this happens] because God wishes that his death happens in that hour? Moreover, sometimes a house falls upon him and he does die; and sometimes they throw him down from the wall and he does not die.

Then there are those who fall from the full height [of a man] and his soul flies away. Look, is it not evident that every person goes according to his [allotted] measure of [days], as it is written, 'Behold, you have given us days with measure and our existence is as nothing before you'.[22] On account of this we beseech you as people who have freedom for whom the Law is laid down and the Kingdom promised to us—Gehenna too is prepared for us—(c.169) let us guard our souls and draw back our hands so that we do not strike anyone, not even with our finger, lest his soul depart and his blood be required by our hands and we descend to the Gehenna of unquenchable fire.

Also whoever stumbles and murders, if he repents and sits in mourning, in prayer and in humiliation, in remorse of soul and with tears before the Lord, [God] will forgive him as he forgave David when he repented and

21. Lk 15:7   22. Ps 39:5

poured out his soul before the Lord. For David said, 'My Lord, see my submission and my toil, and forgive me all my sin'.[23] God saw the obedience of his lowliness and the labor of his request, and forgave him and raised him to honor. Then, let us deeply love our God and love and honor every person so that we may inherit the kingdom—which is promised to us—whose rest does not pass away nor is its delight ever dissolved, neither is its feast ended nor do its wreaths wither, nor is its bridal feast done away with.

14.   Let us petition the Lord concerning all our trials, as it is written, 'Every sickness the Lord heals'.[24] He reviled and condemned the utterance of the lips of the unrighteous,[25] that is, of magicians and soothsayers, and of charmers and writers of amulets, snake charmers and diviners.

But if you wish to be healed without sins, wait for the Lord (c.172) and pray to him, and he will heal you from numerous human and satanic temptations. If it is right that in this world you shall be healed, in this world our Lord will heal you. If he does not heal you in this world, then it is to your advantage, for in that [other] world he will give you rest, extol you, and make you cheerful, because you have waited for his redemption until your departure from this world. Do not be frightened by the stress of your illnesses so that for the sake of physical health you go killing your soul, whether your body is healed or not. It is better for you to endure a little temporal affliction rather than go to that affliction of which there is no measure.

If it happens that your body is healed by being with these false people, you will not know that your soul has become ill, a sickness that will last until the day of judgment. Your condemnation will be then because you have fled from illnesses and afflictions of a short duration; you will go to the affliction from which it is not possible for you

23. Ps 25:18
24. Ps 103:3
25. Ps 59:12

to escape, because you have transgressed against the commandment of God. But if you have a disease and there is a doctor near you, ask him the following, 'Are you a magician or a charmer, or one of these who deal with deceitful doctrine of error? May the Lord witness (c.173) against you, to whose judgment we will go. If you bring something to calm me, [do it] simply in the name of Jesus, and if not, do not bring it to me.' Let him confirm to you that [it is] in the name of Jesus he will make you healthy and [only] then let him approach you.

15. So I advise those who would kill whomever is mad and insane, that if they are able to control him, [well and good]; otherwise, they should let him loose to dwell among the tombs until our Lord heals him or gathers him,²⁶ lest you die along with the charm makers. On account of today's crisis, [which] tomorrow could be gone or [even] disappear completely, we continue associating with the diviners and do not imitate the ancient ones who sought from the Lord until the thing that they lost was found, and if they did not find [it], they praised our Lord all the more because he gave and he took away, just as Job said. In all his sufferings and illnesses, the loss of his possessions and the anguish of his children, [Job said], 'The Lord gave and the Lord has taken away. Blessed be the name of the Lord'.²⁷

[Job] endured blows to his body until the Lord healed and delivered him. The Lord wrote down the deeds [of] Job and placed [them] before the whole world so that they might imitate him when their possessions are destroyed and their bodies fall ill (c.176) and their sons die, in order that like him, they might wait for the Lord and praise his name, just as Job did.

For something worth [only] a hundred dollars we fight and kill one another and do not imitate the ancient ones

26. Mt 8:28ff
27. Jb 1:21

from whom their wives were taken and yet they did not quarrel. When they had taken from them the well of waters they did not fight, but called the place in which they had quarreled with them: Esek and Sitnah.[28] They neither quarreled nor fell from Uprightness and the thing that they had hated they did not do to others, and the thing that they had loved, thus they did to everyone.

16. [In] what [way] should this contemporary marriage imitate that marriage of old? It is not appropriate for the Upright to sing of sin and to exult before Satan. God gave to humanity citherns and lyres, tambourines, timbrels, cymbals, horns, bagpipes, trumpets and everything used for singing, because they were not capable of singing with spiritual citherns and lyres. Because they did not know the truth, [God] gave them visible instruments so that they might sing with them spiritual music to God, because they did not know [how] to praise his name with their own [bodily] parts, these being the instruments of worship and spiritual song. On account of this, instead of the songs (c.177) of Satan, [God] gave them spiritual songs by which they might sing along with all that is sung by him and not sin. God, however, forbid that the Upright act in the way that our generation does. For see, the holy ones no longer sing to God with these instruments. How is it that those who receive the body and blood of our Savior do not fear to serve secretly the secret idols? Do we not understand that while we may have uprooted the idols of our fathers, we have not yet uprooted their laws?

17. When God avenges every impure word that we speak with the [same] mouth that receives his body and blood, he said, 'You have loved the harlot and have done such and such things, which God hates'; indeed, what answer can we give to him? For that matter, what fruits do impure

---

28. Gn 26:20; Syriac: ʿaskā and sātānā

words and dirty songs and hateful psalms and deceitful
tales bring in for us? Indeed, do they produce wheat or
clothes for us? Only sins and pitfalls. Because of this let us
avoid these so that we shall not be condemned along with
the world.

18. Also, God gave us a simple medicine, so that we might
put oil and wine upon (c.180) our wounds,[29] as our Lord
said, worshipping him. Or wax and honey, or a poultice of
figs, as Isaiah said.[30] Or roots that we know are good for
tumors, as Bar Sirach said.[31] Or [like] a wise man who cuts
away our diseases and washes away our cancers, because
not everyone knows how to cut the body on account of the
nerves that should not be severed, except he who has taken
care to learn how to cut. When a bone is broken, he knows
how to set it or to remove it. God gave knowledge of these
things to people so that they might work for one another,
because God promised us illnesses on the day that we transgress against his commandments, as it is written, 'Numerous of years are labor and illnesses'.[32] This [medical] ministry is given to whomever desires to become an Upright
one. May he serve and not sin, nor fall from Uprightness,
as our father Adam fell from Perfection.

19. Let us beware also of divination lest we pay attention
to chance meetings or [bird-]calls, for we do not associate
with idol-worshippers. Our Creator also gave us the knowledge on the day that we sinned to make clothes and skins
for ourselves as shelter for the winter, and vessels of wood,
brass, and iron for our frugal service. But sin caused us to
err (c.181) with trinkets and images for which there is no
requirement.

Instead of doing our work in summertime, so that in
winter we may rest and serve our Lord and know his truth,

---

29. Lk 10:29-37   31. Si 38:4   32. Ps 90:10
30. Is 1:6, 38:21

[sin] has subjugated us to labor in summer and in winter for mammon and for something unnecessary, to prevent us gaining knowledge and returning to the house of life. We do not remember the Lord and his Law, not even during the fast days, and so 'we eat, but are not satisfied. We hurry [in order to put money] in a purse with holes in it, but it does not profit us', as the prophet said.[33]

Did not the first couple, who did not work, also possess [goods] like you? Did they not take wives and did they not eat and drink wine like you? Is it not written that they were considered corrupted like us? Or did you not know that because the people sang and danced in the days of Moses, and did not praise him who filled them with his good things, after their meal the Lord caused them to perish in the desert, because they fornicated and sang to sin and [so] their corpses fell?[34] Or did you not know that for our own education these things were written so that the Lord would not always be destroying us? 'Behold, they have Moses and the prophets, let them listen to them (c.184) and go do [what they say].'[35] If not, Gehenna will take vengeance from them as from you, [as] the Upright one said to that wicked rich man who did not keep the Law and the prophets during his life. When he got into deep straits, he realized he would have been able to keep these commandments if he had so desired. His word shows [this]:

> Let him send [a message] to my brothers, that if they desire they are able not to enter this torment. I was capable of keeping [these commandments], but I greatly neglected them. But let someone from the dead go and speak to them that this is how I am afflicted, and they will not despise the commandments as I have despised [them], and they will be delivered from Gehenna.[36]

33. Hg 1:6
34. Ex 32:28
35. Lk 16:29
36. Lk 16:27-28, 30

They have this Law, which today we do not even really want
to hear and learn. Today's God, is he not the same one as
of old? Does he not hate these evil deeds? Or, because he is
patient and does not kill us as [he did] these, do you not
realize that in Gehenna he will remind us about all of them,
as in the case of the rich unrighteous man? All his patience
is due to the fact that the time for the punishment of our
judgment is near.

20. Why do we not fast twice a week as it is written for the
Upright?[37] The Perfect fast everyday. Why do we not pray
(c.185) three times a day—as well as in the morning and in
the evening—as it is written for the Upright? The Perfect
praise [God] the whole day[38] Why do we not keep the Law
of God and do alms, nor do we pray with them, as it is
written for the Upright? While, on the hand, the Perfect
perform the rites all their days and pray unceasingly before our Lord.

But when Sunday comes, in order that we do not learn
about righteousness, sin directs us to say, 'Our business
has suffered loss'. When the time for prayer comes, in order that we do not worship our Creator, we say that 'our
profits have perished'. Those who wish to be raised up from
the world and perfected, why do they not perform for themselves the rites of weeks, fast and pray, learn the truth and
be humbled, and after a while they will perform the rites of
the months, and then of the seasons, and then of the years
until they are strengthened and are raised up completely
from the earth and live in heaven? There they will pray
and serve before our Lord, and not below on earth.

21. Thus God desires that all humanity act, each one according to the stage on which he stands. They should treat
one another well and love their Creator. Whoever (c.188)
is able, let him treat well with food and clothing someone

37. Didache 8:1
38. Didache 8:3; Clement of Alexandria *Stromata* 7:7

who is needy. Whoever desires to leave all he possesses and come to Perfection is the brother of our Lord, and he desires him more than thousands and ten thousands. Whoever does not come to this [higher] portion let him remain in this Uprightness, which our Lord commands, and let him not do evil or fall from Uprightness and be condemned.

God desires that all people should live. For this [reason], he gave major and minor commandments so that all might endeavor according to their strength. With the major ones, one becomes Perfect and with the minor ones one, becomes an Upright one. 'I am living,' says the Lord, 'I do not desire the death of sinners.'[39] For, if he had delighted in their death, he would have established neither the major Law nor the minor one. Because if they are not able to attain the major Law and be perfected, then they can still live by the minor one and not be destroyed.

The end of the seventh *Mēmrā*, which is about the commandments of the Upright and the Righteous ones.

---

39. Ex 18:32

Mēmrā Eight

ON ONE WHO GIVES ALL HE HAS
TO FEED THE POOR

Summary: Again directed to the Upright, particularly to one who gives all he has to feed the poor. Demonstrates that while the Upright is nothing in the eyes of the Perfect if he does not empty himself and renounce the world, the Upright still receives the profit of salvation, albeit a lesser portion. (c.189)

1. For the apostle [Paul] said, 'If I give all I have to feed the poor, but do not have love, I gain nothing'.[1] That is, I do not grow much at all. Our Lord said, 'Whoever offers a cup of water will not lose his reward'.[2] Moreover, he said:

> Come, my father's blessed ones, because I was hungry and you fed me, and I was thirsty and you gave me drink, and I was a stranger and a foreigner and you took me in. I was naked and you clothed me. I was sick and you took care of me. I was in prison and you visited me. Come, inherit the kingdom which has been prepared for you.[3]

1. 1 Co 13:3   2. Mt 10:42   3. Mt 25:35

But to those who did not do these things he said, 'Be gone, you cursed ones, to the fire that is prepared for the evil one (c.192) and his angels. I do not know you.'[4] Be gone to your leader because you have not done these things to me and because you have served unrighteousness. Moreover, the blessed apostle said, 'If I understand all heavenly mysteries and all knowledge, but there is no love in me, I am nothing'.[5] And our Lord said, 'If you know the truth, the truth shall free you'.[6] Even though the freed may not be Perfect they shall immediately know the truth from falsehood and shall be separated from the bondage of sin. They become the Upright and do not come to judgment. But if they use their time in the world and advance day by day they will attain Perfection.

2.   In what way did the apostle mean, 'they are nothing'? For he said, 'If I give my body to be burned, but do not have love, I am nothing'.[7] What indeed is this for which the apostle yearns, which is better than everything? Our Lord said, 'Whoever offers his cheek to the one who strikes him and endures,[8] comes to perfection if he loves the one who strikes him and prays for him'.

Does the apostle refute the words of our Lord? Absolutely not! He does not refute them at all but actually builds upon them. The apostle is not saying that [the words of the Lord] are inappropriate; rather he introduces something of even more importance (c.193) there. For he who gives all he has to feed the poor on account of God and renounces— as [the Lord] said to him—all he possesses, but does not have in him that humble love that loves his murderers and washes the feet of his enemies and considers everyone better than himself, giving heed to heaven and not to earth, his mind serving there in the heavenly Jerusalem, bound there to our Lord, [then, without this, he is nothing].

4. Mt 25:41; 25:12   6. Jn 8:32   8. Mt 5:39
5. 1 Co 13:2   7. 1 Co 13:3

[On the other hand,] the lowliness of one [who] goes to someone inferior to him and submits himself before everyone is evident to all people. When they curse him, he blesses [them]. When they strike him, he bows down to them. Wherever they stripped him he goes [back] to them as one whom they clothed. He goes to one who has done him harm as though he had treated him well. He understands the height and depth and length and width,[9] yet is humbler than everyone else.[10] When he does these and other such things, he considers those who are sinners better than himself, neither being anxious for daily life nor having a place on earth to lay down [his] head.[11]

3. Therefore, the apostle did not say that there is no profit for that person who gives all he has to feed the poor, but that he is nothing in the eyes of one who empties himself, having in him this love that does these deeds and [achieves] this (c.196) complete lowliness. But it can happen that people give away all they have and become indigents on the earth on account of our Lord but do not attain this lowliness. But, if they love more or less, and are humble before such and such a person, but not before everyone—that is why they are much smaller than the one who reaches perfect love. The one who does not lower himself in this way does not become Perfect; and the one who does not lower himself is much less than the Perfect.

4. There are some people who, on account of our Lord, have given their flesh to the fire, living in faith and in Uprightness. There are many who have wives, are involved in business, and [possess] male and female servants like Abraham and Job. The apostle did not say that they do not gain a thing, but that they are much inferior to the martyrs who emptied themselves and are humble like our Lord,

9. Ep 3:18
10. Hermas, Mandate VIII:10
11. Mt 8:20

resembling the apostles and Stephen. There are even some who are sinners, yet believe in our Lord. Persecution comes into their lives and [the persecutors] say to them, 'Renounce Our Lord [i.e. Jesus] and worship idols'. They do not understand what is perfect love, just faith and baptism only. [The persecutors] burn them and throw them to the beasts and unto the edge of the sword; yet they endure and do not renounce the Lord. Is there not, therefore, a reward for them? (c.197) They do not reach Perfection, however, [so] in the eyes of Stephen and the apostles they are nothing. Nevertheless, their failings are forgiven and they do not come to judgment.

Indeed if all people are gathered before the judgment seat of Christ, as the apostle said, 'All of us must stand before the judgment seat of Christ',[12] there are some of us who come to judgment and some of us who will come to glory and sit upon thrones. As our Lord said to those who have done all of his perfect will, 'You who have left everything and have come after me, on the day when I shall be revealed in my glory, you shall sit upon thrones and judge the tribes of humanity'.[13] Therefore, you see that they come to glory before the throne and not to judgment. As a person is found on the day of his departure, so he stands before the throne on the Day of Judgment.

5.　　Moreover, there are people who have left all they possessed on account of our Lord, loving our Lord and desiring him, but they do not have the love that loves God and people. Because they have desired our Lord, he reveals to them the heavenly mysteries and the complete knowledge of faith. But they do not comprehend the truth of love, nor do they comprehend the height and depth and length and width that love understands.[14] Yet they understand all mysteries and all knowledge (c.200) of faith, which is less than love that loves all and reconciles all.

12. 2 Co 5:10　　　　13. Mt 19:18　　　　14. Ep 3:18

For faith loves our Lord and his friends and his household, but love loves our Lord and his enemies and his murderers and unbelievers and idolaters, as it is written, 'Consider everyone better than yourself[15] and let your lowliness be evident to all people'.[16] Love him who hates you and you shall be imitating your Father in Heaven who makes his sun rise and his rain fall upon the just and the unrighteous, upon the good and the evil.[17] So may your love shine especially upon the household of faith. Therefore, the apostle did not say that there is no profit for those who know the mysteries of faith, but only that they are nothing in the eyes of those who attain love and Perfection.

The end of the eighth *Mēmrā*, which is about the one who gives all he has to feed the poor.

15. Ph 2:3
16. Ph 4:5
17. Mt 5:44-45

Mēmrā Nine

ON UPRIGHTNESS
AND THE LOVE
OF THE UPRIGHT
AND THE PROPHETS

Summary: An extended biblical exposition to explain how the violence of the Old Testament prophets—reducing them below Uprightness— is ordered by God against his enemies. The prophets are eventually admitted into the kingdom following the apostles. (c.201)

1. Now let us show how the prophets who were among that stubborn people had a love that conformed to the Ten Commandments[1] and the New Testament. They walked according to the will of the almighty Lord, and whatever he said to them, that is what they did. But when they pursued love and reached Perfection the Lord held them back from Perfection because he had sent them to kill his enemies. But our Lord, who came into the world, came not for the prophets, nor for the righteous, but on behalf of the sinners and the lost[2] and on behalf of those who no longer

---

1. Literally, yōd—tenth letter of Syriac alphabet used as symbolic name for Ten Commandments.
2. Lk 5:32; 1 Tm 1:15

have hope, to call them to repentance and turn them around toward the house (c.204) of life.

For, the prophets and all the Upright were able to live or to be perfected by the living and Holy Spirit, which is the Lord. But for the sake of the whole world, which was lost, our Lord appeared physically so that he might win the whole world and so that the world might know the will of God from God himself and from his footsteps. The word of our Lord indicates, 'I have not come to call the righteous but [to call] the sinners to repentance'.[3] Therefore, our Lord was born for the education of everyone so that all might learn the truth of his lowliness and love in a visible way, because not everyone is capable of hearing the will of the Lord through his Holy Spirit. Therefore, his advent was for the sake of everyone so that everyone might learn of his lowliness, his kindness, and his gentleness; and so that people should not excuse themselves from this love and lowliness and patient suffering, because they see that the Lord of all endured everything before them—for the sake of everyone in view of all—so that they marvel and say, 'If our Lord endured everything for our iniquity, how much more necessary is it for us to endure for our own iniquity, even more than what he endured for our sins?'

2.   So that both sinners and righteous might profit (c.205) by the good example that our Lord was to everyone, [and] that everyone might imitate him and the good and the bad might benefit through him, God held back the prophets from Uprightness according to the situation because he had need of them during that time, for through them he subdued the rebellious by force as it pleased his will. On account of this, [God] also held them back from love—He who loves his neighbor as himself, because our neighbor is all of humanity.

For he sent [the prophets] during that era when there was enmity between God and human beings in order to go

3. Lk 5:32

kill his enemies because they had defied the Lord, saying, 'What is the message of the Lord?' Just as the Pharaoh had said, 'What is this king to me, the Lord of Moses and Aaron his messengers?'⁴ On account of this, God sent his prophets and killed through them, sometimes with and sometimes without the sword, sometimes by fire and sometimes by hail, and with all kinds of trials. On account of this, the Lord held back the prophets occasionally from that commandment of love which [leads] toward Perfection. For if the Lord had killed [the rebellious] without the prophets, they would have said, 'Our idols killed us, not the Lord', and they would have [continued to have] sacrificed their sons (c.208) to their idols in order to appease them and they would not have known the Lord. Because of this, God subdued them through the prophets until they confessed that the Lord is God in heaven and on earth, and above heaven and below the earth, and in the width and the length, and that no place is far from [God].

Therefore, on account of this, the Lord also occasionally held the prophets back from love. For these pursued Perfection with patience, as Jeremiah said, 'I do not owe anything, nor do they owe me, yet all revile me'.⁵ While longing for solitude he said, 'Blessed is one who lifts up your [God's] yoke in his youth and sits by himself and is silent. He places his mouth in the dust and [gives] his cheek to whomever strikes him and his life is filled with insult.'⁶ [By] this Jeremiah sought this yoke of our Lord Jesus.

The Lord held him back because through him he was destroying his enemies. [Jeremiah] said, 'The Lord is sending me violently against them and they revile me'.⁷ David also said, 'My enemies and those who hate me without cause are more numerous than the hairs of my head and what I did not defraud I was restoring'.⁸ So also all the prophets hoped and waited for that hope that was to be

4. Ex 5:2
5. Jr 15:10
6. Lm 3:27-30

7. Jr 15:10
8. Ps 69:4

revealed. For the rest, the prophets got as far as the love of Perfection, but the Lord did not allow them to become Perfect.

3. (c.209) Sometimes the Lord cast them down even below Uprightness, [the stage] that fulfills these two great commandments of love, because Uprightness does not curse or harm anyone. But because the Lord had sent them, they went cursing and hating his adversaries and raged against those who defied him and [in that way] became lower than Uprightness. But the rest of the time, as long as the Lord did not send them, they remained [faithful] in these commandments: 'Love the Lord and your neighbor', which means all humanity.

They pursued Perfection when they ceased from passion and anger; when they sought and pursued peace; when they departed from evil things and did good things; when they made a sacrifice of thanksgiving to God and not of victims; when they said, 'An evil heart has passed away from us and we have not known evil'9; when Samuel prayed for those who had rejected him10; and when Jeremiah prayed for those who threw him into the muddy cistern, the Lord said to him three times, 'Do not pray for them'11—but he did not listen to him. These behaved toward their fellow human beings as they wanted to be treated. But the Lord held them back (c.212) because it was appropriate.

4. Moreover, Jeremiah said, 'I held myself back from going out and cursing them', the [very] thing I hate someone doing to me. 'The Word of the Lord came upon me like fire and it set me on fire and I was not able to endure it and not curse them'12—until he had descended from Uprightness and then he cursed them.

Of what were the prophets guilty? They killed and cursed—the [very] thing that they hated lest someone curse

9. Ps 101:4

10. 1 S 12:25

11. Jr 7:16, 11:14, 14:11

12. Jr 20:8

and kill them. They did to others what they themselves hated, and transgressed against Uprightness. But did not the Lord himself force them to transgress unwillingly? On account of this, they were not to blame in everything the Lord commanded them, [for] as yet our Lord had not been born of Mary [when] he would make lowliness, peace, and welfare a better covenant than the first [covenant]. How much did the mind of the prophets expect this covenant—but it did not come during their days. Because of this, 'God was not ashamed to be called their God'.[13] This means, he is not ashamed to call them his brothers as he had called the apostles. Because of this, 'He prepared for them a holy city'.[14] This means, he perfected them in the sight of the apostles. But today (c.213) God asks people to love one another and not do to their brothers, the sons of Adam, whatever detestable thing a person may do to them, the sons of Adam, and if not, they shall not enter the kingdom.

5.   Moreover, when our Lord sought to kill the Israelites, Moses said in his prayer concerning these who were embittering his spirit every day and abusing him, 'If you blot them out, blot me out from your book of life'.[15] Look, what did Moses do to the evildoers? As he wished that the righteous might do to him if he had done wrong, that they might pray for him. See how the Upright pursued Perfection! But God said to him, 'No, but I will blot out whoever sins against me'.[16] Moses prayed with his love, [for] he loved humanity as himself. Thus, through his Uprightness, he desired that a person should pray for him if he did wrong, until the Lord forgave the transgressions of his brothers, the sons of Adam. In what way do we resemble these Upright ones whom [misfortune] grieved—we [who] rejoice at one another's misfortune—and [who] prayed for him upon whom misfortune came on account of his sins?

13. Hb 11:16   15. Ex 32:32
14. Hb 11:16   16. Ex 32:33

In another place [in Scripture], the Lord brought Moses down to [a stage] lower than Uprightness when he said to him, 'Command (c.216) the Levites to slay their brothers and fathers because they worshipped the calf',[17] exchanging [God] for a dead calf. When Moses saw that evil had targeted him, and it was no use if he prayed for them, he did to them that thing he hated for someone to do to him if he sins; that is, [he acted] by the word from the Lord's mouth, and not by the will of Moses. When he slew the sinful Amalek,[18] the Lord brought him down from Uprightness and he did the thing he hated for someone to do to him and to his brothers, the sons of Adam. For in that time, there was enmity between God and humanity.

6.   Also when the Jews acted wickedly, God raised up the Assyrian scourge against them and chastised them with it. But, since the day our Lord dissolved enmity and reconciled with the blood of his cross what is on the earth [with] what is in heaven, causing wars to cease from the ends of the earth,[19] no longer when the Assyrian wakes up is it our Lord who awakens him; nor when the Roman descends to battle, is it our Lord who makes him descend; nor when the prophet becomes a zealot and kills the sinners is it our Lord who sends him, but [it is] evil rising up today in all of them.

For our Lord made peace, but the sons of Adam do not wish to be peaceful and a person is not reconciled with his brother, as the apostle wrote, (c.217) 'If one has a disagreement with his neighbor, let him forgive, as Christ forgave all humanity'.[20] But if these had desired to turn away from evil things, [they would have had peace]. Our Lord no longer makes wars today as in former times, but it is these people who fight today by their own desire. Whoever rises up against his neighbor, the Lord pulls him down, as

17. Ex 32:27   19. Ps 46:9
18. Ex 17:8-16   20. Col 3:13

he had said, 'Whoever raises his hand against his brother will not be guiltless'.[21]

Therefore, in this world the two antagonists [i.e. Persian and Roman empires] may raise their hands against one another with a sword and be slain, but in that [other world] to come, they will be tormented, because they did not build upon the peace that our Lord Jesus had made on earth and in heaven, and because they raised up these wars that he had caused to cease from the ends of the earth. He said to them, 'If you thirst for blood, look, my blood is yours: drink and live. But do not drink the blood of one another or you shall die'.[22] They killed him, drank his blood, and were not ashamed, and see, here they are again drinking the blood of their brothers, a thing that God hated and despised since the first day.

7.   David also pursued Perfection when the Lord delivered his persecutor Saul into his hands, yet [David] did not kill him, but repaid him good things instead of bad.[23] But when David commanded Solomon to punish Shimei,[24] it was the Lord [who] spoke through his mouth, so that through that forceful judgment (c.220) he might take vengeance from Shimei [for] all he had unjustly done and carry out the judgment on himself. Look, whoever is angry against his neighbor is reminded of death and will set aside enmity.

Therefore, that discerning and righteous prophet harbored enmity at his death, but during his life when Shimei reviled him, [David] forgave him his error. When he was departing from the world did [David] think again about this evil? Absolutely not! But if Shimei had reviled him, Joab, who waged all the wars wherever the Lord sent David, went instead of [David], because the kings and righteous ones who reigned in Israel did not do anything unless the Lord spoke to them—except when they transgressed against

21. 1 Sm 26:9
22. Jn 6:52
23. 1 Sm 26
24. 1 K 2:8

the commandment and sinned. What did Joab do to David
who commanded, 'Do not let his old age descend in peace
to Sheol'?[25]

But this is clear: the Lord judged the unrighteous
through the word of David; and through the hands of
Solomon the Lord exacted vengeance from the hands of
Shimei who had cursed and defrauded that humble spiritual prophet, and from the hands of Joab who had shed
blood when the Lord had not told him. The Lord had vengeance on them through Solomon just as he had vengeance
on his enemies through the hand of the holy prophets.
But today, since there has been (c.221) peace in the land
and reconciliation between God and people, God has reconciled himself to his creatures through his son Jesus the
Savior. If all humanity feared the Lord and departed from
evil and thought of good things, yet one or two evil ones
were found in the land, our Lord would not kill these two
evil people; and through the good ones, evil does not come
upon anyone and they would all become perfect human
beings. But as it is, today we are pleased to become instruments of anger, and all of us provoke and cause evil against
one another and against ourselves, until we totally consume one another, because the Lord has not told anyone
today to do evil things and become a zealot [for God] as in
ancient days.

8.   Abraham also pursued Perfection when he made clear
his love for all who had crossed his way, good or evil ones;
he supplied all who were needy and afflicted with food and
clothing, not allowing his servant to serve them, but he
stood before them himself like a servant and said to his
servants, 'Make for yourselves alms in your dwellings from
your fields'.[26] He imitated our Lord and washed the feet of
foreigners, good and bad, even while our Lord had not yet
written the Law for him. (c.224) He gave heed to God who

25. 1 K 2:6   26. Apocryphal

makes his sun shine upon the good and the evil²⁷ and upon the ungrateful and upon Sodom and such like it. The law of love was in his soul and his love shone upon everyone when he squandered his property on account of the needy. When they took his wife from him, he bowed down to them and lowered himself before them and asked after their health and called them 'my lords' in his love for them.²⁸

In another place, God brought down from the love of the Perfect [this same] man who loved the good and the bad, sending him as [he had sent] the prophets; he went to slay the evil kings who had intruded into what did not belong to them. So that we might know that the Lord had sent him, [God] met him, after he had chased many peoples with a small number of men, and said to him, 'Your reward shall be very great, because you have come and gone at my word and you did not covet spoils'.²⁹ Also Melchizedek met him with bread and wine and blessed him because he had kept the commandments.³⁰

9.   Elijah also pursued Perfection when he girded his loins with love and with kindness and became a messenger of peace. He ran many miles (c.225) ahead of Ahab,³¹ his enemy and persecutor, who had thirsted for his blood and had sought to kill him in all [the neighboring] kingdoms, though Elijah had not injured a thing, except when the Lord had compelled him to do these things. He bore witness and said while offering up a sacrifice, 'Answer me, Lord, answer me so that all the people may know that you are God, and by your word I have done all these things'.³²

Therefore, because of the wrongdoing of the people and the kings who had denied God, [God] destroyed them by means of the prophets. For Elijah prayed and rain fell and he ran to [seek] the honor of the wicked king so that he might enter his house with honor. You see that the prophets [too] desired the life and honor of the world and of its

27. Mt 5:45
28. Gn 12:20
29. Gn 15:1
30. Gn 14:8
31. 1 K 18:46
32. 1 K 18:36-37

kings—while they denied God and offended the prophets.

10. Elisha also pursued Perfection when he fed and gave drink to his enemies as he wished that his enemies would do to him. He sent them to their lord peacefully after they had dined.[33]

But in another place, the Lord brought him down from Uprightness and from love when he did to these children the thing that he would have hated that someone should do to him if he transgressed. To those who sought to kill him he did good things instead of bad, as is appropriate for one who seeks (c.228) Perfection. [But on the other hand,] to those children who laughed and said, 'Go up, bald-head!',[34] he did the thing that love and Uprightness do not do. But it had been the will of Elisha when he fed his enemies. Yet when he killed the children, it was the will of God.

Then there is a place [in the Scriptures] in which the Lord brought the prophets down from Uprightness and from love, while the rest pursued Perfection. If they were overcome [by temptations] here and there, and transgressed Uprightness without a commandment, the Lord reproved them and it was obvious that they had acted foolishly. They [then] washed away their offenses and ascended to love and were confirmed.

11. Abel pursued Perfection when he submitted to his murderer and did not violate love and Uprightness by striking [Cain], the thing that he hated lest someone should strike him. Adam demonstrated his [love of] truth when he did not require vengeance for Abel from the hands of Cain, because he wished that every person would forgive him whenever he would sin. Thus the Lord was content to forgive [Cain] on the day he went astray and did not kill him.

33. 2 K 6:22-23   34. 2 K 2:23-24

12. Each one of them acted in this way in his generation and endured sinners, but did not do evil to them because they hated that a person should do evil to them. They did not do to others the thing that they hated. As they wished for someone to do (c.229) to them, so they did to everyone, to one who treated them well and to one who treated them badly—[all this] so long as the Lord did not force them to do evil to his enemies. They waited for peace in their days, and to be perfected and completed in the Spirit, the Paraclete, and then they would depart from the world.

But God did not desire to make peace in that time, because humanity had not wanted to acknowledge him. On account of this, long beforehand they saw the peace that would come to exist through our Lord Jesus Christ, they asked about this peace and longed for it and our Lord promised them, 'I will give to you this Perfection, which I shall bring about. When I send the Paraclete to the apostles, I will also perfect you because you have waited for me and have pursued the Perfection of the heavenly angels from which Adam your father fell. I will make you and your father Adam ascend to the height from which you have fallen.'[35]

Because of this all the prophets and righteous ones were comforted and all of them slept in faith, love, and Uprightness even though they had not received their promise. Our Lord said to his disciples, 'The prophets and righteous ones waited to see the peace that you are seeing, yet they did not see; and to hear the thing (c.232) that you are hearing, yet they did not hear; if only people would have acknowledged me, I would have made peace in their days, [and] they would have become like you'.[36]

13. For the Lord slew the sinful peoples by means of the prophets so that they might fear and acknowledge him by their own will, but due to their accursed will they were not

35. Apocryphal   36. Mt 13:17

persuaded. All of them fell by the sword until our Lord appeared and won them over by the force of his love and lowliness. He restored them to conviction through his lowliness, [so that] they professed that the Lord is God. Whatever is on the earth was reconciled with whatever is in heaven, though some still rebelled from the love of Jesus by the hardness of their heart.

Our Lord said to his chosen ones, 'I promised the prophets that I would come and perfect them. For the reason they were not perfected is not that they were less than you in being perfected, but because there was no peace in their days. On account of this, Uprightness will arrange [it] so that even those will be perfected.'[37]

Because of this the apostle said, 'We do not have more than they; he foresaw that they would not be perfected without us'.[38] Even more than that he said, since we are the first, He hurried to perfect us before them and not them before us. The Perfect ones of today are the image of the apostles, which is a great gift. The prophets and the first Upright ones, those who were perfected after they had departed from this world (c.233) in the sight of the apostles, were perfected because they had pursued love and Perfection in this world. From Uprightness a person ascends to love and from love he is elevated to Perfection.

14. As for the rest, anyone who is not perfected in this time and then departs from the world is not perfected in that [other] world. But everyone inherits Perfection and whatever level is lower according to his manner of life: teachers who teach many [students], and the strong who bear the diseases of the sick and reconcile many,[39] and everyone as he is found in simplicity of gifts, cheerfulness of mercy, diligence of leadership, or in the tranquility of love that loves without turmoil.

Then each person according to his level, if he empties

---

37. Apocryphal   38. Heb 11:40   39. Rm 15:1

and consecrates himself, will receive the Paraclete and be-come Perfect. The apostle showed that God placed the Per-fect in the Church, after them the prophets, and after them the strong, the teachers, the builders, and the administra-tors, and after them [those who have] the gifts of healing.[40] He showed that one level is better than [another] level. The apostle spoke concerning these contemporary gifts that God had placed in the Church.

For the ancient prophets and apostles together take delight in the kingdom according to the word of (c.236) our Lord, 'The sower and the reaper shall rejoice together',[41] [for] these are the prophets and apostles, and all who are perfected rejoice with them and depart from this transitory world.

15. Today, because our Lord came and by the blood of his cross reconciled that which is on the earth and in heaven, people are also persuaded by the prophets and by our Lord and his apostles, by the teachers, the strong, and the ex-horters, and everyone has declared that the Lord is God, whether sincerely or not, whether truthfully or wrongfully. Our Lord has been proclaimed today throughout all the creation. Some confessed the Father and some the Son and [others] the Holy Spirit, whether they adhered correctly or not. But they did not talk like these earlier accursed ones, 'What is the message of the Lord?'

On account of this, the Lord reconciled himself with them at this time—even if they were not sure in faith—until the future judgment comes and the Lord Jesus repays everyone according to his deeds and his faith. Therefore, the Lord Jesus does not need anyone today to become a zealot and chastise anyone who acts wickedly, because the Lord himself chastises today whoever transgresses against him, for all the peoples knew that there is a God in heaven who gives death and life.

40. 1 Co 12:28   41. Jn 4:36

Therefore, [the Lord] does not need (c.237) today the prophets as previously, because the evil ones did not understand who killed them nor who saved them. For if the Lord had killed them without the prophets, they would not have known whether the Lord killed them or their idols. They would have kept on supposing that their idols had killed them and they would have offered their supplications all the more. Wherever the Lord had saved them, they would have thought that their idols had saved them and they would have loved them again all the more. [Their] chastisement would have been worthless. They did not know who had punished them, and were not instructed why. Blessed is our Lord Jesus who by the compulsion of his love has redeemed them from the desolation of the idols.

16. Therefore, God does not hold back a person today from love and Perfection. Let us then pursue love, for if a person departs today from the world while he is not [yet] Perfect, our Lord does not perfect him as [he did] the prophets. And if a person does not walk today in the steps of our Lord and of his apostles, he will not go with the prophets. Because after the prophets departed from the world, our Lord perfected them in the sight of the apostles and elevated them to the place of Perfection, they and all the righteous ones who had pursued (c.240) Perfection like them. The compulsion of Jesus' love guided every creature and turned them around to understand that there is a God in heaven, that he created and sustains them.

17. Moreover, this Word greatly excited the creation and it was turned around because they heard that the Son of God had died on account of sinners in order that they might repent and live. All the worlds were stirred; he who gives life to all died on account of his creature. The Gentiles heard of the care of God for them and they trembled and knew that he had died on account of them. They were afraid and discussed with one another, 'How shall we make a defense

to him who formed us and whom we have forgotten? He died for us and yet we do not listen to him. What torment do we deserve?' Or, 'How will we have his compassion unless we repent?' Through this idea the Gentiles repented and were converted—people who were unwilling to be persuaded through the prophets.

18. It is one thing when people hear that a son of Adam died for his companions, but another thing when they hear that the Son of God died for his creation and for his servants. It is not extraordinary that the sons of Adam die on account of their colleagues since their nature is imperfect. But as the Lord, whose (c.241) nature transcends death, died for the evil sons of Adam, human beings were captivated by this love because of this and loved him.

19. Next, let us talk about the love of our fathers because we should imitate their love and their lowliness. Abraham and Isaac pursued Perfection when their wives were taken from them and they did not quarrel or fight. When the well was taken from them, they neither quarreled nor became their enemies. They endured the rape of their riches with joy, and were held captive neither by their possession nor by their wives, as [they were] by the love of and desire for God.

If the Lord had said to them, 'Renounce your wives and let go of your property', as he had said to the apostles, they would have done his will, just as when he had said to them, 'Go out from your land and from your family, and go where I tell you'.⁴² Because they loved him and loved [fellow] human beings, they went gladly even while they knew that they had been plundered and cheated and had their wives taken, in order that they might fulfill the commandment of him whom they loved, and in order to continue honoring those whom they loved. Also, whenever

42. Gn 12:1

he asked (c.244) them to sacrifice their sons, they gladly sacrificed, because his love was fixed in their heart and they did his will in all he commanded them.

But had [God] said to them, 'Give up your wives and your sons and your possessions, and go proclaim me wherever I will tell you', it would have been easier for them to leave their wives in celibacy and their living children in their homes and their wealth and everything that belonged to them with their families and go wherever the Lord sent them; much more easily than what he did say to them, 'Go with everything you have with you', because their women were carried away by force to be dishonored before their very eyes, and their sons to be sacrificed in the face of [their sense] of compassion, and their possessions were to be plundered every day as they looked on with their own eyes and endured it—because of the hope of truth, which is to come. But all whom the Lord held back from renunciation and from physical celibacy were to become an example to all who are married in this world, so that they might live like them.

20. Jacob also pursued Perfection when he humbled himself before Esau his brother. He gave the fury of Esau an opportunity to calm down. When his anger had calmed down a little he sent [a message] to him, 'I am your servant'[43] by means of the offerings (c.245) he delivered to him. When Esau approached to meet Jacob, Jacob bowed down to him seven times upon the ground.[44] The enmity of Esau was put to rest and he embraced Jacob, kissed him, and was reconciled to him. Where is our own lowliness today? Who among us is humbled like this before his enemy, bowing down to him and reconciling himself with him?

21. Joseph also pursued Perfection when he repaid good things for bad to his brothers who had sought twice to kill him. The Lord delivered him from their hands, but they

43. Gn 32:18   44. Gn 33:3

sold him into slavery and he endured great sufferings on account of them. 'His feet were bound in chains and his soul entered into irons',[45] as it is written. He repaid them all noble deeds instead of spiteful things and did not keep a grudge, nor did he become their enemy.[46]

It is also written in [another] place: when he did good things to them in Egypt, they repaid him bad things and plotted to kill him. He endured the evil things like a good worker and did not do evil to them, but instead did good to them, and [so] he excelled and triumphed over every evil with good things. When Israel died, they came beseeching him, 'Our Father gave [this] commandment before he died, "Say to Joseph my son, forgive (c.248) the transgression of your brothers"',[47] because they thought that Joseph had held a grudge and enmity against them, yet, because of his father, he had not treated them badly. Then Joseph raised his voice with sighs and tears and said to his brothers, who were his murderers, 'Do not fear me, for I am subject to God'.[48] And [so] they realized that he was a friend of the Lord like his fathers, and would keep his commandments. For just as his mercies are many, so also his friends increase their kindness.

Just as he makes his sun shine and the rain fall upon the good and the bad, so also his friends shine their love upon the good and the bad. But because people exalt themselves and grieve the heart of their brothers, standing against the commandments of God, he overthrows them here and there in this world, as well as on Judgment day. But if we are sincere, God is kind and good, forever and ever.

The end of the ninth *Mēmrā*, which is on Uprightness and on the love of the Upright and of the holy prophets.

---

45. Ps 105:18   47. Gn 50:16
46. Rm 12:21   48. Gn 50:19

Mēmrā Ten

Summary: A sermon arguing against a spiritualizing asceticism in which physical fasting is disdained by those who believe they have superseded anything physical.

(c.249) Concerning the advantage we have when we endure evil things while perfecting good things; and concerning the fasting and lowliness of the body and the soul, [written] by this same holy person. May his prayers help us all, Amen and Amen.

1.   It helps us, brothers, to endure evil things while doing good things because Satan opposes us, and whenever we do something good, he schemes against us to cause us afflictions, so that we may not do what is good. Whenever we treat strangers or our brothers well he brings his disciples, wolves in the likeness of lambs, and troubles us through the likeness of our brothers to prevent us being hospitable to strangers or treating our [own] brothers well. But we should neither fear, nor be irritated, nor hold back from all good things, because if we persevere the Lord will defeat him in front of us, and he will not be able to tempt us all the time. (c.252)

2.   'Pray that you do not enter temptation.'[1] If [the evil one] threatens us through adversities or afflictions and we

1. Mt 26:41

flee from good things, he will also strive to frighten us so that we will not do what is good, in order that we will depart without fruits from this world. For nothing from this world accompanies us except the good that we have done and our fasting and our continual prayer.

3. Let us examine closely our death and see what will go with us from this world to that [other] world. For see, we would not want to travel a short distance or even to some-place nearby—[in] which a person has to do business and is able to work and live—without provisions in this world. For, if in this [world] a person has a hundred resources and still does not wish to proceed without provisions, how shall he travel to that [other] world?

Because if a person does not take anything with him here, no one will give him [anything] there, for they will call him a poor man. We do not wish to become humble in our heart and in our body; through our heart our lowliness and servitude shall be known to God, and through our body our lowliness and servitude shall be revealed to everyone, as it is written: 'Let your lowliness be evident to all people'.[2]

For if a person greets people spiritually,[3] bowing his spiritual head, but not bowing his [physical] head and heart before them, (c.253) his lowliness is evident only to God and is not evident to people, nor does he teach them. If he greets people with external lips, bowing his physical head, his lowliness is apparent to people and he pleases them, but not God, because the Lord is served spiritually and people [are served] through these visible things.

But if we wish to work and teach and be called great ones,[4] we have to wash and purify the inner [self] as well as the outer and the outer as the inner.[5] Our bodies and souls become equally worthy through fasting and prayer

2. Ph 4:5
3. Literally, 'in his heart'.

4. Mt 5:19; Didache 3:3
5. Mt 23:26

and lowliness. Let our bodies fast from foods and pleasures and from every pride of clothing and pleasures of life. Let our souls fast from spiteful words and from controversies and jealousy, zeal, curses, and anger, even enmity and from everything evil and similar to these.

4. Gluttony harms bodies [even] when they are healthy, and hateful words and everything evil harm the soul. In other words, if the soul is harmed, the body is harmed; and if the body is harmed, the soul is harmed. For there is no inner person without an outer [person], and there is no outer [person] without an inner. But if you wish to become perfect and be made pure, pursue justice of the heart and of the body (c.256) and [pursue] sincerity, lowliness, and peace of the heart and body. Because soul and body mutually succeed and fail with one another, together they are praised and together they sit down at table, and those who keep his commandments with their bodies and souls will rest together on the day of the Lord.

But let us lower ourselves before God and people, just as we see our Lord and all his preachers who lowered themselves and became great on account of their lowliness, and bowed down to their enemies; [just as] Israel bowed down to the one who sought to kill him, and humbled his soul and body and bowed to him many times;[6] and as our Lord was humble in his body and his spirit so that he might teach us; and as the prophets and apostles became humble in their bodies and in their souls, that is, they fasted with their bodies from ornamental clothing and all pride, and fasted with their souls from sustenance and from all pleasures. 'Do not be concerned about things belonging to your bodies, or what you shall wear, nor about things belonging to your souls, or what you shall be nourished. The soul is more than food and the body more than clothing.'[7]

6. Gn 33:3   7. Mt 6:25

5.   The Lord commanded those here who are involved in the labor and profit of this world to fast from the bonds of iniquity and from the ties (c.257) of deceit, to release the captives to freedom and fast from injustice and from slander, from fraud and adultery, from usury, pride, and luxury,[8] and from everything that is hateful to them, so that they might not do them to others, lest they find themselves sealed with the names of strangers; but rather, in the name of Jesus let them do everything[9] and heal every disease.

He commanded them to do to all people whatever they wish everyone would do to them. 'Break your bread with a hungry person and invite the strangers into your house and give a garment to the naked and do not turn away from your fellow human being.'[10] When you do these things, then be assured that the Lord will establish you upon the strength of the land and fill your soul with rich food and make your salvation shine like a light; and your righteousness will shine like a lamp, and the glory of God shall overcome you and his salvation will shine upon you.[11]

This is the fast the Lord commanded to almsgivers. But our Lord commanded the solitaries, that is, the merciful ones who do not harm anyone, [both] the ancients and the contemporary ones, to fast from all pleasures, saying through Paul, 'It is better for us not to eat meat or drink wine'.[12] And 'Be careful lest your hearts become heavy through intemperance and intoxication, through the anxiety of the world and through thinking (c.260) about wealth.'[13] Be careful not to be enticed because the peoples [Gentiles] seek all these things.[14] But he commanded the peoples [Gentiles] in this way, 'Be careful not to possess by iniquity, nor to build in sin, nor to build or to acquire as [if] forever; and do not deal with debauchery in the world, because the form of this world will pass away.'[15]

---

8. Hermas Mand.   10. Is 58:7   13. Lk 21:34
VIII:10, Sim. V:3   11. Is 58:7   14. Mt 6:32
9. Col 13:17   12. Rm 14:21   15. Apocryphal; cf. 1 Co 7:30

6. God could have made all the world rich and healthy and life-long residents,[16] and not needy people; but he made some rich and some poor and some strangers and some sick. He tempts those who have by those who have not [in order to see] if their affections are for their fellow human beings. If the rich take care of the poor and the healthy [take care of] the sick and the clothed [take care of] the naked and the life-long residents [are hospitable to] the strangers, and if they will do this and have compassion upon those who are worse off than them, those worse off will be able to find relief with the powerful ones and the powerful will be justified through those worse off.

But if they will not do as our Lord commanded—to have compassion on those who are worse off than they— [the Lord] will provide for the poor according to his mercies and will have pity 'like a poor person' on this world. These who have not been compassionate will be without fruits and without righteousness on the day of our Lord. For Lazarus was ill-treated and lived (c.261) in this world, but he went to that [other] world and was given rest.[17] But, woe to that rich person who has gone without [spiritual] provisions, because his stomach will not be full with the rich food of the new world.

7. My brothers, take care of the strangers and the needy and the poor and the bereaved and the sick, and let us prepare provisions for ourselves for the long road and for that great world, lest when the doers of good deeds find enjoyment and rest, we shall be tormented in front of them and be afflicted. But when we wish to throw ourselves upon food, we dispute [the validity of the words], 'It is not what enters the belly that defiles a person, but what issues from the mouth that will defile a person'.[18] And if we desire to be slack from prayer we dispute the words, 'In our heart let

16. Literally, *bnay bēt abā*—'sons of the household of the father'—i.e., 'local natives' belonging to the patriarchal establishment of the community.
17. Lk 16:19ff   18. Mt 15:11

us please our Lord'.[19] If we wish not to be diligent for the church, we dispute the words: 'our heart is a church'.[20] If we wish to adorn ourselves, we are [in effect] saying, 'Inwardly we shall mourn. God does not desire these visible things'. If it pleases us not to comfort one who is naked or poor, we are saying, 'In our soul we shall be justified and shall heal our own illnesses'.

8.   Evil teaches us all of these things, so that we might falter and not be diligent in our body and in our soul. But just as [evil] makes us believe that we work in our hearts, it makes us work neither in our heart (c.264) nor in our body. For there is no one who accomplishes righteousness with his heart and does not [also] accomplish [righteousness] with his body, because, from the fullness of the heart, lips speak[21] and, after the thought of the heart, the body moves. As the heart is humble, so the body will [also] be humble.

Moreover, if we wish to possess and to build, we should say, 'we possess while not possessing, and we own [something] but our mind is not bound by it'.[22] But wait. If a person should demand from you your possession, I will watch whether you will give [it] to him and are not bound by it. Or if a person takes it from you, are you not indignant against him, do you not go to court with him and do you not part in anger and become his enemy?

Woe to us who walk in falsehood and cunning. Liars are similar to demons.[23] For, everyone who empties his heart of the land also empties his body of its possession. Therefore, if a possession can be acquired while not being possessed, and a building can be built while we are not attached to it, then even a theft could be committed while [we are] not being robbed, and hateful deeds could be done while not being done. Moreover, we could say, we are heaven and earth and all that is in them—we are [even]

19. Rm 14:8; 2 Co 5:9   22. 1 Co 7:30
20. 1 Co 3:16, 6:19   23. Jn 8:44
21. Mt 12:34

Paradise and Jerusalem. As we do not ardently desire nor are enslaved to that excellent place of which the world is not capable, nor to that household of the Father that only sons (c.265) who have kept the commandments with their body and soul and have become holy ones in the heart and body [are able to] enter there; indeed, just what is the source for this weakness in people, unless it is the contrivance of sin? This doctrine, which is so enfeebled, has the tastes of death hidden in it.

9. But this we have known, that there is nothing in food that defiles and whoever eats is surely not defiled. But his body will become exceedingly heavy and he will live extravagantly,[24] bearing himself with pride and ceasing from the pursuit of Perfection.

Whoever dresses lavishly does not defile himself, but becomes really puffed up and extremely haughty and is brought down from the pursuit of Perfection. Error enters between pleasure, pride, luxury, and haughtiness, these that are not derived from love, and a person becomes fat and petulant, just as the Israelites were petulant. At first, one forgets that he is a covenanter[25] and after a while one will [even] forget that he should serve God, just as the Israelites forgot the Mighty One who had saved them.[26] After he had grown fat with riches and pleasures, then he defiled himself. [He was] not immediately [defiled], but little by little, because he enjoyed delights and lived luxuriously. Gradual, moreover, are the excellent deeds of fasting and asceticism; righteousness increases with lowliness; (c.268) while, [likewise], little by little, spiteful deeds, pleasures, and the delicacies of food defile.

10. When our Lord and the apostles emptied themselves, they emptied themselves completely and fasted fully with

24. Lk 6:45
25. Literally, 'son of the Covenant' (*bar qyāmā*).
26. Dt 32:15

[both] their bodies and their souls. For they never said, 'We fast' while they lived luxuriously, enjoying delicacies. Nor [did they say], 'We renounce', while possessing. Nor, 'We build as if we do not build'. May no one turn us away from the ascetic discipline of our Lord and his apostles, not even from the fast that the prophets fasted, while they lay upon each side three hundred and sixty days.[27] They bore the iniquity of sinners upon themselves, each for forty days and for all days.[28]

The apostles and the prophets constantly fasted, in order to be an example for us. Our Lord fasted so that he might become an example for us through his fasting and his prayer. Who does not hear and tremble? He who forgives debts and pardons sinners has fasted and made supplication on account of our own iniquity. How much should we ourselves fast and supplicate on account of the wickedness in ourselves and the adversaries we have in the world, and on account of the inheritance that we will have in that world, so that we may go and receive it (c.269) through the grace of our Lord, with our faces uncovered before his face, seeing that we will have kept his commandments?

The end of the tenth *Mēmra*, which is on the assistance we have when we endure evil things, while doing good things; and on the fasting of the body and the lowliness of the soul.

27. Ezk 4:9
28. 1 K 19:8

Mēmrā Eleven

Summary: One must be able to distinguish between the major and minor commandments. The author defends his position that Scripture is intended for and may be interpreted by two or more levels of Christians among its readers.

On the hearing of the scriptures when the Law is read before us. (c.272)

1. Just as we examine the food for the body, knowing which is good and which is bad, which is impure and pure, and knowing that there are foods that are fatally poisonous, we are concerned to distinguish [one] food from [other] foods; so also when the scribe reads the scriptures. If there is someone who will interpret for us, [well and good]; if not, let us not be in need, but rather let us distinguish the commandments of Perfection from those of vegetable and milk, and the humble commandments from the harsh ones, and the major ones from the minor, and these by which one will not be saved when he keeps them from these by which one will be saved while keeping them.

When the Law says, 'Love the Lord your God more than yourself and your neighbor as yourself',[1] you should say, 'This commandment is mine'. When [it says], 'An eye for an eye and hate your enemy',[2] and things similar to

1. Dt 6:5; Lv 19:18   2. Ex 21:24; Lv 24:20; Dt 19:21

these, say, (c.273) 'These are not mine, but belong to harsh and evil people'.

For our Lord established humble commandments for the humble ones so that they might become even more humble and be perfected, as I wrote above. When David said, 'I hate, O Lord, those who hate you',[3] you should say, 'This was not mine. The Spirit desired to speak against those who hate the Lord so that they might hear and fear and repent and be saved.' When [David] said, 'Who is the man who desires life? Come, children, listen to me and I will teach you the fear of God. Hold back your tongues from evil and do not let your lips speak deceit. Depart from evil and do good. Seek peace and pursue it.'[4] 'Cease from anger and rage. Remove from me an evil heart. And evil I do not know.'[5] You should say, 'These are my commandments because through them and those that are similar in all the prophets and apostles I will become gentle and humble of spirit'.

As the apostle said, 'Choose for yourselves these [commandments] that are humble from among these that are harsh, and in that way you will be made Perfect'.[6] When the apostle and the Gospel are read, pursue all of these commandments of the Perfect, which I have chosen for you above and those which are similar to them, and you will be raised [above] these that are vegetable and milk, for [the scriptures] were not addressed to [only] one [type of] person. (c.276)

2.   Do you want to become Perfect? Pursue the great commandments. But pay attention, because if you prescribe these minor and major commandments to a person, he will not be able to observe them all at once, unless he leaves one in order to observe the other. Notice how the words of Jesus become the opposite of one another. So that you shall

3. Ps 139:21   5. Ps 101:4
4. Ps 34:12-14   6. Ph 4:8

recognize that they were spoken to two [types] of people, our Lord said, 'Do not judge';[7] and he [also] said, 'Shame a person before the whole church'.[8] If both of them are [intended] for you, which one will you choose? If you judge, you have isolated yourself from that major commandment, 'Do not judge'. And, if you do not judge, you will be blameworthy because of that [other] commandment, 'before the whole church shame him'.

3. Moreover, our Lord said, 'Forgive your brother seventy times seven,[9] [even] if he does you wrong [that many times] in a single day'. Yet again he said, 'Think of him as a Gentile'.[10] If these were spoken to [only] one [type of] person, which one would you choose? That one, 'Forgive him seventy times seven'; or that [other] one, 'Regard him as a Gentile and keep away from him'?

For in that first one, 'Forgive him', he tells you not to distinguish yourself from your brother. In this way, the major and minor commandments contrast because they were not spoken to one person, but to everyone according to the power in him. For example, that commandment 'Do not (c.277) associate with immoral people'[11] contrasted with that [other] one, 'Be all things with all people'.[12] Therefore, these commandments, which do not judge anyone and love everyone, are spoken to the strong, of whom it is said, 'We the strong ought to bear the infirmity of the weak, visit them everyday and teach them with humility'.[13]

These minor [commandments] are spoken to the young and imperfect whose conscience is [easily] offended. Paul said that one with a weak conscience is greatly offended when seeing one with a healthy conscience eating with Gentiles'[14] and instructing them, just as our Lord instructed them. In the same way, the Jews were offended by Jesus; 'this one receives and eats with sinners'.[15] 'To the pure,

7. Mt 7:1	10. Mt 18:17	13. Rm 15:1 ˙
8. Mt 18:17	11. 1 Co 5:9	14. 1 Co 8:9ff
9. Mt 18:22	12. 1 Co 9:22	15. Mt 9:11

everything is pure'.[16] In other words, he whose heart is pure from Satan does not think evil of anyone, but [thinks only] good things of all people. He whose conscience is mixed with Satan [can only] think of impurity about people.

4.   Moreover, he commanded the healthy, 'Do not be an obstacle to the sick while they are being healed; and if not, they may die and you will be offending Christ who died for them'.[17] Another time the apostle said to the healthy that they should regard everyone as better than they.[18] To the infant, however, he said, 'Do not eat with (c.280) immoral people',[19] so that they may not make him like themselves at a time when [he is still] immature regarding truth.

Which of these commandments does the one who says they are spoken to a single person choose: the major one or the minor one? [Would you choose] that major one, which [says] 'Make your soul lowly' and 'Consider your brother better than yourself', or that minor one, 'Do not eat with immoral people'? If you keep that major one, you shall receive a blessing from God. If you choose that minor one, the greater part of the world will become impure in your eyes. Satan even will make the pure ones [appear] defiled in your eyes because you permit him to have power over you. Therefore, if you keep that major commandment, you will ascend from the minor one. If you choose that minor one, you will fall short of that major one.

Further, [Paul] said, 'Be all things with all [people]', and 'Do not associate with immoral people'.[20] The opposite of that minor one is that major commandment. The major one says, 'Be all things with all people and instruct everyone'. The minor one says, 'Flee from being with whoever is sick and join with whoever is strong'. For he said, 'May the lame not be pushed down'.[21] He sends all the sick to the strong and the strong to the sick, as it befits the strong

16. Tt 1:15   19. 1 Co 5:11
17. 1 Co 8:12   20. 1 Co 5:9
18. Ph 2:3   21. Heb 12:13

to bear the illness of the sick. To the person who is not able to teach, not even himself, he says, 'Do not go to the sick, but to the healthy', lest [the sick] go (c.281) to one another and die because there is no one who will heal them. Therefore, if a person does not discern why [the commandments] were spoken, he does not help at all nor is he truly healed.

5. The Spirit wrote excellently: the sick will be healed without being aware, but the healthy person knows which commandment is his. Because our Lord said, 'Whoever breaks one of these minor commandments, and teaches people [to do so], shall be called the least',[22] do not ever break these minor commandments and reside in the major ones. You will surely grow up from that minor one and reside in the major one.

Therefore, when a person has become an adult, since he no longer sucks the milk of infants, shall he do away with milk? [God] forbid! Infants go on sucking, but he does not come near to milk. In addition, when the spiritual infant grows strong and comes to what is greater than milk, he will attain the solid food of these who are well trained to understand and discern the higher ministry from what is inferior. 'As children in Christ I have given you milk to drink. Come now to solid food, that is, [come] from the minor commandments to the major ones.'[23] As milk is a torment to an adult to suck and bread can choke an infant (c.284), so the minor commandment is the opposite of Perfection. For a person will never rise up above that [commandment], 'Put your brother to shame before the church and regard him as a Gentile',[24] nor will he attain Perfection, unless he approaches that [commandment], 'Forgive him seventy times seven'[25] and 'Think of him as better than you'.[26]

The end of the eleventh *Mēmrā*, on the hearing of the Holy Scriptures.

22. Mt 5:19   23. 1 Co 3:1   24. Mt 18:17   25. Mt 5:22   26. Ph 2:3

Mēmrā Twelve

ON THE HIDDEN AND
PUBLIC MINISTRY
OF THE CHURCH

Summary: The Church exists on three levels— the Visible Church, the Church of the Heart, and the Hidden Church. The Visible, physical, and earthly church is, nevertheless, the true church through which one must travel to the Church of the Heart and the Hidden, heavenly Church. (c.285)

1. My brothers, since we believe that there is a hidden renunciation of the heart, which forsakes the earth and is raised up to heaven, let us also physically renounce our possessions and our inheritance. Then we will be keeping the commandments of the one who gives life to all, knowing that there is a hidden prayer of the heart for that one who is bound up in our Lord and meditates on him ceaselessly. Let us pray with our body as well as with our heart, just as Jesus blessed and prayed physically and spiritually.

The apostles and the prophets [also] prayed in this way. Let us not be witless ones who resist being instructed by their fathers, or do away with our spiritual fathers, adopting new ones in the flesh who are not genuine, leading us astray from the truth of our Lord and his preachers. Since we know there is (c.288) a hidden fast of the heart from evil thoughts, let us also fast openly just as our Lord fasted [along with] his first and last preachers.

Since we know that the body becomes a hidden temple and the heart a hidden altar for spiritual worship, let us be diligent in this public altar and before this public temple. Although we are weary in these things, we shall live forever in that great freeborn and heavenly church, and in that altar that is adorned and erected by the Spirit, before which the angels and all the saints serve and Jesus celebrates and offers up [his sacrifice] before them, and above them and on all their sides.

Since we know that the Perfect are baptized in Jesus Christ and are inwardly pure, let us believe and affirm this visible baptism, which is of the Spirit and is the absolution and pardoning of sins for whoever believes in it and is baptized in it and performs good deeds.

2.   For our Lord and his first and last preachers did not erect in vain the Church and the altar and baptism, all of which are visible to physical eyes. It is through these visible things, however, that we shall be in these heavenly things, which are invisible to eyes of flesh, our bodies becoming temples and our hearts altars.[1] Let us open [the door] and enter into this (c.289) visible church with its priesthood and its worship so that [our bodies] may become good examples to all people who imitate [the church] in the vigils and fasting and patience of our Lord and his preachers—let us act and teach.[2]

Then, when we are in great lowliness and honor all people—great and small—that heavenly church and spiritual altar will be revealed to us and we will sacrifice praise upon it through the prayer of our hearts and the supplication of our bodies while believing in this visible altar and this priesthood, which serves [the altar] true for us. Everything in this church is established in imitation of that hidden church. But if we doubt and treat with con-

1. Heb 11:3   2. Mt 5:19

tempt this public church and this public altar and the public priesthood and the baptism that brings forgiveness, our body will not become a temple, nor will our heart become an altar and a fortress of glory. That higher church and its altar, its light and its priesthood, will not be revealed to us. Whither are gathered all the saints who are pure in their heart and dwell in its glory and luxuriate in its light for they do not treat with contempt this blessed nurse who gives birth everyday and educates good envoys and sends [them] to that great church (c.292) in heaven.

This visible church is revealed to everyone for our Lord established its altar, its baptism, and its priesthood, because our Lord and his apostles prayed in it, baptized in it, and they sacrificed in it his body and his blood and ministered in it truly. It is the true church and a blessed mother, which brings up all the children and the body and heart in which our Lord dwells. Because of the Spirit that resides in it, it is the true temple and altar. Because our Lord dwells there, as it is written, 'Your bodies are temples of the Lord and Christ dwells in your interior humanity'.[3]

From that heavenly church originates everything that is beautiful and from there the light shines on us on all sides. Because its image was the church on earth and its priests and its altar, and through its type of service the body serves outwardly and the heart ministers from within, they imitate and pursue it when they are diligent in this visible church. Because of this, that church is greater than all and is the mother of all the baptized, especially since the person of our Lord shines through it and gives it light.

3.   This church—with its altar and baptism—gives birth to people as infants, (c.293) [who] suckle milk until they are weaned; then, they come to education and the understanding of the body and the heart, making their bodies temples and their hearts altars, eating food that is stronger

3. 1 Co 6:19

and better than milk until they become Perfect and truly
eat our Lord, as he had said, 'Whoever will eat me will also
live on account of me'.[4] When they have eaten the true
food, as the apostle said, 'Solid food is for the Perfect who
have the strength to train to comprehend[5] what is the height
and depth and length and width',[6] then they will reach that
church on high and it will perfect them and they will enter
that city of Jesus our King. There they will work in that
great and excellent palace, the mother of all the living and
the Perfect.

Therefore, let us not despise the visible church, for
it is the teacher of all infants, nor let us despise this [church]
of the heart that is the fortifier of all the sick, and let us
desire ardently that higher [church] that perfects all the
saints.

4.   There is life in each of the three churches and their
ministries, but one glory is better than another. Whoever
departs from the ministry of this [visible] church and does
not attain that [church] of the heart and that (c.296) higher
[church] departs without sins from this world, his good
deeds accompanying him—that is excellent. Whoever departs from that [church] of the heart, [that is] even better.
Whoever attains in his heart that heavenly church and then
departs, blessed is his spirit that becomes Perfect and he
will go see our Lord face to face. When, however, a person
is diligent in this visible church, he is living in that [church]
of the heart and in that higher [church]. Just as when a
person is baptized in visible waters, some are baptized in
fire and in the Spirit, which are invisible. Just as when a
person has faith he loves, and when he has loved becomes
Perfect, and when he is perfected he will reign.

But without this visible baptism a person cannot be
baptized with fire and the Spirit; and without this visible
church a person will not live in that [church] of the heart

4. Jn 6:58   5. Hb 5:14   6. Ep 3:18

and in that higher [church]. If a person has separated himself from [the church] and has served on the mountain,[7] he will be guilty or lost. Wherever he is, however, the true [church] is faithful to him because it is alive and its covenant will not be dissolved.

5. For just as a wet-nurse who raises an infant teaches [the infant] to eat bread which is better than milk, so this visible church teaches its children to eat something better and much greater so that through it (c.297) they may grow. It is not that the nurse of the infant does not have food; it is that the infant is [too] weak for food and milk is [still] needed by it. It is not that the Spirit that serves the visible church is weaker than that [church] of the heart and that of the Spirit, because one Spirit serves the three of them. The descendants of Adam, however, are very weak, and if [the church] does not instruct them as infants they are not able to receive the solid food.

But what sort of nursing mother is it who has many children of which some are thirty years old and some are thirty days old; how is she able to place before them one kind of food? If she places before them the same solid food only, the child of thirty days will die and the son of thirty years will grow; and if she offers milk only, the thirty day old child will live and grow fat, and the thirty year old son will be tormented [by hunger] and die.

Because of this, even our Lord and his preachers who are the tutors of all people command the thirty day old child, 'Do not eat with adulterers nor have anything to do with prostitutes and gluttons and cursers and with any whose deeds are evil'.[8] And they say to the thirty year old son, 'Take up the misfortune of the sick[9] and be all [things] to all [people][10] and do not talk about anyone (c.300) that he is pagan or unclean or evil,[11] even if this is so, and con-

7. That is, worshipped
in a pagan cult.
8. 1 Co 5:9-11

9. Rm 15:1
10. 1 Co 9:22
11. Ac 10:28

sider everyone better than yourself and in this way you shall grow'.

6. They commanded each person whatever was fitting for him. Because, if the child of thirty days goes to the house of evil people he will perish. If, however, the thirty year old son goes to the house of evil people he will convert them, and if they are not converted, he will not perish because he has become an adult in the Spirit.

Moreover, in this way, they will command one whose nature is childish and not conscious that he must work,[12] and then he will eat until he grows strong. Not on account of bread was the apostle fearful, but lest ceasing from visible work and not knowing how to do hidden work, he might learn lackadaisicalness and falsehood and slander, fall into decrepit discussions and into games and laughter and in stories that are not virtuous, and forget that he is a Christian.[13]

But to him who is greater in his mind and repentant in his heart and knows how to accomplish an invisible deed, our Lord and his preachers said, 'Do not be anxious for your body, about what you shall wear, nor even for yourself of what you shall be nourished',[14] but 'seek that which is higher and meditate upon it'.[15] Because a person in this way is able to correct, reconcile, admonish, and teach people to please the one who gives life (c.301) to all, and to extricate people from stories that are not virtuous and discussions that are not profitable and amusement and inappropriate laughter and hateful words and evil deeds.

Because of this conduct and profit, our Lord did not allow this person, who is a helper for all people, to work on the land, because he said to him as [he had said] to Simon, 'If you love me, feed for me my flock and my sheep, my ewes and my lambs'.[16] This one who feeds the sheep of

12. 2 Th 3:12   15. Col 3:1
13. 1 Tm 4:7; Ep 5:4   16. Jn 21:15-17
14. Mt 6:26

Christ is not able to go guide the plow and work the visible land, but gathers, feeds, and reconciles the sheep who were delivered to him, and his face will be revealed on that day before the one who commanded him, 'Feed my flock and my ewes and my lambs'.[17]

7. Blessed is whoever has entered that heavenly church upon which our Lord shines openly, just as this visible sun shines upon this visible church and upon these temples of the body. How many times will this sun set on these? The light of the face of our Lord and Savior Jesus Christ does not depart from that [church] that is above. For even if our Lord is everywhere, he is clearly visible [only] in that heavenly church, but [only to] those who have lowered themselves and have become calm and gentle with everyone, and have fought and made war only with the evil spirits, and have purified their hearts from evil thoughts (c. 304), just as the apostle said, 'Your struggle has not been against people of flesh and blood, but against the principalities and the powers and the evil spirits',[18] and against Satan the destroyer.

Those who have struggled against Satan and have defeated him will deserve this church upon which our Lord openly shines, which is above all, and they will receive that light of his glorious presence. Because our Lord said, 'Blessed are those who are pure in their heart, for they will see God'.[19] For even if there are other beatitudes and other places, to each according to his deeds, that great place is for those who have been purified from evil things and from despicable thoughts. They will be exalted and will see him and be glorified with our Lord Jesus and will receive blessings from his clergy. 'Who shall ascend the mountain of the Lord and who shall dwell on his holy mountain'—which

17. Jn 21:15-17
18. Ep 6:12
19. Mt 5:8

is the heavenly church? 'He whose hands are clean and is pure in his heart. This one will receive a blessing from the Lord and righteousness from God our Savior',[20] who is our Lord Jesus Christ. Praise be to him forever and ever. Amen.

The end of the twelfth *Mēmrā* about the hidden and public ministry of the church.

20. Ps 24:3-5

Mēmrā Thirteen

BY THE SAME AUTHOR
ON THE WAYS
OF THE UPRIGHT

Summary: The most detailed description of the Upright. The step of Uprightness is personified throughout the *mēmrā*. The focus is upon the Upright's social obligations and ministry to others, particularly marriage, commerce, and providing for the needy.
(c.305)

1. Uprightness[1] is sincere in whatever concerns it, but does not approach whatever does not concern it. [Uprightness] claims what belongs to it according to its [fair] measure, but does not get involved in usury or approach a bribe. [Uprightness] possesses wealth righteously and buys and sells as is appropriate before God. [Uprightness] neither deceives nor borrows something it lacks, but claims only what it has loaned without interest, even if it will be one hundred years [before it is repaid].

Whatever [Uprightness] hates it does not do to anyone. In addition, as it desires that a person treat it well whenever it is needy, so it will fill the needs of everyone as it is capable. If a person defrauds it, [Uprightness] will speak

1. Uprightness (*kēnūtā*) is used throughout this sermon as a personification —'the person who lives in Uprightness'.

its judgment before one or two and then three [others]. If [that person] is not persuaded to repay what belongs to Uprightness without usury, then [Uprightness] will speak before the whole church. If (c.308) he is not persuaded before the church, [Uprightness] will commit its judgment to God and turn away from him, while still speaking with him and not murmuring against him.

But neither does [Uprightness] approach nor harm nor reproach the person who harms [it]. It is not permitted for [Uprightness] to strike and swear lest it slip from the law. In addition, [Uprightness] is not permitted to expect that God will do evil to anyone at all.

For [God] said, 'Do not rejoice in the ruin of your enemy lest a double [portion] shall happen to you.'[2] This commandment is spoken to whoever harbors enmity. Uprightness, however, has no enemy, unless a person desires to become its enemy through iniquity.[3] [Uprightness] is not permitted to call a person by another name and to grieve him or [to call him] fool or contemptible or stupid or spiteful, for if it is able to give him honorable names [it does so]; yet if not, [Uprightness] does not give him insulting names, but calls a person simply by his [regular] name.

2.　　Uprightness honors its parents who have given it birth and they do not hear from [Uprightness] a harsh word. [Uprightness] honors the elders and greets them [respectfully]. [Uprightness] honors the priests, heeds their words,[4] and goes to them. It gives the best of all its crops to its priests and the best of its dough and the first-born of whatever it possesses[5] and it brings [all of that] to the house of the Lord (c.309), without being envious of the tranquil life of the priests, who bury its dead, visit its sick, and teach and edify its living.

On Sunday, [Uprightness] places in the Lord's house some of [the fruit of] its labors for the needy because [the

---

2. Pr 24:17
3. Didache 1:3

4. Didache 4:1
5. Didache 13:3-7

latter] visit the house of our Lord. During the observances of fasting, [Uprightness] brings to the house of the Lord whatever it saves. [Uprightness] is concerned to go and pray at the right time and to see whether there are [any] needy there it could help so that it might receive a reward from our Lord. [Uprightness] loves its friends, but does not hate its enemies. If a person hates [Uprightness, Uprightness] keeps it to itself, while making peace with him and with everyone. If it cannot speak good things about a person, neither [will it say] bad things. If [Uprightness] does not become a person's friend, neither will it become its enemy.

If a person is unjust and is afflicted—and [even though Uprightness] knows that he does not repay [what he has borrowed]—[Uprightness] will give him freely as much as it is able to give. If a person's reckoning is evil, [Uprightness] keeps it to itself and does not harm him and, if possible, [Uprightness] will do something beautiful for him. It does not requite the evil action of a person in order to treat him badly. [Uprightness] reconciles the house of brothers and honors the entire community of the Lord. [Uprightness] distributes honor to everyone as is appropriate, honoring the elders and the old women and its deaconesses, and that is good, and [Uprightness] is honored by them as is just.

3. [Uprightness] takes [only] one wife without songs, (c.312) foul language, and commotion. [Uprightness] worships the Lord and his Son and his Holy Spirit. [Uprightness is] neither a glutton nor a drunkard nor a boastful one nor a cheat, but [even if] it is greatly wronged, it speaks [only] what is right.

[Uprightness] is not envious of a person who lives comfortably nor does it quarrel in the fellowship of Uprightness. Its love reconciles a woman to a man; he reconciles [himself] to her; and they comfort everyone who is troubled and a stranger in whatever way they can. [To Uprightness] a man and a woman are equal, or a man and a man, or a woman and a woman.

They clothe the naked, just as our Lord said. They open the door to the strangers on a cold or hot day, and they have pity upon [other] people as upon themselves. In short, as they desire that people do to them, so they treat [others], knowing that [because] they do not want anyone to do evil to them, [so] they should not do evil to others. The Upright have observances of fasting, and [other] observances to keep and learn the law of the Lord their God, and to give alms through them. In short, on the day when they have ceased from their labors, they have prayed, fasted, or given alms. If this were not so, why would they be idle?

The Upright have [particular] hours of prayer so that they might worship the Lord their God three times a day, once in the morning, and in the evening, and in the middle of the night, as it is written, 'They shall stand up and praise you for your righteous judgments'.[6] (c.313) Such is Uprightness. And so God commanded Adam on the day he left heaven and loved the earth.

4.   Uprightness' love does not withhold any possession it has, whether of food or drink or clothing; but it will give liberally to everyone, to the good and the bad. Once evening is come, [Uprightness] reconciles with whoever is angry with it,[7] [and] if the [angry person] is persuaded, [well and good]. If not, however, it commits the judgment to our Lord. Between him and his neighbor he seeks [only] what is owed him, and does not put him to shame before the community. If someone steals from him and he catches him, he takes back what is his and releases him without dishonor. If he has nothing, he releases him without disgrace and does not despise the person who sins against him.

With 'yes' or 'no', he swears concerning every dispute. He does not lie or practice divination or consult oracles, use magic or charms, and he does not use spirits or soothsayers, amulets or phylacteries. He lives blamelessly and

6. Ps 118:62
7. Ep 4:26

gives alms out of his own [possessions]. He neither emulates nor imitates a man who commits iniquity and his path prospers. In the middle of his years—if he wishes—he becomes holy, [celibate,] and pleasing like Enoch, who after he had begotten Methuselah,[8] became holy and did not taste death.[9] That is, if he will renounce all he possesses, he will become like Enoch while bearing the Cross.

5. Whoever journeys in this Uprightness and in this love, while he is in his house with his property and with (c.316) his wife, is living in the ways of the first Upright ones. If he desires to become Perfect, he [must] empty himself, become celibate and abandon everything and become attached to our Lord in heaven and become dead from the use of the world. He will ascend to these great commandments and receive the Paraclete and know all truth as our Lord makes known to him. Quickly he will be perfected and bear the Cross. But, if he departs from the world in that Uprightness and in that love while he has his house, he will increase in Uprightness and inherit the portion lower than that of the Perfect.

6. Those who act this way and keep these commandments of Uprightness are virtuous, [even] while they are in trade and commerce, taking one wife as is appropriate for Uprightness and for the ways of the world, treating well every person as they desire that everyone should treat them well, in as much as possible.

Whoever has a good word should give a good word to whomever has need of it. Whoever has food and clothing should give food and clothing to whomever has need of it. Just as they hate that someone should do evil to them, so they should not treat anyone badly. As they wish that everyone should forgive them, in word and in deeds, they should forgive evildoers. Those who live this way are

8. Gn 5:21   9. Heb 11:5

subordinate [only] to the Perfect. If they desire to leave everything (c.317) and empty themselves, they shall quickly understand all truth and be perfected. If, however, they depart from the world while they are Upright, they are subordinate [only] to the Perfect.

7. [One who possesses] the love of Perfection does not possess anything except clothing and food for the day, does not desire anything earthly, and does not get involved in earthly matters.[10] Moreover, he avoids everything that is on earth and possess nothing of earthly things, teaching and treating well every person with a just and true word, becoming a servant of everyone through love.

That means, however, he will admonish this one and teach that [other] one, loving and honoring everyone and praying for everyone.[11] In this manner, he will become a servant—observing our Lord in heaven the entire day, and not being able to labor at anything physical without being greatly tormented in his conscience if he works in the transitory world. Rather, he will be fastened on to the Cross, all his members being bound up [in order not to do] evil things, yet being free for the service of good spiritual matters. His mind is bound up in our Father in heaven, and in every time and in every place praises and worships him. [One who possesses] the love of Perfection is not allowed not to love and pray for everyone.

The Perfection of the apostles says the following, 'We desired to die and bring to our Lord the evil and sinful ones, even by force in order that they might praise him'. Because (c.320) greater is the love of Perfection than that of Uprightness, the Perfect desired to die [so that] sinners may live. Whoever is like this will mature greatly and will know this as it is written, 'Whoever loves our Lord loves everyone more than himself';[12] that is, he will know the truth according to the will of our Lord Jesus.

10. Didache 11:6   11. Didache 2:7   12. 1 Jn 4:21; Didache 2:7

8. As for [one who possesses] the love of the prophets, as the Lord had spoken to him, [so] he lived; and as he was commanded, so he walked. As for the love of the apostles, our Lord will command him to consider everyone as better than himself. As for the love of the prophets, wherever the Lord had told him to love, he had loved; and wherever he commanded him to hate, there he had hated. The prophets, however, desired that they should love completely and be perfected, [yet] the Lord held them back from Perfection because he had sent them to kill the wicked, his enemies, through them. It is not right for the love of Uprightness to give to the good, but to hold back from the evil ones, but [to do] as God commanded him—love his neighbor as himself, which means all people.

9. Uprightness, which is complete in its knowledge and in its deeds, has some of its ways mixed in the love of Perfection. Because of this, [Uprightness] falls short of Perfection (c.321) because it has not emptied itself and become celibate, and because anxiously it loves bodily things and refreshes itself. [Uprightness] does not reside in the joy of spiritual things and enjoy [them], nor does [Uprightness] increase in the holiness of the wisdom of God, nor is purified, nor exults, nor grows strong, nor rejoices, nor refreshes itself, nor is fed, nor lives spiritually.

It is not right for [one who possesses] the love of Uprightness to give disreputable names to people, but [he should] call [them] honorable ones, 'my lord' and 'my mistress', and older people 'my father' and 'my mother', and his neighbors 'my brothers' and 'my sister', and the younger ones 'my son' and 'my daughter'.

If they do not like to refer to everyone in this way and become Upright ones, they should call a person by his [regular] name,[13] but not give him hateful names and grieve

13. Mt 5:22

him and so sin. For the evil one teaches people to call one another names.

The end of the thirteenth *Mēmrā* on the ways of Uprightness.

Mēmrā Fourteen

ON THE UPRIGHT
AND THE PERFECT

Summary: A series of dichotomies describing first the Upright in terms of duties—avoidance of evil actions and emotions. The Perfect are juxtaposed, always transcending these worldly parameters and conflicts. (c.324)

1. The Upright do not commit adultery and are not condemned; but the Perfect do not [even] lust and are not diminished.[1]

The Upright neither plunder nor cheat nor take advantage [of others], nor seek what is not their own; but the Perfect neither possess nor build nor plant, and they do not inherit the land nor work for food and clothing, but live like a pauper in grace.

The Upright do not swear, except 'yes' or 'no', about anything; but the Perfect speak only what our Lord wishes, because not even with 'yes' or 'no' will they transgress and be diminished.

The Upright are sanctified from the evil (c.325) of the earth, [but] not from its possessions, its benefits, or its fellowship; but the Perfect rise above every inheritance of the visible earth and above all its evils and its possession and

1. Mt 5:27-28

riches, and above temporal intercourse and all its delights.
The Upright distinguish impure animals from pure
ones and eat from the latter; but the Perfect rise above pure
and impure things.

The Upright build and possess, not as [if] forever, but
live in the world as strangers; the Perfect neither build nor
possess, nor do their minds abide on the earth.

The Upright discern good people from evil ones and
are moved with compassion upon the latter; the Perfect
consider [others] as better than themselves.

The Upright uproot anger and are at rest from it; the
Perfect not only are at rest from anger, but also love their
slayers and pray for them and for all people.

The Upright exact what is theirs from wherever they
lend or buy without usury or contracts; but the Perfect do
not borrow or possess more than meager food and humble
clothing. (c.328)

2.   The Upright reproach, but are not angry, admonishing with lowliness and teaching with love. The Upright
feed   the   hungry   and clothe the naked and rescue the
afflicted with their [own] possession and riches; but the Perfect give away all of their possession at once to the needy
and the afflicted, taking up their cross and following their
Lord spiritually,[2] and spiritually they serve him loving all
people and praying for them.

The Upright have one or two doors in heaven and
knock on them five times a day; but [for] the Perfect all of
heaven consists of doors before them and all day they look
there, praising and glorifying our Lord and walking spiritually from glory to glory and seeing our Lord as in a mirror in their heart.

The Upright inherit this side of the city of the Perfect;
but the Perfect live with our Lord in Eden and in heavenly
Jerusalem because they have become similar to him.

2. Mt 19:21; Mk 10:24; Lk 18:22

The Upright are not able to do all the will of our Lord, unless they come to holiness³ and empty themselves; but the Perfect do these things and live with our Lord. The Upright do not know (c.329) today all the ways of our Lord, unless they come to holiness and empty themselves; but the Perfect do [know] and act and hear the voice of our Lord, as he said, 'My sheep hear my voice and follow me, but do not know the voice of a stranger'.⁴

The Upright glorify God with trembling and turn aside from evil; but the Perfect understand the height and depth and length and width. With all the saints who have been perfected they have understood and triumphed and ascended to the supernal Jerusalem. The Perfect reach Zion and Jerusalem, which is in heaven and the spiritual paradise.

The Upright just barely attain this side of [the Perfect], and are much lower than the Perfect.

3. The Upright are not troubled and do not wander from the commandments of our Lord, which are [established] in Uprightness; but the Perfect are better and rise above them and convert all those gone astray, and because their hearts are pure, they see the Lord. Whoever is not pure of heart is not able to see him, but will inherit the place that is right for him.

The Upright do not curse anyone, nor call a person a fool or stupid or contemptible and do not lie against anyone; but the Perfect honor and bless everyone, teaching everyone not to lie against his neighbor.

Everyone (c.332) is exalted according to his manner of life and according to his rank, his wearied mind, and the lowliness of his soul. As for the rest, everyone is rewarded in that world, whether good or bad, according to what he has done—whether good or evil—in this world. As the

3. celibacy
4. Jn 10:16

apostle said, 'We must all stand before the tribunal of Christ in order that each one of us may be rewarded [for] whatever he has done in his body'.[5]

There are some whose torment is more severe than that of his neighbor; there are some [others] upon whom it is fitting there should be mercy,[6] because he was compassionate and will escape from torment. Whoever hears the word of our Lord, however, whether about Uprightness or Perfection, will not come to judgment, unless he does so in order to be glorified before the tribunal of Christ in the sight of all the world, or to judge the sinners, as our Lord said, 'Whoever hears my words will depart from death to life'. 'But the person who is in the Spirit, that is, he who knows the truth and has become Perfect, will judge everyone and by no one is judged.'[7]

4.   Blessed are you, Lord Jesus Christ. (c.333) How upright and how good you are, for your greatness is immense and your grace is immeasurable. Everyone as he seeks you, so he will find you. As he compels his disposition to keep your law, so he will grow. As much as one increasingly lowers himself, so he will be glorified.

The end of the fourteenth *Mēmrā* on the Upright and the Perfect.

5. 2 Co 5:10
6. Mt 5:7
7. 1 Co 2:15

Mēmrā Fifteen

ON ADAM'S
MARITAL DESIRE

Summary: An extended discourse on the origins and consequences of the human sexual drive. Celibacy, a principal requirement for Perfection, is the proper channel for sexuality. Sexual lust is not innate in human beings, but derives from the temptations of Satan. As a result, marriage is provisionally sanctioned. (c.336)

1. So now let us explain this marital desire that came into being through Adam, how it came to be in him and how it might be removed from his children. After he had sinned and was censured, a law was established for him, inferior to that first [law]. By this same law [God] permitted him to marry. Because he had desired to become physical and not spiritual, that is, earthly and not heavenly, it was then that carnal desire came to exist in him, for Adam desired intercourse as a result of the teaching of the evil one who had plotted to make him fall from the sanctity[1] of the angels and imitate wild beasts.

   Now Adam had turned his thoughts to these [things] before [God] had permitted (c.337) him to marry, seeing that the evil one had taught him while he was [still] without

---

1. *qadišūtā* = continence, abstinence from intercourse

lust, and Adam and Eve supposed that everything that the evil one had taught them would come to be. But if God had not had compassion upon Adam, the evil one would have cast him into the pit; Satan desired that [Adam] become like him and be subservient to him.

Blessed is the Good [God] who opens the door to every one who repents.

2.   At first Adam and Eve accepted the evil idea and coveted the beauty of the earth. The woman saw the tree—how it was desirable to eat from[2]—and it became an object of lust to the eyes, just as today we know that gold and silver, property and clothing, and the delicacies of the earth are desirable. They initially desired these things in the hope that they could become like their Creator, through the deadly appetite that the evil one had put into their ears and after which their mind speedily followed. There did not exist in them any lust to desire intercourse, but they greatly desired it because the evil one had directed their gaze [to it] through cattle. That is why David said, 'A person who has not taken notice of his honor',[3] because he was holy like the angels and peaceful like the heavenly ones. But he saw an animal and wished to imitate it in sexual intercourse.

They had not had any desire (c.340) of the instinct for [sexual] union until they had been persuaded by the evil one to become earthly people and to acquire earthly toil and wealth. So God permitted them to marry and to labor after he had cursed them. Lust and the procreative instinct[4] was in them because they had sinned and·violated his commandment. They hated holiness[5] and loved intercourse. They did not really desire it, but [they did so] in that hope that they could become great like God.[6] Now let us show from this that Adam and Eve had no lust while they had not yet sinned.

2. Gn 3:6   5. That is, celibacy.
3. Ps 49:12   6. Rm 8:20
4. Literally, 'the instinct of the seed'.

3. It is written, 'Adam and Eve were naked, but they could not see their own nakedness',[7] that is, like infants who are bare and do not know what nakedness is. In this, they did not have a despicable thought, but if they had known, they would have put on clothes.

Therefore, what man or woman is able to stand before one another naked and not have the lust in their heart aroused, seeing one another naked, apart from those whose heart is pure from lust and who are holy in their heart and bodies, just as Adam and Eve were before they had sinned? On account of this our Lord said, 'If you do not turn back and become like these children, you will not become like that first creation of Adam',[8] who had not yet (c.341) transgressed against the commandment of his Maker.

Before Adam and Eve had sinned, they were naked like infants, but since the lust in their heart was not aroused they were not ashamed, just as infants are not ashamed. Once they had sinned, and sin existed in their heart, directing them to desire intercourse, [then] 'They saw that they were naked';[9] that is, they knew the shame they had not known. Just as from the [moment] sin existed in the heart of Adam and Eve, and they desired intercourse. God allowed them to marry—the instinct and lust of intercourse being in them; so today when the descendants of Adam, who love holiness, have striven against and killed the sin from the heart with lowliness and love, then they will abandon physical lust and turn away from it, ascending to the desire for God. Then God will command that lust be removed from the heart and the instinct from the body completely. Then they will become 'holy' like children, as our Lord said, 'If you do not turn around and become like these children, you shall not become as you were[10] before you had sinned, in this purity in which I created your father, while he had not yet transgressed against my command-

---

7. Gn 2:25   9. Gn 3:7
8. Mt 18:3   10. Mt 18:3

ment. And if you do not become like this, you are not worthy (c.344) of me to be perfected and glorified with me.'

4.   Now infants neither lust nor judge, nor are they anxious, but they may cry at any time. We who are purified, however, judge and are anxious, but cannot cry at any time since we fall short of our Lord. Our Lord said, 'Those who are worthy of the resurrection are like the angels of God and are not able to die'.[11] That is, those who know my words and keep them are like the angels.

How therefore can we say that lust is not going to be removed from people? Do, therefore, the angels have lust, since our Lord said, 'You will become like them'?[12] If you say that [only] in that [other] world will we become like angels, then let us listen to what our Lord said, 'as you are found, so shall you live'. However great you are in this world, so you shall be greater in that new world. If you say that there are people in whom lust remains until they depart from this world, then will lust rise up with them on that Judgment Day? I say, 'Not so!' But if a person does not adopt the image of the angels—who do not have fleshly desires and carnal lust—(c.345) in this world, he will not become like them in that world, as our Lord said.

5.   Our Lord promised, 'Everything that you ask, you shall receive. There is nothing that you shall ask while believing in me that shall not be yours.'[13] Therefore, why do we not ask our Lord for us to become like angels without passions and physical lust, and [so] live according to the perfect will of our Lord?

Perhaps you will say to me, 'I will be glad to ask him, but let him give me this request, which is a great gift given in love and prayer, in fasting and in lowliness. But we ask

11. Lk 20:34
12. Clement of Alexandria *Stromata* II, 12, 87.
13. Mt 21:22

and do not receive.' Because we do not do the perfect will
of our Lord and do not keep these major commandments
of his, because we do not love or lower ourselves like our
Lord lowered himself, he does not give us our perfect request unless we become dead to [this] world and judge and
kill our bodies because of the sin which inhabits us until
we kill it. 'Those who have put on Christ crucify their flesh
against all desires and lusts', and then they put him on. See
how people who have put on Christ subdue their bodies
and do not allow their bodies to rejoice and rest in the ease
of this world, in its pleasures (c.348) and in its lust. Then
their bodies die from sin, yet they have put on Christ. Because of this he said, 'If Christ is in you, the body is dead
on account of sin, but the Spirit is alive on account of righteousness'.[14]

6.   'Food', Paul said, 'does not commend us before God',[15]
because those who have walked this way have not been
helped, but have forgotten God after they had eaten and
reveled, and the anger of God rose up against them. Do
you see how food and pleasures do not allow us to stand
before God? Therefore, on account of that hope, the evil
one had taught Adam and Eve, 'In this way you shall become as great as God', and then 'There is a way for you to
be fruitful and multiply,'[16] and to do everything you desire,
as does the Creator'.

    Adam wanted to rebel and consented to imitate the
intercourse of animals. Adam did not know, however, that
if they had kept the commandment they would have been
fruitful and multiplied, as he had made Eve fruitful by the
word of our Lord without lust. Although they would not
have been able to do a thing without the word of the Lord,
still they believed that without our Lord what the evil one
had said would come to be. Adam sinned and erred in this
because he obeyed the advice of the evil one. He was not able

14. Rm 8:10   15. 1 Co 8:8   16. Gn 1:28

to perform a deed without the Creator, but was overthrown and departed from the Paradise (c.349) of the Kingdom.

Perhaps you will say, 'Since he was not able to do a single thing without the Creator, why did [God] drive him out and close the door of Paradise so that he may not reenter?' Was his error small, seeing he desired to become an opponent to his Creator, to sit opposite him and resist him, since he thought he could become like [God] and challenge him with power? For had he not thought, 'I take no account of him', he would have been afraid of his commandment and would have listened to him. But he was also defiled without lust by what the evil one had placed in their ears. Immediately after they had obeyed and had given their attention, the evil thought made the taste of death enter and it was impressed on their heart.

If you say, 'Look, the [genital] members were meant for intercourse', but you [really] do not desire intercourse, [you should say] that the Creator made them in order for you to urinate.

7.   Therefore, keep the commandments today as [God] has spoken to you and come to that Perfection that Adam had wasted. When you have come to that thing from which Adam fell, see, it has removed the lust from you. When you became a celibate without lust you will see that these members are for urinating and not for intercourse. Because when you become a celibate, lust will never ascend again upon your heart, (c.352) and you will no longer desire intercourse just as a dead person whose soul is removed does not desire it.

On the other hand, [if] your freedom listened to the evil one and you desired [intercourse] like Adam, your Creator will angrily give it to you as he had to Adam. [God] is angry because we renounce the celibacy of the angels and imitate the beasts. [God,] however, will have compassion upon you as he had upon Adam and you will observe Uprightness and be alive while you [are involved] in intercourse.

If you say, 'Why did he make masculine and feminine?' Are you going to blame him because he created male and female? He will respond to you, 'In no way does it harm you, if you do not desire to become like the beasts, nor like the angels'. 'A person watched the animals and desired to become like them',[17] and hated the celibacy of the angels—that is, in the hope that he will become greater than the angels and be like their Lord. The angels were in distress because of the fall of Adam and because of the anger that he received from the evil one. There was in that time enmity between the heavenly ones and the mortals because Adam despised the word of his Creator. So today, therefore, once we have kept the words of our Lord, the heavenly ones will be reconciling with us. After (c.353) Jesus revealed himself, he revealed to whoever wishes to become like the first creation of Adam. Before the advent of our Lord, the kingdom of Heaven was difficult [to enter] because it was not revealed to everyone, and there were few who disciplined and lowered themselves and did the will of God and attained it. Today, however, it is revealed to all who love him.

8.   Therefore, when Adam and Eve left heaven and loved the earth and these visible things, they transgressed against the law of the Creator. God came to find fault with them but had compassion upon them, establishing for them another law after they had transgressed against the first [law], and God allowed them to marry. Then the lustful instinct of marriage came to exist in Adam and Eve, and, because of all their transgressions, they were married.

It is written that after God had indicted Adam and allowed him to acquire that thing he had desired, Adam departed from Paradise and worked the soil from which he was taken.[18] [Adam] knew Eve and she gave birth to Cain.[19]

17. Clement of Alexandria, *Stromata* III, XVII, 102
18. Gn 3:17,23
19. Gn 4:1

There are different kinds of lust: the lust of intercourse is one, and the lust of 'you shall not desire whatever belongs to your neighbor'[20] is another. So also today, when the descendants of Adam have desired heaven and left the earth and everything in it, they have drawn their mind and bodies away from transitory abundance (c.356) and their mind was humbled, in contrast to how [Adam] knew to exalt himself and to leave heaven and inherit the earth.

9. Therefore, once they have emptied and lowered themselves, as they were exalted in the beginning, the instinct of lust is uprooted from them. Just as when their mind loved the earth and all in it—God allowed lust to be in them. So today—when they have abandoned the earth and all in it, and have given heed to our Lord in heaven, and attained that thing that Adam had lost, and have known what is the truth, the height and depth, the length and width[21]—they will be freed from the instinct of lust. God will sever it from them and they will become like the angels in heaven who do not lust.

The apostle said, 'These things I say: as you have prepared your members as a weapon for sin, so prepare the ear to hear Uprightness'.[22] And now, just as we know [how] to leave heaven and inherit the earth, so let us leave the earth and inherit heaven, and see, we will triumph over the exhortation of the evil one. Since evil is mixed in the intercourse [permitted to] Uprightness, as a result of this [evil], adultery and fornication have increased and something more evil than fornication—something that God hated, which makes the descendants of (c.357) Adam fall even from Uprightness.

Therefore, those who empty themselves from the world, and give heed in heaven to their Lord and worship their God and love everyone, will become 'holy' and dwell

20. Ex 20:17
21. Ep 3:18
22. Rm 6:19

with our Lord in the higher realm. Those who bind and loose in the world and buy and sell, owning possessions justly and treating the needy well while not treating anyone badly, are the Upright who are inferior to the Perfect. For the Uprightness of people does not treat poorly anyone who treats it badly, but it does away with its goods and flees from evil, just as Isaac had left behind his father's water wells when they quarreled with him. He named [the wells] 'Satan' and 'Contentious' because they had quarreled and contended with him,[23] and he migrated from there; and just as Abraham and Isaac had given up their wives and neither condemned nor quarreled, yet God administered their judgment.

10. Therefore, those who do good and are honest some of the time, but sometimes treat a person poorly, do not abide either with Uprightness or with evil, being familiar with both. As with today, we see people who do what is below the Upright, these who are inferior to the Perfect. The Upright are those who utilize the good things, while not treating anyone badly. Those who do good half [of the time] and [do] evil [the other] half, even if they are chastened, God is (c.360) merciful to them because they have been merciful to people. Those whose good deeds are fewer than their evil deeds, God is not unjust in forgetting their [good] deeds; just as he will repay them for their evil deeds, so also [God will repay them for] their good deeds.

Those who were without good deeds and without evil actions, and who neither treated anyone well nor badly, will not descend to Gehenna nor will inherit the Kingdom. They are considered better than Gehenna and live in the place that suits them and our Lord does to them whatever he wishes. While they have not treated anyone badly, still they have withheld from everyone their compassion. They have kept that word, 'Whoever does evil will be tormented',

23. Gn 26:19-22—*Sāṭānā* and ʿ*Asāqā,* (Syriac)

but have abandoned that [other] word, 'Whoever does good will inherit eternal life'. Therefore, they deprived their souls of pleasure and guarded their souls from torment.

However, this Uprightness, which is honest with its own, treats everyone well as best as it can, not doing evil to anyone. This [Uprightness] is subordinate to Perfection, because it has not emptied itself from the earth nor attained the height and depth, the length and width.[24] These people, who have neither treated a person well nor badly, are between those who are tormented and those who are in the place of life. As they have lived in this world between those who do virtuous things and those who do evil things, and have done neither good nor evil things with these, (c.361) that is so because 'In the Father's house there are many rooms'.[25]

11.   Our Lord said, 'Whoever is unrighteous in a little is unrighteous in much; and whoever is faithful in a little is faithful in much'.[26] Whoever cannot discern this word, or justifies or condemns all creation through it, is not one of these who are perfected because they do not consider themselves subject to it, since all their mistakes are taken away. These who act impiously and avoid all good things do not consider themselves subject to it. Not even the Upright consider themselves subject to iniquity, but they are greatly inferior to the Perfect. Because they have neither emptied themselves nor have become celibate, they have not been able to do the perfect and acceptable will of God.

Because the Perfect are fulfilled and do not have faults, not [even] a little one after they were perfected, and [because] the impious were not in the least righteous after they became impious, these [two groups] are not part of this word. This word, however, includes everyone who has a little righteousness or a little iniquity, but neither to allow one to ascend higher nor to descend with the impious.

24. Ep 3:18   25. Jn 14:2   26. Lk 16:10

Therefore, those who argue that our Lord has only one place of Life and a single Gehenna, where do they place these people who are a little unjust and a little righteous? (c.364) For, see, the word of our Lord does not allow them to ascend to the upper realm where there are no faults, nor does it allow them to descend to Gehenna where there is no life.

Whoever does not get rid of all faults, and loves all people, good or bad, will not be able to reach the level of Perfection. Whoever lacks even one is less than the Perfect. Therefore, every person is repaid according to his deeds. One who commits a hundred murders is not equal to one who commits only one murder. However, if that [latter] one answers to one soul, the other answers to one hundred; and if one is tormented once, the other is tormented a hundred times. Do not say that they are tormented the same way, but when the torment of the one who killed one person is completed, then, after him, the other will be tormented a hundred times more.

12. All the prophets and the Upright and the righteous who had attained Perfection, but died before the coming of our Lord without becoming Perfect, [our Lord] perfected them in the eyes of the apostles, as Paul said, 'Without us they should not be made perfect'.[27] For not even the Paraclete, who teaches lowliness before everyone and love for all, was sent to them just as he had been sent to the apostles. They waited all their lives for there to be peace, but it did not happen. (c.365) They knew that the Savior would come to the world through the spirit, which was in them and give peace to all.

[This spirit] was promised also to Adam when he wept and prayed and made supplication, 'I will come and perfect those who pursue love and Perfection' from which he had fallen. Therefore, since there was no peace in their time,

27. Heb 11:40

they were not perfected because the Father and Lord wished to bring about reconciliation by the Passion and Cross of his Son.

But if before his coming, all the world wished to become like Moses or Elijah, our Lord would have allowed them to become Perfect and he would not have needed to come to birth and to the dishonor of the Cross. He would have broken down the wall of enmity, due to the transgression of the commandment, while sitting in heaven with great honor, and the prophets would have ceased from the slaughter of the heathens and the wicked and been perfected.

If the first covenant had been found blameless—that is perfect—why would the second covenant have been required? In the latter covenant, the Lord broke down the ancient wall of enmity. The first Upright who are found blameless are those who had walked in the word of our Lord.

13. The Perfect do not take wives, nor do they work in the field, nor acquire possessions, nor (c.368) have a place to lay their heads on earth like their teacher.[28] The Upright and the righteous used the land and sometimes reached Perfection when they had emptied themselves and became holy. When some of them practiced virginity they matured greatly, but they were not perfected, because the Lord had held them back even from Uprightness, when he had sent them to kill his enemies. But all these died in Uprightness and in faith, though they did not receive their reward,[29] and he foresaw the apostles who are greater than them. The apostle had said, 'Without them they should not be made perfect'.[30]

Therefore, our Lord perfected in front of the apostles these who had died while not being perfect, because he had held them back from Perfection. On account of this,

28. Mt 8:20   29. Heb 11:13   30. Heb 11:40

he did not act unfairly but perfected them in front of the apostles, and God exalted them after he had perfected them, 'They were seen with him in the heavenly cities',[31] they and the apostles.

The rest of the righteous whom the Lord had not held back from Perfection, as he had held back the prophets, preferred to remain in Uprightness, just as the contemporary Upright do. But [they do] not [remain] as the Perfect, since they were not perfected like the prophets whom the Lord perfected with the apostles, because they had not pursued (c.369) love and Perfection like them.

14. When the apostles departed from their bodies from this world they were with our Lord; when Jesus perfected the prophets in front of the apostles, they entered and dwelt with them in the heavenly cities and rejoiced with them and with our Lord. For our Lord himself had held them back from Perfection, because at that time it was right, as it was written, 'After the resurrection of our Lord, [some of] the righteous who had died ascended and were seen in the heavenly cities'.[32]

Today, whoever desires to journey to reach the prophets, unless he lives in the ways of the apostles, however, cannot be like the prophets, because the Lord greatly exalted the prophets and the righteous ones—those who had pursued Perfection—after he had perfected them. God has not allowed his laborers today to conduct themselves like the prophets. This was written in the Gospel, 'Some of the righteous who had died rose up and were seen in the heavenly cities with our Lord'.[33] He did not say, 'All of them', because our Lord did not resurrect from the graves with himself the bodies of all the righteous. He made ascend with him [only] those who had pursued Perfection, to show the higher and lower [beings] the resurrection that is to come and the glory that is prepared for their bodies and

31. Mt 27:53   32. Mt 27:52-53   33. Mt 27:52-53

souls—all who had died and are dying in the love of our Lord and of all his preachers, (c.372) the first and the last ones. For it was necessary that their bodies and souls were perfected together, just as the apostles were perfected while they were yet wearing their bodies.

15. So that you may know why Paul said, 'Before our eyes all the prophets and Upright and righteous who have done the perfect will of our Lord are perfected, but have not received their promise',[34] he said:

> You Perfect ones have reached the mountain of Zion and the city of the living God, the Jerusalem in heaven and the camps of the myriads of angels, the church of the first born who are enrolled in heaven, and God the judge of all, the spirits of the Upright who have been perfected, and Jesus the mediator of the New Covenant.[35]

He demonstrated by this that their souls are changed, because he showed that they were perfected.

Paul also made known that the prophets and the apostles are with our Lord today by what he said: 'When we depart from the body we shall be with our Lord until that judgment day comes [when] the bodies of all the Perfect will be resurrected in glory; and they will be swallowed up in the light of their spirits, and glorified with our Lord forever and ever'.[36] As they had suffered with him, so they will be glorified with him. 'If a person suffers with him', said (c.373) Paul, 'he shall also be glorified with him'.[37]

34. Heb 11:13
35. Heb 12:22-24
36. 2 Co 5:8
37. Rm 8:17

16. If today a person observes Uprightness and attains it, the advent of our Lord will be revealed to him just as it happened, as well as the way of life of the apostles. He will discern the commandments through which the apostles were perfected and he also will know by which [commandments] that the world will love. If he comes to the way of life of the apostles, he will receive the Paraclete and be perfected. He will go to the prophets and the apostles and be exalted there, to the degree he has thought little of himself here.

If he lowers himself more, the Lord will be revealed to him in this world and he will hear the voice of God and be able to distinguish the voice of God from the voice of Satan. When he understands the whole truth, the voice of our Lord will be distinguishable to him from that of Satan.

Yet, if a person remains in that Uprightness of the ancients, yet does not leave the earth as the apostles left it and fasted to the whole world,[38] he will not be able to receive the Paraclete. The whole truth will not be revealed to him, nor will he be able to hear the voice of God like the prophets, but a pledge of the Holy Spirit[39] exists in him. He knew how the apostles had left the earth and fasted to the world,[40] and then had received the Paraclete, but he is not able to attain the thing that the Paraclete had revealed to them. But he knew the power of these commandments of Uprightness, 'Love the Lord your God with (c.376) all your heart and people as yourself,[41] and that thing that you hate, do not do to your neighbor, and as you wish that people do to you, so also you should do to them'.[42] He knew that in these four commandments there is all Uprightness. Moreover, he knew that these [commandments],

38. Cf. Gospel of Thomas 27
39. Literally, 'an intermingling'; cf. A. Guillaumont, 'Les 'arrhes de l'Esprit'dans le Livre des degrés' in *Mémorial Mgr Gabriel Khouri-Sarkis* (Louvain, 1969) 107-113.
40. Cf. Gospel of Thomas 27
41. Mt 22:37,39
42. Lk 6:31

'An eye for an eye and evil for evil',[43] were not spoken to him. He does not do them and will go out from this world in Uprightness and will be gathered to the place of the Upright.

17. People should really know about this: everything that our Lord had spoken to the prophets in that time while they were not yet perfected, [is] because [he] had held them back from Perfection, since he had known that they would be perfected with the rest of the righteous. [God] does not speak openly today with anyone because no one is yet Perfect, nor will [God] speak with anyone until they come to Perfection and [God] knows that they will be able to hear him. As he had said, 'Whoever loves me keeps my commandments and I will love him so that I will show myself to him and reveal about myself to him and he will understand the power of my mysteries in what I manifest to him'.[44]

[God] spoke with these righteous ones who had not yet been perfected, because the Road had not yet been walked by the footsteps of our Lord. Because of this, (c.377) he spoke with them at that time in order to show them, lest they perish and stray from what was necessary in that time, to walk on [the Road].

But today the way of life of the righteous is written down before us, and the Road of our Lord and of his apostles is trodden for us. It is not necessary that God openly speak with anyone unless it is right that God should call him to his Road. As for the rest, until one comes to enter into the commandments of our Lord and journeys in them and arrives at the house of our Lord like that son who had squandered his wealth,[45] then [God] will go out to meet him and receive him like the kind father who received his penitent son.[46]

43. Ex 21:24; Mt 5:38
44. Jn 14:21
45. Lk 15:13
46. Lk 15:20

18. Whoever is able to hear our Lord, our Lord calls him to embark upon his Road; and whoever is not able to hear our Lord, a Perfect one of our Lord will show him the Road of our Lord. If a person is able to hear our Lord from the beginning of his vocation, [God] will reveal his truth to him; but if [God] delays and does not reveal himself to him, let him know that by a fulfilled person he will be able to hear the truth.

There are people, who by their own accord, are able to hear the word of our Lord through [spiritual] reading, lower themselves, and call upon our Lord Jesus until our Lord answers them and shows them what is his perfect and acceptable will. For not (c.380) everyone is capable of being called by God, and not everyone is able to hear the spirit. On account of this it is written, 'There are eunuchs[47] whom our Lord has called and made'.[48]

There are others whom someone has called for our Lord and there are some who have lowered themselves and prayed with great boldness in their lowliness until they were ready for our Lord and he revealed himself to them and showed them what is his acceptable and perfect will.

This is what it involves: a person first journeys on the Road of our Lord, whether through one's vocation or through the lowliness of one's being, and then our Lord will reveal himself to him. David clearly explained, 'I will walk on your road blamelessly until you come to me'.[49] He also said, 'My soul thirsts for you, the Living God, when may I come to see your face?'[50] 'Whoever loves me keeps my commandments and I will come to him, I and the Father and the Holy Spirit.'[51] See how both sides go back and forth until the mind of the person transcends the place of evil and reaches the place of peace in which our Lord resides.

---

47. Literally, 'faithful ones'.
48. Mt 19:12
49. Ps 101:2
50. Ps 42:2
51. Jn 14:21

Just as the son had departed to that place where he had fed hogs, and then when he reached his father's house, his father came out to meet and receive him,[52] so when a person has abandoned the earth by his mind, which is the place in which a person feeds (c.381) evil with the lusts that he commits, he then hungers for Uprightness and for holiness. No one can give [them] to him unless his mind keeps on ascending to heaven, the peaceful place of his father's house where the servants abound in Uprightness and virtuous things. So when the penitent has traveled and arrived there by his mind, mercy goes out to meet him and says, 'This [is] my son [who] left me and [who] has tasted death, but now has come back alive'.[53] Then he fills him with the holiness for which he was hungry and clothes him with Perfection, the best garment of the higher level. While he is standing physically on the earth, his mind lives everyday in spirit in heaven and our Lord speaks with him there as the father [had spoken] with his son. He becomes a distributor to others of the heavenly wealth, the food of the Spirit, instead of having wasted away here from his hunger while he was made of flesh, regarding the earth without the knowledge and truth with which he had sought to fill his stomach here with life. 'And no one gave it to him.'[54] That is, he had sought to know at least the integrity of this world or how he was created and why he was created, and why he was made a slave to sin, but no one revealed it to him. He who then had been hungry and had nothing, that is, he had not known a thing, see him, he [now] teaches others the thing that they have not (c.384) perceived and he turns them toward the house of life.

19.   Therefore, if there is a person who is in the conjugal state while he is in the Uprightness of the Upright, a pledge of the Holy Spirit exists in him. If he elevates himself above

52. Lk 15:15ff
53. Lk 15:24
54. Lk 15:16

marriage while he is in the Uprightness of the Upright, he will grow even more above marriage. If he has elevated himself above marriage, he will elevate himself above intercourse to the way of life of the apostles, [then] quickly he will be perfected and receive the Paraclete and hear the voice of God.

If virginity comes up to the [level of the] way of life of the apostles, it will be much superior and will receive the Paraclete and become perfect and hear the voice of God. If marriage sanctifies and lowers itself more than physical virginity, it will be superior to it, but if it is only a little ahead of [virginity] in lowliness, it will [only] be equal to it.

If, however, physical virginity becomes spiritual and empties and lowers itself more than everything, there is nothing surpassing it among people. Yet marriage, which, like it, has lowered and sanctified itself spiritually, can reach it while still being inferior to it.

20. If a person from a higher level is seen in that [other] world among those of the levels lower than him, they will seem to be as nothing in his eyes. If one of the lesser degrees is seen with the higher ones, he will be as nothing in their midst. It is better for each, in the place that our Lord has prepared for him according to his station, to struggle to keep (c.385) the commandments, so that he may rise in the eyes of the great ones in the new world of our Lord Jesus Christ, King of all ages, to him be glory, Amen.

The end of the fifteenth *Mēmrā*, which is about marital desire.

Mēmrā Sixteen

ON HOW A PERSON MAY SURPASS
THE MAJOR COMMANDMENTS

Summary: One can continue to grow above the step of Perfection by superseding any quantifiable definitions of Perfection. The model of the holy fool is presented as an ideal of the Perfect life. (c.388)

1. [This *mēmrā* is] about how a person may surpass the major commandments in love. If you wish, listen to me and I will show you how you may grow and be elevated above even these major commandments. Our Lord said to you, 'Whoever strikes you upon your cheek, offer him the other.[1] Moreover, give him your whole body and, look, you will grow greater than him who only offers his cheek.' [Jesus] said to you, 'Whoever compels you [to go] one mile, go with him two more. In your case go even more because he told you, "Look, you will surpass one who goes only as he was commanded"'.[2] He said to you, 'Forgive a wrong-doer seventy times seven, but in your case, do not require anything at all for a wrong, and look, you will surpass the one who forgives seventy times seven (c.389) only'.[3]

   [Jesus] said to you, 'Do not judge lest you be judged,[4]

1. Mt 5:39; Lk 6:29   3. Mt 18:21
2. Mt 5:41   4. Lk 6:37

but in your case do not put your brother to shame; and look, you will also surpass one who offers only his cheek'. For he said to you, 'Do not call [anyone] "contemptible", crazy, hateful, or fool, lest you be condemned to Gehenna. Whoever calls [anyone] "fool" or "contemptible" will be condemned—that [very] day—by the whole congregation. Because he called his brother "empty", he himself became empty the entire day'.[5] 'With that [same] judgment by which you have judged, you will be judged.'[6] If he talks [like this] tomorrow, then he will be empty. If he continues to talk like this until he dies, it is because he is lacking in intelligence and will not acquire a normal intelligence until he uproots these faults, as our Lord said.[7]

2.   One wrong can be more tolerable than [another] wrong, and one Gehenna more [tolerable] than another. Everyone will be judged according to his works, but you should call whoever is like you, 'my brother' and 'my sister'; and whoever is younger than you, 'my son' and 'my daughter'; and whomever is older than you, 'my father' and 'my mother'; and those who are clergy, 'my lords' and 'my patrons'; and the male and female celibates, 'my lords' and 'my ladies'; and to whom honor [is due, give] honor; and to whom love [is due, give] love; and to whom fear [is due, give] fear;[8] (c.392) [act thus] with honor and with diligence, and so you will be above the first and last law, which means, you shall be with the Lord of the laws.

If you call someone 'my brother' or 'my sister', consider him as you would a brother or sister. Do not be false in your word. It is not right for you to treat him badly, not even if he treats you badly. If he goes astray, do not let yourself go astray because he is your brother in love.

5. Mt 5:22ff
6. Mt 7:2
7. Mt 7:5
8. Rm 13:7

Whomever you call 'my lord' and 'my lady', remember that you are his servant by your own will. If he treats you badly, do not stand up against him, but suffer him as a master. That one whom you call 'my son' and 'my daughter', remember that they are your children in mercy. Educate and encourage and love them as much as you are able. If they forget that they are your children, do not yourself forget that they are your children and neglect them.

Whomever you call 'my lord' and 'my patron', remember that he offers offerings and prayers for you and for all people, and because of their deeds live peacefully with them and submit yourselves to them.

3. [Our Lord] also said, 'When you pray, say, our Father who is in heaven, forgive us our debts as we also have forgiven our debtors'.[9] Forgive your brother and then pray. Say (c.393) in your prayer, 'Forgive me, my lord, because I have forgiven whoever has owed me, and you forgive those who have done wrong to me. I ask [this] of you, being ashamed because I have been extremely angry', and so you will be above the major and minor commandments and above the Law and the prophets, and you will understand our Lord, that is, his way of life through which you will journey to him and to his apostles.

But if you attain these major commandments, it will be easier for you to transcend them. If you refuse [to call anyone] 'contemptible', immediately you will call [him] 'my brother'. If you refuse [to call anyone] 'fool', immediately you will call him 'my son'. If you refuse [to call anyone] 'crazy', it will be easier for you to call him 'my friend'. If you forgive seventy times seven, it will be easier for you to forgive absolutely. If you are reconciled and then pray, it will be easier for you to no longer get angry. If you wash the feet of your enemies, it will be easier for you to kiss

9. Mt 6:9-15

them. If you offer your cheek, it will be easier for you to offer all of your body. If you go two miles, you will also be able to go as much as you want. If you give up your coat, you will also be able to give up your cloak. If you attain the commandments, you will be above them and it will be easier for you to surpass and progress in that time. (c.396)

4.   At first you will feel under constraint, but at the end you will be relieved. For he said, 'I will observe your law forever and I will walk about freely'.[10] Again he said to you, 'Love your brother more than yourself. From here you shall understand what is love—whoever will put himself in the place of his friend. If my love is true for you, offer yourself in place of your brothers.'[11] However, if you love the evil ones, your despisers, more than yourself, you are much greater than he who [only] loves his neighbor more than himself and his despiser as himself. In this way, you will greatly surpass the major commandments and be glorified with our Lord.

For whoever does these major commandments will become Perfect. However, if he does more than the major commandments, loves [and] lowers himself greatly, and suffers with our Lord, he will be glorified with him, because he sees him in the Spirit and suffers with him, as he had said, 'I have given you this example so that you may wash the feet of your brothers and of your betrayers'.[12] Kiss the feet of your betrayers, and look, you will surpass one who [only] washes the feet of his betrayers.

5.   Our Lord called all people his friends, [including both] his despisers and his friends, (c.397) and he loved them more than himself, since he had offered himself in their place. Whoever would become his disciple should act like him in this way. If your Master, [who is] without sins, makes

10. Ps 119:44-45
11. Jn 15:12-13
12. Jn 13:15

himself Sin—that [Sin] that brings about the sins of all sinners—think of yourself as something even worse than Sin, and look, you will not judge anyone. For if you say, 'There is no one who is [more] guilty than I', and you are found to be judging and condemning someone else, then you have considered yourself greater than he, and your actions are not the same as your words. Act this way and you will be found with our Lord, and because you have considered yourself like Sin, you will not judge sinners.

Because the Sin of all creation makes sins, your sins will not be measured. Because your sins are not measured, do not judge him whose sins are measurable. 'For if I, who am your Lord and your Teacher'[13] have made myself Sin through my lowliness, how much more still must you lower yourself? 'For he who had not known Sin made himself Sin on account of you';[14] that is, he made himself [Sin] and lowered himself so that he might become an example for us to imitate.

If our Lord greeted (c.400) women in his lowliness, it is right for us to bow down before men and women. Our Lord told us to become humble like that infant who suckles milk or [who] is being weaned. Where will you find a child who judges in the village or who knows who are adulterers or thieves in it? So not even the adulterers really hide from the children of whom our Lord said, 'become like them', because they do not know how to put them to shame, nor even is uncleanness revealed to their intelligence. But bring the child to the house in which there are adulterers and thieves and say to him, 'Enter and see what is inside,' and notice that he does not perceive them as evil or whether they are naked or adulterers. We also should become infants with regard to these evil things and become Perfect ones in knowledge, in love, and in lowliness.

13. Jn 13:15
14. 2 Co 5:21

6. Now I will explain to you what you should take from the children and what you should leave. When you see from now on a child who is not concerned about how to dress and feed himself, say, 'This is my [way of life]'. When (c.401) you see him not desiring a wife and capable of crying at any time, say, 'These are mine, I will become without desire and cry at any time'. When you find him neither judging nor perceiving [anyone as] evil people and adulterers, say, 'These are mine'.

But if you see one who curses or gets angry or does evil or strikes [others], say, 'These are not mine,' and do not imitate these. So do not allow your mind to be so childish to go after evil things like that child who when someone tells him, 'Curse', he curses. Also whenever someone tells him, 'Hit [someone]', he hits and becomes angry because sin is born with him, and sin is crafty and he is naive. But [as for] you, defeat [sin] and uproot it and become a child amidst the company of evil, just as [Paul] said, 'Become infants among evil things and become Perfect ones in knowledge'.[15]

7. Let me describe for you a crazy person, so that when you see a crazy one who treats himself with contempt and does not own a house or a wife and any property, not even [extra] garments besides his clothes, nor food apart from a day-to-day [supply], say, 'These are my [ways of life] and I should imitate them'. When you see him talking insanely with everyone—and [if] he establishes a law for himself so that he may not become angry in order not to be found at fault, (c.404) and [if] he despises the wisdom [of] the wise sage of the world and the philosopher because he is contemptuous of whatever is visible—say, 'These are mine, this is the madness of the apostles'.

[But] when you see that he uses magic or practices divination or fornication or consults oracles or that he bows down before idols, say, 'These are not mine'.

15. 1 Co 14:20

The fools of the world, in their foolishness, are not able to distinguish between whoever is dishonoring them and whomever is honoring them, and they would be talking first thing in the morning with that one who struck them in the evening. Imitate them in this way. Enter [the home of] the people who are insolent to you as a fool and talk with them and honor those who honor you. Look at the fool who cannot distinguish good people from bad in his foolishness, and in the same way you should love the good and the bad while knowing them [for who they are].

When you see that he is acting foolishly, if someone says to him, 'Go, fornicate or steal or curse', and he does so foolishly, do not imitate him. Because [it is] by the cunning of worldly wisdom he will say to you, 'Become a fool', not by heavenly wisdom. Do not become like these cunning sages, seeing evil ones and judging them, but become like these fools, seeing [the evil ones] and disregarding their follies. Like a heavenly sage advise them to repent, and do not judge them like an earthly sage (c.405) lest through evil ones they might die.

Imitate the grace of God and treat everyone well and do not imitate him who repays everyone according to his deeds, because you are neither Being [Itself] nor one who is without law like him. Because if he does not establish justice for the oppressed, who will do it? Do you wish to become like him? Make for yourself a creation like him and do not become a god in his creation, lest he overthrow you as [he has overthrown] Satan.

8. The law does not have power over a person who in the Spirit pursues love, for he is above the law. Therefore, [if] you desire that the first law not judge you, do not sin physically. If you desire that the last law not find fault with you, do not sin in your heart by a sinful thought about any person. If you wish to be with the Lord of the Scriptures, love your Lord and love every person who is from the children of Adam, and look, you have encompassed the law.

9. The fulfillment of the law is love from a pure conscience and an unshakeable faith. These are the commandments people have deserted and they have forgotten the truth and the purity of the heart. 'The written [law] will kill you',[16] because you do not know how to distinguish his commandments and to take love from them (c.408) and our Lord Jesus will give you life in that you are associated with him. Christ dwells in lowliness and in the love of the lowly ones, revealing to them his mysteries. If you wish, come to this rest and taste this sweetness.

Look, when were you [more] contented—when you judged everyone, or now [when] you forgive everyone and love them? See, when did the power of sin begin to be driven from you? When you had enmity with your fellow believers and with [other] religious, or now when you love all people, good or bad, and have no enemy, except Satan, and have no strife with flesh and blood, descendants of Adam, but make war with evil spirits, the powers of sin?[17] Abandon mammon and iniquity and all that passes away and distance yourself from it as an enemy. Every person, and our Lord, should be seen by you as friends, beloved ones, neighbors, fathers, and lords. You will be a servant to them by your love, and [like a] son and brother, friend and heir.

10. Therefore, let us be like this and pray for all people since Adam and until the end [of time] so that they may live and praise the Father and the Son and the Holy Spirit, the perfect Trinity.

11. The Lord witnesses to me. If all (c.409) people who have existed and who will exist—the children of Adam, from the beginning until the end—were alive—each having ten thousand mouths, and each mouth having ten thousand

16. 2 Co 3:6   17. Ep 6:12

tongues, and each tongue having ten thousand words, and each word having ten thousand praises, and each praise having ten thousand blessings—they would be too few to confess and to praise the kindness of God toward people, whether at first, in the middle or at the end. [The number of] people would be too few in comparison to the places of rest that are prepared for everyone, in accordance with his works and his level, and with how he has afflicted himself, was humbled, and tormented; and [even] if they progress more than the apostles and [more] than the example of lowliness that our Lord had shown them, they would be too few for what our Lord has prepared for them.

'I consider that the sufferings of this time are not comparable, and the life that the Perfect are pursuing, to the glory and the beauty that we will come to receive.'[18] 'The thing that eye has not seen and ear has not heard, and the thing that God has prepared for them has not ascended to the heart of a person'[19] in the higher levels, for those who loved him and left everything that passes away and loved what does not pass away in order that they might be with him in the Kingdom (c.412) and be glorified with him, because they have suffered with him and with him have not possessed anything which passes away. Lest the spiritual ministry cease from their soul, they have not done earthly work and have not[20] abandoned heavenly work ever since the day they came to know Him.

12.   Glorious also is that which is prepared for the Upright and those who perform good deeds, and that [other] world is an absolutely glorious and excellent one for whoever enters it. But one glory is better than [another] glory. There are some who, like the glory of the sun, increase and some who are like the moon and some who are like the stars. There is one that will inherit a great and hidden

18. Rm 8:18
19. 1 Co 2:9
20. The negative has been omitted in several mss.

glory, which is better than the sun and moon and stars. 'Another one is the heavenly glory and yet another is the earthly [glory], and one is of the sun and the other is of the moon and still another of the stars. One star is brighter than another star; so [it is] with the resurrection of the dead.'[21] The glory and the light of each person will be different from that of his neighbor.

But that heavenly glory is what our Lord said, 'The eye of the flesh has not seen and nor does it ascend to the heart of a person, the thing that God has prepared for those who have loved him',[22] and have kept his words, [something] that is much better and more glorious than all the glories. These who lower, sanctify and empty themselves from this world will be perfected and attain (c.413) [this glory], observing their Lord in heaven as in a mirror in their mind, and imitating him in all his lowliness. When they depart from this world they will be with our Lord.

The end of the sixteenth *Mēmrā* on how a person will surpass the major commandments.

21. 1 Co 15:40-42
22. 1 Co 2:9

Mēmrā Seventeen

ON THE SUFFERINGS OF OUR LORD
WHO BECAME THROUGH THEM
AN EXAMPLE FOR US

Summary: A discourse on the distinction between sufferings and signs. The imitation of the sufferings of Jesus is the way for those who believe that Jesus is God, while signs are used for those who do not believe in God. The prime example of Jesus' suffering is when he washed the feet of Iscariot before those of Simon Peter.
(c.416)

1. [This *mēmrā* is] concerning the sufferings of our Lord who became through them an example for us, so that we might imitate him, because if we suffer with him, we shall also be glorified with him.

Therefore, when you read the New Testament, distinguish carefully the sufferings from the signs and you will suffer as our Lord suffered so that you might be glorified as our Lord was glorified. That is, you will suffer with our Lord. For even today when you suffer he will suffer with you, as the apostle said after our Lord had suffered and was lifted up, 'If we suffer with him we will also be glorified with him'.[1]

---

1. Rm 8:17

Look, is it not evident that our Lord suffers secretly with us? He was tempted, but he did not abolish our temptations. He suffers with those who suffer and are tempted. See how he suffers (c.417) secretly, as our Lord said, 'Whoever dishonors you, dishonors me; and whoever honors you, honors me'.[2] Certainly, [our Lord] had suffered well before Paul spoke about it, so then this could only mean that our Lord will come again, suffering physically. But if we give ourselves over to sufferings, our Lord is there to suffer secretly with us.

Therefore, when you read that our Lord purified the lepers and opened [the eyes of] the blind, made the crooked straight, strengthened the paralyzed, calmed the people with dropsy, healed the sick, caused the lame to leap as harts,[3] and straightened the tongues of the dumb, these are signs that our Lord did for whoever does not believe so that they may believe. But signs are not necessary for whoever does believe, yet suffering is necessary for him so that he may be perfected and suffer and mature and be glorified.

Therefore, if you believe that Jesus is God, signs are not necessary for you. Do not inquire 'how' and 'why', but bring yourself to sufferings and love, and watch, the 'how' and 'why' these things happen is revealed to you. 'If a person thinks that he knows something, he does not yet know anything in the way he ought to know it. Whoever loves God will know this.'[4] Notice that with love a person will know everything. Because you see that our Lord has performed the signs people are not able to do, (c.420) [so that] if something is hideous to you on account of its lowliness, which does not resemble God, know by his signs that he is the Lord and understand that he is not as despicable and lowly as this. He is teaching you, however, to become as lowly and despicable as him, so that once you have lowered yourself like him, you will be exalted as he himself was exalted. Distinguish, therefore, sufferings from signs.

2. Lk 10:16   3. Is 35:6   4. 1 Co 8:2-3

2. These are the sufferings of our Lord: when he gives his cheek to whoever strikes him and speaks peacefully with him and prays for him. But if you control your propensity [to strike back] and pray for whoever strikes you and are reconciled [with him], you will be suffering with our Lord and will be glorified with him.

3. [Here is] another [form of] suffering: when our Lord submitted himself and washed the feet of the person who was going to sell and deliver him to death, becoming a neighbor to his murderers. Our Lord made him sit and [then] stood before him like a servant and washed the feet of the one who hated him before he washed [the feet of] his friends.

[For example, here was, on one hand,] the dreg of the disciples, that is, [Judas] Iscariot the thief; and [on the other], Simeon the chief [disciple]; but he began with Iscariot and finished with Simeon. Therefore, if you know who are your betrayers and your sellers and the companions of your murderers, control your tendency [to strike out] and make them sit down and wipe their feet, before [going on to] the feet of your loved ones, and do not make [it] known that they are your enemies, just as (c.421) our Lord did not expose Iscariot. However, he said, 'One of you is Satan, and the hand of the one who will betray me is in the dish with mine',[5] in order that his disciples would not be offended and say, 'How can he say, "I am the Lord", without knowing who is going to betray him to death?' [Our Lord, however, did not identify his betrayer] so that they would [not] be led astray once these things happened and he physically departed [from them].

But in our case, no one is going to blame us, nor will anyone be offended by the fact that you do not expose your betrayers. Notice that our Lord did not expose.[Judas],

5. Mt 26:23; Mk 14:20; Lk 22:21; Jn 13:26; cf. Jn 6:70-71

but he made it thoroughly known that he knows everything. In your case too, when you know that your killer is eating with you among many, if you should say, 'My murderer is eating with me', do not say his name and put him to shame. See how much his disciples pressed our Lord to tell them his [murderer's] name.[6] However, he refrained with difficulty when his confidant[7] pressed him, the one who first had entered into his mystery [of Christ] before his companions. Our Lord trusted in him because his heart was like his. He had only just told him in secret when Judas would say, 'Is it I?'[8] He exposed himself while our Lord had not exposed him. When you have behaved this way to your sellers and your betrayers, then you will suffer with our Lord and mature greatly.

4.   [Here is] again another [form of] suffering: when our Lord was healing the ear of the one who took the sword and came to kill him.[9] Therefore, if you can control yourself and do what is pleasing (c.424) to him who wishes to kill you, in this way you will be perfected.

5.   Again another [form of] suffering [is] when our Lord says in prayer, 'Father, forgive them',[10] those who have covered my head and have struck me with a reed and slapped my cheeks derisively and made me drink vinegar and gall with hatred and cursing, having stretched me out upon the Cross in anger and pierced my hands and feet with hatred and stabbed me with a spear in enmity. In this same way, if you can control your propensity [to strike back] and say, 'My Lord Jesus, forgive these who have done evil things to me, as they have done to you, the Lord of the two worlds', you will be greatly glorified with our Lord.

6. Jn 13:21
7. Literally, 'that son of his mystery' = the Beloved Disciple.
8. Mt 26:25
9. Lk 22:50-51
10. Lk 23:34

6.   Yet another [form of] suffering [occurs] when our Lord says to his disciples, 'Come, let us go to those who stoned me yesterday and teach them lowliness'.[11] They said to him, 'Our Lord, the Jews sought to kill you'. He replied to them, 'Come, and do not remember any evil they have done to you in the evening and in the morning'.[12] The disciples imitated him and said, 'Let us go die with him so that we might live with him'.[13] Therefore, if you die with him, but are raised up after a little while, you will be above death. For whoever suffers these [kinds of] sufferings will be afflicted [only] until death.

7.   These and such like them are the sufferings: If you bless whoever curses you and love (c.425) whoever hates you and pray for whoever persecutes you[14] and forgive whoever does you wrong seventy times seven in one day,[15] all this because our Lord said, 'Never be angry against one who sins against you'.[16] In case you are not persuaded that his purpose was to prevent you from getting angry altogether, he said, 'Forgive all these offenses in a single day'.[17] But then, if you have the idea that when these four hundred and ninety wrongdoings are completed you may be [permitted to be] angry against the offender, you must count from [one] morning to [the next] morning, night and day, and [even] if your fellow human being has committed four hundred ninety faults—that is the reckoning of seventy times seven—if you find an offender after all these faults night and day, will it even so be permissible for you to become angry with him? Now if you cannot find someone who offends [you] even five or ten [faults], look, is it not evident that our Lord has held you back with this word, 'Do not become angry against an offender'? That is, when you love [the offender] and requite him good for bad, washing his feet and praying for him, then you will become

11. Jn 11:7-8   14. Mt 5:44   16. Mt 5:22
12. Cf. Ep 4:26   15. Mt 18:22   17. Lk 17:4
13. Jn 11:16

perfect, submitting yourself to whoever seeks to kill and harm you. You will become all [things] with all [people], making disciples of sinners and harlots. You will loathe neither the impure nor the impious nor those who have (c.428) the gangrene of sin; and, you will heal all who come into your care like the good doctor.

8.   If you suffer in this way, blessed is your soul because your heart will be purified and you will see our Lord. For thus did Stephen, saying in a prayer for those who stoned him,[18] 'Do not count this sin against them on account of me',[19] lest you think that only our Lord prayed for his murderers. All these apostles spoke to those who gnashed their teeth against them, 'Men, brothers, listen to us and be saved. We ask you on behalf of God to obey'.[20] Up to the point [their opponents] had killed [the apostles], they prayed for their murderers as our Lord had done in front of them. When they went to kill them outside of the city, [the apostles] stood up and admonished them so that they might be saved, and then [the apostles] gave themselves over to be killed. When they hung [the Apostles] on the cross, look, [the apostles] admonished them, teaching them while being crucified.[21] Praise to our Lord Jesus Christ who suffered apart from them, and they suffered with him and in him. That is, he suffered by himself and became an example for us to imitate and to suffer with him and in him. Let us walk in his image. Glory to him and blessed are they. (c.429) Our Lord, do not deprive us of you and of being with them, but with you and with them may we rejoice in your presence.

18. Literally, 'imprinted stones upon his brain'.
19. Ac 7:60
20. *Apocryphal Martyrdom of Paul 4* in J. K. Elliott, *The Apocryphal New Testament* (Oxford: Clarendon Press, 1993) 387.
21. *Acts of Peter 39* in Elliott, 425-426; *Martyrdom of Peter and Paul*, 59-62.

9. If you wish to know these mysteries, however, do not cease to pray and ask every person, nor despise anyone, for perhaps the one whom you despise will know the truth and will explain [it] to you. Be humble and self-deprecating before God and all people. Just as the man who goes to a far-away place or to such and such a city, despising neither child nor elderly person, nor cripple nor one whose appearance is ugly, nor does he despise a woman, but he asks everyone whom he meets to direct him to wherever he seeks to go. In this way, because you also seek to travel to the heavenly city, do not despise one of the least and worthless,[22] but ask with lowliness until you find someone who will show you the heavenly road, so that you may journey to the house that is in heaven and enter [to be] with God who will give you joy.

The end of the seventeenth *Mēmrā* on the sufferings of our Lord who became through them an example for us.

22. Mt 18:10

Mēmrā Eighteen

ON THE TEARS
OF PRAYER

Summary: Meditation on the necessity of agony and struggle in prayer, that is, the mournful tears of prayer that eliminate sin from within and enable one to be perfected.
(c.432)

1. Consider carefully, my son, what I am saying. There are tears that come from sadness and tears that come from joy. As our Lord said, 'You shall weep and mourn and grieve, and the world will rejoice; but later your tears shall be changed to joy'.[1] A person weeps on account of his sins and he [thus] acts well, as it is written, 'Sorrow on account of God is remorse that leads to life'.[2]

There are some who have defeated sin, and have transcended sins and have done good deeds, weeping with joy on account of their love for their Lord who has dealt very kindly with them and has removed them from the servitude of death and made them free because they have lowered themselves (c.433) and have kept his commandments.

As David said, 'This is the day that the Lord has made. Come, let us exult and rejoice in it. O Lord, save us! O Lord, deliver us!'[3] Let us exult and rejoice in this day of our

1. Jn 16:20   2. 2 Co 7:10   3. Ps 118:24-25

salvation. When a person is rescued from the servitude of death he serves the Lord with joy and not with sadness. As David explained, 'Serve the Lord with gladness and come before him with praise'.[4] Moreover, he said, 'Serve the Lord with fear and take hold of him with trembling; and kiss the Son lest he become angry and you perish from his path because in a little while his anger will be kindled and all the wicked ones will be burned. Blessed are those, however, who are trusting in him from this world'.[5] He redeems them and then, departing from [the world], they are perfected by the love of our Lord Jesus. Moreover, they will be glorified with him on the great and fearful day.

2.   Concerning the tears of which I have spoken: A person will weep for his companion because he loves him, [but] lives far away from him. Therefore, if a person distant from his companion weeps for him, it is either on account of his love or on account of his sadness. But when a person sees his beloved he will weep in front of him, his tears flowing upon his [beloved's] neck and everyone near to him will see him [doing this]. Is it not evident to all that these are tears of joy, because seeing his companion, (c.436) whom he had not thought he would ever see [again], he weeps and groans, his tears flowing? In this way also people who sin and are distant from our Lord and his righteousness will weep in sorrow, just like a person who is far from his companion and is sad for him and weeps.

These [people] are also sad because of their sins because they fear the judgment of our Lord and weep so that God might have compassion upon them and forgive them. If they turn away from their sins and become righteous, they will approach our Lord and their tears will be turned to joy. When they become sinless and are rescued from sin they will proceed to weep before our Lord with joy. Just as

4. Ps 100:1
5. Ps 2:11—Hebrew text is obscure; *Peshitta* reading indicates 'paying homage to the Lord'.

when a person sees his beloved whom he had not thought
he would ever see again, and falls upon his neck and weeps
for him with groans and tears of joy, so it is necessary for
us to work diligently to become sinless and to entreat our
Lord to rescue us from sin, as Paul said, 'I am a wretched
man! Who will deliver me from this body of death, except
the grace of God, which is through our Lord Jesus Christ?'[6]

3. So now, let us leave behind everything visible because
it is transitory, and let us turn away from external sins.
When we cut off all our visible sins we shall rise up in the
struggle against the Sin that dwells in us internally, because
they are (c.437) the evil thoughts that Sin devises in the
heart. With power may we pursue the struggle that is set
before us and let us do battle with prayer just as our Lord
did before us. He showed us that with a mighty groan and
many tears Jesus offered a petition to him who delivered
him from death. He was heard[7] and made perfect.[8]

But our Lord taught us these things, so that when we
are without external sins we should approach the struggle
of prayer, as our Lord said and did. Paul said to the brothers who are [living] in our Lord,[9] 'Epaphras does battle for
you with his prayer'.[10] This means, our Lord groaned mightily and was afflicted in prayer; his sweat became as clots of
blood and he shed many tears so that he might show us
that when we are without external sins and open faults, we
should offer petition and prayer.

But until we are afflicted in prayer like him and shed
tears as he shed and powerfully implore as he implored,
we will not be rescued from the sin that dwells in the heart,
or from the evil thoughts that we inwardly think. So it is
fitting for the men who are in Christ to raise their hands in
every region and in every place without anger and without
evil thoughts,[11] having (c.440) shed tears in their love for

6. Rm 7:24   8. Heb 5:9   10. Col 4:12
7. Heb 5:7   9. Col 1:2   11. 1 Tm 2:8

our Lord and in their yearning for him. At that time let us go see him face to face, as it is written, 'Blessed are those who are pure in their heart for they shall see God'.[12] In this world, as Paul said, we see our Lord with the eyes of our hearts as in a mirror; but in that [other] world, [we will see him] face to face.[13]

4. Therefore, the heart is not purified unless the hidden sin has vanished from it and [the heart] has put an end to evil thoughts hidden and buried in it through the power of sin dwelling in [the heart]. Sin will not be rooted up from our heart nor will the evil thoughts and their fruits pass away unless we pray as our Lord and all of his preachers prayed.

When we pray to the Lord with our heart, let us greatly rejoice, [both] with our lips [and] inwardly. We inwardly rejoice when our heart does not condemn us with sin and when we have no need to be ashamed before our Lord because we have kept all of his commandments. So we rejoice as David said, 'My heart shall rejoice in you, O Lord, and in those who fear your name. I will give you thanks, my Lord and my God, with all of my heart, and I will glorify (c.441) your name forever, because your grace has increased toward me and you have delivered my soul from the lower world of Sheol.'[14] You see how God redeemed our fathers from the hand of Sheol and how their heart rejoiced in the Lord and in those who fear his name. Moreover, as Mary said, 'My soul magnifies the Lord and my spirit rejoices in God my savior who has given heed to the lowliness of his handmaiden'.[15] You see how she rejoiced in her inner spirit and was glad in her mind because she had found grace and mercy before the Lord.

12. Mt 5:8
13. 1 Co 13:12
14. Ps 86:11-13
15. Lk 1:46ff

5. Now, let us be a law unto ourselves and pursue Perfection. When we hear the word of truth and of mercy, let us become a fertile ground for it, and may it establish roots in us and entwine a root in our soul and spring forth and bear fruit thirty- and sixty- and one hundred-fold.[16] Let us not be a ground of thorns, and choke the seed of truth and be choked of life on that day of judgment of our Lord. Let us not be soil on the path of the evil one, because it does not allow a person to bury the good seed in it, for a bird will come and glean it and [the seed] will not sprout.

Therefore, let us not become harsh people, lest the Word of life enter us without taking root, allowing the evil one to rob the good seed from our land. Our mind is not far from knowledge, like the shallow earth whose seed withers and does not spring up in the brilliance (c.444) of the sun. Let us be diligent to bear fruit lest when the children appear, the doers of the acceptable and perfect will of our Lord, we shall indeed wither in the new sun of righteousness,[17] in that sun of compassion which carries healing upon his wings.[18]

So then, when we hear the Word that summons us to come to the way of life of our Lord and of his preachers and become Perfect, let us establish our own law and imitate them saying, 'Why are we not like them, because even they were like us?' Let us listen to Paul when he says, 'Everything visible I despise and every advantage remaining here I consider as refuse',[19] and it will not accompany me to that true and glorious world. 'Become like me'[20] because I have also become like you. You will see that, if we desire, we can become like Paul.

The end of the eighteenth *Mēmrā* on the tears of prayer and their interpretation.

---

16. Mt 13:23
17. Mt 13:3-9, 19-23
18. Ml 4:2

19. Ph 3:8
20. Ph 3:17

Mēmrā Nineteen

ON THE DISCERNMENT
OF THE WAY OF PERFECTION

Summary: The longest *mēmrā* depicts the metaphor of a steep, narrow, and difficult road to the heavenly city of the Perfect. Twenty-five pairs of biblical citations distinguish between the steep road of the Perfect and the paths diverting to the side of the road intended for the 'sick' and 'children' until they gain enough strength to resume travel on the road. (c.445)

1.   Give me now your full attention, O one who wishes to become a solitary and is anxious to travel quickly to the city of our Lord Jesus. I will show you how you may go directly to the city of our king, if you have the strength to journey as I will show you. Because the steps are difficult to climb, I will guide you [how] to climb. Since, however, there are also numerous paths that deviate from the straight road—on which many mountains loom about you, and day after day you are blocked until the day of your death comes—it will find you on [one of] the paths (c.448) that turn off from one side or the [other], seeing that you do not know how to go directly on the road to that city. If during your life you do not investigate about that road, traveling diligently in order to reach that city, you will not be able to go to it when you have departed from this world, for the

end of your road is Perfection and its beginning is when
you begin to uproot from yourself all faults.

For just as this road to these cities in this world is visible, if there is no one who will direct you to the cities that
are not visible to you and you do not know them, the paths
that depart from the roads to them will lead you astray and
you will wander in circles for a long time and not reach
wherever you wish to go. So [it is] also [with] that hidden
road leading to that hidden city from which many paths
branch off in all directions. If there is no one who knows
that road leading to that place to direct you and point out all
the paths deviating from it, you will not be able to journey
directly and will cease from a rapid pursuit of Perfection,
and depart from this world not being Perfect. Moreover,
you will not be able (c.449) to live with our Lord in his city
and kingdom in that [other] world, and you will not enter
the city of the saints.

2.   These paths, veering from the Perfect road, which
leads to that place in which our Lord is visible face to face,
are not despicable, but our Lord and his preachers made
them deviate from that great road because of the infants
and the sick. Because the steps that confront a person on
that road leading to that city are difficult, straight, and narrow, so toward the top it is much steeper and narrower and
toward the bottom it is much broader. If you lean to one
side it will be fire, and if you lean to that other [side] it will
be full of water; and if a person falls underneath he will be
crushed and if one enters the fire he will be burnt; and if
one falls into the water he will be drowned. However, it is
very steep towards the top and the step is difficult and narrow. If you want to go to that city, however, but are anxious
climbing up to that great height and not veering to the right
nor to the left nor even to the depths, lest you perish, go up
straightway so that you may go quickly to that great and
glorious place.

I will explain to you these parables (c.452) of the difficult steps, which [are] of fire and water and great depth. If you believe the words of Jesus and have established a covenant to obey his words and keep his great commandments, from that hour, whether in the body or in the spirit, you will come to this road of the commandments and enter these steps. If you desire to ascend them in order to confirm your covenant with Jesus and see and receive from him what he promised you, 'Refresh yourself with me at the table of the Kingdom',[1] but do not lower yourself like a servant before all people, good and bad, you will not be able to ascend these steps and complete that road leading to that place our Lord promised you, 'Refresh yourself there'. If you turn back on your covenant, you will fall into the great deep that takes [you] down to Sheol; and if you transgress his commandments you will go to Gehenna, which is the fire; and if you renounce him, you will be drowned[2] like Iscariot in the stifling hidden waters which are the teaching of the evil one.

3.   But listen to what our Lord said, (c.453) 'The road that leads to life is narrow';[3] but how much more narrow is that [road] that leads to Perfection and to the greater glory? Moreover, Ben Sira said, 'If you would hand yourself over to the service[4] of God, lower yourself more than all there is in the land, [for] you hand yourself over to all [kinds] of trials'.[5] But make yourself the lowest of all people and endure temporary suffering so that you may go to the rest that does not pass away. Do not break your covenant lest you go to the suffering that never ends.

---

1. Lk 22:30
2. Syriac verb usually means 'to choke', 'to suffocate', and often 'to be hanged'. But here the context implies 'to drown'; certainly a heterodox detail from the biblical narrative.
3. Mt 7:14
4. Literally, 'fear of God'.
5. Ben Sira 2:1

4.   Our Lord and his preachers divert the paths that veer
to [one] side or the [other] away from that summit that ascends straight up, not in order to inhibit the powerful from
ascending, but for the sake of the sick and the infants who
are not able to go up higher on these steps in as much as
they are young and ill. Because of this, [our Lord] made
the paths go along near the borders of these steps, so that
[the sick and the young] might travel near the road that
goes up toward heaven, until they are fortified and become
mature, in order to have through [these paths] the strength
to ascend this narrow road and onto these steps, not being
afraid and never turning (c.456) back; nor will they become dizzy on account of their youth and illness and fall
into that great depth nor stagger to one of the sides and
perish.

   Since these paths are not as difficult as this great road,
people love them, not understanding that if they do not get
onto this difficult road, they will not enter that city of great
peace. However, let us not prolong our illness and delay
too much our education. Let us heal ourselves diligently
and grow strong and go onto the road that valiant people
travel. For however much we walk back and forth on the
paths that are easy for us, we mock ourselves in our soul,
because if we do not get onto the difficult road we will not
become Perfect ones.

5.   The paths are the minor commandments, given like
milk to infants and like vegetables to the sick because they
are not able to receive the major commandments that are
the solid food of the Perfect. 'That solid food of these who
by practice are trained [to discern good from evil].'[6] See
how the sick and the infants are not able to ascend these
steps. 'I, my brothers, am not able to speak (c.457) with
you as with a spiritual person, but as infants in Christ[7] I
have given you milk to drink.'[8] Therefore, come to solid

6. Heb 5:14   7. 1 Co 3:1   8. Heb 5:12-13

food. 'When I was a child I lived like a child by the minor commandments. When I became a man I ceased my youthful mind, that is, I left behind the easy paths that are the minor commandments and I became a man and was perfected.'[9] Imitate me,[10] my brothers, as I have imitated Christ and was perfected. You see that he was not able to show [them] while they were young and ill how to ascend to that heaven, but he showed them these paths, the minor commandments, and look, he called them after they had grown strong and were healed, 'Come, go on to the straight road that is the major commandments', because the powerful Perfect eat this food and travel on this great road.

6.   Up to what point are we [still] children? Indeed, are we not healed from illness and do we not become adults after youth? 'There are some who believe that they may eat everything and whoever is sick will eat [only] vegetables.'[11] Why, therefore, (c.460) did the apostle speak about these visible foods? Look, whoever eats everything is the least among the solitaries and is not excellent like them. Notice, the apostle commands us, 'This way would be better for us, that we neither eat meat nor drink wine'.[12] Our Lord also cautions us, 'Do not allow your hearts to be weighed down with meaty foods and with drunkenness of wine and with the anxiety of living'.[13]

Look, is it not evident that Paul called 'sick' whomever is ill in his mind and whose understanding is little, but does not call 'sick' whoever fasts and eats bread and vegetables and salt? Because if one fasts and prays he is better this way [than one who eats]; but [Paul] reviles and calls 'sick' whoever does not keep the major commandments. On the other hand, there are some who have the

9. I Co 13:11
10. I Co 4:16
11. Rm 14:2
12. Rm 14:21
13. Lk 21:34

power to obey all the commandments and receive, keep, and discern the major and the minor. Yet, there are some who are not able even to hear these great commandments, because [their] understanding is immature or [their] mind is ill.

The major commandments are these steps about which I have spoken [which he cannot receive],[14] but he is able to receive the minor ones that are these paths about which I have spoken, and he travels on them until he becomes strong and healthy. But if (c.461) he departs from this world while he is [still] on the paths, he will live in the place of life and will not perish like that one who turns back from that difficult road and falls into the great depth of Sheol. Even if he travels on these paths, which our Lord and his preachers prepared, which are the lesser commandments directed to infants and the sick, he will be in that place of rest and rightly obtain his salvation. However, he will not enter that great city and that place in which our Lord is visible face to face, unless he comes to ascend these steps that are the major and promised commandments.

7. Concerning the way of life of the prophets and the Old Testament, it was explained to us above how we should obey the writings of the prophets and the Law of Moses.[15] But it is then proper for us to adhere to the Spirit and agree with it and to observe the New Testament, which is Jesus Christ, and imitate him because he is the head of and the one who perfects our faith. Look, the apostle said, 'He made the first and last Testaments one (c.464) Testament. He eliminated the law of the commandments, which were not necessary, by his own commandments so that in both of these testaments of which he had made one Gospel, he might create people anew.'[16]

Until Christ comes, we are under the Law that was over us, just like a guardian over the household of God.

14. Corrupt text.   15. Cf. *Mēmrā* 9.   16. Ep 2:15ff

Just as [in the case of] the guardian presiding over the household of a great person until the heir matures[17]—when the heir whom the master of the household has left becomes an adult, the children of his household do not live under the hand of guardians or stewards; so also we who are the household of God, so long as this New Testament was hidden, were under the Law, the Old Testament, just like [being] under guardians. But today the heir of the household is revealed, we are no longer under guardians, but under the hand of the master of the household, who is the Son, the Christ in the New Testament, who is our Lord Jesus Christ.

Just as [in the case of] this heir of this world, as long as he is young, his activity is placed under guardians.[18] When he becomes an adult, however, he will claim and take up (c.465) from the guardians the inheritance that his father had written down; so also as long as Christ was hidden, his servants and the children of his household were under guardians. Today, however, just as that heir has been revealed, who had grown up and taken control of the possessions of his father from the guardians and stewards, so also those who belonged to him recognized that they had acquired their Lord [so] they followed him and took refuge in him. This is to say, he freed us from the yoke of servitude of sin and from the heavy burdens of the Old Testament. He yoked us with a sweet and light yoke and with the light burdens of the New Testament.[19] For he took these major commandments of the Old Testament, these upon which hung the whole power of the Law and the prophets, and fixed them in the New Testament and gathered all of its power, the first and the last, and placed them in a single New Testament so that we might see and discern what is the power from the Law and the prophets that conformed with these two commandments and how we might join it with the power of the New Testament and travel on the

17. Ga 4:2   18. Ga 4:1   19. Mt 11:28-30

road that our Lord Jesus had prepared before us in order to walk to that place from which our first father had departed.

8.   Therefore, my son, ground yourself upon the New Testament and it will be greater in your eyes than all (c.468) the [other] testaments, since it is [so] great, for through it the acceptable and perfect will of God is accomplished in the Spirit. Paul wrote more, 'Woe to those who consider the testament of the Son of God like [that of] any [other] person. They treat the Spirit of grace shamefully, because they treat the testament of our Lord equally with that of any [other] person.'[20] These [other testaments] were consummated by the blood of dumb beasts, but this [testament] was consummated by the eloquent blood, pure and holy, of the mediator, our Lord Jesus Christ.

Therefore, love the New Testament in order that it may show you the straight road issuing from it by which a person may quickly travel to the city of saints and to that place in which the Perfect are refreshed, those who journey by the major commandments, which I will explain to you so that you [too] may travel by them directly and quickly.

9.   The Perfect road is this, 'Whoever does not leave his family is not capable [of walking on this road]'.[21] But the path that leads you away from it is this, 'Dwell with your parents and honor them while their mind is entangled in earthly matters'.[22]

Now what he said, 'Dwell with your parents and with (c.469) your teachers and honor them',[23] [was intended] for children who are also attached to earthly matters; in this respect, it is good that they live with their parents and honor them and live among them.

10.   This is the Perfect and straight road, 'Consider every

20. Heb 10:29   22. Ex 20:12
21. Mt 10:37; Lk 14:26   23. Dt 5:16; Ep 6:1-2

person better than yourself'.²⁴ The path that goes near it for the sake of the infants and the sick is this, 'If there is a brother who fornicates or curses, is greedy or drunken, do not even eat bread with him'.²⁵

In order that the infant and the ill person might not fall from this commandment, which is the great step, the Spirit made this path deviate so that near this step one might travel until he becomes strong or is healed in order to climb on to it directly. As the apostle said, 'Come, now that you have become adults to this solid food'.²⁶ For if he had allowed the infants and the ill to consider sinners better than themselves, they would have intermingled with them and committed their deeds and fallen from the great height of the step of that major commandment. He, however, caused them to turn (c.472) a little toward the borders of the step until they grew up and were made whole. That is, he separated them from evil people until they received power from on high²⁷ so that they might not enter powerless among evil people and perish. However, this is so lest they ascend that step powerless, and becoming dizzy, fall from it.

11.   This is the Perfect road through which the strong become Perfect, 'Blessed are those who make peace with everyone for they shall be called the children of God'.²⁸ In addition, 'Let your lowliness be known to all people'.²⁹ However, the path that makes you turn away from it is this: 'Do not greet anyone on the road'³⁰ and 'Admonish the offenders'.³¹

This was spoken to whoever is feeble in his conscience and immature in his understanding, lest, on account of salutation, a young child shall fall and be injured; or because the offender is not corrected, another [offender] will become arrogant to imitate him and whoever will come to imitate him will succumb. Therefore, when someone

24. Ph 2:3   27. Ac 1:8   30. Lk 10:4
25. 1 Co 5:11   28. Mt 5:9   31. 1 Th 5:14
26. Heb 5:14   29. Ph 4:5

young gives a greeting where he is not confident, he shall quickly pass through and go to a safe home, and remain with the strong one who teaches him, lest he become subject to and be injured by someone whom he does not know is good or malicious. (c.473) Because of this, [our Lord] held the infant back from salutation so that others would not take him captive where he does not know. Therefore, the peacemaker is [in the company of] good and bad, but will not lend them his conversation or ear except where he is confident after examination, and knows that they will teach him honestly and raise him up truthfully.

12. This is the Perfect road, 'Bless him who curses you and love him who hates you, and pray for whomever harms you and persecutes you'.[32] However, the path that will lead you away from it is this: 'Consider whoever does not listen as a Gentile and as a tax-collector'.[33] This is said to the sick one, 'Consider whomever does not listen as a Gentile', lest he strike back and kill him.

13. The Perfect road is this, 'Do not be anxious about what you shall eat and what you shall wear'.[34] The path that leads you away from it is this, 'Work and eat the bread [you have earned] and do not be a burden on anyone'.[35]
    This is said to whomever is dissolute because he does not work [for] heavenly things with fasting and prayer, with vigils and with lowliness. He said to him, 'Work, (c.476) even if in earthly matters, and give alms; do not cease completely from either one, [for] evil could triumph over you and you could contrive all sorts of evil'.

14. This is the Perfect road: 'Men who do not take wives and women who do not belong to men are like angels and cannot die. Whoever does not leave his wife and his children and his family and everything he has in the land, is

32. Mt 5:14   33. Mt 18:17   34. Mt 6:25   35. 2 Th 3:12

not worthy of me.'³⁶ However, the path that leads you away from it is this: 'Whatever God has joined together do not separate'.³⁷

This was directed to whoever does not judge himself and subdue his body, for it would be better for him to marry and not be corrupt in adultery and fornication. This is because he does not lower himself and fast from all foods as long as he is alive and his body is young, and because he is not persistent in prayer and does not guard himself from everything evil and from every hateful word, [thus] making himself blessed and not cursed, a humble person and not one prideful and hard, a child of peace and not an enemy or an angry person. Because of this, he will also be defeated by physical desire, become corrupt and be conquered, and do evil.

15. This is the Perfect road: 'A virgin (c.477) who does not marry a man and a man who does not take a wife are pleasing to our Lord in body and in spirit, while those who do marry please one another'.³⁸ However, the path that leads you away from it is this: 'Marriage is [held] in honor and their bed is pure'.³⁹ This, again, is written for whoever does not subdue his body from food and is [not] constant in fasting and in prayer. Because [Paul] knows that the person who builds up his body and is void of spiritual work is overcome by desires; it is better for him to marry and not be licentious and corrupt.

16. This is the Perfect road: 'Seek what is above and think of what is above'.⁴⁰ However, the path that leads you away from it is this: 'If a person does not work, he shall not eat'.⁴¹

This too is spoken regarding the dissolute and whoever does useless things, slanders, devises evil, and does

36. Mt 22:30
37. Mt 19:6
38. 1 Co 7:32
39. Heb 13:4
40. Col 3:1-2
41. 2 Th 3:10

not work spiritually nor meditates on the truth in his heart. For when someone does not supply them [with food] they will have to work on the land and be occupied with transitory work and cease from slander, and evil and useless things.

17. This is the straight and Perfect road: 'Offer (c.480) your cheek to whoever would strike you and pray for him. Let loose and you will be loosed. Forgive and you will be forgiven.'[42] The path that will lead you away from it is this: 'Whatever you bind on earth will be bound in heaven'.[43]

Look, my son, see how he speaks to the Perfect One, 'Pray for whoever treats you badly', and he prays. He commands the rulers, 'Bind whoever goes astray and drive him out from among you, but never strike him'. They, however, are not able to be patient and [so] strike him and sin. Now, in that they bind the offender so that he may be chastened and so that others may fear lest they imitate him, [they] do not sin. But as long as [the rulers] have authority they remain apart from Perfection. For, when they strike him, they sin, so that they will go astray even from Uprightness that is lower than Perfection. This is directed to the rulers so that with this word, which binds people who act wrongly against heaven and earth, they will subdue all who rebel against the ways of Uprightness of the church.

18. This is the Perfect road: 'Whoever forces you to go one mile, go with him two more and make peace with him'.[44] But the path (c.481) that leads you away from it is this: 'Separate yourself from whoever [acts] this way, lest you get mixed up with him'.[45] This is directed to the infants so that they might distance themselves from evil people lest they give themselves over to their evil will.

42. Mt 5:39; Lk 6:37   44. Mt 5:39
43. Mt 18:18   45. 1 Co 5:11

19. This is the Perfect road: 'Do not acquire anything on earth'.[46] But the path that leads you away from it is this: 'Whoever has stolen, let him work and acquire in order that he has [something] to give to whoever is needy and be saved'.[47] Now everyone knows this, that it would be much better for a person to work and acquire and give alms than to steal and grieve the heart of his neighbor, and be condemned in the Judgment and tormented at the last. If he is seized in this world, he will be beaten and die; or he will be stripped of everything and be imprisoned and convicted in judgment, here and there.

20. The Perfect and straight road is this: 'Whoever wishes to become great in the Kingdom of Heaven, let him think of himself as less than everyone and let him honor everyone like a good servant who honors his masters'.[48] But the path that leads you astray from it is this: without having understood the word of our Lord, you declare, 'The rulers of the Gentiles are their lords',[49] (c.484) having forgotten that word of our Lord that said, 'Whoever becomes the chief among you shall be a servant to you'.[50]

Did you not understand what he said, it shall not be among you like that leadership of the Gentiles that makes them the lords and potentates, but [that you shall be] as servants honoring one another? Are you to be exalted like earthly kings, those who have no fear of God in their hearts and before their eyes and [who], without hesitation or compassion, judge and condemn the people who are under their control, and condemn without pity, kill without justice and mercy and the fear of our Lord? In this way they commit evil and [so] go down to lower Sheol and to the deepest part of the pit of lower Gehenna.

46. Mt 10:9
47. Ep 4:28
48. Lk 22:26
49. Lk 22:25
50. Mt 20:26

Do you dare, you who have been called a disciple of Christ, who was a servant of everyone through his love and was struck and did not strike [anyone] and loved his murderers and prayed for them on account of his great mercy and his lowliness without limit to teach us to imitate him? Did you say this word, and are not troubled, that you are imitating the rulers of the Gentiles, these who make the whole world wail under their control, because they plunder and kill without (c.485) mercy? If you seek these [things], you shall not be a disciple of Christ. Depart then from the church of our Lord and join the kings of the Gentiles and their chiefs, and do your evil will and commit evil. Because the law of Christ is far from these and those similar to them, it pursues every benefit of good and virtuous things, and of love and lowliness so that it may save everyone and make them great in the kingdom of our Lord Jesus Christ, the Lord powerful and mighty.

21. This is the Perfect road, 'When the bridegroom is taken up the disciples shall fast continually in the sincerity of their heart and their body.'[51] But the path that leads you away from it is this, 'It is not what enters the mouth that will defile a person, but what comes out of his mouth and [whatever] evil his heart devises [which] will defile a person'.[52]

It is not food [by] its nature [that] defiles, but a person reveling, going astray, and being defiled in debauchery through misguided and deadly passions, death and by sinful deeds. This is so, even if he guards himself from foods that are impure in the Law, (c.488) while enjoying and taking pleasure in others that are pure as far as the conscience is concerned, yet his heart and mouth are full of evil thoughts and hateful words. [This word] was spoken so that he might understand that unless he purifies his mouth and his heart, he is unclean even while fasting from whatever defiles his conscience. It would have been better for

51. Mt 9:15; Mk 2:20; Lk 5:35; Gospel Thomas 104
52. Mt 15:11; Clement Alexandria, *Stromata* 2, 11, 50

him if he had purified his mouth and heart and [then] had taken food, rather than fasting while he is unclean. This means a person is not able to become pure without fasting, prayer, lowliness, and love.

22. The Perfect road is this, 'Do not allow a spiteful word to come out of your mouth'.[53] But, the path that will make you turn back without coming near to the road is this: 'When you seek to imitate our Lord and call the people, "Brood of vipers, how can you do what is virtuous, being evil ones and sons of the evil one?"';[54] or, [if] you imitate the Spirit, which spoke through Paul, and you call people, 'Fools and those lacking in intelligence'.[55] This authority was not given to you. For our Lord is not under a law, and in Paul's case the Holy Spirit allowed him to speak this way. But our Lord called people in this way in order to make them understand that he is their Lord (c.489) and has power over them and to make them understand that he is going to judge them at the last, but by his [own] will lowered himself to give an example to his disciples to imitate.

In order that people not accuse them and say, 'As our Lord was humble in his words and his deeds, so he will be gentle on the day of judgment', and sin without fear, our Lord cast fear upon hearers through his words and said, 'Woe to you hypocrites, to whom on that day the King will say, "Go, you accursed to the fire that is prepared for the evil one and his servants"'.[56]

Yet, [our Lord] was humble toward everyone through his way of life. But if it had pleased our Lord that he should not lower himself through his way of life and [yet] to say to all, 'Lower yourselves by your words as well as by your way of life', who would have bidden him [to do otherwise]? Can the servant find fault with his creator? No! O human

53. Ep 4:29
54. Mt 12:34
55. 1 Co 15:36
56. Mt 25:41

being, do you dare to find fault with the commandment of God and say, 'As he has done, I will do'? Then, create creatures and make them grow and rear them like him.[57]

Therefore, our Lord has the power of life and death; he who is above authority lowered himself. Wherever he said a harsh word (c.492) it was because it was right for him to speak in that way at that time before [his] listeners. But to us he commanded, 'A spiteful word should not come out of your mouth'.[58] Therefore, like obedient and submissive servants, let us speak, as our Lord commanded us, with dignity and lowliness, so that he will not put us to death justly because we have transgressed his commandments.

23. This is the Perfect road: 'Forgive the offender four hundred and ninety faults, [even] if he offends you on a single day.'[59] But the path that leads you away from it is this: 'If he is not obedient to you, in the presence of the church let him be separated from you so that you do not associate with him'.[60] This was spoken on account of the wrathful and the dissolute, lest the wrathful destroy through their rage and the dissolute be encouraged in [their] sin, because no one rebukes them and [so] they become corrupted. But once they have separated themselves, there will be peace on both sides: on one side, in that they will not cause harm in their anger seeing the indignation of the offenders; and on the other side, in that they will not be harmed through their indolence because they see that no one rebukes, chastises, or warns them lest they come to these.

24. This is the Perfect road: 'Blessed (c.493) are those who are pure in their heart, for they shall see God'.[61] But

57. Cf. Jb 40:1-42:6   60. Mt 18:16; 1 Co 5:9; 2 Th 3:14
58. Ep 4:29   61. Mt 5:8
59. Mt 18:22

the path that leads you away from it is this: 'If he does not say to you, "I repent", do not forgive him'.[62]

This is written to whomever is stiff-necked and corrupt so that he may be humbled and avoid the evil road and say, 'I will not act like this', and then he shall be forgiven and become a warning and a chastisement to others not to become presumptuous and slack.

This is [the task] of the leaders and not of the Perfect. The Perfect do not come near the positions of leadership, but if they are [in] leadership positions and are pursuing Perfection, they should leave these positions. Then they can be perfected because the Perfect teach everyone with lowliness and are not able to coerce a person like the rulers [do]. But the leaders, who have authority over each place, are allowed to demand everything justly and to chastise appropriately whoever rebels against [his] companions and exile him until he repents. And because of this, it is said, 'Speak and exact [punishment]'.

Those who exact judgment and raise charges are not able to be perfected and become peaceful and kind ones. But if they wish to become upright and pursue (c.496) Uprightness through these minor commandments and be virtuous on that day of our Lord, but are not able to do the Perfect will of our Lord, as long as they are managing the congregations, they are not able to leave these minor commandments and come to the major commandments. It is in these [major commandments] that the perfect and acceptable will of our Lord resides, and [through them] they will eat solid food and be perfected through suffering, lowliness, and spiritual service.

25. This is the Perfect road: 'If you remember that a person holds a grudge against you, go and be reconciled to him,[63] and then come and pray saying the following—Our Father who is in heaven, forgive me as I have forgiven,

62. Lk 17:3   63. Mt 5:23

and do not allow me to enter into temptation[64]—and love covers sins.'[65] But the path that leads you away from it is this: 'When you have rebuked him between the two of you and before three [persons], yet he does not listen to you, put him to shame before the whole church'.[66] Or, 'Separate the evil person from among you lest he stand with you in prayer'.[67]

This is addressed to the wrong-doers and the offenders and to those who imitate them. (c.497) Our Lord allows the injured and the leader of the church, 'When you have censured the oppressor and the offender personally, or before one, two, or three, or before the whole church and he does not pay any heed, that person is a rebel.'[68] Get rid of that matter and forgive that offense and you will not ruin yourself nor be impoverished, because you will have brought to an end that matter. It will be an advantage for you to no longer demand requital for that fault. Our Lord will judge your judgment. Evict [the offender] lest another like him will be daring and become an oppressor and an offender like him.[69] From then on, distance [yourself] from whomever does not fear our Lord, from his sins and his destructiveness; even excommunicate him from your congregation without blows and without chains and our Lord will take vengeance from him if he does not repent and become ashamed, and being regretful, turn away from his evil deeds.

26. This is the Perfect road: 'Be all [things] with all people and teach everyone that you may win over everyone'.[70] The path that leads you away from it is this: 'Do not eat bread with adulterers'.[71]

This is addressed to him whose (c.500) understanding is immature, lest on account of the nourishment of bread he will keep company with adulterers, and they cor-

64. Mt 6:9,12   67. 2 Co 6:17; 2 Th 3:14   70. 1 Co 9:22
65. Pr 10:12; 1 P 4:8 68. Mt 18:17   71. 1 Co 5:11
66. Mt 18:15-17   69. 1 Co 5:13

rupt him like themselves, and in his childishness he will be carried away and be captured and perish.

27. This is the Perfect road: 'In every house you enter, proclaim peace over it and pray for its residents'.[72] But the path that leads you away from it is this: 'If they do not receive you, shake off your dust against them in anger,[73] and ask who [else] is worthy? Enter and proclaim peace there.'[74]

If this is the way it is, we will love only whoever loves us and we will falter from that fast pursuit of Perfection. This is addressed to the disciples who are young, lest they get into a quarrel or get injured with words, as these disciples who were still too young for Perfection said there, '"Our Lord, do you wish that we should call out and have fire descend and burn up these who did not receive us?" But our Lord rebuked them,[75] "Do not talk like this. Instead, love your enemies and those who hate you and your murderers"'. Because of this, he permitted them to shake off the dust (c.501) and leave. Our Lord knows what he is to do and how to lead his servants into peace and quiet. Also he will be merciful to all people in order that they should receive the assurance of his truth.

28. This is the Perfect road: 'Do not call a person impure or defiled', as Simeon said, 'God gave me this that I should not call a person impure or defiled'.[76] But the path that leads you away from it is this: 'Do not associate with fornicators'.[77] This is addressed to [spiritual] infants so that they will not draw near to fornicators through their immaturity, lest [the fornicators] corrupt them, before they possess spiritual power and their minds grow up and are perfected. Then they will have the authority to be all [things] with all [people].

---

72. Mt 10:12
73. Mt 10:14
74. Mt 10:11

75. Lk 9:54-55
76. Ac 10:28
77. 1 Co 5:9

29. This is the Perfect road: 'You ought to take up the sickness of the ill'[78] and 'he who is lame will not be rejected'.[79] But the path that will lead you away from it is this, 'Do not travel on the road of pagans'.[80] This is addressed to the infants so that they will not enter the house of pagans in as much as they are too young for the knowledge of truth, lest [the pagans] scandalize them or they stumble and are greatly injured. (c.504)

30. This is the Perfect road: 'When our Lord calls the tax-collectors and fornicators and converts all the sinners and the lost ones'. But the path that will lead you away from it is this: 'Distance yourself from every brother who walks wickedly'.[81] This is addressed to [spiritual] infants so that they might distance themselves from evil people and follow the powerful and the Perfect, until they become strong and receive the strength of truth and are perfected. Then they will have the authority to become lambs among wolves.

31. This is the Perfect road: 'I am sending you as lambs among wolves'.[82] But the path that will lead away from it is this: 'Do not enter the villages of the Samaritans'.[83]

This is addressed to the imperfect ones, lest they enter with just anyone, until they receive the power from on high.[84] When they are perfected in Christ, they will be able to be with any person and with whomever they wish to travel. For as long as they are inferior it would be good for them to follow the Perfect and not stray from their teaching, until they can establish themselves as Perfect in Christ.

But the Perfect, since they are fulfilled in every aspect of truth and are without fear, do not say because of this: (c.505) 'This is our place' and 'this is not ours' or 'this person is ours' or 'this [person] is not one of us'. Because [the

78. Rm 15:1
79. Heb 12:13
80. Mt 10:5
81. 1 Co 5:13

82. Mt 10:16
83. Mt 10:5
84. Ac 1:8

Perfect] invite everyone by their word, since the truth of
our Lord wins them over at all times, they do not follow the
teaching or word of [any]one. Because of this, they are
capable of being with everyone, for their intelligence rules
in Perfection and in truth and is complete in the knowledge of our Lord. Because of this, they are all things with
all people and know how to instruct every person as it is
helpful for him.

But the leaders have only such and such a region
where, as is necessary, they may discipline with mercy and
wherever it is right they may separate justly what is better
for the congregations in each place, and what is helpful for
the infants and also for the sick, the corrupt, and the rebels.
For the Perfect, because they travel to many places, speak
to each one the word that is helpful to him and leave them
for another place. For leaders reside in each place and if
they do not rebuke and chastise these, the rebels will rebel
more and the corrupt will assail even more in sin. The ill
will become weak, the infants will be scandalized, the oppressors will be ignored, (c.508) the robbers will be arrogant, the oppressed will be blasphemed, and those who are
robbed will wail. Therefore, let us understand, my brothers, what concerns the leaders, but does not apply to us
because we are Perfect ones or because we seek Perfection.
You also, the leaders, take notice of the ways of Perfection
and do not complain about us, nor accuse us in matters
that concern us, nor hate us at random and chase us away
for nothing from the ministry in which it is right for us to
walk—going to everyone, instructing and teaching everyone in love and in lowliness—which is what our Lord Jesus
taught and showed us in his person and revealed to us by
his grace and his mercy.

32. This is the Perfect road: 'Leave the tares growing with
the wheat until I convert them in the harvest, lest you root
up the wheat with the tares, because you do not know which
are the tares, since the tares may be transformed and be-

come wheat.'[85] The path that will lead you away from it is this: 'Separate those who sin from being in the congregation, so that they may not stand among the wheat, in order that the infants may not imitate them and the ill not be scandalized by them.'

33.   This is the Perfect road:

> If you love only the one who loves you (c.509) and you greet only your brothers, what is your righteousness? Because even tax-collectors and heathen and sinners act in this way.[86] But, love whoever hates you and persecutes you,[87] and your peace will increase toward the good and the evil, and you shall be imitating the Father in heaven who makes his sun shine and his rain fall upon them equally.[88]

But the path that will lead you away from it is this: 'Love your neighbor and your acquaintance'[89] and 'whoever will do [this] to one of those who is called in the name of the discipleship of Christ, his reward will not perish'.[90]

Because of this Paul explained, 'Do good things for everyone. But if you wish to do [good] especially to the children of the household of faith of Christ, you may do it, and this is most excellent because you are doing [good] for the disciples of Christ.'[91]

85. Mt 13:30
86. Lk 6:32-35
87. Mt 5:44
88. Mt 5:45
89. Lv 19:18
90. Mt 5:43; Mk 9:41; Mt 10:41
91. Ga 6:10

34. But the Perfect road is this: These lowly and major commandments of love, and those that resemble them or are [even] greater than they and like them, are addressed in the New Testament to whoever wishes to become strong; so that by all means they might be instructed to understand and comprehend what is 'the height and the depth and the length and the width with all (c.512) the saints',[92] and they might be able to ascend with power these steps of that narrow, difficult, and confining road that goes up to that city in which the saints dwell with our Lord Jesus, King of glory.

35. But these paths that travel near this road are the minor commandments, which are given to infants as milk and to the ill as vegetables, because as long as they are immature in their intelligence and ill in their minds, they are not able to come to these major commandments of love and Perfection.

Because of this our Lord and his preachers prepared for them paths so that—by these minor commandments and those less than and similar to them in the New Testament—they might walk near this great road until the infants grow up and the ill are healed so that vigorously they might grow and immediately they might be healed and enter this great road of the major commandments, journeying and ascending on it to that city of the saints.

For as long as they are immature and ill, they are not able to go up on these great steps and it is better for them to walk on these paths (c.513) near the road and not turn back and perish completely or grow dizzy and fall into that great depth and descend to Sheol while living, because they have no strength, some of them being immature and some of them ill.

36. Love loves all, which the apostle extolled more than all [other] good gifts.[93] It is acquired by these major com-

92. Ep 3:18   93. 1 Co 13:13

mandments, and that Perfection, which our Lord said is like the angels,[94] is accomplished on this difficult and narrow road.[95] Now this road of the major commandments leads to the house of our Lord and enters his bridal chamber. But these paths of the minor commandments do not reach the house of our Lord, nor enter his bridal chamber, but are held back in places of life that are on this side of the bridal chamber of our Lord. But those who travel on that perfect road will rejoice in the joy of our Lord and be glorified with him as it is written, 'I will rejoice in your joy and be glorified also in your heritage'.[96]

But these who journey on these paths will remain in places of life that are prepared for everyone according to his deeds, and they will not enter that joy of our Lord, nor also be glorified with him (c.516), nor even see him face to face in the bridal chamber of glory and in the joy of his presence. But see what I am showing you that in as much as the infants and the ill are not capable of the power of this road, the paths have been prepared for them.

37. Say to him whose mind is still immature, 'Go work for our Lord in fasting and in prayer and learn his truth and confirm also the others, and when you have made ready, do not be concerned about food and clothing'. Look, see how heaven and earth perish before his eyes, and he says to you, 'If I do not work, [how] will I live?'

Say to whoever is sick and is tormented and has not yet become strong, 'Go reconcile with your enemies, these who have treated you badly for no reason', and see how he is confused and falls from this step if he goes to ascend on it. For when he goes to be reconciled, [if] that enemy makes him hear a spiteful word, he is not able to endure it. Because he is upset and quarreling with him, he will really be confused and fall, if not into the lower depth of Sheol, at

94. Mt 22:30
95. Mt 7:14
96. Ps 106:5

least between the cliffs that are in this step, and [his bones] will be broken and he will hardly be able to stand. Or, he will not listen to you at all to go be reconciled, and out of fear he will not ascend (c.517) even a little on to that step, for he has no strength in his feet as a result of the great illness that is with him. [This illness] causes him pain because he has not asked our Lord and has not yet received power from on high to reconcile by it his enemies as the apostles had asked and received. He has not yet been healed so as to [be able to] stand upon his feet and put water in the washbasin and wash the feet of his mockers and of his betrayers, just as our Lord had done for Iscariot. Because he is tormented by a great illness, he is not able to stand upon his feet when a person has struck and pushed him down and look up into heaven and say like Stephen, "'Our Lord Jesus Christ, let this sin not be accounted to him",[97] to this one who has defeated and thrown me down and now wishes to kill me'.

38. You see how infants are not capable of the power of these major commandments because they are young, and those who are ill are not able to ascend on these hard and difficult steps because they have not yet received power from on high. But whoever (c.520) is immature in his understanding and wishes to grow up quickly, will seek out for himself a nurse.

Whoever is sick should request from our Lord to be able to receive the true word. Also he will give an opportunity to whomever is able to bear the illness so that he may quickly heal him in order that he might have strength, requesting and praying that God or a spiritual person of our Lord might teach him how he should spiritually serve our Lord by these major commandments of love and see this road spiritually with the eyes of his mind and travel on it spiritually unblemished to that spiritual city. For spiritually

97. Ac 7:60

he is able to be with the Lord of the commandments and [the Lord] will give him the power to love him and keep his commandments and be perfected. That is, the Lord creates in him a perfect will; otherwise, he is not able to exist according to his perfect will.

But, my children, let us step on to this difficult road, enduring a little affliction so that we may reach that place of rest. Look, we have explained earlier everything in this *mēmrā* that is entitled 'the Discernment of the Commandments'. Read and learn and understand everything in lowliness, and pray for me and remember me before our Lord when you go (c.521) and reach that great place of peace, holiness, and love.

39. Therefore, my beloved, see how people flee from the Perfect road, which is the major commandments by which a person serves our Lord spiritually, on account of the difficulty of these steps that are on it. They walk back and forth on the paths that are the lesser commandments because there is not on them the great difficulty as on this road. Because [the lesser commandments] lead [one] away from the steps that are very high, all [these people] travel on the borders near the great road.

For when a person has separated himself from one who has offended or bound him or has become his enemy or considered him a heathen he is contented, because he has done only a little of what he wants, but he remains behind Perfection. It would be better for me not to chastise the offenders and fall short of Perfection and deprive myself of the city of the saints and of the person of our Lord Jesus. Those who flee from difficulties do not know that these are the difficult and narrow steps that ascend directly to the city of our king. But in order not to suffer afflictions, they seek the lesser commandments (c.524) so that they might take refuge in them. When a person said to them, 'Come, endure a little affliction and you will depart to relief', as it is written, 'You made me enter through fire and water and made me go out to a wide-open space; then I will go to your house in honor'.⁹⁸ Do you see how people travel between fire and water, enduring many difficulties, and then they come to the house of our Lord and enter his tranquility?

40. But people are content to wander on the paths without being challenged as [on] the road and [without] wishing to become Perfect and inherit the great portion, but not understanding that unless they make their soul enter into the affliction of these major commandments while there is still time for them in this world, they will not be perfected. Because suddenly there will be the day of their death and as a thief it will come and they are not able to attain that great city of our king, clearly visible face to face.

But even if they inherit their life in other places according to their deeds, yet they will be deprived of that city of the saints who have kept the major commandments and love and are perfected and have ascended from this world, (c.525) and they are not able to enter it because they did not know his law and did not live according to the acceptable and perfect will of its king.⁹⁹

Do you not know that whoever does not know the law and commandments and all the customs of this earthly king, and does not do all of his will, cannot enter his palace; so also with that heavenly king who is [both] hidden and revealed, whoever knows all his acceptable and perfect will and does it, it is he who will enter his city and dwell with him forever without limit. Its days are not reckoned nor are the years of that new world counted, but a thousand years of this world are not like one of the years of that new world that is prepared for the righteous ones who have kept his commandments. For its days do not pass away and the years of that world are not numbered, because it is built

---

98. Ps 66:12-13   99. Hermas, *Similitude* I:1-4

and established on the light that has no limit and does not pass away.

The end of the nineteenth *Mēmrā* about the commandments of the road of Perfection and about the discernment of these commandments, by the same author.

Mēmrā Twenty

ON THE DIFFICULT STEPS
THAT ARE ON THE ROAD
OF THE CITY OF OUR LORD

Summary: Continuing the same metaphor of the steep road to the heavenly city of the Perfect, the pilgrimage intensifies with the three most difficult steps. Reconciliation with one's enemies and not working in order to divest oneself of everything are the first two. The last step is the uprooting of the root of sin that Adam had experienced in Eden. One must be prepared to adopt the affliction of prayer in mounting the last step, as witnessed by Jesus before his disciples in Gethsemane. (c.528)

1.   There are three very difficult steps on this road leading to the city of our Lord Jesus. One is this: if a person has enemies, even though he does not offend or annoy anyone, he should go meet these enemies—and those who hate him for no reason—and reconcile with them.

The second [step] is this: one should not work, either for nourishment for oneself or for clothing for the body, in order to divest oneself from all one has.

The third [step] is this: 'It is right for people to raise their pure hands before the Lord without anger and without (c.529) evil thoughts'.[1] That is, while their heart is pure

1. 1 Tm 2:8

from sin, just as the heart of our father Adam was pure
before he transgressed against the commandment.

2.   Indeed, a person may climb that [first] step, in which
one should humbly reconcile with his enemies who [hate
him] for no reason through much fasting and powerful
and lengthy prayer. Then a person may ascend that [sec-
ond] step in which one should not be anxious or work,
trusting in our Lord [and saying], 'If I climb up, good; if I
remain [on the same step], so be it'. That is, [we receive
sustenance] from our Lord as well as from begging food
and clothing like a poor person. 'If I die, I will die; and if I
live, I will live', as long as I do not abandon the journey of
that great road on account of nourishment and clothing. A
person may climb this step in this hope, knowing very well
that he must endure because his soul will be cast down to
death, as our Lord said, 'Whoever loses his soul on account
of me shall find it'.[2]

3.   This other step, through which a person shall come
to reach the city of our Lord Jesus Christ, is harder than all
the [other] steps. Because through this one a person en-
counters (c.532) murder and perseveres until blood [flows]
in the struggle against sin. Along with it there are many
[other] steps on the road of our Lord, which were described
to us above, and all are hard so that one may climb them all
[only] with endurance.
     But these three are especially hard and this is the last
step: when a person has kept all of the commandments, he
uproots all sin, its [evil] thoughts and fruits from the heart,
that [very] sin that was planted in our father Adam and in
our mother Eve on the day they sinned. [Sin] entered and
lived in all their children. This is the most difficult step.
The nearer one comes to the city of our Lord, the harder
and steeper [the road] becomes, so that no one is able to

2. Mt 10:39

climb it except with difficulty. But if a person does climb it, he will triumph and escape from captivity and death. On the other hand, there are people who travel these steps and upon reaching this step are amazed and pull back from its severity, remaining silent in front of the city of our Lord, and do not enter into it because they are shaken by the severity of this step, or they turn around, or distance themselves a long way from the city of our Lord, in which he dwells openly with his saints. (c.533)

4. This step is difficult because through it a person does battle against sin, and if he does climb this step he will enter the house of our Lord. Ardently and defiantly, [sin] stands in front of him: either it kills or is killed. Because of this, even an athlete, who sees [sin] standing menacingly before him preventing him from crossing over to the place our Lord promised him, battles desperately, struggling with sin. Concerning this step Paul said, 'You have not yet encountered murder nor stood up in the struggle until blood [is shed] against sin.[3] While you have not yet cut off the leaves of a withered tree, its shoots and its branches, you have not yet approached the root, nor do you know how difficult it will be to uproot it.' That is, while you have not yet conquered even the visible sins, which are the leaves and shoots and branches of sin, when you reach its root, then you will see murder and the battle by which sin and the powers of Satan engage you, as it is written, 'A battle outside and fear within'.[4] Externally, the powers of Satan do battle (c.536) and internally sin attacks.

Therefore, all the difficulty of this step lies in that a person uproots the hidden death, which Adam experienced in the transgression of the commandment, [as well as] all the [evil] thoughts of sin, everything that is considered spiteful in a person, as our Lord said, 'In the heart exist all the thoughts of murder, adultery, and false witness, and of all

---

3. Heb 12:4   4. 2 Co 7:5

the evil things a person does'.[5] Within and without, this sin
entices him, for it is that [same] death that our parents Adam
and Eve experienced in the transgression of the first commandment. For as long as a person commits despicable
deeds external to himself, [derived] from the sin inwardly
thought about, the sin inside him is not very hard on him.
But when he eliminates his despicable deeds, and fights
and defeats the evil spirits that struggle against him externally, and eliminates these external sins, then he will reach
that inner root that makes the flower bloom from within
and strikes many from without, as Paul said, 'Watch out,
lest the root of bitterness push the flower out and harm
many'.[6] (c.537)

5.   Therefore, a person may journey all the steps of the
road of our Lord Jesus, yet come to do battle to the death
on this last step. That is, a person may eliminate all visible
sins when he lowers himself and loves, but come to do
battle to the death and great struggle with the very root of
sin and its thoughts. But if a person uproots sin and
ascends these steps of which I have spoken, then he will
enter to be with our Lord spiritually, taking refuge in our
Lord, as the prophet said, 'A fortified tower is the name of
the Lord our God and may the rich man and the poor man
run to it'.[7]
       For a person reaches the city of our Lord when he
climbs this step; that is, when he has uprooted every root
of sin and its fruits that confront him. Because this sin con-
fronts him in the door of this step, he will not cross over,
unless our Lord comes to rescue him, and one will not be
rescued except by great battle. But this step is hard because
on it all the deficiencies belonging to the body and soul
vanish.

6.   Understand this also, my brothers: unless one performs all the commandments as our Lord and his apostles

5. Mt 15:19   6. Heb 12:15   7. Pr 18:10

did and as our Lord commanded to do, one will not (c.540) be able to cast off all outer and inner faults. If one does not become full of our Lord, his heart will not be emptied of sin and its fruits.

Therefore, in the killing of sin and in that lowliness, renunciation, love, holiness, and asceticism, and in these ways of life that our Lord has shown [us] how to do as he had done, a person, possessing that living soul that belonged to Adam while he had not yet sinned, and in the fulfillment of this step, will enter Eden, the house of his salvation. While this sinful thought and its fruits [still] exist in him, which you see he still struggles to uproot and kill, he has departed from the paradise of the Kingdom; but when that sin and its fruits that are completely evil and hateful cease to have effect on him, he will enter the bridal chamber of the Kingdom. For toil and evil anxiety are also its fruits.

For by the transgression of the commandment Adam and Eve[8] descended to these [fruits], and if they did not abandon the wealth and possession of the earth and all its beauty, they would not be able to live as [they were] at creation. Because by these [fruits] the evil one carried off humanity at the very beginning and made it fall from Perfection, as our Lord had said, 'If you do not turn and become as you were (c.541) before you had sinned, you will not be perfected into the glory of the Kingdom'.[9]

If a person compares the deeds of the Upright with those of the Perfect, they amount to very little in his eyes. Even if the Upright defeat evil, prevailing over sin and purifying their heart of evil thoughts, yet some of the fruits of sins are still living in them, since their heart was not purified from anxiety, toil, and marriage. For these [three] things happened to Adam by the counsel of Sin, and on account of this these are its fruits. For when Adam listened to Sin and neglected the word of his Creator, [God] gave him toil, anxiety, and marriage. While he did not have need of these

8. Literally, 'the house of Adam'.   9. Mt 18:3

things, he had great need after he had sinned. Because the Upright have neither emptied nor sanctified themselves from all there is on earth, they cannot rise higher than that by which the evil one had seduced Adam in the beginning, because he had longed for the earth and all in it and fell from heaven.[10]

Therefore, because the Upright have not separated themselves from everything there is on earth, nor from marriage and anxiety and toil, they are still eating (c.544) from that same tree from which Adam ate and have many faults [separating] them from Perfection. But our Lord desired through his mercy to give them [the opportunity] to keep Uprightness, which is lower than Perfection, so that while they are married and [involved] in these visible things they will be in good condition on the day of our Lord.

7.   Therefore, when we have climbed these steps and have rooted up sin and its fruits from the heart, then we will be filled with the Spirit, the Paraclete, and our Lord will dwell in us completely. We will eat freely from that tree of life that is our Lord, from which we were deprived by the transgression of the commandment; and then, we will be able to love and be merciful to all people, even our murderers, and be able to pray with love for all people and for our murderers. When we [are able to have] mercy upon and love everyone in this way, including our murderers, our heart being pure, then we will increase in Perfection and live according to that great, acceptable, and perfect will of our Lord.

8.   In this way a person may climb this difficult step with that prayer and example that our Lord has become for us when he gave out in prayer (c.545) a powerful shout and shed many tears[11] and 'he was afflicted in his prayer until

10. Cf. Mt 4:8-10; Lk 4:5-8
11. Heb 5:7

his sweat became like drops of blood;[12] and then a protector came and an angel appeared to him, strengthening him and saving him as [if he had only been] a man'.[13]

The Perfecter was perfected so that all who followed his example would be perfected. For it was not that he was not perfect—he who is able to perfect all if he so desires—nor even was he subject to sin so that he prayed to be saved and be perfected, nor that he needed the power of his angel, who is his own creation, to come and strengthen him while he was praying to make the time of affliction pass away. Rather, our Lord took on our image in these things because we are under the servitude of sin and death, and through these many afflictions of sin he showed us how to climb this step.

For there is no other ascent to this step that athletes may cross in battle except by this ascent that our Lord has shown us: with much watching and fasting, lowliness, and powerful crying out with many tears, much supplication and with the sweat (c.548) of afflictions; and, then our Lord will come and save us according to that example which was written, 'An angel came to the aid of our Lord and appeared to him, strengthening him as [if he were only] a human being'.[14] Because of these and similar things in the conduct of our Lord, Paul wrote, 'The Lord of creation took the form of a servant while he was in the form of a human being, his creation',[15] for the sake of his creation, so that all flesh might observe his death and his submission. For so it was written, 'Our Lord made such supplication, while he did not need to, much prayer and severe prostrations',[16] and 'then his angel appeared to him'.[17] Our Lord rested from this hard battle, snatched victory from death, and lifted up the crown of his victory. He showed people how to defeat and snatch victory from death.

---

12. Lk 22:44
13. Lk 22:40
14. Lk 22:43
15. Ph 2:7
16. Heb 5:7
17. Lk 22:43

9.   So you see, my son, how our Lord became an example for us. See how he went back and forth praying and rousing his disciples so that they might see how he triumphed and [how] they might win like him. For if he himself had had need of prayer, he would have prayed by himself, and he would have been heard as he was in fact heard. But so that he might make everyone know that he himself had no need of prayer, he went back and forth (c.549) to his disciples and roused them to teach them how they should pray like him, as he had taught them fasting and battle in his forty days' fast and in his battle with Satan, being tempted by [Satan] as if he were a human being. Our Lord was patient in order to be an example for us to imitate.

Moreover, see how much our Lord prolonged his prayer; in this way he wrestled mightily in his prayer so that from evening until that time when the cock crowed, when the crucifiers seized him, 'he prayed intensely and went back and forth three times to his disciples and said to them, "Stay awake and pray lest you enter into temptation"'.[18] See how I pray and I win; you should pray like this and defeat death and sin.

Sin fought during that night with the disciples, and lulled them with the burden of sleep and anxiety, in that [our Lord] had said to them, 'Today I will be delivered up'.[19] In this way, [sin] burdened them and did not allow them to see how our Lord wrestled in his prayer. Our Lord had it written down about the struggle he had made with death and placed it in the New Testament so we might act like him and conquer as he had conquered. But, nevertheless, every (c.552) day our Lord had wrestled in this way with powerful groaning and tears, with great supplication and many prostrations.

18. Mt 26:39-41
19. Mt 26:2, 21

10.   Supplication, as we have demonstrated above, is the patience [we have] when we bow down for a long time before our Lord and pray and request of him. A prostration occurs when a person is patient, bowing down and standing before our Lord and worshipping him spiritually many times; this is what our Lord then did when he led his disciples, going out to the mountain away from the great crowd, and showed them how to fast and pray, defeat death and kill sin, and to teach these things to others, as our Lord had taught them.

Therefore, our Lord acted in this way for a long time in front of his disciples, praying and crying out in his prayer even though he had no need [to do so], except in order to give us an example to imitate. For on that particular night he went back and forth to his disciples, since he would be seized during it. He roused them to stand up and keep vigil with him and to see how the deliverer comes to him, (c.553) strengthening and helping him to conquer, so that in this way when they were as diligent as our Lord himself, the deliverer would come to them, who is our Lord, and rescue them and all who imitate this exhortation of our Lord, his lowliness, and his poverty: 'There was no place for him to lay down his head on earth'.[20] He walked on the earth as a stranger and an alien as long as God walked among people as a human being.

So then, if the deliverer had not openly appeared to our Lord, that would have irked us and we would have said, 'Is a person abandoned in this way until he departs from this world, and [only] later will he be rescued from sin?' The deliverer does not come to this world, but do we depart from this world such as we are? But as it is, the deliverer openly appeared to our Lord and to his apostles and everyone was comforted, as it is written, 'When the apostles had prayed and made supplication as our Lord had

20. Mt 8:20

shown them, the place in which they were shone and the odor of the sweetness of the Spirit, the Paraclete, forcefully came upon them'.[21]

Therefore, in the case of every one of us (c.556) to whom the Paraclete did not come as to our Lord and the apostles, and the odor of its sweetness did not diffuse, it is because one was not rescued from evil thoughts and his heart was not purified from sin, and we should understand that the deliverer has not yet come to him. Instead, let him walk in the steps of our Lord Jesus and imitate him and impoverish and empty himself, and let him pray like him and fast continually; [then] look, the Victor and the Savior will come to him, as he came to our Lord. And see, he will become great and be glorified in the manner in which our Lord magnifies all his listeners and his friends with his great love.

For our Lord answers those who keep his words, as David said, 'Answer your servant so that I may live and keep your words. Open my eyes that I may see the wonders that are in your law. I am a sojourner with you; do not hide from me your commandments, because my soul desired and longed for your judgment at all times.'[22] You see how our Lord answers those who confess to him in prayer, 'We do all your perfect will and we become sojourners with him'. He opens their eyes, and seeing his glory and comprehending (c.557) all his truth, they explain the wonders in his law and he does not hide from them the truth of his commandments. On account of this they impoverish themselves, longing all the time for that great day of judgment of our Lord, and are not afraid of that judgment to come. For our Lord saved and exalted them so that these who have done the perfect will of our Lord might judge the wicked ones on that great day of judgment.

21. Ac 2:2
22. Ps 119:17-20

11. Our Lord, even though he was not in need of prayer, prayed—was heard and perfected—and the deliverer came to him even though he was not subject [to anyone]. Therefore, if our Lord [prayed] while not needing prayer, since he had no sin and no lord to whom he should pray, for he was not subject [to anyone], but is in his person the savior of all who seek and wait for him, [how much more ought we to pray].

Therefore, if our Lord, while not needing to, labored and fasted and prayed, how much more ought we to pray—even more than when our Lord prayed—and to fast continually, as he had said, 'You will defeat this kind of Satan [only] with fasting'.[23] How much more ought we to cry out, even more than (c.560) when he cried out with power and many tears, because we are in need since sin still resides within us. Our Lord was not in need in the same way, for there was no sin in him as there is in us.

From this point let us understand that our Lord had no need of a savior, but was the savior for himself and for all who took refuge in him. For in this way, it was written,

> Sing to the Lord a new song, because he
> has done a wonderful thing. His right hand
> and holy arm saved him. The Lord has
> shown his salvation and has revealed his
> righteousness in the sight of the nations.
> He has remembered his grace and his faith
> to the house of Israel. And all the ends of
> the world have seen the salvation of our God.
> Praise the Lord, all the earth. Exult and
> break forth in singing and praising. Sing to
> the Lord with lyres and with the sound of
> music.[24]

You see that our Lord did not have need of the deliver-

23. Mt 17:21   24. Ps 98:1-5

ance of angels: 'Look, his right hand and his holy arm saved him'. See, my child, what the prophet said, 'The Lord showed his salvation and revealed his righteousness before the eyes of the nations'. You see that he emphatically demonstrated to us how one should fight with Satan and defeat him, and see (c.561) how he revealed his righteousness to us so that we might imitate him. He made supplication with prayer and beseeched with a powerful cry like a person in whom sin remains, even though our Lord was holy, as it was written.

12. Therefore, our Lord shows us how a person might become pure from sin. Notice how he died on account of sinners and if it were not on account of us—so that he might teach us how to fight with Satan—he could have breathed on [Satan] and made him cease [to exist]. See how, on account of us, he lowered himself in order to fight against Satan, an unworthy fox. For just as when a righteous person is seized, condemned to death on account of God, and the Lord sees him, turning away so that he may endure a little suffering and be victorious, that person, seeing that there is no one who will help him, is filled with sadness and cries for his murderers so that they may not be killed on account of him. In this way, our Lord desired to be afflicted by evil people and endure sufferings, and his heart was filled with sadness for our iniquity. This is due to his love for his creature [and his desire to save it] from perishing. Because, in this way, he had a means whereby you might be convinced and turn around to the house of life. In the same way, our Lord was sad for his betrayers and crucifiers and he wept and prayed with tears for them so that he might become for us an example and that we should pray for our murderers (c.564) with tears and should request from him[25] as he had requested from his Father to forgive his murderers, because he and his Father are one

25. Variant reading from Ms E (British Library Add. 14621, A.D. 802).

in each other and the Holy Spirit is one in them. Whenever he said, 'Forgive them',[26] it was to teach us also to say what he had said to his Father.

13. See how our Lord persisted and became an example for us in everything: even how we should defeat evil and sin, [and] how we should defeat evil people who come upon us in iniquity.

> May you be patient and pray for them so that they may live. If they repent, look, they will be ashamed of their faults and will come to you and be saved. But if they do not repent, remaining in their wickedness, be comforted in this: that on that day of judgment I will reveal myself in my glory, and you will be glorified with me before all creation and they shall be humbled before me and before all creation of the heavenly beings and those below. However, you shall not rejoice in their ruin, but pray for them that they might be raised up.[27]

Look, my child, notice that while our Lord did not need one of these, for our sake he desired to become needy. That is, on account of his great love for us, he wished (c.565) to save us, and, on account of us, he endured everything to teach us how we may defeat the cruel lord whom we had earlier acquired through our freedom by the transgression of the commandment that Adam and Eve had transgressed against the word of him who gives life to all and feeds all with his mercy. Glory be to him, Amen.

14. But let us also know this: if a person does not become poor and empty himself and sanctify and lower himself,

26. Lk 23:34   27. Apocryphal

according to that example that our Lord showed us in that he kept all the commandments and loved those who hate him and his murderers and prayed for them with mercy, he will not be perfected and become great.

If we do not pray as our Lord prayed with crying out and with tears and making supplication for a long time, the deliverer will not come to us. Our Lord said,

> If you love me, keep my commandments[28] as I have kept the commandments of God,[29] and you will remain in his love, as I have kept the commandments of my Father. I will love you and my Father and I will come to you.[30] I will make you my brothers and my abode and the place of my rest[31] and I will lead you to me and I will not leave you orphans.[32]

Therefore, while we are attaining Perfection, if we do not make supplication and are not afflicted in prayer as our Lord had done, (c.568) we will not be perfected and the deliverer will not come to us. If the deliverer does not come, sin will not be redeemed. And if sin is not redeemed, evil thoughts will not be removed from the heart. If [evil] thoughts are not taken away, the heart will not be purified. If the heart is not purified, our hands will not be raised with purity. If we do not raise our hands purely along with our heart,[33] being full of love for every person and the love of our Lord, we will not be able to enter with our Lord into his bridal chamber, even if we stand beside his bridal chamber. As it is written, 'The king entered to see the guests, but he saw there a person who did not have the fine garments

28. Jn 14:15
29. Jn 15:10
30. Jn 14:21
31. Jn 5:23: literally, 'the house of my dwelling'.
32. Jn 5:18
33. 1 Tm 2:8

appropriate for that wealthy feast and for that glorified bridegroom. The bridegroom commanded his servants to bind up his hands and feet and cast him into the outer darkness',[34] because he had dared to enter while his heart was not pure.

But the wedding garments of the Lord's feast are the purity of a perfect heart, as it is written, 'Blessed are those who are pure in their heart, for they will see God'[35] so that they might enter the bridal chamber of our Lord Jesus, our king and our glory, (c.569) our crown and our kingdom; and see his face inside his bridal chamber and dwell with him and be glorified and refreshed with him. Because they suffered with him and loved him, they will rejoice with him and be comforted and glorified in his light, the inheritance, and in the place he chose and prepared for them, which is better than all the [other] places of the house of life.

15.   Even though there are many places prepared for every person according to his works, that place is exalted and not everyone will be able to climb it, as our Lord has said, 'Not everyone is able to comprehend this word'.[36] That is, not everyone accomplishes things worthy of this word. 'Whoever does not lift up his cross and journey in my footsteps and in my ways of life is not worthy of me.'[37]

From then on will not people beat themselves once they have gone into that world, and see that they are to be deprived of the presence of our Lord and of that city of his glory, because he had already told them here? Therefore, whoever wishes to see the face of our Lord and dwell with him must take up his cross and imitate him in this world, so that once he has departed from this world, he may be with our Lord, as Paul said in the Spirit, 'When we depart from (c.572) the body we will be with our Lord'.[38].

34. Mt 22:11
35. Mt 5:8
36. Mt 19:11

37. Mt 10:38
38. 2 Co 5:6

But if you do not know how to carry the cross and walk in the footsteps and ways of our Lord, read the Gospel, come to this *mēmrā*, and you will learn. Ask whoever knows and he will show you. Or, lower yourself and make supplication before our Lord and he will reveal [it] to you. Be humble with everyone, for where you would least expect, you might find there a people of knowledge who can show you the way of our Lord Jesus, for the disciples of our Lord are despised, lowly, and mean in their appearance.

Just as our Lord established the Perfect ones on the earth, so his Perfect ones establish [other] perfect ones on earth in our Lord, because it is through them that our Lord creates Perfect ones. If everyone had been capable of hearing the Holy Spirit, our Lord would not have appeared physically as a human being, nor also would he have sent the prophets and the apostles to be his preachers and to show people his truth and glory. Paul said the following, 'This is my labor and my struggle according to the energy that works powerfully in me: to present every person perfect in Christ'.[39] As Christ established and perfected us by his power, (c.573) so I will hurry to present every person perfect in Christ. And so, I will run so that I may reach the thing on account of which he reached me.

Therefore, 'Do not despise one of these least',[40] because perhaps through him you shall come to receive Perfection from our Lord Jesus Christ, king of glory. Praise be to the Father and to the Son and to the Holy Spirit, the Trinity without division, forever and ever. Amen.

16. Concerning the feast of which I have spoken: the king who gave the feast for his son[41] is the King, the Lord; and his son is our Lord Jesus, our heavenly king. The feast represents the kingdom of our Lord. The guests are all the apostles and the prophets. But this is the invitation—the

39. Col 1:29, 28   41. Mt 22:2
40. Mt 18:10

Father desires to reconcile all people through his Son. Their arrival to the feast indicates that whoever repents will be received, whether 'the good or the bad'.[42] That is, our invitation is the one that summons them in this world with plenty of time to get dressed with fine garments, which are excellent actions, and to go to that feast, which is the kingdom of our Lord.

But these guests who excused themselves[43] are the people who excused themselves from the arrival of our Lord and did not desire to believe in him. These (c.576) who entered and were received wearing fine wedding garments are the ones who believed in our Lord and kept his commandments and did all of his acceptable and perfect will. The one who entered but was thrown out and had to leave represents these who believed in our Lord, but did not keep all his commandments, and carried his body and his blood to condemnation, as it is written, 'Whoever eats the body of the Lord and drinks his blood while not being worthy of him will carry [this disgrace] to the judgment and the fire that burns on the day of Judgment'.[44] But they will never be able to enter the kingdom on that day of Judgment and then depart from it.

But those who entered are those who believed in our Lord and are baptized in his name. Those who have left are those whom our Lord will reject on that day of judgment and they continue in their evil works for they have not kept his commandments just like that man dressed in filthy garments, which are the evil deeds of human beings.

17.   Now listen to me and let us prepare good works that are the wedding garments received as [proper] garments at the house of our Lord. Our Lord invites every person, the rich and the poor, despising no one, but receives the good and the bad, everyone who repents (c.577) and turns back

42. Mt 22:2
43. Lk 14:18
44. 1 Co 11:27

to him. On that great day of Judgment, there will be his treasury from which he will reward every person according to his deeds. He answers directly whoever keeps his words and seeks him, just as the Holy Spirit appointed David and said, 'The Lord will appear in his glory and will regard the prayer of the poor and not despise their prayer. May this be written for another generation, [so that] a people [still] to be born may praise the Lord. Because he looked out from his holy height from the heavens, the Lord looked at the earth to hear the groaning of the prisoner and to set the children free from death.'[45]

You see how the Lord regards the prayer of the poor, neither despising their prayer nor their supplication. That is why this will be recorded so that people may see it up until the final generation and they will seek from God his truth. 'He will reveal to them the depth of wealth of the wisdom of Jesus Christ',[46] and they will believe in him and say the following, 'Hear, O God, our prayer and do not turn away from our supplication; listen to us and answer us and regard our groaning and hear us because of our enemy and because of the difficulty of sin'.[47] They will say patiently:

> Be merciful to us, O God, according to your grace and the greatness of your mercy, blot out our sins. Wash us thoroughly from our iniquity and purify us from our sins. (c.580) For, we know our faults and our sins are always against us. Against you only, Lord, have we sinned and done evil things before you. My Lord, see how sin is mingled in us from the womb, but you desired truth. You have taught us the hidden things of your wisdom and we have been justified by your

45. Ps 102:16-21
46. Rm 11:33
47. Pr 55:1-3

word. Sprinkle the hyssop of your mercy upon us, purify and make us clean with it and whiten us more than snow. Turn your face from our iniquities and observe our lowliness and our repentance. Blot out our faults and give us your gladness and joy and let our bones, which were humbled before your brightness, rejoice.[48]

Let that old person who was corrupted by lusts of error be humbled in truth. Let us put on that new person who will be renewed by good works in imitation of our Lord Jesus Christ who created him. Our bones will be humbled until our Lord listens to us, answering and turning us toward him, binding us with his mercy and redeeming us from the oppression of the bondage of death, and creating in us a pure heart and renewing in us his steadfast spirit.

We will become a new creature and will praise our Lord who has had compassion on us in the later generation. 'For he looked down from his holy height and heard our groanings, we who were imprisoned (c.581) in the bondage of death.'[49] He has adopted and saved us from the hard oppression of death and 'he has returned the children to their own countries.'[50] That is, they will become the people who will be a new creature in Christ in the purity of the heart just as Adam was before he sinned and transgressed against the commandment of his Creator. These children who return to their countries are the ones whose heart is purified from sin and love everyone.

The end of the twentieth *Mēmrā* on the difficult steps that are on the road of the city of our Lord.

---

48. Ps 51:1-9
49. Ps 102:20
50. Jr 31:17

Mēmrā Twenty-One

ON THE
TREE OF ADAM

Summary: Jesus, the Tree of Life, is the fulfillment of what Adam was meant to be in the Garden before he sinned. Perfection recaptures the status of Adam and Eve possessed before the Fall. (c.584)

1.   Now I will begin to explain about the good tree, how it exists and how it stands, and concerning the tree of the knowledge of good and evil, which is the evil one, toil, anxiety, and the thought of transitory things by which Adam and Eve tasted death. For through it they came to know evil, which they had not known. After they ate from it they knew evil, which is death, [which] they had not known. After they obeyed the evil one and observed the earth and saw this thing on [the earth] and loved it, evil had power over them and they knew it, as it is written, 'On the day when you transgress against my word, you shall surely die'.[1]

Because (c.585) God had only taught what is good to Adam and Eve when he created them, they did not know evil until they had obeyed Satan and he taught them evil. Because of this Satan is called the 'Tree', through which Adam and Eve knew evil and good. They learned good

1. Gn 2:17

231

from God, and evil from Satan. They became 'knowers of good and evil'[2] and from there the enmity of impiety bound Adam and his children.

Because of this, God said to them, 'Do not eat from the tree of the knowledge of good and evil',[3] that is, do not listen to it because it will teach you all sorts of evil things and take you away from heavenly things and from the kindness of your Creator. It will bind you up in transitory things and in toil, anxiety, and pride; and it will make you renounce your Creator and slay one another. You will become children of the curse and children of darkness and [the Tree] will become a lord over you and feed you the poison of death.

And look, today the children of Adam still eat with the hardness of their heart from this tree, which makes known [to them] evil and teaches them to be bound on the earth by transitory things. Now they are bound and strangled by anxiety and the thought of these transient things because they have not lowered themselves (c.588) and sanctified and emptied themselves of those things that pass away with the earth. The whole [reason] why they are bound to the earth is because they have not emptied themselves of it. Neither do they learn from God nor from a person of God how they may be bound up with our Lord in that world in which there is no death where they will eat the life-giving words of our Lord. They shall eat our Lord and live and become great and be perfected through him.[4]

2.   Therefore, if you wish to be saved from the death of the Tree, which has killed our father Adam and us as well, and, moreover, [if] you do not wish to die, renounce and distance yourself from Satan and his teaching: that is, from Satan, from everything evil, from the world, from its anxiety, and from everything that Jesus had said to abandon through lowliness, prayer, and fasting while keeping the commandments.

2. Gn 3:5   3. Gn 2:17   4. Jn 6:58

Moreover, I will explain what the teaching of the evil one is, who harms the Upright ones because they are held fast in this world by transitory things and are far removed from the Perfect, for [the Perfect by contrast] are spiritually bound in that world of light. I will explain how God first commanded Adam to become a perfect saint, just like the watchers and angels in heaven, so that while living physically on the earth, being stripped (c.589) of everything in it, he might dwell spiritually in heaven with the angels while his mind is clothed with the glory of his Creator and the earth is not seen by him.

The good tree, in that world of light invisible to the eyes of flesh, is our Lord Jesus. He is the tree of life who gives everything life by its fruits wherever the perfect will of God is, as our Lord said, 'Pray so that the will of God might be on earth as it is in heaven'.[5] That is, as there is quiet and peace and harmony between the great and the small, making a joyful noise together, and there is no one there who is superior to one smaller than him, nor one who despises someone greater than him, so pray that all people may become like this.

3.   The fruits of that good tree are these spiritual fruits of which the apostle spoke, 'Let us cling to the Spirit and submit ourselves to it, and let us not be vainglorious, making light of each other and envying one another for evil [purposes]'.[6] Everyone who imitates [our Lord] yields these fruits and becomes perfect. 'It is excellent to be jealous for good things at all times.'[7] But these spiritual fruits are: 'Let us put on mercy, pity, harmony, peace, and the glory of our Lord';[8] that is, let us submit ourselves to one another through these spiritual fruits with love, patience, kindness, lowliness, endurance, moderation, (c.592) and holiness without desire. These are the spiritual fruits on which the

5. Mt 6:10   7. Tt 2:14
6. Ga 5:25-26   8. Col 3:12

saints feed in Eden while separating these from the [commandments] that are hard for infants, so that may see these and, leaving [alone] the hard [commandments], cling to things that are humble. As the apostle said, 'Choose things that are humble and associate with them'.9 'Conduct yourself in these things', the Creator commanded Adam, 'your mind being in heaven as an inhabitant, but your body being on earth as a stranger and a sojourner. Above, serve and glorify [me] by these deeds as an angel among angels.'

That you were originally thus, our Lord and his apostles witness, for they came and showed the children of Adam [what] to do after he who was raised up had broken down by means of this way of life the fence of enmity, which stood between him and people. The apostle pointed out, saying, 'Everything is made new again in Christ',10 as [God] had wanted Adam to become, and as he had been created before he transgressed against the commandment.

The latter will of our Lord matched the original one, the one of which I have spoken. See what is similar between the latter and the former: in the former, our Lord made Adam without anxiety and without [evil] thoughts; and in the latter, our Lord and his apostles commanded, 'Become without anxiety and without (c.593) [evil] thoughts'.11 The former, God created Adam pure; and the latter, he commanded in the same way, 'You must become pure in your heart and you will be happy'.12 He spoke in this way to Adam while he had not yet transgressed against the commandment, lest he obey the evil one and desire the earth and all in it. The latter will witness from above, 'Whoever does not get far away from the evil one and abandon everything on earth and look into heaven while being crucified will not attain that thing which Adam lost'.

4.   When the apostle said that Christ has come again to make everything new13—as he has wished that Adam

9. Rm 12:16   11. 1 Co 7:32   13. Ep 1:10
10. Ep 1:10   12. Mt 5:8

and Eve might remain—understand that God desired that people conduct themselves according to these commandments of Perfection, which I have explained to you above, and according to these spiritual fruits, which the apostle distinguished from the fleshly,[14] God was wanting human beings to conduct themselves just as [God] desires today. The whole [reason] why Christ came and lowered himself was in order to teach us how we might lower ourselves in imitation of him and to show [us] that original truth. It is written, 'He approached and was tempted [by Satan]'[15] in order to show us how Adam was tempted in the first place. It is written, 'He defeated Satan'[16] in order to show us how if Adam had wished by a [single] word, he would have been able to demolish [Satan], as God had overthrown him by that word to which he did not listen when [Satan] cajoled him to look out over the earth like Adam (c.596) so that he might lust for the wealth of the earth and its transitory beauty as Adam and Eve had yearned for.

They exchanged heaven for earth and left heaven and loved the earth. They exchanged that thing that does not pass away and is imperishable and acquired what passes away and is perishable. They exchanged the perfect original for the shadow, as the apostle said, 'Everything visible is a shadow of that thing that is invisible and does not pass away'.[17]

Just as neither the ministry that Moses showed to the Israelites nor the Tabernacle were the perfect reality, but are a shadow, as it is written, 'That true sanctuary that Jesus Christ entered first before us, so that in his footsteps we might also enter into it, is in the heavenly heights'.[18]

As Paul said, 'I know a man who was carried away above the third heaven to the spiritual paradise'.[19] The whole

14. Ga 5:22
15. Mt 4:3
16. Mt 4:10-11
17. Col 2:17
18. Heb 9:24
19. 2 Co 12:2-4

[reason] why he said 'a man' was so that he might not boast that it was he, because it is not advantageous for a person to boast, 'I am perfect', not even when he is perfect. However, he should condemn himself with sinners before everyone and think less of himself than all who are on the earth lest he not be lifted up and fall like Adam. But now, that one who trod out for us (c.597) the road to the heights does not wish that we live in the shadows, but cling to that perfect reality, 'Seek what is above and think about what is above where Christ sits in the heavenly heights'.[20]

5.   Therefore, see that that thing that the Lord desired at first is what he also desired at the last. Because of this he said, 'I am the first and I am the last';[21] that is, my great and perfect will, the first and the last. May a person not become earthly, nor return to the earth, but may he become heavenly and his mind die from the earth. Just as Paul had died from all there is on the earth and said, 'If you have died from the uses of the world, why do you conduct yourself like those alive in trade and commerce, these things by which no one is perfected, unless a person dies from the world?'[22]

If they say to him, 'You eat and drink and talk', he will answer them, 'Those who speak in this way are dead from the world. Food and clothing are given in abundance.'[23] This word that I speak, 'No longer is it I who am alive, but Christ is alive in me who speaks in me'.[24] It is in the word of Christ that I stand, sit, eat, and drink, go to sleep and am awakened. Not with foreign speech nor with senile tales,[25] (c.600) nor with stories that are useless for Perfection, nor with accounts of commerce nor with transitory wealth, but Christ is alive in me who thinks about what is is in heaven and not what is on the earth.

20. Col 3:1-2
21. Is 44:6; Rv 18:17
22. Col 2:20
23. Mt 6:33
24. Ga 2:20
25. 1 Tm 4:1

6.   See how Paul died from everything visible that is the opposite of Perfection, which pursues something that is invisible to fleshly eyes. For, he was not even living by food and clothing, because he was not anxious for something visible. But while considering what is above, sometimes he was hungry and sometimes he was naked without clothes, as he said, 'I am trained in everything, in famine and in plenty, in cold and nakedness,²⁶ in honor and in dishonor with many torments.²⁷ For while half of the world curses us and half blesses us with blessings and curses, while we love everyone, and in the sight of everyone we are disinherited as imposters, still we are true.'²⁸

7.   Therefore, Adam lived at first according to the perfect will of God. This one who came, Jesus, showed to whoever wishes how to imitate him and be perfected. He looked into heaven and not on earth and rejoiced with the heavenly angels without anxiety and pains, and was neither concerned about clothing nor food. But God fed him, as (c.601) it was appropriate to the wealth of his kindness with heavenly bread, as it is written, 'A human being has eaten the bread of the angels'.²⁹ They did not have this labor and the pains of childhood and of the body, as David explained, 'Because people rendered bitter the word of God',³⁰ which is what he said to them, 'Do not transgress against my commandments', and 'they rejected the counsel of the Most High',³¹ in which he desired that we become like angels. Because of this 'he discouraged them with labor and they became ill and there was no one to help them'.³² But if they had kept the commandments of our Lord and made supplication to him, the Father would

26. 2 Co 11:27
27. 2 Co 6:5
28. 2 Co 6:8
29. Ps 78:25
30. Ps 107:11
31. Ps 107:11
32. Ps 107:12

have reconciled with them in his Son and saved them on account of his name and with the love of our Lord Jesus Christ.

And so our Lord would have made for them children as he had made Eve from Adam, without lust and without marriage, or if he had wanted he could have made children by the hairs of their heads or by their finger nails, and the people would have become the images of angels. He who created them would have prepared food for them [if] he had wanted without labor. He would have carried their burden, as our Lord said, 'Do not be anxious for your body or for your soul, because that one who created you is greatly concerned about you'.[33] Therefore, 'Cast down your anxiety upon the Lord and he will nourish, comfort, and keep you'.[34]

(c.604) Thus people would have been on earth physically and in heaven spiritually until it pleased their Creator to elevate them to on high. Nothing on earth would have harmed them: neither reptile, nor wild beast, nor Satan, if their [free] will had not wished to listen to the reptile and Satan.[35] For he said to them on the day he created them, 'I will throw the fear and dread of you upon all that exists on the earth'.[36] The hand of the Lord was on Adam and the hand of Adam tamed all there was on the earth beneath him by the power of our omnipotent Lord. They were created without earthly passions; that is, let us not place weakness upon God because he wanted it this way, but his will was not [effected] as he desired.

8.   It was not the case that Adam and his children vanquished God, but through his grace and kindness [God] gave them freedom and choice in order not to subjugate them like the rest of the other subjugated creatures who do not have the freedom that Adam had, nor will they come to judgment, for they do not have either a soul or freedom as

33. Mt 6:25   35. Gn 3:1ff
34. Ps 55:2-3; 1 Pt 5:7   36. Gn 9:2

Adam had. For if [God] had desired to limit their freedom, as in the gesture of the blinking of an eye, he could have brought them to his will. However, [God] gave Adam freedom and established for him a law for the aid of his soul (c.605) lest he let go of heaven and inherit the earth. For he held him back from labor, anxiety, and evil, but not from Perfection and heaven.

In order that you are assured that the earth was not visible to [Adam and Eve] because they did not even know that their bodies were naked, but as it is written, 'Adam and Eve were naked and their nakedness was not apparent to them'.[37] But after they ate from the tree, that is, after they had abandoned heaven and loved the earth, their mind came from heaven to their bodies, [and] then they saw that they were naked. For they were in heaven while they were walking on the earth. They were speaking by their bodies as our Lord had shown them in this last will of which he spoke, 'I have come so that I may carry out your will, O God',[38] that one that Adam had done away with at creation. He said concerning this last will that it is similar to that first one, 'The spirit blows wherever it wills and you will hear its voice', [and] 'in this way are those who are born of the Spirit, and as you can only hear the voice of the Spirit, you will not know from where it comes, nor where it will go'.[39]

In this way, the voice of Adam and Eve was heard by their bodies, while their mind stood before God in heaven. Like today, there are spiritual people who speak with worldly people, while (c.608) watching the majesty of our Lord, how much it is humbled, and their mind is with our Lord in heaven. While they are praying on earth, their voice departs from their bodies, [and] they are looking spiritually into heaven, [seeing] whatever is born of the Spirit,[40] and resembling our Lord in lowliness. While they are in heaven like this, because they have lowered themselves and

37. Gn 2:25
38. Heb 10:7; Ps 40:8
39. Jn 3:8
40. Jn 3:6

renounced everything visible, they turn their vision and
mind to what is above. But if they desire to be haughty and
return to the earth in order to possess and use it, they will
remain and the door will be closed in their faces. They will
depart from the heavenly Jerusalem just like Adam from
the spiritual Eden, which is the spiritual Jerusalem, the city
of God. Therefore, by a similar explanation that we have
[already] given, the mind of Adam was in heaven purely
and sweetly with these spiritual fruits that the apostle had
explained.[41]

9.   But when the deceitful one approached Eve and
Adam through his deception, he seduced them as he would
have seduced Jesus, and said to the Creator of the Uni-
verse, 'Look, see how the earth is attractive with its possession and its kingdoms. Listen to me and take possession
and rule and you will not become poor and empty yourself
and become a stranger on the earth.' Our Lord said to him,
'Go behind me, Satan'.[42] Immediately, his battle and temptation wasted away (c.609) and he was overthrown and
vanished.

     In this way he also seduced Adam with deceit and
approached him as someone concerned [for him] and a
bearer of [his] burden and he counseled Eve to advise Adam
and commanded her to speak to Adam so that he might
acquire wealth and become a king. 'Look, gold and silver
are on the earth and all sorts of pleasures. Possess and
enjoy yourself; rule, increase, and multiply', the evil one
counseled. 'Cast off from yourself asceticism and renunciation and holiness, also lowliness, and know evil as well
as good things and grow and become like God who created
you.'[43] Eve advised Adam, 'That rebel advised us well, if as
much because he preceded us and is older than us, he
knows'. Adam said to Eve, 'Go back and say to him, "Our
Creator commanded us not to obey you, nor eat from [the

41. Ga 5:22ff   42. Mt 4:8; Lk 4:6; Mt 4:10   43. Gn 1:28

tree], nor be united with earthly things"; that is, we should not labor or possess anything on the earth.' The tongue [of the evil one] again persuaded [Eve], 'Because [God] did not wish and was not content that you become like him'. Adam said, 'If he does not desire that we become like this, will he not punish us because we have dared [to do this]?'⁴⁴ The evil one said, 'When you become like him, what can he do to you?' (c.612)

10. See, O man, what [kind of] thought Adam had about the one who created him from dust and mingled him with the heavenly angels. Adam and Eve listened in the hope that they would become like their Creator. For Paul had said, 'The creatures were subjugated to vanity, not by their own will, but on account of the one who subjugated them in hope'.⁴⁵ That is, not of their own accord did they think this, but by the counsel of others.

However, in the end, Adam had a will, and if he had not so desired, the evil one would not have oppressed him [during] the thousand years he lived on the earth. Therefore, Adam and Eve were persuaded and turned their minds to the earth and descended from heaven, and their mind was on the earth like their bodies. They decided to descend from the heavenly Paradise that is the perfect original, and lived on the earth that is the shadow of what is invisible to the eyes of the flesh; that is, the shadow of that heavenly Paradise. Adam descended and stood in the earthly paradise that is the shadow of heaven. They became poor from the supernal wealth and departed to pursue the lower wealth, which is whatever passes away and is dissolved in one hour.

Not (c.613) before God cursed them had they labored on the earth, but immediately after they accepted the counsel of the evil one and despised the word of God, [God] cursed them and they departed from the spiritual Paradise.⁴⁶

44. Gn 3:1-5   45. Rm 8:20   46. Gn 3:17

Then they worked the earth from which they were created for the sake of transitory wealth. After they saw that they were naked, after their mind stripped off that higher glory, they went on to worry about clothing because they knew the shame that had been invisible to them while they were looking at heaven.⁴⁷ They saw that the heavenly bread was withheld and went on to labor on the earth for food and were all alone. They were separated from the angels and the great hosts, these who surround the keepers of the commandments, but not those who despise the word of God. They went on to desire [conjugal] union and to give birth like the animals. They looked at the earth and imitated it so that they did not consider their higher honor⁴⁸ or their intimacy and their love with the heavenly angels.

11.   Adam and Eve desired all these things but were humbled through the mediation of the evil one and they abandoned heaven and the heavenly wealth and loved the earth and all that is in it. However, Adam and Eve were naked without this visible clothing in this world. Adam and Eve had been like this (c.616) before they had sinned, and it was not that they did not know they had sinned by their rebellion. In this they, however, were foolish for they had hoped to become like God. They erred because there is nothing that is able to become like the Creator of all the worlds, that one who is the Creator, and who is our Lord Jesus Christ. But God saw and averted [his eyes] and was patient and forbearing while Adam despised his words and broke his commandments and sought to usurp, to become the equal of God in majesty, but not in lowliness.

Because of this the apostle said, 'Christ did not by force desire to become the equal of God like Adam, but he emptied himself,⁴⁹ even from this thing that Adam loved and sought to become God through earthly wealth. He took the example of a servant while he was in the image of that

47. Gn 3:7   48. Ps 49:20   49. Ph 2:6

creation of the first human being, through his obedience, his love and his lowliness so that he might show us how a person becomes a brother and a son and an heir and a neighbor, for [God] desired ungrudgingly that the earthly ones dwell with him, 'He took the image of servant so that he might obey his father like a servant'—not in the way Adam took the image of majesty in order to be the opposite and adversary to his Lord and Creator and to sit opposite him and resist him.

For nothing brought down Adam on the day he fell, except the pride by which he desired to become (c.617) the equal of God in his majesty. Too much [pride] forced him to depart from the Paradise of the Kingdom and humbled him down to earth. My brothers, let us flee from pride lest we become salt whose flavor is lost, for it is not useful even for fertilizer,[50] because it does not have any taste in order to salt from it offerings[51] and no field is fertilized by it nor is any wheat produced by it as our Lord said, 'Whoever exalts himself - like Adam - will be humbled; and whoever humbles himself—like Jesus—will be exalted, just as he was exalted'.[52]

12.   On account of the pride of Adam, God closed the doors of Paradise before him, that is, the doors of heaven. Therefore, just as with the pride of Adam God made him depart from Paradise, so by his lowliness [God] will make him enter, that is, he will make him ascend to the higher heavens, where God dwells and is visible there.

For he said, 'With what will you try to appease me after you have angered me? With possessions or with offerings of dumb animals? My own sacrifice from now on, my reconciliation, will, and rest is the person gentle and lowly in spirit upon whom I look and in whom I dwell. He will ascend with me when I ascend to the place of my rest'.[53]

50. Mt 5:13
51. Lv 2:13

52. Mt 23:12; Lk 14:11
53. Is 66:2ff

Again he said, 'God chose Moses because he was the humblest of all people'.[54] Lowliness (c.620) was weighed with everything and it was heavy. For God weighed Moses against six hundred thousand swordsmen with their wives and children and placed that lowly one on one side of the scale. Harshness and pride weighed light, and lowliness and gentleness were heavy. The Lord said to him, 'Go out from among this people and I will lay them waste in one hour'. But Moses said, 'If you are going to blot them out, blot me out with them'.[55] And [God] said, 'No, Moses. I will blot out [only] whoever has sinned against me'. Moses said, 'No, my Lord. If you forgive them as you forgave them from Egypt until now, [good,] but if not blot me out with them'.[56] Because of this, Moses became great for he had placed his soul with the sinners who were sinning every day. 'Forgive them as you forgave them from [the time] inside Egypt until today. He loved the sinners as himself and did not separate himself from them.'

13.   In the same way, only Noah pleased [the Lord], 'Because I have seen that you only are guileless and the most humble of all the earth'.[57] The Lord said to him, 'Go out from among them, because I will blot out all flesh I have created because all flesh has corrupted its way'.[58] Noah said, 'No, forbid it that you would destroy all the earth'. (c.621) The Lord said to him, 'Look, I will place all the earth on the scale with you. If they weigh heavier than you I will forgive them'. The Lord weighed them with him and Noah weighed heavier by his lowliness than all of them. The Lord destroyed all flesh, which was proud and lightweight in that time.

14.   Again in this same manner, in the days of Job [God] weighed everyone with him and Job weighed heavier by his lowliness and no one was found like him in his days.

54. Nb 12:3   56. Nb 14:19; Ex 32:33   58. Gn 6:7, 12
55. Ex 32:33   57. Gn 6:9, 7:1

Our Lord witnesses when he said, 'O, who is [like] my servant Job who is guileless and upright and turns away from evil? There is no one like him on earth.'[59] Concerning what I have said about the scale the following is written, 'All false people are like vapor, who are weighed on the scale and together are weightless'.[60]

What do we say? Because these people alone became humble ones, were the [rest] led to pride and to the lasciviousness that has filled all the earth? Today when we say to someone: 'Become lowly and avoid evil, and do good like the first ones', he says, 'There is no one who acts this way today'. 'But why do you and I not become like Noah and Job and Daniel—for he too was lowly like them—because the Lord placed his portion with them?'[61] [You may reply,] 'But because there is no one like these I will not be humbled.' But there are persons who are more humble (c.624) and excellent than these today, one among many, but if there is no lowliness and kindness in a person, he cannot be known to the lowly ones of old and God does not dwell in him, nor does he understand truth.

15.   Paul was also a very great person who loved wicked people more than himself. He said, "The Lord will witness to me that I wished to die [in order that] the evil ones might glorify the Lord of Glory'. If the Lord wishes to receive me and exchange my death for their salvation so that I may imitate our Lord who died for sinners.'[62] All the apostles died on behalf of sinners with numerous deaths by torture, sword, and the cross. Therefore, how can we reach [their level] if we do not even forgive sinners? How much are we left behind by Perfection if we are not even anxious for our souls? How much are we guilty of this because we persecute and kill our souls so that [instead] we become the persecutors and not the persecuted?[63]

59. Jb 1:8
60. Ps 62:9
61. Ezk 14:14

62. Rm 9:3
63. Mt 5:10

16. In the same way the angel spoke to Mary, 'Peace to you, blessed among women';[64] that is, the lowliest of women. 'My Lord is with you on account of your lowliness.'[65] Mary said, 'I give thanks to God who has seen the lowliness of his maid-servant'[66] and not beauty or (c.625) wealth. If there had been another woman who was more lowly than Mary, Christ would have been given birth by her—he who is the lowliest of all people who is the friend of lowliness.

17. From then on Adam lived on the earth, the heavenly became what is lowly, the spiritual became physical, [and] the breath of life became the taste of death. Majesty bent down and spoke with Adam, but Adam and Eve fled and hid themselves among the trees standing on the earth. The Lord said to Adam, 'Where are you, Adam, are you not among the heavenly angels?' [Adam] said, 'I heard your voice and I hid myself from your presence because I am ashamed to see you on the earth, before whose face I continually stood in heaven. Now you see my shame.'[67] That is, I am ashamed of what I have thought, despising your word; and I did not know that the dust is not like its maker. That which is made is not able to dwell with its maker except with love while lowering itself.'

The Lord said to Adam, 'Look, you have used the thing of which I warned you'.[68] That is, you have cast aside heaven and chosen earth. You have left the good tree, that one by which you did not know evil, and you descended to that one by which you have come to know evil and good. In other words, you fell from heaven to earth. 'Why, Adam?' [Adam] said (c.628) to him, 'Eve advised me!' Eve said, 'The serpent advised me!' And the serpent said, 'The Rebel allured and sent me!'[69] Because God commanded Adam not

64. Lk 1:28
65. Lk 1:42
66. Lk 1:46-48

67. Gn 3:9-10
68. Gn 3:11
69. Gn 3:12-13

to listen, neither he nor Eve, to the one who rebelled against the word of his Lord—as we have explained above how he rebelled—on account of this [the Rebel] sent[70] the serpent because he had allured and subjugated him.

18. Because [Satan] rebelled and God overthrew him, Satan became the son of darkness by his own will. However, [God] turned away and did not kill him because of his patience, yet [Satan] did not repent on account of his stubbornness and rebellion, because he had not worked for the Lord as our Lord had said, 'It is written: you shall worship the Lord your God and you shall work and pray to him only.'[71] However, [he did] the opposite of this, alluring other creatures encouraging rebellion, as he had taught the serpent and Adam and Eve to rebel. Adam fell from heaven with that [same] fall by which the Rebel slipped and fell. For, the idea came upon the Rebel to become God. When he was ruined he came to allure Adam so that he might slip and fall to become his son and disciple. But God did not give him rest according to what he had thought, but had pity upon Adam and Eve on account of their repentance, and established a law for them on earth, for if a person does it (c.629) he will be saved thereby.

Because of the fact that [Satan] was corrupted and corrupted others, the right [hand] of Jesus does not have pity on him nor upon his corruption, nor upon his torture, but as he destroyed [so] he will be destroyed, and every soul that he incited to rebel and made perish, [God] will require from him, soul for soul. Everything that he seizes from his creatures [God] will require [of him]. For the torment of all the impious ones will pass away, but his own torment shall remain forever and ever, and it will become the sharpest of all torments and the most despicable of all of them.

70. Kmosko's text reads 'šadad'—typographical error. Read 'šadar' (he sent).
71. Mt 4:10

19. Far be it that our Lord would light [the fire of] Gehenna for a person like [Satan] because no one has destroyed like him, except the impure spirits who were his children subservient to him, for even these were created for [heavenly] service for which God had desired to create them. They were obedient to Satan like the serpent and became impure ones, becoming [like] Satan, and were never again sanctified. For everyone who has committed evil acted provocatively for a generation or two. However, [Satan] did so in every generation as long as this world exists, seeing that through the teaching of the evil one Adam and his sons liked to exacerbate the spirit of our Lord. So, as long as that world to come exists, [Satan] will be embittered and tortured through the fiery deluge, just as the deluge of water came upon the descendants of Adam through his word and his deception. (c.632)

20. From then on God began to have compassion upon Adam and Eve. God made coats of skin and clothed them with his compassion[72] and [God] the creator did not treat him according to his transgression nor according to what Adam had thought. For if [God] had treated him according to his transgression, he would have utterly destroyed and annihilated him. However, Adam, in his freedom, chose labor, which is the opposite of Perfection, and through his own choice he bore anxiety—something that stifles those who seek to ascend to the higher realm. For he heard the advice of him who acted as if he cared for virtuous things, and so deprived him of heavenly graces and bound him with the beauty of the earth. Adam longed for the lower beauty and deprived himself of the heavenly. Because this transitory one is visible to the eyes of flesh, it is very agreeable to him who does not have spiritual eyes to observe the heavenly beauty. Adam,

72. Gn 3:21

who had [spiritual] eyes, saw it, [but] the evil one blinded them, saying to him, 'You will become even greater and be with your Creator'.

The end of the twenty-first *Mēmrā* on the Tree of Adam.

Mēmrā Twenty-Two

ON THE
JUDGMENTS
THAT DO NOT SAVE
THOSE WHO
OBSERVE THEM

Summary: Uprightness is not merely the application of 'an eye for an eye'. God has appointed evil judges and kings to judge people harshly, while restraining their evil tendencies and restricting them to the *lex talionis*. The Ten Commandments and the Gospel are sufficient for salvation. (c.633)

1.   Now let us explain the judgments that do not save one who has kept them. 'An eye for an eye, a tooth for a tooth, a blow for a blow, an insult for an insult, a wound for a wound, a soul for a soul.'[1] In other words, everything evil for evil. 'Love him who loves you and hate your enemy.'[2] 'If you strike your father bring an offering into the temple.'[3] 'Let whoever wishes to leave his wife give her a writ of divorce while she has not committed adultery',[4]

1. Ex 21:24; Mt 6:38
2. Mt 5:43; Lv 19:18
3. Mk 7:11
4. Mt 5:31

something not admirable either to our Lord or to people.

These are the commandments that are not virtuous and the judgments by which we will not be saved. Why did our Lord give them? Indeed, it was because [people] desired [them]. Why (c.636) were evil judges established over them? Why did he allow them to repay one another evil for evil? Because there are still people today who, seeking to rebel from being under the commandment, walk by their own will and say, 'Uprightness is not 'not doing evil' to anyone, but this is Uprightness: to treat well the good ones and to treat badly the evil ones, as God will also do on the day of judgment and on the day of admonition.'

2.   If we do not understand [Uprightness] from the Scriptures, will we not recognize Uprightness from the world when people complain against one another, crying out saying, 'A certain one seeks to wreak evil consequences upon me, upon my possession and resources'. Everyone says, 'Such a one does not act justly, but unjustly'. Look how everyone cries out, 'Uprightness does not do harm'.

Whoever has treated a person badly or injured him or has taken away his property will ask everyone and say, 'I have erred, forgive me and I will repay, have mercy on me'. But if he does not pardon him, everyone who hears will say, 'Woe to such a one who does not act as he should to God', because God had said, 'Forgive one another seventy times seven, for if you do not forgive, I will not forgive you'.[5] He had sinned and repented. On account of (c.637) sinners our Lord said, 'Blessed are the merciful, for they shall receive mercy'.[6] If a person is not merciful to him who has harmed [him], who will be merciful to him who is better than him or like him? For he says, 'Why do you have mercy upon me? Am I not better than you?' And if he says, 'It is written that a person should have mercy upon the hungry and the naked'.

5. Mt 18:23   6. Mt 5:7

Not upon the hungry and the naked alone is the word limited, but also upon whoever errs in any way. If he has mercy and forgives, a person is also giving alms through this. Therefore, whoever is merciful in this world upon a wrong-doer, they will have mercy upon him in that [other] world and will forgive him his errors and sins. Therefore, if an evil person harms someone, let his love shine upon him, just as the Father makes his sun shine upon the evil ones.

3.   See how God and human beings cry out that Uprightness does not reward evil. Uprightness is falsely accused and does not reward evil for evil. But if [Uprightness] blames [someone] before one or two or three, or before the whole church, and still a person does not wish to give back to you, consider what is yours to be lost, and do not fall into evil. The Lord will make your judgment if you do not make the judgment for yourself.[7] You will not be deprived of that thing that you lost.

If there is someone who says, 'I (c.640) will not attack a person, unless someone attacks me, [then] I will stand up against him and treat him badly'. This is not Uprightness, but evil. All the battles and wars occur because both sides oppose one another, [for example,] when a man stands up against his neighbor and neither of them yields before the other. Because of this, Uprightness abandons both sides and evil reigns.

For God commanded neither the oppressed nor the oppressors to sin against each other, but said the following to the oppressed one, 'If you remain in Uprightness and do not make a judgment by yourself, I will make your judgment',[8] says God. See how he commanded that not even when you are oppressed should you do evil to anyone, lest you fall from Uprightness. But if someone says, 'I am imitating God who requites the unjust', this is more evil,

7. Rm 12:19   8. Rm 12:19; Heb 10:30; Dt 32:35

because by your imitating God and comparing yourself to God who is without law, who even [suppose] he were to sin there will be no one to reprove him, though far be it from him that he should do injustice. Do you, then, want to become a judge of God? In that case, become a creator like him and make by yourself a heaven and an earth where there is no Lord; and create by yourself human beings where no power of the omnipotent Lord exists. Do good to the good ones and treat badly the evil ones when (c.641) you have become the Eternal and the Not Made and have become without the law like him.

4.   O feeble one, remember your father Adam and Satan who because they thought that they might become gods came to that fall. You who have not openly strayed, look out, the evil one will make you stray secretly, so that you will say, 'Just as God does, [so] I will do', in order that you will incur an incurable wound. For the wound of Adam was healed, but look at me, is not your own wound incurable? If you say, '[God] commanded the first righteous ones to take vengeance on the unjust, so I will imitate them', you have no authority to imitate them, [for] God did not speak to you as he did to them.

God did not destroy them by the prophets because they had sinned against each other, but because they were saying, 'What is the news of the Lord?'9 On account of this, [God] punished them until they proclaimed, 'The Lord is God Almighty'.10 In order that you may know that this is so, see that from the day when they proclaimed [God] did not send the prophets against them, but rather, if they do not desire to repent, he was reserving for them the day of judgment.

But today God does not send a person as [he had sent] the prophets. Yet if you desire on your own accord to become a murderer, that is your problem. The Lord said,

9. Ex 5:2   10. Ex 7:5

'Do not let even a [single] hateful word come out of your mouth'.[11] If you say, 'I will imitate the judges for "there is no (c.644) authority that does not exist apart from God",'[12] notice that they have authority over evil, and they administer judgments by which no person is saved. See how evil judges judge the evil world, and this is because God raised evil judges and gave evil judgments so that neither the judges might be put into the right, nor these who are judged might be comforted. Since people also rebelled from Uprightness that is the commandments [given] after our first rebellion of our father Adam, just as our father rebelled from grace of the heart and from serenity of the mind, and acquired the heart that knows evil by its own choice, so we too rebel from Uprightness, which our Creator commanded us, for even if [Uprightness] knows evil, unless it wishes, it will not do it.

5.   Thereafter, God saw that we had rebelled even from [Uprightness], not only requiting evil for evil, but many evils for one evil, something that the Lord did not say—He who is not even pleased with 'evil for evil'. They receive bribes and show preference—something that the Lord did not say. Not even by these judgments is a person saved because they were given in anger. The Lord said, 'I will establish evil rulers (c.645) who have no pity',[13] because people were crying out and saying, 'Give us a king and these judges who will oppress us harshly'.

6.   The Lord said to Samuel, 'Tell them how the king will oppress them, because he will take their sons and their daughters and tithe their property and their harvest'.[14] They cried out, 'These are judges who will go for us, who will kill with the sword all who do wrong, for otherwise we will devour one another'. God said, 'Just as they have rejected

11. Ep 4:29   13. 1 S 8:5
12. Rm 13:1   14. 1 S 8:11

my commandment, so also they have rejected me; I will establish over them evil rulers', so that the unjust one will take vengeance on the unjust ones and I will take vengeance on both of them. Because neither the rulers are able to be saved by these judgments of 'evil for evil', nor are the doers of evil, both of them will die by their own choice. If people do not wish they will not become judges or doers of evil, but because they love money and honor and transitory glory, they bribe and become governors and take up the power of the sword to kill whomever they desire and for a bribe they become executioners in order to be murderers. Through bribe[s] they become all that they desire (c.648) in order to do evil and plunder.

If a person desires to flee from evil, he must not become either a king or a ruler, nor even an executioner. Those to whom [such a position] has not come will sit and wait for [the time] when they will become evil rulers in order to do their evil will. For if people desire that someone should walk on his road in Uprightness, they would not be waging wars or killing, or plundering one another, or have had need of judges. But as it is now, the judges do not flee from evil, nor are the doers of evil impassive. All of them destroy one another—everyone who does not repent in his life and flee from evil. Where have you seen a righteous person desiring to become a king or a governor, or one of the rulers of the evil world, after our Lord has ceased anointing the king and raising up prophets and rulers [as God did] for the first people?

7.   If you say that the Lord incites them against one another or [provokes] kings or anyone else, as in earlier times, you really should not say this or anything similar to it. The one who asks for peace from people is the one who said, 'Allow yourselves to be beaten and do not strike [back], become the oppressed and not the oppressors'.[15] If earlier

15. 1 Co 6:7

there had been enmity between God and people, today God has made peace through the blood (c.649) of his cross, whether on the earth or in heaven, and he said, 'Let wars cease from the ends of the earth'.[16]

Therefore, if our Lord said, 'Let there be peace in all the ends of the earth',[17] then it is people themselves [who] do not wish to become peaceful and die at each other's hand. Did God say to one person, 'Love your kinsman as yourself' and 'pray for him who strikes you',[18] yet to another did he [not] say, 'Do evil to whomever does evil to you, and wage war and kill him?' Far be it from the Lord, [for God] is blameless in these things, because the evil ones by their own will do evil things and the avengers by their own will avenge one evil [deed] with many evils.

Nevertheless, these judges are useful for this world, since people are unrestrained from evil things and devour one another, and a people who proceeds even worse than this loves a requiter of evil to requite yet further, since it is pleased with evil.

Because of this, when God saw that in this way there are people who do not even repay one another one evil for only one evil, neither the people nor its judges, [God] wrote and showed them that they should repay evil for evil in the first law as [God] had said, 'I have given them judgments by which no one may be saved'.[19] [As for] evil people (c.652) I have given them commandments that are not virtuous and judgments by which they will not be saved, just as they themselves desired, that is, because they neglected the virtuous commandments of love, by which is accomplished the whole power of the law and the prophets, 'Love God and your fellow human being'. Because, if we or they had stood by them, Satan might have been defeated. For, a person sins in relation to [another] person and is justified by a person. 'They loved murder and enmity and hidden

16. Ps 46:9
17. 1 K 2:33
18. Mt 5:44
19. Ezk 20:25

hatred.'[20] Because of this, I have given them commandments so that when they keep them they shall die. 'If you
walk with me contentiously, I will walk with you contentiously.'[21]

8.   He also said, 'They loved the curse and did not desire the blessings',[22] because they have rejected the blessings promised to these who journey in Uprightness that
does not harm anyone, guards itself from evil and flees
from the judgment. It is afraid to speak harshly against a
person lest he strike [Uprightness]. But, if it happens that
someone strikes [Uprightness], it will endure and our Lord
will judge its judgment. There is no way for whoever walks
in Uprightness, love, and Perfection to avenge himself from
whomever leads him by coercion, unless our Lord avenges
him and brings upon him a great difficulty until he lowers
himself. (c.653)
        Therefore, because we have loved curses, we have put
them on like armor. Because we have walked contentiously,
the evil judges have stood up over us, for they have no
compassion and make blood flow like water and require
for one evil action one hundred evils and love bribe[s] and
judge with iniquity. We increased the punishment, we who
are not disciplined, and these [judges] were condemned
who had become avengers of anger. We did not remember
the true judge,[23] neither we nor [the Israelites], who repays every one according to his deeds. But the evil judges,
who judge and kill the evil ones and by whom they die,
resemble Satan who kills the people who obey him, and
does not escape from the fire.

9.   The apostles also instructed the murderers until they
were murdered, but [the latter] did not repent. These people
were not afraid to become evil judges rather than Upright

20. Ps 109:17 (*Peshita*)   22. Ps 109:17
21. Lv 26:23-24   23. Jr 11:20; 2 M 12:6; Esdras 14:32

ones who do not harm anyone like Adam. For, it is not written that he even struck the cheek of Cain who had killed his brother, but made him go on his way. The Lord judged the judgment of Abel at the hands of Cain.

For, if each of us went on his [own] way, even if it is in this world, which we love like Adam, because of the transitory beauty, which is visible; and if each one were just in what is his own, working and living, and not doing whatever we hate (c.656) to our fellow human beings; but [if] we were to do what we desire that everyone should do to us, there would be no murders or wars or blows. There would be no need of evil judges or kings and no one would hate his fellow human being. But God saw what people themselves do to one another, that they rob one another, no one is restrained from evil, and 'all flesh has corrupted its way',[24] as it was written of old and today as well. 'Each one who has sharpened his sickle',[25] as it is written, and made for themselves swords; and [so] they have raised up for themselves kings and judges, that is, lords and murderers. They fell upon one another and fostered enmity and waged wars, until in the end God gave himself to them for their sakes, so that through his blood we might be pacified whether on earth or in heaven. They did not have pity for his life and were not ashamed of his blood and were not persuaded by the Son to make peace on earth as he had done.

10. Woe to us, for if we do not repent, [God] will not be persuaded by us on Judgment day, just as we were not persuaded by him. 'Everyone who does not obey the Son the anger of God will remain on him.'[26] For [God] said in the Law, 'Cursed is everyone who does evil to his fellow human being whether secretly or openly, and let (c.657) all the people say, Amen'.[27] You see how everyone who harms

24. Gn 6:12
25. 1 S 13:20
26. Jn 3:36
27. Dt 27:24

his fellow human being becomes a cursed one like Satan. 'It is necessary for the disciple to become like his teacher',[28] and whoever has become a servant of sin and listened to it in order to become like his teacher [will be cursed like Satan].

When he submits to the lowliness of Christ, he will become like his teacher and his instructor. But the Law was not established for the Upright ones for they will become a law unto themselves. A person is able to become a law of love for oneself, just as the ancient fathers became. They imitated God who makes his love shine upon the good and the bad, and makes his rain fall upon the just and the unjust and they were not reproved by God, but were greatly glorified.

11.   In the proper place in our *mēmrā* we will explain about the love of the fathers, because by these virtuous and good deeds God desires that all people should imitate him and in this way they should observe and imitate him, when he lowers himself and asks every person to become reconciled with him and be saved, by means of the prophets and the apostles, as he washes the feet of his mockers, as he greets his betrayers, as he kisses Iscariot and calls him 'my companion'.[29] He did not say to [Iscariot], 'Where are you going, murderer?' But (c.660) he lowers himself and kisses him in order to be an example for us, so that we might act in this way to whoever mistreats us and triumph over evil just as our Lord had shown us.

He has 'become the head and perfecter of our faith'[30] so that by imitating him we might be perfected and thus come to resemble him when he prays for his crucifiers, and covers over through his love the sins of those who were baiting him with vicious names, whose hateful character the apostles were not able to explain. They just wrote the following, 'They called him Son of adultery and a

28. Mt 10:25   29. Mt 26:50   30. Heb 12:2

deceiver;'[31] while the apostles were silent about other abuses from their hateful character. He had in mind that time the adulterers who had been there and the murderers and thieves and the oppressors because he knew where they had killed and where they had stolen and where they had performed all kinds of evil things, and he concealed their sins and did not put them to shame. These spat at him on his face and struck him upon his head. They pierced his hands and feet and gave him vinegar and bitter herbs to drink, a thing that they had not done even to murderers, and they stabbed him on his side. When they had done to him all these evil things, apart from the evil things that had been done by them to others, instead of hating them and putting them to shame, he loved them deeply and prayed for them, 'Father, forgive them',[32] in order that he might be for us an example of Perfection, so that (c.661) we, all the children of Adam, might imitate him.

12. In this way again let us imitate him, when he calls and has pity upon the tax-collectors and the prostitutes, while submitting himself before one who is inferior to him and is baptized—although [he did] not need [to be]—to be an example for us, so that we might be blessed by one who is less than us and needy of us. Let us imitate him, when he greets his servants and women-servants, preceding them in greeting, and when he impoverished himself and had nowhere to place his head upon the earth,[33] so that we might become rich in his poverty;[34] and when he makes himself a sinner and prays and makes supplication as an offender and makes himself Sin on account of our iniquity so that we might become righteousness through him.[35]

It is fitting in this way that people should observe God

31. Gospel Thomas 105; Origin, *Contra Celsus* 1:28
32. Lk 23:34
33. Mt 8:20
34. 2 Co 8:9
35. 2 Co 5:21

and imitate him in all the good things he has done and is doing with all creatures, and let them do likewise to all the children of Adam, good and bad. And so the Upright and the Perfect are authorized to become a law unto themselves and imitate all the good deeds of our God.

But it is not lawful for anyone at all to imitate God, either when he judges or kills or curses or hates and is angry or condemns and calls [them] 'the brood of vipers',[36] or when he calls 'the sons of the Evil One, he who from the beginning was a murderer'.[37] (c.664) It is not authorized for a person to imitate God in one of these deeds without being utterly condemned. But let us imitate him by these things: when he calls his servants 'my brothers and my sisters, and my mother, and my sons and my daughters;'[38] when he calls a daughter of the world 'my daughter'.[39]

13.   For God lives without law and has authority over his creation. The creation is fit to be under God and subservient to him. 'If I, who am without law, am your Lord and Master, have humbled myself in this way, how much more ought you who are beneath God to bring yourselves to be humbled more than me, the Lord and Master.'[40] But not even when we imitate the lowliness of our Lord is our lowliness comparable to his. When we offer our cheek to blows according to our tangible nature, this lowliness is smaller than that lowliness, because that nature, which was neither tangible nor wounded, became limited and was wounded.

When we become poor just as our Lord became poor, as when we are poor ones, this lowliness is less than that of him who enriches everyone who has became poor, 'for through his poverty we shall be rich'.[41] When we are in

---

36. Mt 12:34
37. Jn 8:44
38. Mt 12:49

39. Mt 9:22; Mk 5:34; Lk 8:48
40. Jn 13:14
41. 2 Co 8:9

need as our Lord was in need and he asked Zacchaeus for bread[42] and the Samaritan woman for water,[43] (c.665) our own need is smaller than that of him who feeds everyone who is needy. When we die for the evil ones just as our Lord had died for evil ones, our lowliness is [still] less than that of our Lord, because our nature is mortal, not like that nature [that] gives life to all, which has tasted death.

In brief, if the totality of our lowliness is compared with that of our Lord, it is smaller than his. Through his grace he makes us equal to the level of Perfection of his stature[44] when we lower ourselves just as he lowered himself. Because of this he said,

> When you have done everything that I have commanded you, say, 'We are unworthy and useless servants[45] because we have done the thing that you commanded us by your power, because you have set us free from the strings of death for we were calling you at all times so that you might set us free. Now, because you have freed us from the flaming arrows of the evil one, by your grace accept us with you and make us forget everything we have seen in this world, and then we will have left it.'

14. So let us not be audacious as Adam was and fall just as he did. But God gave the authority to people to do good and virtuous things, as much as they desire and as it pleases them, (c.668) because the limit for love and good deeds has not been set,[46] as Paul said, 'If all the people had acted in this way, the law would not have been defined, but the law was established for all doers of evil':[47] for murderers and adulterers, thieves, deceitful ones, fornicators and

---

42. Lk 19:5
43. Jn 4:7
44. Ep 4:13
45. Lk 17:10
46. Ga 5:23
47. Ga 3:19

oppressors, slanderers, idol worshipers and magicians, diviners, soothsayers and people who curse, contentious ones, wrathful ones and violators of agreements, coveters, drunkards and singers, speakers of filthy words that are impure and foul, for those who commit adultery with ridicule and mockery, and with fables and stories that are useless.[48] 'Do not let any hateful and vain word issue from your mouth, but all matters that grace gives as edification for your personality.'[49]

Therefore, the law is not established for the Upright or the saints, or for those who bless and the compassionate, or for those who love and do good things, for those who have pity, the gentle, and the blessed. The law is not established for these, because they are a law of love to themselves in that they love their God and all people, good and bad, and imitating our Lord have compassion upon them and make peace with them, even when they are not worthy of peace, just as Iscariot was not worthy. (c.669) Our Lord made peace with him, so that all his loved ones might learn this from our Lord and imitate him.

The whole reason why our Lord and his preachers— the first and the last ones—wrote a great deal was in order that people should be good among evil ones, as our Lord Jesus our Teacher had been. But if a person says, 'I will imitate God, doing good and doing bad like him', he will go greatly astray, and the Law will convict him on the day of judgment, for the Law does not allow him to imitate the misfortunes that God does, only the good.

Moreover, this [Law] allows him to teach lowliness to all people in imitation of our Lord only, so that this idea might not occur to him to curse as God cursed, or to be angry or to hate as God has. Therefore, whoever imitates God in these harsh deeds will fall from the kingdom of our Lord Jesus Christ.

48. 1 Tm 1:10
49. Ep 4:29

15.   But when our Lord saw that we repay and judge not only [one] evil for evil, but many evils for one evil, and are not persuaded to avoid evil and do good and be saved, because of these things he put down for us in the Law that we should only repay [one] evil for [one] evil, so that the torment will be a little more tolerable for us on that day than (c.672) for whoever repays many evils for one evil. 'I have given them commandments that are not virtuous and judgments by which they cannot be saved.[50] Because not even by these—'an evil for an evil'—do they persist so that their punishment may be more tolerable, but [instead] why do they do many evils for one evil so that their Gehenna will be grievous?'

For our Lord explains:

> It was said to the ancient ones, 'an eye for an eye'. But I say, 'Whoever strikes you on your cheek, offer him the other one',[51] and you will become Perfect.[52] It was said to the ancient ones, 'Love your neighbor and hate your enemy'. But I say to you, 'Love your enemies and bless whoever curses you'.[53] Whoever leaves his wife, while she has not committed adultery, and takes another [wife], it is he who commits adultery.[54]

The scribes say to him, 'You are breaking the law of the Lord God,[55] how are you his son?' Jesus said to them, 'I do not break the Law'. They say to him, 'Why did Moses say to us, "Thus says the Lord", and you say, "The Father desires thus"?' Jesus said to them, 'Because your heart is hard the following is spoken to you'.[56]

50. Ex 20:15
51. Mt 5:38
52. Didache 1:4
53. Mt 5:43-44
54. Mt 5:32
55. Mt 19:7
56. Mt 19:8

16.   But another way of saying this, the Father did not desire that you do thus, but because the heart of your fathers was hard they were not persuaded (c.673) by 'an evil for an evil'. For this reason this God allowed them that [one] evil suffices [for another] evil. For the one to whom it was said, 'an eye for an eye',[57] really wanted to kill that one who stumbled and put out [his] eye. Because of this God said to him, 'An eye for an eye' is sufficient for you in order that his death will be a little more tolerable for him than that of a murderer.

What do you say, did he do well to give them these judgments by which no one can be saved or not? Then they began to understand that it is right to pass on from these [judgments] as Jesus had said. The one [to] whom [it was said], 'a cheek for a cheek',[58] wished to cut off the hand of the one who stumbled or struck [his] cheek, or was prepared to strike a hundred cheeks for one. Because of this, it was said, 'a cheek for one cheek only', so that it might be more tolerable for him on the day of judgment than for the one who cuts off the hand of his neighbor or strikes a hundred cheeks. With skill and artfulness the Lord restrains them from a greater wickedness so that it might be a little easier for them on the day of judgment.

17.   See what is written, 'I have considered the work of your hands and I have considered your contrivances, God. Your way is holier than all the evil ones, requiting good things for evil.'[59] Because of the hardness of the heart of people [God] wrote 'evil for (c.676) evil', as though this was his way, in order that the judgment will not be too severe upon him.

[Concerning] 'a wound for a wound' and 'a burn for a burn',[60] [this was said since] he was wanting to do many

57. Ex 21:24
58. Ex 21:24 (*Peshitta*)
59. Ps 77:11
60. Mt 5:43

things to whoever does thus to him. Because of this [God] said the following to him, '[One] burn is sufficient for a burn; a wound is sufficient for a wound', in order that his torment might be a little easier on the day of judgment than [for] him who inflicted numerous burnings and wounds. The one to whom it was said, 'a soul for a soul',[61] had wished to kill many souls instead of [just] one, so that his torment and death might be easier than for him who kills many souls. The one to whom it was said, 'Hate your enemy',[62] really wished to kill him. Because of this he said to him, 'Really hate your enemy and treat him very badly, but do not ever kill him', in order that his torment might be a little easier on the day of judgment than that of a murderer.

18. Again he said, 'Be angry with one another'—a thing that is not virtuous—but do not treat one another badly and do not sin.[63] Because it is better that they should be angry and not do evil rather than being angry and commit evil while they are angry, in order that they might be better than the evil doers. For just as he who does many good things is excellent, so whoever (c.677) commits many evil things will be brought low. Our Lord Jesus is just in his judgment, so that by many torments he might punish the person who does much wickedness. He whose fault is little will endure light blows and our Lord is good in his kingdom so that he might promote each person according to his labor, up to the level he has attained.

19. The one to whom it was said, 'Leave your wife',[64] desired the wives of his neighbors. Because the Law did not allow him to leave his wife and take another—that [woman] he desired—he killed his wife by poison or by some other

61. Ex 21:23
62. Mt 5:43
63. Ep 4:26; Ps 4:4
64. Mt 19:7; Dt 24:1

means, and went to take that one he desires. By the hardness of his heart he killed the husband if she had one, as David had stumbled and killed Uriah on account of his wife.[65] [God] said to this one, 'Write [a divorce], dismissing without a fault, but never kill her', so that the death of him who dismissed her might be easier than for him who really killed her.

In order that you may be assured that this is so, the following was written in Malachi, 'I will reject your offerings, because I have been a witness among you and the women of your youth, that you have been unfaithful to, those who are the women of your covenant. But I will be true with you.'[66] The men who follow these rules (c.680) are not victorious, but like a deadly poison [the judgments] torment their doers if they do not repent and avoid them. As our Lord had said in the Gospel when he commanded them that he did not desire this [rule],[67] but with difficulty he permitted those who are stubborn, 'an evil for an evil'. As today, if a person transgresses and strikes him who is stronger than he [with] a single blow, he may strike him a hundred blows and not be persuaded, or with a rock splitting his brain open on account of one blow. Look, 'a cheek for a cheek'[68] would have been better, as it is written for one who does not triumph, and avoids striking him with many blows and his torment is grievous on the day of judgment if he does not repent and avoid evil. But if a person has repented or repents, whether among the first ones or among the last ones, our Lord has forgiven and will forgive him.

20. As for the one to whom it was said, 'When you revile your father or your mother, present an offering in the temple',[69] there was a reason why he had commanded him

---

65. Mt 19:7; Dt 24:1

66. Ml 2:14

67. Mt 5:1ff

68. Ex 21:24

69. Mt 15:4

in this way. As for the rest, can he be absolved when he reviles his parents, unless he repents and avoids evil? For he said in the Law, 'Whoever reviles his parents will surely die'.[70] But why did they command this? Was it for his lack [of intelligence], or in order that he might be ashamed before the priest and the congregation, (c.681) for the priest says to him everyday, 'Are you not ashamed that you strike your parents who bore and raised you?' If he reviles [his parents] again on another day, and goes to present an offering, the priest and the congregation will spit in his face, for the offering of each person was known and why he offered it. The cause was known for which the holocaust and the vows were burnt. And the reason for the sin was known. The priest asked, 'What is the sin?' and then he offered it.

That is why it was said to him in this way: whether [it be] for his lack [of intelligence] or so that he might be ashamed on account of the priest and the congregation and not revile his parents, in order that his death might be a little easier than for him who really strikes his parents. For if a person reviles and hates his parents and abuses them, he will surely die. But if he transgresses and errs, yet repents from his sins and does good things, the Lord will spare him on account of his mercy.

21. When he said, 'He made both of them one Testament',[71] and he annulled law of the commandments by his commandments, so that he might make everything new with one testament. 'From now on not a single letter *'iota'* will pass away from the Law and the prophets.'[72] As for the rest, (c.684) 'The whole Law and Prophets up to John were established in order to serve and then pass away'.[73] 'For the thing that has become old is worn out and close to destruction',[74] and from then on we ought not to speak about

70. Ex 21:17
71. Ep 2:14
72. Mt 5:18

73. Mt 11:13
74. Heb 8:13

these.[75] From then on, that one letter *iota* will remain—which is the ten commandments,[76] which are called *'iota'*, for there are ten commandments in the number of the signs. These ten commandments, which I will enumerate here, are *'the iota'* that do not pass away from the Torah or from the prophets.[77] 'Hear, O Israel, our Lord and our God is one.'[78] 'You shall love the Lord your God with all your heart and with all your strength and with all your soul.[79] And you shall love your neighbor as yourself.[80] You shall not kill. You shall not commit adultery. You shall not steal. You shall not bear false witness.'[81] This is the letter *iota*, and look, it is recorded in the Gospel.[82] So from then on let no one serve these other commandments that have been abolished, or these by which a person is not saved, because they were given on account of the outcry of the people and their contentiousness.

22. In summary, these ten commandments are sufficient for the salvation of people, so that whoever (c.685) does them will be saved by them. For all the wearisome-ness of the Law and the prophets [was intended] so that people might come to these commandments of this *iota*. As our Lord said, 'All the power of the Law and the prophets hang upon these two commandments, and whoever does these two commandments fulfills the whole law'.[83] As Paul said, 'The whole [Law] is spoken with a few [words], "you shall love your neighbor as yourself" '.[84]

23. Know this, my friends, that all the beauty of the virtuous commandments, which you find in the Law or in the

75. Heb 9:5
76. *'ptgāmīn'* instead of the more usual *'pūqdānē'*.
77. Mt 5:18; Aphrahat, *Demonstration* 2:7; literally, *'yōd'*—equivalent of Greek *'iota'* and the tenth letter of the Syriac alphabet.
78. Dt 6:4
79. Dt 6:5; Mt 22:37
80. Mt 22:39
81. Ex 20:13-16; Dt 5:17-20

82. Mt 5:18
83. Mt 22:40
84. Ga 3:19

prophets, that is their sense, these commandments, which are called *iota* as our Lord said, 'You shall love the Lord God and the people who are all descendants of Adam, who are your neighbors, relatives, and family'.[85] Therefore, let us fulfill the Gospel and the *Iota*, which are one testament by which people conduct themselves in a new way. But whatever is outside of this *iota* is in the Law and in the prophets, being called the testament of debts, for on account of the debts of the people is designated the testament of debts.[86]

24. Therefore, the fact that some of the ancients spiritually served this *iota* was glorification for them, as Paul said, 'In the righteousness of the Law of which I was found blameless',[87] which is *iota*. For (c.688) the Spirit saw their lowliness, and taught them to leave the commandments that are not virtuous and the judgments by which no one is saved, and showed them these commandments upon which hang the sense of the Law and of the prophets through which people are saved. The Spirit taught them how to practice them spiritually, and in this way the testament would become glory for them. All who are outside the *iota* were serving physically on account of their contentiousness. The Spirit did not teach them to fulfill spiritually the commandments of righteousness and of salvation. The commandments that are not virtuous and the judgments by which a person is not saved became debts for them, [namely] the testament that was designated on account of the debts of the stubborn people.

25. Hear [this] argument, O hearer of truth, and see all the harshness that is in the Law and the prophets. It is contained in that great commandment, 'Love your fellow human being as yourself'.[88] Where have you seen an

---

85. Mt 22:37,39
86. Ga 3:19

87. Ph 3:6
88. Mt 22:37-39

offender who kills himself after he has offended? When he kills his neighbor, whom he has offended or not offended, but kills and has no pity? Whom have you seen among the offenders, or among those who have not offended, who has gouged out his own eye because he had gouged out the eye of his neighbor since he had sinned or while he had not [yet] sinned? Who have you seen striking himself and putting himself to shame because he has sinned, striking his neighbor (c.689) and denouncing him? Who is without pity for himself just as the children of Adam treat one another, abusing the souls of one another?

If we loved our neighbors as ourselves, just as we do not do evil to ourselves, we would not treat our neighbors badly. If we loved our neighbors as ourselves we would do to our neighbors all the good things we have done for ourselves. But [as it is,] we desire that everyone should forgive us while we are not compassionate, taking vengeance on our neighbors. At no time have we ever sharpened the sword and prepared to strike ourselves, but [instead] we prepare armor to protect ourselves, preparing for ourselves a sword to strike the souls of our brothers, the descendants of Adam.

The end of the twenty-second *Mēmrā* about the judgments that do not save those who do them.

Mēmrā Twenty-Three

ON SATAN AND PHAROAH
AND THE ISRAELITES

Summary: An extended biblical exposition on how God permits free will in evil people, Pharaoh in the case here. God did not predestine the hardness of heart of Pharaoh, for such derived from Satan. God's kindness actually elicited the rebellion of Pharaoh, just as Jesus' humility brought out resistance among the Jewish leaders.
(c.692)

1.   [This *mēmrā*] about Pharaoh and the Israelites who sinned by their own [choice, for] the Lord did not compel them.[1] For the Lord does not inhibit anyone from believing in him and doing good things, except for the prophets alone whom he held back at that time from Perfection so that they might be zealots for him.[2] But as for the rest, [God] did not hold back anyone else from good things, neither at the first, nor at the last.

Our Lord revealed this so that everyone might understand how Adam was created. Our Lord showed us through his person the creation of Adam and how Adam became like the heavenly angels, without anger and without lust, and without [bad] thoughts and faults. According to that image (c.693) of [Adam], our Lord was born. For by the

---

1. Cf. Rm 11:32   2. Cf. *Mēmrā* 9

imitation of Adam, our Lord came in order to show people their original nature [and] how they were created. As the apostle said, 'Everything is made new again in Jesus',[3] that is to say, as from the beginning.

Our Lord made [it] known that Adam was created in purity through that parable in which his servants approach and ask him, 'Our Lord, did you [not] sow the good seed in your field from where have the tares [come]?'[4] Our Lord replied, 'The field is the world.'[5] In other words, 'You have created Adam well. From where have these evil things he has committed come to be in him?' And he said to them, 'An enemy has done this.'[6] That is, Satan has caused him to stray. For it is written, 'Everything that God created, look, it is very good'.[7]

2.   Now God did not make anything that is an opponent, but God did create this one who today is an opponent. [God had created him] as one of the higher powers and made him [sit at his] right hand, as he had raised up Iscariot on his right. By his own will, however, [Judas] crossed over to the left side; so also this wicked ruler, under the pretext that God had given him power like the angels, and [that God] had promoted him and placed him on [his] right, yet he acted wickedly with his authority, and desired to become God. The Lord cast him down from heaven to earth and light departed from him and he became (c.696) the son of darkness. His power was cast out from the light and he became a dweller in the darkness.

For it was written, 'God made him make war',[8] as it was also said, 'I have raised up Pharaoh for controversy', while Satan established himself against the Lord so that his son might become as his own. God was not unjust because having established [Pharaoh] in controversy in order that he might not be persuaded, [God] turned around and killed

3. 2 Co 5:17   6. Mt 13:28
4. Mt 13:27   7. Gn 1:30
5. Mt 13:38   8. Jb 40:19 (*Peshitta*)

him. But there is an explanation for these words, as the apostle said, 'God compelled the Israelites not to obey',⁹ while God up to our day [still] asks them to obey, yet they do not want to do so.¹⁰

3. [God] sent his messengers to Pharaoh until the messengers wearied and [Pharaoh] did not submit.¹¹ He did not create Satan with the intention that he should not serve his Uprightness with his angels; [Satan] sought by his own will to become a god and fell. Likewise, Pharaoh died by his own will. The Israelites, by their own will, did not obey and they killed the Son, the Christ. Because of this, Satan was judged justly and not unjustly. The Pharaoh was judged justly and not unjustly. And the Israelites were judged justly and not unjustly. If they had committed wrong not by their own will, they would be being judged unjustly, and our God would be found (c.697) not to have [judged] justly.¹²

But far be it for the Upright One to be unjust, he who became good for the sake of the unjust ones and died for them. Injustice has not existed among the Upright. Is this, then, to be understood that Pharaoh had been just and the Lord perverted him and [that] the Israelites were just and the Lord perverted them? Whatever the Lord commanded Satan, [Satan] did. And just as [the Lord] created [Satan], he will stand and judge and destroy [Satan] at the end. At all times [the Lord] calls [Satan] an enemy and a rebel, hating him, and sentencing him into the unquenchable fire that will burn him up.

4. If God tells a person to do something evil, [God] will not judge him, for [God] commanded him [to do so]. But if a person treats another badly without the commandment of our Lord, he will be judged according to his deeds. But if God had told him to become Satan, [God] would not have judged him. Is this not understandable to those who have

9. Rm 11:32
10. Ex 9:16
11. Ex 9:16
12. Dt 32:4

the intellect and [are able to] comprehend with the holy ones what is the height and depth, the length and width?[13]

This is what Scripture said, 'Fear the evil one because he was created for evil'.[14] A human being is the one whom our Lord created, his heart being full of good things, [but who] obeyed Satan and [Satan] upset his creation through his evil teaching. [Satan] filled his heart with all [kinds of] evils and made him contrary [to good]. Because of this he said, 'Deliver me, Lord, from the evil person',[15] (c.700) but he obeyed Satan and became Satan. But the Lord caused Satan in this to make war while being patient with him and overthrowing him when he wished to become a god in heaven, an evil example in good places and a division in the midst of unanimity. Because of this, he allowed him to fight, for he knew that he would do these evil things on the earth, and [so] he did not kill him, but offered that evil one an opportunity for repentance. When [Satan] stood before our Lord on the mountain, [Jesus] said to him in the Spirit, 'You shall worship the Lord your God with good things and you have not served him'.[16] Satan did not repent at the mention of the written book[17] so as to worship the Lord with good deeds; instead he did not do [them].

If you say that [our Lord] spoke to him as [he would have] to a human being in the Law, that he should worship the Lord his God, then it is as you have said, Satan rebelled by the desire of his own soul and did evil things just like an evil person. He did not worship the Lord in righteousness like a good person. That is, while he had a higher authority he [did not] worship, [nor] did he [obey] the Law with the heavenly angels, and he was found unjust and not true in his authority as the [other] angels are true.

5. The worst of all of this [is that] he sought to become a god, but he was defeated and fell, just as Iscariot had not

13. Ep 3:18
14. Pr 16:4
15. Ps 140:1

16. Mt 4:10
17. Literally, 'a bottle of ink'.

been true in his ministry that (c.701) our Lord had given him, but he had become a thief, and at the last rebelled, resembling his master Satan and not Jesus. For he had accepted the teaching of Satan and not of Jesus. Our Lord also said, 'I chose you, yet one of you is Satan'.[18] Therefore, it is right that Satan and Iscariot were compared with one another. As in the beginning Satan was found among the sons of the right [hand], so at the beginning of the second creation in Jesus, Satan was found among the sons of the right [hand]. For our Lord had known that Iscariot was Satan. He selected him so that through him he might inform us how Satan rebelled from the right-hand side in the beginning. For Jesus made everything new from the beginning and showed us [how to understand everything].[19]

6.   In this way the kindness of the Lord effected it so that Satan became an opponent, because he allowed him to be free and did not kill him. His kindness effected that Iscariot betrayed him, because he had not breathed into him and consumed him. If it is hard for you to imagine how God saw Satan, disregarding [Satan] and being patient and enduring, while he planned these things and did [them] by his own choice, be persuaded by this: he knew what Iscariot was thinking and doing but did not kill him; instead, he called and brought him close, honored him and washed his feet and greeted him with love. (c.704)

7. Be persuaded also by the following: Adam desired, with the advice of Satan, to become a god, yet our Lord did not kill him because of his loving kindness, but our Lord increased his love all the more, and had compassion and pity for him and saved him. See, moreover, how they rebelled and [how] people [in general] rebel against the kindness of God. However, [God] is patient and does not do away with them, but takes them by their hands and offers them

18. Jn 6:70   19. Ep 1:10

repentance. See that not only have they renounced [God], but people also challenge the Lord, yet [God] does not blot them out and does not wipe out their memory on account of his mercifulness.

8.   If you should say what [often] is said about [Satan], that Satan desired to become a god on earth, he wished to become [so] in the days [when] paganism [ruled] over the earthly corporeal creation, not over these heavenly spiritual beings. Understand what I say, 'Everything visible is the shadow of what is invisible'.[20] However, if Satan had wished to cast out his shadow upon the earth, it is because he wanted to cast it [also] in heaven. For, whatever he did on earth [is] due to the fact that we human beings listened to him and he was able to rule over all those who do his will. He was called a god, as it was written, 'The god of this world has blinded the minds (c.705) of the wicked, lest they obey the Lord of Glory'.[21]

As it is said, 'You are slaves to whomever you incline the ear to hear, whether [it be regarding] sin or whether righteousness'.[22] If you should say, 'By the nature of his creation iniquity existed in Satan', since he was called 'the ruler of iniquity',[23] you should not talk like that, for if God had created iniquity in him, [God] would not have hated him with [such] anger, and would not have reviled him with [such] rage, and the Prophet would not have written in the spirit this way, 'Everything which God has created, look, it is very good'.[24] Everything that is created is better in the [original] nature of its creation, everything in its kind, but [if it had been otherwise] he would have said, 'Everything that he created is good, except Satan', if God had created something iniquitous in him, whatever is not good.

9.   He also had said regarding Pharaoh, 'I have established him for a controversy', in that when [the Lord] sent

20. Rm 1:20   22. Rm 6:16   24. Gn 1:31
21. 2 Co 4:4   23. Cf. Ep 6:12

punishment upon him, he said to Moses, 'Pray that [this plague] may pass and I will obey and allow you and your people to go in peace'.[25]   This is how the Lord hardened him: in that [God] had heard everything [Pharaoh] had called upon him through Moses, and he had healed the land from wounds; thus, the listening ear and tolerance of the Lord hardened Pharaoh. For when the suffering arrived, [Pharaoh] was humbled; (c.708) but when respite came, he was hardened. In misfortune, he was humbled and in health he was hardened. As if someone might say, 'I have raised up the head of this one who was sick and healed him; he was naked and I dressed him; he was poor and I made him rich; and look, today he opposes me'. In this way, the Lord hardened Pharaoh through the good things he did to him and was compassionate upon him and by this gave him an opportunity for repentance. Because of this, it was written, 'The Lord hardened the heart of Pharaoh—so that he would not obey'.[26] That is, by means of compassion and [good] health Pharaoh was hardened.

10.   With regard to this, God constricted the Israelites through his lowliness and despicableness. Isaiah said, 'He was scorned and the most humbled of people. He had no form and no brightness. We saw that he was despicableness and humble and we held him to be false.'[27] Now, then, the despise and lowliness of Jesus constricted them—that is, because they condemned him and did not obey him. Some say that 'God imprisoned them so that they might not obey'.[28] It is for the reader to discern whether [God] constricted them by his lowliness or by his hardness. The matter seems as if there was iniquity on God's part, even though God is blameless with all his servants. So, then, his lowliness does not constrict (c.709) anyone, but it prays powerfully, yet his hardness leads by force.

25. Ex 8:8
26. Ex 11:10

27. Is 53:2-3
28. Rm 11:32

Every [time] our Lord performed the first signs for
their sake, and told them, 'If I am not doing the works of
the Lord, do not believe me',[29] they said, 'This is the son of
Joseph and is he not a human being like us? [Why] should
we believe him?'[30] Our Lord replied to them, 'At least believe [by] these deeds that the Lord has sent me'.[31]

Where did you see that God constricted them? But
they constricted themselves because they despised him,
because he thought little of himself and lowered himself.
For our Lord came to show lowliness to people and the
way and door of the spiritual Paradise from which Adam
had departed, [and] to which Paul was caught up above the
third heaven.[32] Therefore, the whole reason for his coming was to show lowliness and he saw that they constricted
themselves on account of his lowliness and were not obedient by their own choice, while fatiguing [him] with their
own iniquity. He performed [some] signs, but they did not
believe, saying to him, 'Give us a sign from heaven'.[33] He
called them 'an evil and adulterous generation',[34] in order
to show that he is the Judge. He used this word and those
like it, not to establish by it an example for his chosen ones,
but to show that he will recompense everyone according to
his deeds, lest some should say that he does not repay evil
deeds on the day of judgment and they despise them and
not fear his judgment and not keep his commandments
and be saved. (c.712)

11.   It is written, 'Dishonor them here and then execute
them before me'.[35] He said, 'You are the sons of the evil
one'.[36] He said, 'Go, you cursed ones, into the fire',[37] while
he commands us not to utilize harshness nor a spiteful
word.[38] And he said to them, 'I have performed all these

29. Jn 10:37	34. Mt 12:39
30. Jn 6:42	35. Lk 19:27
31. Jn 10:38	36. Jn 8:44
32. 2 Co 12:2	37. Mt 25:41
33. Mt 12:38	38. Col 3:8

signs and [yet] you seek [another] sign for yourself?' From now on, as you have not obeyed the first [signs], you will not obey others.

But I will give you a despised and small sign by which you may stumble, because you were not persuaded by the great ones. Because I was lowly, you were scandalized, for you despised becoming lowly ones and imitating me and becoming my disciples. Moreover, I will die by your hands while making my soul lowly. I will be three days in the heart of the earth,[39] so that those who believe in me might lower themselves until [their] death. And those who are scandalized by me shall be constricted by my lowliness. They will say with a hard heart, 'God did not lower himself in this way and could not have died by the hands of his feeble creatures'. For they know that there is no one who can defeat the one who triumphs over all. They do not understand that because of their iniquity and their pride—that of Adam and his children—he lowered himself in order to teach them so that they might revert to their first image from which they had fallen.

The end of the twenty-third *Mēmrā*, which is about Satan and Pharaoh and the Israelites.

---

39. Mt 12:40

Mēmrā Twenty-Four

ON REPENTANCE

Summary: Repentance and redemption are required for all below the step of Uprightness. God's mercifulness, which is contrary to reason, created Uprightness as a way to escape the taste of death. The Perfect are beyond the need for repentance and mercy, having no enemies in their hearts upon whom to be merciful. (c.713)

1.   There are people who say that if a person should sin after he is baptized, he has no opportunity for repentance. As the apostle said, 'If a person should turn aside and sin after he has received the knowledge of truth[1] and tasted the sweetness of the world to come,[2] there is no other sacrifice that may be offered for his sins'.[3] 'But there will come a fury of fire which will consume the people who have become an obstacle to their soul and do not repent.'[4]

We know that not everyone who is baptized receives at that time the knowledge of truth, but only one out of many receives the knowledge of truth. So therefore, it is not that they are unrepentant, says the apostle, but 'they have no other sacrifice'—as though someone might say, 'there is no God besides the one against whom they have sinned and there is no other knowledge (c.716) besides

1. Heb 10:26   3. Heb 10:26
2. Heb 6:5   4. Heb 10:27

283

that truth, which they have known, but have not lived by'.
They have no place or foreign location [away] from this
God to go offer him another sacrifice, unless they turn back
toward this God in whom they first believed and to whom
they sacrificed this knowledge and faith that they have previously sacrificed. It is not that they are not saved, he said,
but that they have no other worship except that truth that
they have known and from which have departed. But if
they do not return to sacrifice just as they had sacrificed at
the first, the fire will come to consume them for they have
become an obstacle to themselves.

And they said, 'From the time we have sinned, God
will no [longer] receive us, [for] one is equal to one hundred'. That evil teaches them to talk this way lest they repent and are saved, just as it taught Iscariot and he strangled
himself.[5] For if Iscariot had repented, our Lord would have
received him because [our Lord] 'does not seek the death of
[any] person, but [wishes] that they might repent and be
saved'.[6] There are some who say, 'If a coat is torn and [then]
is repaired, the spot is recognizable; and if a wall is dam-
aged and is built up, the place is recognizable'—and [in
this way], they break the heart of the penitents, when all of
us are penitents, and all of us have sins. But let us speak
plainly with everyone, 'Whoever is standing let him watch
out lest he fall',[7] and whoever (c.717) falls, let us show him
repentance and pick him up, [for] 'If you, O Lord, keep
[track of] sins, who would be able to stand?'[8]

2.   See how the Holy Spirit has spoken, 'If the Lord re-
tains the former sins, no one is able to stand up before
him, because everyone sins, but by repentance all will be
received. Is there anyone who has defeated sin from the
womb of his mother?'[9] But human beings sin and repent
and then they defeat sin, [that is,] those who continually

5. Cf. above, regarding Iscariot   7. 1 Co 10:12
drowning.   8. Ps 130:3
6. Ezk 33:11   9. Jb 14:4

battle strenuously and valiantly with [sin] everyday. A penitent person should not be compared to a coat or a wall, but
we should compare them with something entering the fire.
For, people are baptized in the Spirit, which is love and
truth. Then, if they are prone to sin after they have been
baptized, each time that they repent love is found for them
to be baptized and purified. Just as when vessels of gold or
of silver, brass, glass or iron, are broken, the worldly[10] craftsman puts them into the physical fire, making them new
and mending their features, and they are called 'new ones'
after they had been worn out—how much more will God
[do], the master craftsman, so that he might make them
new (c.720) in the fire that is love, and his spirit that is
truth, and his waters [that] are faith?

However, if we are baptized, and these things are not
in us, we are baptized for judgment and condemnation;
we must be baptized and acquire love and truth and faith.
Yet, if we should slip after we are baptized and repent, there
is the love of Jesus, a living fire, that will purify our dirt
and our foulness. He will labor and give birth to us anew,
and will mark us as at the beginning. Not even the seal that
the priests gave us will pass away from us until our death.
But on the day of death, as one is found [so] he shall be led
away. If he has walked in sin until death, the lord of the
flock will snatch from him the mark [of the cross] that the
priests have given him and he will remain naked. 'Whoever has, to him will be given and added to him, and whoever does not have deeds of righteousness, but only the
seal, even he who has it shall be taken from him.'[11]

As for that one who received silver so that he might
trade with it but went to wrap it [in a napkin], buried it and
did not add to it, our Lord called him 'an evil servant'.[12]
'Because you have known that I demand of you the commandments I have delivered to you, you have taken up my

10. Literally, 'transitory'.
11. Mt 25:29
12. Lk 19:22

covenant with your words,[13] but have cast down (c.721) my law behind you. You have been sealed with my name, yet you have transgressed against all my commandments. My apostles and I have pleaded with you everyday, but you did not repent.' On behalf of God, we ask you, be reconciled with God.[14] 'Take from him that money', that is, that seal, 'and give [it] to him who keeps my words.'[15] 'And regarding the evil servant, cast him out into the darkness and the gnashing of teeth.'[16]

See that the seal of baptism is established even upon the unjust until death. For Jesus was concerned for sinners so that they might repent and he might accept them, as he had said, 'There shall be [more] joy in heaven for one sinner who repents than for ninety-nine righteous ones who have no need of repentance'.[17]

3.   Therefore, we admonish discreetly the healthy lest they become weak, and the sick in order for them to become strong and be healed, to stand up and not fall down.

4.   Moreover, the following was written with regard to the marriage state, 'If your enemy is hungry, feed him. And if he is thirsty, give him drink.[18] When you act this way, you will be greater before our Lord, but if that [other] one does not repent, it will be hard for him.'

But as for the Perfect, they have no enemy, except Satan alone. They do not even possess anything. Look, is it not evident that this was directed to [those involved in] marriage, (c.724) those who transgress on account of their possession, yet have food in abundance in order to feed their enemies?

---

13. Literally, 'with your mouth'.
14. 2 Co 5:20
15. Lk 19:24
16. Mt 25:30
17. Lk 15:7
18. Gn 50:19; Pr 25:21; Rm 12:20

5. Again, 'If the ass of your enemy is lying underneath its burden, lift it up with [your enemy]. If his bull strays or if you see something that has gone astray from his possession, gather it together. When you do these things you become for me a just and holy people.'¹⁹ For in this way, Uprightness treats well all who treat it badly, just as though [Uprightness] wished that they might treat it well, even those whom it had transgressed against and treated badly. [Uprightness] too repents from evil and treats well whoever does evil.

By these [commandments], one man may become greater than [another] man; the one who has compassion upon his enemy and gathers in his property when it strays and reconciles with him, [while] another does not gather in his property, but does not actually harm him—that is, without doing either good or evil to him—is better than one who heaps evil consequences upon him. And the torment of whoever heaps evil consequences on him will be less than one who murders him. But of all these, it is the one who treats him well and reconciles with him [who] will become Upright. As for these others, everyone is rewarded according his deeds, whether good or bad.

6.   Moreover, whoever becomes enraged, his offense is less than [for] one who assaults a person. (c.725) Whoever assaults a person, his torment is less than [for] him who murders. Whoever is angry against the one who has injured him, but reconciles with him [at] sunset does not sin like that one who is angry against whoever sins against him, but does not reconcile with him [at] sunset. 'If you are angry, do not sin.'²⁰ That means, an Upright one is not permitted to become angry, but he should control his anger and endure whoever treats him badly and suffer a little wrong and depart from being with him in friendship. Whoever does not reconcile in the evening but does not

19. Ex 23:5; Dt 22:1   20. Ep 4:26

treat his enemy badly is better than whoever does not reconcile [with him] and treats him badly. And whoever treats him badly and does not reconcile, his death will be less [painful] than [for] the one who does not reconcile and kills him.

However, all of them are slipping away from Uprightness. Two of these are deserving of death—that one who treats someone badly or strikes him or curses him and that one who kills him. The torment of the murderer will be terrible. But if they repent, they will all be saved. If they pursue the major commandments, they will become very great and be perfected.

7. Whoever gives straight-forwardly to everyone who is poor and does not ask who is worthy and who is not, (c.728) his love is greater than one who chooses which people to whom to give. For whoever gives to the needy, good or bad, imitates our Lord. Just as [God's] sun shines and his rain falls upon the just and the unjust, upon the good and the bad,[21] so [God] causes his love to shine upon the good and the bad, upon the just and the unjust. Just as our Lord sent his servants, commanding them to invite everyone, good or bad, and to put on [them] wedding garments, '[so that] my house may be filled'.[22] However, whoever shines his love upon each person is better than whoever does not even have compassion for a person. Whoever is not merciful to someone, but does not treat him badly, is better than whoever treats [someone] badly, plunders, and defrauds [him]. And whoever treats [someone] badly, plunders, and defrauds, his death will be more tolerable than [for] one who kills.

But, whoever does not treat anyone badly and treats everyone well is an Upright one, inferior [only] to the Perfect. If he empties himself and is celibate, he will quickly be perfected. However, whoever has compassion upon every-

21. Mt 5:45   22. Lk 14:23

one, whether good or evil, is a blessed one,[23] because he is much greater than that blessed one who is compassionate only upon the good. Whoever lowers himself before good and bad and considers them as better than himself—he is (c.729) a man greater in the Spirit, the Paraclete, than him who lowers himself before good and evil and does not consider them better than himself.

8. 'Blessed are the merciful ones'[24] who are merciful to and forgive everyone who offends them, for they will receive mercy by [being] with God. Because we are sinners, and if we forgive whoever offends us, our Lord will forgive us who have offended him. Even if we sinners taste death because of the offenses and faults we have, we will still be revived on the day of our Lord. For, [real] death is the sins and offenses and faults. For someone to cast off the body is one [thing], while to taste death is another. 'On the day you transgress against my word you shall taste death',[25] said his Creator to Adam. That is, on the day when you go astray you will have an evil thought. As much as you transgress against my word, the more [transgression] will increase and you shall die. For Adam cast off the body on account of that word, after which he tasted death. For God said to him, because [Adam] had disobeyed his commandment,[26] 'I will make you return to the earth from which you have been taken', since he had said to him, 'You [have come] from dust and to dust you shall return.[27] If you repent you shall be saved and resurrected by my word as the Lord.' (c.732)

[God's] mercies do not follow according to our offenses. If [it were] according to our own faults, [God] would have dispersed us like smoke. But [God] was merci-

---

23. Mt 25:34
24. Mt 5:7
25. Gn 2:17
26. Literally, 'he had embittered the word of his mouth'.
27. Gn 3:19

ful to us and established for us these minor commandments that are on this side of Perfection—on the day when
Adam transgressed against his word and fell from Perfection—so that through them we might become Upright ones
until the day when that one who showed us Perfection
would come in person. For he said to those who are not
strong enough:

> if you can not exert yourselves to come to
> this Perfection, keep these commandments
> of the first Upright ones and you will re-
> ceive eternal life. Whoever is strong enough,
> let him endure and enter through the nar-
> row door and arrive at this good and excel-
> lent portion. If he does not leave everything
> he has, [then] while remaining with what is
> his, let him do as it was written for the Up-
> right above. Everyone will be rewarded ac-
> cording to his deeds. But if he becomes an
> Upright one while he is with his children
> and with his inheritance, he will be blame-
> less on the day of our Lord. But as for the
> rest everyone is rewarded according to his
> deeds.

The end of the twenty-fourth *mēmrā,* which is about
repentance and forgiveness and about the fact that one
should not discourage a person; and about compassion and
how one man becomes greater than [another] man through
his compassion and love.

Mēmrā Twenty-Five

ON THE VOICE OF GOD
AND OF SATAN

Summary: A sermon calling upon both the Upright and the Perfect to distinguish correctly the divine or satanic motives behind their manner of life. The author cautions the Perfect not to be seduced into adopting the worldly ways of the Upright. The Upright are exhorted not to cease their upward journey to Perfection.
(c.733)

1.   Even in our day the evil one treats in this way anyone who is childlike and seeks to empty and sanctify himself from the earth, [the evil one] scheming to give him advice, secretly or openly. Because he is yet a child in the wiliness and knowledge of that higher world, he does not know [how] to discern the voice of God from [the voice] of Satan. The evil one makes him stray by the many promises he guilefully gives him. [The evil one] changes the snares every day for him, and if he figures out that one, he will fall into others. Because he does not understand the truth in any way, the evil one makes [him] stray and binds him onto the earth, yet that person is convinced that, in fact, he is bound in heaven. For from the beginning even [up to] our day evil habitually makes Adam and his children descend from on high by the image of beautiful visible things.

2.   For from the start, [the evil one] made Adam fall and few (c.736) could ascend to the place from which he had fallen until our Lord summoned them by his mercy, and by his many assurances made those who were persuaded return. God tried all means in order that people might be saved. By all [kinds of] mysteries, God told the truth; and by all kinds of parables, he depicted [the truth] through his prophets, from the beginning until the time God wished to be reconciled with human beings[1] and sent his Son who came to establish a reconciliation of heavenly things with earthly beings.

He demonstrated clearly through his person Perfection and the holiness of the first creation of Adam. Just as he said, 'Everything old has been made new in Jesus'.[2] You see that no person has shown clearly how Adam was created, except Jesus through his way of life. Whoever, therefore, wishes to ascend to Paradise, let him walk according to the lowly, renouncing, kind, and [self-]contemptible steps of our Lord, because he has been good with everyone and humbly he admonished everyone and assisted them. If a person does not have work in heaven, he is not able to cease from earthly labor. Therefore, after he saw that Adam loved such things, [God] allowed him to be married and to become Upright in this world which he loved and to be saved and not utterly perish. Because of his compassion our Lord, even if we desired something through sin, (c.737) effected that we might be [involved] in it without sins, if we become Upright.

3.   Therefore, if the matter is not such as I have said from the beginning, why does our Lord when he teaches us holiness and Perfection say, 'If a person does not separate himself from everything there is on earth,[3] he will not be able to become for me a disciple of holiness; but whoever works the earth in Uprightness will become an Upright one

1. Heb 1:1   2. Ep 1:10   3. Lk 14:33

and inherit eternal life, but will not become a Perfect one'? Why did the apostle and all who became Perfect ones not desire the earth, and not pursue the world, nor become married? Our Lord commanded them, 'Your Father knows that you require food and clothing'.[4] Do not be anxious, because I will tell the Upright who work the earth to nourish and clothe you and they will live the life of the new world on account of you, and will do for you these things by their labor while not treating anyone badly. If it were not on account of you that [the Perfect] were to live among you, I would have rained food and clothing upon you from heaven. If all the earth had practiced Perfection and holiness without having worked or having possessed, I would have fed all without toil as in the beginning.

In the same way, I would have wished that all people might live, but Adam your father brought you to this toil. If all people desire to become holy (c.740), I would create for them children just as I made a daughter for Adam from himself, without marriage and without lust. Only let there not be an obstacle or blame against me for anyone. For if the Upright live and labor on the earth, and not treat anyone badly, and do to the needy as I have commanded them, they will inherit the kingdom, even if they do not attain Perfection.

4. Even today by means of something virtuous, evil leads astray those who seek holiness and Perfection and inhibits them with luxury and they do not ascend to Perfection that our Lord had shown them. When our Lord said, 'Lower yourselves and separate yourselves and become celibate from the world and from intercourse, love everyone and follow me. Do not be of the world as I am not of it and do not labor in it, but follow me and become Perfect ones.'[5] The evil one will come to make them see earthly things in order that they not see heavenly things and be reconciled

4. Mt 6:32   5. Jn 15:19, 21

with what is higher and defeat him. For unless he has made them see earthly things, he will not be able to make them descend from Perfection.

But [the evil one] inhibits them through the toil of Uprightness, so that when they stand in the labor of Uprightness, he might do his will with them, even if he is not able [to do so] completely, at least partly. For when they have emptied themselves and have become celibate and have observed heavenly things, he is not able to contend (c.741) with them, for they progress to what is higher [while] he remains below them. Because he is not able to cross over the firmament, let alone to enter that world with God, as their own mind crosses over and ascends up to the supernal Jerusalem, as it is written, 'He shall lead us beyond death[6] and you have reached the mountain of Zion and the city of God in heaven with the hosts of angels and with the spirits of these former Upright ones who have gone to sleep in Uprightness, and were perfected in Jesus[7] and have entered the spiritual paradise.'[8]

5.   The wounds of Adam and of his children are healed by this when they enter spiritually that Paradise from which their father [Adam] had departed. Therefore, even in our day when the road to heaven has been walked through Christ who said, 'Leave everything visible and think about what is above and not what is on earth'.[9] Do not inherit what is on earth but [what is in] heaven and look, you will triumph, the evil one came promising under the guise of fine [actions] these things that our Lord had commanded only to the Upright ones.

[The evil one] deluding the Perfect one, says the following, 'It is virtuous that you should acquire a little [wealth] through Uprightness, sufficient for your own comfort and for whomever comes to you. Build for yourself a dwelling that is just adequate for strangers to come and rest in it.

6. Jn 5:24   8. Mt 27:53
7. Heb 12:22-23   9. Col 3:2

Plant a little (c.744) crop and make for yourself a vegetable garden that will be for the healthy and the sick.' Under the pretext of the comfort of the afflicted [the evil one] schemes to make [a Perfect] one fall from that major commandment that [Jesus] directs to the Perfect, 'Do not be anxious even about yourself',[10] and by that [other] commandment, 'Think about what is above and not of what is on the earth'.[11]

Because he cannot distinguish one voice from another and does not understand that these things were commanded to the earthly[-minded] Upright, and not to one who seeks heavenly things and Perfection, the evil one has made him return unwittingly to the Uprightness, which is below Perfection. That [person] believes he is pursuing Perfection, but he is found below [Perfection]. On account of this, the apostle said, 'If I do not know how to distinguish the power of the voice that calls and makes me ascend to heaven from the voice which forces me down to the earth, I am beating the air like a man who is not aware of what he is pursuing.[12] As for me, I am running in this way, like a man who knows how to discern one voice from another.'

Therefore, in this way the evil one beguiles to make him go back down to the earth as [he had done] to Adam. For even if these things are attractive, the Upright Gentiles of the earth still seek them.[13] For, they are the opposite of the heavenly ones. Our Lord commanded the Upright who labor on the earth to do all these things—alms and the comfort of the weary—so that they might comfort the weary (c.745) and be saved by these means. For those who desire to become heavenly beings should look upon heavenly beings. That is, [look upon] our Lord and his apostles, and upon the Upright who have been perfected. They should look up into heaven and not upon the earth, and should not be captivated by any earthly thing.

10. Mt 6:25
11. Col 3:2
12. 1 Co 9:26
13. Mt 6:32

6.   For there is no way that a person is able to work for
God spiritually while he is bothered by things of the world.
Let him empty himself to please that one [God] who has
chosen him.[14] With their prayer and good teaching let them
approach everyone, the good and the bad, and treat everyone well who is afflicted.

Look, [God] commanded the heavenly ones that they
treat every person well with heavenly things. Where did
you get the idea that no one should speak with a worthless
or deceptive [person], because it may be [the case] that he
will become a Perfect or an Upright one? As our Lord said
to Ananias, 'Go, speak with Paul'.[15] And Ananias said to
our Lord, 'My Lord, he is an evil man, and I have heard of
the affliction he has laid upon the saints who are in Jerusalem'. Our Lord replied to him, 'Go speak with him, because he is my chosen instrument, for you do not understand.'

Therefore, in this way, [if] you have a word with anyone, speak, and you will not [thereby] sin. 'I have made
you a watchman[16] to see the judgment to come and warn
first the sinners and then the righteous ones.' Therefore,
once (c.748) the evil one has made a person turn away
from heavenly matters and beset him with the toil of Uprightness and he has acquired gardens and earthly Para-
dises, properties and buildings, then the evil one begins to
pull him down also from Uprightness. Once [the evil one]
had gone to encourage others to treat him badly, he went
to attack the Upright one who had fallen short of Perfection while not knowing that the evil one would trouble
him and make him do [evil].

He begins by saying to him, 'They have plundered
your house that you have built with great effort'; then the
person will go quarrel and fight [against them]. Here is
one profit he has gained. Again he says to him, 'Grasping
people who are not satisfied have picked through [your]

14. 2 Tm 2:4   15. Ac 9:11-15   16. Ezk 3:17

plants and vegetable garden', and the person goes off to struggle [against them]. Here is another profit that the evil one advised him to do. Once more he says to him, 'They have struck and killed and led away your flock[17] while it was feeding on your mountain', and then he wrings his hands and is disturbed. Here is another profit that the evil one advised the heavenly ones that they should own and build.

7.   Do you see how the virtuous things the Evil One promises will become evil things? Unless a person resists and endures his temptation like Job, the [Evil One] will drive him from Uprightness, because the Upright do not treat anyone badly. Even if the Upright one does not treat anyone badly, the evil one will torment him with labor and anxiety and not allow him to comprehend the truth. And if he is not contented and neither observes the rites (c.749) nor prays during them, nor gives alms nor fasts by them as something appropriate for the Upright ones, he is not able to thoroughly understand Uprightness. But he is not able to attain Perfection unless he has abandoned the earth according to what our Lord has commanded him and has taken up the cross, has emptied and lowered himself and become celibate; and has become like a servant in his obedience, and not like a lord in his supervision. Let him have compassion on the sinners and the righteous; and let him love to give himself up for the evil ones, as [did] our Lord and his apostles. Then he will comprehend the height and the depth, the length and the width[18] along with the saints, these who have understood the Holy One in everything he has shown them, with compassion and love and peace for all people, good and bad.

8.   These, then, are the tricks that the evil one contrives against those who are becoming solitaries and [who] seek

17. Literally, 'your possession'.   18. Ep 3:18

to leave everything and ascend to the higher realm in the steps of him who ascended before them. For those who have chosen the manner of life of Uprightness and marriage, let them give out of these earthly things alms and virtuous things from what they possess and become Upright in their ways. If they desire to leave behind the earth, as our Lord commanded, and journey in the footsteps of his lowliness, they will quickly ascend to Perfection, for they are not very (c.752) far from it.

For the Perfect are like angels, as our Lord said, 'Those who are worthy of that resurrection are not able to die, but are like the angels'.[19] From then on they become like angels. Whoever wishes to be perfected should imitate the angels.

Let us see, what is the work of the angels? The angels do not cultivate the earth, nor do they clothe the naked, nor feed the hungry, nor does their mind remain on earth, but with the word of our Lord they admonish everyone as he is capable. As they are continually in [God's] presence and minister to his majesty, they are not anxious for their food, because our Lord is concerned for them and for everyone. It is fitting for these who would become like angels that they should imitate angels and preach the word of our Lord, as he had commanded them, 'Do not be anxious about food or clothing',[20] nor about themselves, nor about their brothers, because our Lord cares for them and for everyone, and he is concerned about his creation so that he might guide it.

By means of the Upright ones he feeds the needy, and they have [thus] become like the angels, constantly in the presence of his majesty. But if everyone desired to renounce the earth and come to Perfection, our Lord would not hold them back on account of food and clothing, but [God] would make manna descend as he had done for the Israelites (c.753) in the desolate desert, [which was] with-

19. Lk 20:35-36   20. Mt 6:25

out seed and had no crop in it. He would have made coats as he had done for Adam and Eve on that day when they sinned greatly. How much more will he do for us on the day when we decide to pursue Perfection and follow [our Lord] and do his great will? Whoever wishes to become like this, [will not] all his creation become like the angels in heaven?

9. For Perfection is above heaven and Uprightness is below on the earth, standing on the boundary of evil. The Upright are being battered by it at all times because they are the children of [evil's] boundary and [the evil one is] the resident of these cursed frontiers.[21] 'Cursed is the earth on account of you', said God to Adam,[22] because from the moment you loved whatever is on the earth and hated whatever is in heaven, look, [the earth's boundary] has been given to you. Only do not slip [and] fall below the earth down to Sheol, just as you have descended from heaven to earth. For when you fell from heaven the earth received you—where you can find life, even if you will not attain Perfection, as long as you labor in this first fall. You have indeed tasted death.

Now, if you fall from the earth, you will be cast down into Sheol, and you will fall from Uprightness and inherit (c.756) torment, as you were deprived of the good tree of life. Because you have tasted the evil thought and have known evil, you have fallen from heaven to earth. But if you really do [something] evil, you will fall from earth to Sheol.

The end of *Mēmrā* Twenty-Five.

21. Literally, 'the daughter of these cursed frontiers'.
22. Gn 3:17

Mēmrā Twenty-Six

ON THE SECOND LAW THAT
THE LORD ESTABLISHED
FROM ADAM

Summary: A discourse directed to the Upright who live by the law God gave to Adam after his transgression of the first law. The Gospel of Jesus is the same one against which Adam transgressed, so there is still hope for the Upright to reach Perfection.
(c.757)

1. [This *mēmrā* is] about the law that the Lord established for Adam after he had eaten from the tree. 'Look, from now on, I am establishing for you a law in this thing that you have loved. Because if you do not transgress this law that I am establishing for you, it will protect you from Sheol and will give you eternal life and the heritage and the resurrection. But if you act presumptuously against it as [you did] upon the first [law], you will see Sheol and suffer torment.

But then if you keep this law of Uprightness and pursue love and Perfection, at the end of the ages of this world I will be revealed and will perfect you and all who pursue love and Perfection and you will enter (c.760) the spiritual Paradise that you left. I will show all who are living during and after my advent how you were created like the watchers, and how they can arrive at that holy creation in which you were created. I will clothe your image and show them everything.

For after you depart from this world, your children will forget your creation, how it came to be, and what is the tree from which you ate. They will liken your creation to everything [else], how it was, and [likewise] with the tree from which you ate. They will not know [anything] except a few things until I come and show them clearly what was my will from the beginning. For your children will stray and fall even from Uprightness, which I am commanding you today.'

2.   God said to Adam when he established for him another law on that day he transgressed against the first [law]:

> Here is the possession that you have loved, oblivious to your [own] honor.[1] Acquire as much as you wish, only walk uprightly. Here is the earth that you have loved. It has been given to you; only do not take what belongs to your neighbor. Look, the [fruit of the] labor that you have sought has been given to you, only do not covet the [fruit of the] labor of your neighbor. Look, the marriage that you sought through the advice of the evil one has been given to you, only do not desire the wife of your neighbor and do not take two wives and do not allow your sons to commit fornication nor let your daughters become (c.761) harlots. Command your sons following you, and let your sons command their sons, until I come and become for you an example of Perfection.

---

1. Ps 49:12

3. He said to them:

> When you acquire, do not possess as [if it were] forever and forget me. When you build, [build] like people who know that you will not be here forever. But you ought to know that I will cause the earth and all that is in it to pass away and there will be a judgment and a rest; and everyone will be rewarded according to his deeds. O Adam and Eve, it is sufficient for you to have fallen from virginity and Perfection. Do not fall again from integrity and Uprightness.

For just as there is an opposite to Perfection: all the beauty of the earth visible to the eyes of the flesh; so there is an opposite to Uprightness: everything evil and harmful to a human being or grievous to everything in which there is life.

4. Therefore, after the first commandment, Adam and all the former Upright ones abided by that Uprightness that God had commanded Adam after he had transgressed against the first word and became an earthly being. But if the remainder of the people had continued in this Uprightness that is written, in which Adam and the Upright ones journeyed, another law would not have been given to them until the Lord came and gave this (c.764) Gospel for now. For the apostle said, 'The law was added to on account of error, this [law], which was given through Moses'.[2]

Therefore, Adam and all the Upright ones and the prophets and righteous ones waited for this peace, which is through our Lord, and died hoping that our Lord would come and make peace on earth. When the time was near in which God wished to reveal himself and bring about

2. Ga 3:19

reconciliation and peace on earth, the Spirit prayed for all people, good and evil, and said the following, 'Remember your word to your servant by which you gave confidence to Adam and to all the Upright ones, by which they were comforted in their humility, because your word[3] gave them life'.[4]

He whose declaration is true and whose promise is trustworthy came and perfected those who had left everything and had done his will and pursued love and Perfection. They died before his advent, but he made them enter the spiritual Paradise as he had promised; and he showed clearly to those who [came] later how Adam had lived at the beginning. He promised them Paradise and ascended from being with them so that they might abandon the earth and follow him.

5.   Now this Gospel, which Jesus gave, is the same one which Adam transgressed and [from which he] fell. That Uprightness that Moses and the prophets gave is the same one that was established for Adam after he had transgressed against the first commandment. (c.765) So the first law became the latter law and the latter [law became] the first one, just as the last became the first and the first [became] the last.[5] Whoever seeks Perfection and loves holiness, out of these things will come the holiness of the heart; he will give everything he has to the needy and ascend above whatever is visible. There will be controversy against him, yet he will neither judge nor demand [anything from] anyone, but will love everyone as a saint of our Lord, for he makes his love shine on everyone like the sun that the Father [causes to shine] upon all there is on the earth, whether good or evil, whether the just or the unjust.[6]

The end of *Mēmra* Twenty-Six.

3. Literally, '*mēmrā*'.   5. Mt 20:16
4. Ps 119:49   6. Mt 5:45

Mēmrā Twenty-Seven

ABOUT THE HISTORY
OF THE THIEF
WHO IS SAVED[1]

Summary: The title bears no apparent relation to the subject matter of the text. A sermonic discourse on one's readiness to suffer like Jesus on the way to Perfection. Concern is expressed for the immature lest they stray into idolatry or paganism. They should not leave home until they are mature enough to withstand the lies, slanders, and injustices incurred on the christian pilgrimage.
(c.768)

1. Our Lord sends one who will show the way of truth to all those whose labor he sees imitating his own sufferings. If they gaze upon the sufferings of our Lord and are wounded as he was wounded and pray for whoever strikes them, just as our Lord prayed for whoever struck him, and 'for whoever called him 'sorcerer' and 'bastard' and 'deceiver of the people'; if they greet whoever hands them over to death and wash his feet, just as our Lord did for Iscariot; if

---

1. The title is the one given to the *mēmrā* in Ms R. Cf. Mar Filoksinos Yohanna Dolabany, *Catalogue of Syriac Manuscripts in St. Mark's Monastery (Dairo DMor Marqos)* (Sidawi Printing House: Damascus, 1994) 379. Kmosko's title is 'About the History of the Robbers', which he admits is not intelligible for the context.

305

they act in this way and imitate his sufferings, our Lord himself will be their teacher. He will show them his way (c.769) and his door. And then, they will be adults and become preachers and teachers for Jesus to all people.

2.   Therefore, when we know the truth and love and lowliness, then it will be right for us to travel from our city to another place. But if they are not weaned from milk and then depart from their city, they will be in need of a foreign wetnurse. Perhaps she will not educate them thoroughly, and perhaps not agreeing with the church, she will make them into idolaters or pagans. These will be led like children [who] stray unaware and die. But as long as they are still young, they should remain in their city, whether man or woman, until they are confident in themselves that they can come and go without perishing.

There [are] good nurse[s] who can educate better than a mother. And there [are] evil nurse[s] who either make a person a servant of sin or a servant to her own children. Should we not also learn from the world, for as long as their children are young, [parents] do not allow them to go onto the road, unless they hand them over to one who will receive and guide them? When they become adults, then [their parents] will be confident about them and will send them by themselves and they will come and go and not perish.

3.   I say to you, my son, until you become (c.772) an adult and establish yourself, knowing how to go and come without being a burden upon anyone, [only] then shall you travel on the way of our Lord Jesus, lest when you have gone out from the world, someone might deceive you and make you a servant of sin or of people. But if your parents are evil and cruel like the parents of Thecla, do like Thecla, whom they beat and tortured and threw into the fire; she did not dishonor them at all, nor did she do the evil will of those who had taught her.[2]

2. Cf. *Acts of Paul and Thecla*

But today the world sits and condemns us, saying, 'Now, because of Christianity, let us reject our son or our daughter, for even when we say to them, "Come and eat", they dishonor [us]. Because of one stubborn word that we say to them as parents, in order to test whether they have any patience, they give back to us ten bad words. Is it because we are sons of the world that we are unaware that Jesus taught his disciples lowliness and tranquility?' [The parents] say, 'We were happy to work to nourish them during their childhood, and would have [wished] only to have seen in them the fruits of Perfection'.

Notice that on account of our stubbornness our parents complain, not on account of our lowliness. When your parents are very stubborn and evil, show (c.773) them your lowliness [for] a year or a month or even ten days, and then depart. Do you think that when you depart, not being humble, you have defeated evil? That is when your struggles will multiply, when you depart from the company of your family. And if you do not have lowliness sin will corrupt you. But if you decide in your mind to endure everything that happens to you—falsehood, slander, and injustice— while they are saying to you that you have committed adultery and fathered a child, and you are silent like a good rock, which is battered by a hundred pickaxes [and] does not say [anything, well and good]. Otherwise, do not depart, because you are still too young.

4. An adult is able to endure things much greater and more hateful than these, even as far as [people] accusing, scourging, and crucifying him, as they did to the apostles. He is able to endure silently, his dignity being between himself and his master. But [first grow up and then][3] depart. [If] your parents strike you because of [christian] teaching and the word of God, which you have gone to hear, and [when] you return they curse you, endure and revere

3. Ms A has a lacuna of five letters: cf. MsR.

them until you become an adult.

From this point [onward], you are examining your soul; if you have the ability to endure strangers, then you will go without anxiety while being dignified between you and our Lord. [If] you say, 'Is it not better if (c.776) they beat me wherever I go, than my parents and my towns-people beating me on account of [christian] teaching and lowliness?'—in this way you will become an adult, in that you bear the burden of your soul and wear out your mind with [christian] teaching and with questions of the Word [of God]. In as much as you are lowly, so you shall grow.

In order that you do not say, 'He holds me back'— since our Lord said, 'Come after me[4] emptying yourselves from anything visible'—I will not hold you back, although I am afraid lest you will perish, yet I am glad that today you are learning and tomorrow you shall be teaching your parents. On the next day, your lowliness [will teach] the priests and on the fourth day the covenant[ers]. On the fifth day [you will teach] the adolescents and on the sixth day you will be a new creation like Adam, and will engage in busi-ness and your lowliness will be known to all people. On the seventh day you shall rest with him who has summoned you to the supernal Jerusalem. It depends only upon you to become lowly and to know the truth and [then] you will become a father to others. But I advise you with love to know what is good for you, [but] I will not judge you. Be a son of wisdom and understand everything and pray for me with the love of our Lord Jesus Christ.

5. There are teachers in our day who when they go to instruct someone who does not know [anything] (c.777) say to him, 'Come on, leave', and when he has gone out [the teachers] say to him, 'Go ask our Lord'. But they leave [the student] to learn [by himself], not knowing who is our Lord nor what is the doctrine. If our Lord does not send

4. Mt 19:21

him a teacher from some place, they will make him useless since he does not know how to pray, and they do not even allow him to learn [by himself]. He will become like an ignorant merchant who does not know how to conduct himself, so that whatever he accumulates he will dissipate in his ignorance.

Perhaps you will say, 'God chose the ignorant ones to put the wise to shame'.⁵ These ignorant ones whom God chose were ignorant in earthly matters, but were wise in heavenly affairs, as it is written, 'Because I do not possess [great] learning, I will enter into the strength of the Lord'.⁶ That is, because I have rejected earthly wisdom, I will acquire heavenly wisdom. But I say,

> Learn the sufferings of our Lord and his lowliness, and in this way you will be bound up with his sufferings, whether you are standing or sitting. Be tied to our Lord in heaven and do not become tethered in a circle like a beast, not knowing anything, and so tie yourself down to the earth. But tie yourself at all times to our Lord in heaven, offering sacrifices of knowledge, whether you are standing or kneeling, whether you are walking or singing (c.780) in the Holy Spirit. No one should doubt the church or its priests, [for] from the catholic church all truth shall be known. Let us love even idolaters and infidels, while the catholic church is great in our eyes.

6.   When you know how to forgive, then pray, saying, 'Our Father who is in heaven, forgive us as we also have forgiven our debtors',⁷ as Jesus our Lord taught us to love one another and all the children of Adam. When we know

---

5. 1 Co 1:27   6. Ps 71:15   7. Mt 6:9-12

how to act in this way, and forgive in this way, let us go pray, for we do not call upon our Lord for condemnation. The disciples of our Lord acted in this way and then went to pray, as he had said to them, 'Pray for all people so that they might not enter into temptation.'[8] As it is written, 'Do not let a spiteful word out of your mouth[9] . . .'[10] no one should hear from our mouth a spiteful word, neither in our city nor in our parents' home'.

Let us bow our head and kneel to everyone. We ought to love everyone as the apostle said, 'Do not owe anything, except to love one another'.[11] We should know what we owe every person:[12] to whoever [requires] honor, [let us give him] honor; to whoever [requires] fear, [give him] fear; to whoever (c.781) [needs] a greeting, a greeting; to whoever [wants] love, love; to whoever [needs] a visit, [pay him] a visit; to whoever [requires] knowledge, [give him] knowledge.

But [if] the one to whom we owe honor is greater than us, let us not give him teaching so that he might find fault and say, 'Are you teaching me?' And to whomever we owe fear, let us not show him a naive love [lest] he should abuse us. And to whomever we owe an ordinary love, let us not show him sadness and distress him. Whomever we owe a visit, let us not greet him from afar [lest] he complain about us. And whomever we owe a greeting, let us not linger with him lest he burden us with his stories and fables. Whomever we owe knowledge, let us not stop being with him until he is assured [of the truth], lest he be scandalized and perish.

7.   Let us be innocent in this world of evil, but wily in order to do all sorts of good things. Let us make peace with everyone and profit from everyone. Let us be of use to everyone and recognize all the voices of Perfection from

8. Mt 26:41   11. Rm 13:8
9. Ep 4:29   12. Rm 13:7
10. Lacuna in text.

those of Uprightness, and those of Uprightness from those of Satan. On account of this, our Lord said, 'Be wily',[13] so that we might know one doctrine from another and one word from another word, not to expel evil people from among the good. For an evil doctrine harms us, not (c.784) evil people. If they murder us, the profit is ours.

The end of the twenty-seventh *Mēmrā* on the thief.

---

13. Mt 10:16

Mēmrā Twenty-Eight

ON THE FACT
THAT THE HUMAN SOUL
IS NOT IDENTICAL
WITH THE BLOOD

Summary: A theological exposition on the inbreathing of the Holy Spirit, the Paraclete, given to the Perfect; and the lesser gift of the Holy Spirit to the Upright. The latter part returns to the theme of the Visible Church as the image of the heavenly church—Abraham is the example of one who was saved while married and having many possessions.
(c.785)

1. Let us now speak about the proposition that is brought forward by some people, that the spirit and the soul in human beings are created. They take the human soul to be blood, just like the animal soul. And they say that the soul dies when the body does, while the spirit then leaves alive. But we shall show that the soul does not die with the body, but leaves it alive, so it can be understood why the soul is sometimes called 'spirit' and sometimes 'soul'.

According to the nature of his creation, a person is body and soul only; the Holy Spirit of God comes to dwell in him when he keeps the commandments of his Creator. This is the way it has been ever since the first day, when God created the body and soul of Adam. It was then that he breathed into him [something] of his Holy Spirit, **(c.788)** and thus Adam became a living soul.[1] As Isaiah[2] says, 'He created the spirit of man within him'.[3] He does not say, 'He breathed into', in order to make clear that the 'inbreathing' was from the Spirit of the Lord and not a creature. The same we know today; 'When the Spirit of the Lord is not in a person, he is rejected'.[4] However, when the 'inbreathing' dwells in him, then he is a living soul, in the same manner as on the day that the Lord breathed into man after he had created him, and in the same manner as our Lord breathed his Spirit onto the face of his disciples, in order that they might be like Adam was before he sinned. For whenever Adam or his offspring sin, this 'inbreathing', which is the Spirit of God recedes from them, and when they repent, [God] comes and dwells in each of them according to his receptivity, that is, according to the measure he has of the gifts[5] of Christ, [who gives] diverse gifts.

2.   One person's gift is greater, another's lesser, in accordance with its measure; our Lord gives him as much as his mind can contain. Therefore, people in whom there is a little of the Holy Spirit are neither rejected nor are they perfect and fulfilled. For if the vessel of the human soul is not full (c.789) of the Spirit of God, it does not receive that total 'inbreathing' by which it becomes a living soul in the beginning. And that gift of which the one—in whom nothing is lacking—is full, is called 'the Paraclete'. How do we know that one has received it? By the fact that there is no defect in him, that he is full of all good things and knows all the truth. This is what our Lord said, 'I shall send the Paraclete to you, who will make all truth known to you'.[6]

1. Cf. Gn 2:7
2. Is 42:5, confused with Zc 12:1
3. 'Created'—Syriac; 'formed', Hebrew and LXX.
4. Rm 8:9
5. That is, 'charismata',
6. Jn 15:26, 16:13

So once one has received the 'great gift', which is the Paraclete, he immediately knows all the truth and begins to grow and to eradicate all his defects. Then he is made perfect in that Paraclete; he is fulfilled with all good things and is serving in the spirit, according to the perfect and acceptable will of our Lord.

3. Now the Holy Spirit is a [Spirit of] many gifts—one gift, however, is greater than another. 'And if you are eager for the greater gifts', [Paul] says, 'I shall show you a gift that is greater than all those,.[7] So you see that one is more excellent than another. Although the Holy Spirit of God and the Paraclete are one and the same, [Scripture] speaks of the Paraclete on the one hand and the Holy Spirit on the other hand, in order to distinguish the greater gifts from the lesser ones; he who (c.792) receives the Paraclete is made perfect by this great gift, but those who receive the lesser gifts are not made perfect, because they are deficient. Unless the Great Gift comes, they are not fulfilled. Yet everyone, according to his works and his gifts, will become great on the day of our Lord. 'You ascended on high,' Scripture says, 'you took captivity captive and you gave gifts to people'.[8] So you see there are many gifts.

4. Consequently, the soul is not identical with the blood, but it leaves the body that then dies. If the Holy Spirit is in the soul, the soul goes with the Spirit to the house of the living, to the stores of light. If the Holy Spirit is not in the soul, the soul by itself leaves the body. When Adam had sinned, the 'inbreathing' was taken from him and thus he tasted death.

5. This is what our Lord said, 'If two of you agree on earth and keep my words, whatever you ask in prayer and

7. 1 Co 12:31
8. Ep 4:8; Ps 68:19

believe, while keeping my words, you will receive'.[9] These 'two' are the interior and the exterior person who agree in the keeping of the commandments; they ask and receive from God the gifts of the Holy Spirit who will be given to them in the form of a pledge, and a person will be established as a trinity and live.

If anyone should say, 'If the Spirit of God has been in Adam, then how (c.793) could he have been so foolish that the Spirit failed to teach him not to obey the evil one, who managed to lead him astray and frustrate his growth, contrary to what he told him?' Well, the Holy Spirit, that is, the Lord on the day he created him told him, 'If you eat from this tree you will taste death';[10] that is, if you transgress the commandment and obey Satan, you will taste death. So you see how the Spirit did teach him but he did not want to obey him, just as he teaches us too and we do not want to obey, but follow Satan who leads us astray with his deceitful promises—exactly as in the case of Adam.

6.   Furthermore, there are people who have an external mind, an exterior understanding, an exterior sense perception, an exterior taste, an exterior order, and an exterior intelligence, all belonging to their 'exterior person'. They are people who have a feeling for the things of this world, who are knowledgeable, experienced, disciplined, and understanding in the visible things here on earth, but for the rest they do not see and hear or understand anything, that is, anything the body and the flesh cannot hear and see. It is not that they have no inner eyes and ears and an inner intelligence, but they have been struck with blindness by sin; they have an inner blockage. That is why such a person does not see or hear the hidden things. Just as he who has injured his visible organs cannot see, hear, (c.796) and understand the visible things that are in this world, so also

9. Mt 18:19, 21:22; Mk 11:24—third person plural used in second part of the Syriac sentence.
10. Gn 2:17

he who has injured his interior organs by sin cannot see, hear and understand those things which appertain to the world of truth and the invisible.

7.   This is how visible organs are injured: either by God or by malicious people or by Satan—by means of violence (in cases where someone strikes his neighbor and harms him), by contrivances, or because it is [actually] advantageous to a person. Someone can be injured by the evil one when he obeys him, but also by God, namely, when he is injured by a punishment, since that is [actually] advantageous to him.

Now the interior organs can likewise be injured by the evil one when one pledges his obedience to him and follows his teaching. One can equally injure the organs of his soul. If the soul is willing to be obedient, he injures it by evil teaching, for by evil teaching one can injure the interior organs. Or when our Lord is looking the other way, a person can damage one of the senses of the soul through magical spells.

But God, since he is going to judge (c.797) people, does not injure the interior organs. Now if the exterior organs have been injured, the interior organs should keep his commandments. However, if there is someone whose interior organs are injured by God, he will not judge him on the day of Judgment, because his is a just judgment, and he will not judge a person to whom he has not given eyes, ears, intelligence, and understanding to know and to understand him.

8.   Therefore a person receives the Holy Spirit from baptism in order that he may obey his commandments and keep them with faith. God has made two worlds and two ministries, so that from the one that is visible the other, which is invisible, may be seen.[11] The same is the case with

11. Cf Rm 1:20; Heb 11:3, 8:5

the visible and hidden Covenant, Church, baptism, food, prayer, altar, and gifts. In short, in every respect the ministry that is on earth is alike to that which is in heaven. And because people did not comprehend the heavenly one, He gave them its likeness on earth so that, when standing in the visible church and eating from the visible altar, they might live (c.800) in eternity in the hidden Church, which is in heaven, and eat from the hidden altar—an ineffable ministry, too great for the human mouth.

Now the visible ministry is like the hidden; everything that is seen is a symbol of something unseen. In the likeness of that which is seen has been formed, that which is unseen; and from the likeness of that which is seen, spiritual people can elucidate to him who believes and desires to see. 'The things that are seen were made from the things that are not seen', says the apostle.[12] This is why God prefigured in the body more than one likeness of salvation to the prophets and apostles and then in the Spirit showed them the perfect exemplar.

9.   But because Adam and Eve had gone astray in transgressing the commandment concerning the heavenly ministry, which they used to fulfill like angels and together with the angels, God gave them the visible ministry on earth in the likeness of that heavenly one, so that they might not all perish together. But now, ever since our Lord has been reconciled to whoever of the children of Adam desires to minister in heaven in the spirit, our Lord shows [the heavenly ministry] anew; that is, to anyone who obeys his words and leaves the earth and all that is visible behind him, following in knowledge him who leads (c.801) day by day; for when such a person has come to know this visible ministry, [God] shows him the hidden and heavenly ministry.

10.   For example, [God] appeared to Moses on the moun-

11. Cf. Rm 1:20; Heb 11:3, 8:5   12. Heb 11:3

tain as a human being and showed him the ministry of the spirit. From then on, Moses knew how to minister in the spirit and to see the glory of the almighty Lord, as it is written, 'The Lord spoke with Moses face to face, as a man speaks to his friend'.[13] He also said to him:

> Go down, show to the Israelites on the physical earth everything that I have shown to you. Show them the whole ministry of the spirit physically as I have shown it to you on the mountain spiritually. In this way, show them first in the body and then in the spirit; teach those who wish to serve in the heavenly tabernacle how to minister in heaven and show those who wish to serve in the earthly tabernacle how to serve on earth.

11.   So you see that the Lord, like a human being, has instructed all the prophets, and then they knew how to see and hear spiritually. Nowadays, the Perfect are baptized as though in a mirror, until they see him face to face.[14] And since the Perfect lack clothing and food, and God sends no manna at all down to them, the Upright can give [them] alms in order to be saved in this way. (c.804) God uses the sicknesses that [the Perfect] have while they are being perfected to chastise them, so that they are brought low and do not exalt themselves; and when they pray to him, they are healed. Because they lack the remedy that Adam did not lack, our Lord made them in want, in order that they should pray more and make more supplication to him. The Perfect today lack those things that Adam did not lack and therefore they are not deprived of the spiritual paradise and of Adam's former glory, because our Lord said to them, 'All the more will [such] things be added unto you'.[15] And

13. Ex 33:11   15. Lk 12:31
14. Cf. 1 Co 13:12

they are more excellent than that earlier creation because they are vexed by evil people but endure them—seeing that had Adam not transgressed the commandment, there would not be any evil ones. If anyone should ask, 'So those prophets and righteous people who lived before the advent of our Lord, who were either married or had possessions, were they under the curse?' [Then he should know that] one should not say anything against them; they did as the Lord had told them during their whole lives.

Consider Abraham and Sarah. After they had ceased carnal intercourse and their bodies were dead to desire, they obeyed the word of God and returned to having intercourse. In the same way, if God had told Abraham when he was young that he should keep himself holy from his wife, he would have kept himself holy, or if God had told him to empty himself, he would have emptied himself. (c.805) Also, Abraham received the needy who did not even believe that God exists. He imitated God, who makes his love rise upon the good and the bad.[16] For although everyone pities the good, one does not pity the bad, unless his love is great like our Lord's.

Here ends the twenty-eight *Mēmrā* on the fact that the soul is not identical with the blood.

16. Cf. Mt 5:45

Mēmrā Twenty-Nine

ON THE DISCIPLINE
OF THE BODY

Summary: A sermon directed to the entire church to conduct their ministry with passion and enthusiasm, not just 'by rote'. The author expresses concern over the lapses of the Perfect and exhorts the Upright to treat others well and follow their own rule.
(c.808)

1. 'I will subdue my body and subordinate [it],' says Paul, 'lest while I preach to others, I myself will be rejected.'[1] I will make my body a servant and discipline it and I will not allow it to clothe, put on shoes, feed, and refresh itself according to its will. And I will not allow it to be honored whenever it wishes, not even to sleep with honor, but I will subdue it with hunger, thirst, and nakedness, vigil, weariness, asceticism, and emaciation, and with much fasting and prayer, with supplication and loud crying, with many bitter tears,[2] and with lowliness, endurance, and patience. (c.809)

    I will subdue myself in order to honor everyone as a servant and in order to stand before and greet everyone before me, bowing [my] head before everyone. I will make [my body] run on foot like a servant in order to reconcile

1. 1 Co 9:27   2. Heb 5:7

with its enemies, while not offending them, and to bow its
head before whoever is less than it, just as our Lord bowed
his head before John [the Baptist] and was baptized by him,
although [John] was less than he, and [our Lord] did not
have need of him. That great one was blessed by that lesser
one—who is his servant and his creature—so that he might
become our teacher, for we might do the same for whoever is lesser than we and has need of us, just as John had
need of our Lord.

I will make my body wash the feet of its enemies and
greet its murderers, just as our Lord greeted Iscariot and
prayed for his murderers. I will make it call [all] people 'my
father' and 'my mother' and 'my brothers and sisters', 'my
sons and daughters', 'my lords' and 'my parents', just as
our Lord called his servants 'my brothers'. For he said, 'I
will announce your name to my brothers'.[3] And later he
said to Iscariot, 'Why have you come, my friend?'[4] If (c.812)
[Jesus] then called his betrayer 'my friend', how indeed did
he call his loved ones, and how [did he call] these who gave
themselves up for him?

I will lead [my body] wherever it does not wish:[5] to its
despisers and to those who are angry against it. Just as our
Lord went to teach his crucifiers and despisers, I will make
it visit as the servant of everyone, the servant of servants,
just as our Lord visited the evil and insolent ones who held
him in contempt, and just as God visited his people with
good intent, although they had malevolently dared to kill
and hate him for no reason, as it is written in the Old Testament, 'They hated me for no reason'.[6]

As it is written in the Gospel, 'To his own he came,
but his own did not receive him. But to those who did receive him, he gave the authority to become the children of
God.'[7] On account of this, Paul wrote to us, 'Examine your
bodies and then eat the body of the Lord and drink his

3. Ps 22:22   6. Ps 35:19
4. Mt 26:50   7. Jn 1:11-12
5. Jn 21:18

blood. For whoever does not chastise his body should examine and subordinate it until he subdues it and it is obedient to him, and then he may eat the body of our Lord and drink his blood. He will eat and drink to his condemnation.'[8] Because you do not restrict (c.813) your bodies from food and nor make supplication to our Lord that he set you free, there are many sickly and ill people among you and many who sleep and many who are drunken, greedy, and unrestrained, because they do not examine themselves and subdue their bodies.[9]

2.   If sin is mixed in people by the transgression of the commandment, it will entice them to acts of gossip and licentiousness, and of pride and pomp, of pleasures and desirable things of all kinds, of avarice, lasciviousness, and drunkenness, of ridicule and games. Nevertheless, the individual human being loves these lowly deeds, just as in the beginning on account of these [lowly deeds] people listened to sin by their own choice. Also sin, because it knows that our individual selves enjoy these deeds, entices us to follow them so that people might be captured through what they like doing, for they will follow whatever they like without a struggle.

If Paul had not known that our body would become a companion to sin and would wrestle against that small breath of life which is [still] in our mind, and seek to kill us completely with sin so that we might not (c.816) return to the house of life, he would have not said the following, 'I will subdue my body',[10] so that it will not immerse me in sin, which fights against people outwardly and inwardly, [along with] its kindred, the evil spirits.

Therefore, as this is written, '[Adam] desired the food';[11] that is, luxury and pleasures. But whoever desires our Lord to dwell in him forces his body to serve our Lord by these

8. 1 Co 11:27-29
9. 1 Co 11:30

10. 1 Co 9:27
11. Gn 3:6

fruits of the spirit that were recorded by the apostle.[12] He protects his body and soul from these deeds of the flesh about which he wrote. But the body in which sin is mixed rests upon the deeds of the flesh, [while] the spirit of God rests upon its fruits. See how Paul commands us to examine ourselves until we have the strength to keep his commandments and surrender to our Lord.

3.   Look, my son, consider how much power is hidden in the praises of our Lord, yet we repeat them by rote without passion. Because of this, the words of God do not effect in us good deeds, for we do not give them a place in our soul to lay down roots in us. For that matter, even pagans, if they want, [can] learn the words of our Lord by rote at the same time they are worshipping in the house of their idols and doing the will of the devils.

(c.817) When one of us teaches his brother a psalm, saying to him, 'Refrain from rage and cease from anger',[13] and [if] that teacher does not take it to heart, nor even does the disciple consider what his master is teaching him, look, are we not going through the motions[14] without passion or knowledge? Because we do not do what we say, it is the same as if we do not know. Because of this, the prophet said, 'I will think with my heart and speak with my mouth and make my voice heard';[15] that is, I will know what I am saying. 'Like a hart that longs for a pond of water, so also my soul longs for you, O Lord. My soul thirsts for you. living God, when may I come and see your face?'[16]. We are not as we teach, not knowing how to do [what we teach]. Even if a person reminds us that we ought to do thus we say, 'Yes', but look, are not the words of God playing in us, just like a dead cymbal in which there is no living soul, and we have learned by rote, and not with passion or with interior understanding?

12. Ga 5:22   15. Ps 77:6
13. Ps 37:8   16. Ps 42:1-2
14. Literally, 'behaving by rote'.

When we say, 'An evil heart has left us and we do not know evil',[17] yet we hate one another so that not even a word of mouth or a greeting of lips do we exchange with one another. And on occasions (c.820) we even throw evil pestilences against one another and repay evil things to one another. Look, is not the truth concealed from our mind, since we do not genuinely learn the words and teach others by rote?

> I have humbled my soul through fasting
> and prayer, and I have made my clothing
> sackcloth,[18] and I have eaten ashes like
> bread,[19] and my knees have grown weak
> from fasting and my flesh is wasted with-
> out oil,[20] and I have become a foreigner to
> my brothers and a stranger to the children
> of my mother.[21] A person of the world was
> not worthy of them,[22] they were clothed with
> the skins of lambs and of goats[23] and did
> not possess anything in this transitory world.

We teach these others, but do not teach ourselves. Instead we eat meat and drink wine improperly, while our former companions ate ashes and drank their tears in weeping. We put on ornamental clothes and adorn ourselves for the desire of our flesh, while our predecessors wore the skins of goats and hideous sackcloth. We have riches and are lords of the domain.[24] We suspiciously watch[25] strangers while our predecessors were made foreigners (c.821) and strangers to their brothers and parents and did not possess anything in this world, aside from distasteful food and despicable clothing. These, our first teachers, were despised and were the lowliest of all people, yet we seek to

17. Ps 101:4
18. Ps 69:10-11
19. Ps 102:9
20. Ps 109:24

21. Ps 69:8
22. Hb 11:38
23. Hb 11:37

24. Literally, 'lords of the house of the father'.
25. Literally, 'we breathe against'.

be exalted above all people. They walked with afflictions, yet we desire to walk in ease and luxury.

When we talk about these [predecessors], but do not act [like them], is it not as if we have not learned [anything] and that we do not know what we have learned? Because of this, it is said, 'Blessed is the people who know your praises. O Lord, they shall walk in the light of your face and exult in your name all day, and be exalted by your righteousness. Because you are the glory of our strength, and by your will may our horn be exalted.'[26] Notice that if we knew and did the praises of the Lord, maybe we would be walking in the light of his countenance and exulting in the redemption of his name, our horn would be exalted in the victory of the righteousness of our Lord Jesus Christ, whom we worship.

4. 'I entreat you, my brothers, by the gentleness and lowliness of Christ, to present your bodies as a living sacrifice, holy (c.824) and acceptable [to God] through reasonable worship.'[27] For the thing that is killed is called the sacrifice, while something living is not called [a sacrifice]. But because we are being killed while we are living, we are called 'a living sacrifice'.

In order that a person might be troubled by prayer and lowliness and by spiritual knowledge, these are the punishments and the death of the body: the trial of hunger and of thirst so that a person might eat bread and salt by weight, and drink water by measure, and be crucified against bread and water and not be satisfied, just as with the example of Ezekiel [who] ate and drank by measure and weight and was afflicted by hunger and thirst and was not satisfied.[28]

5. My brothers, listen and understand. There are many fasts commanded by God to people so that they might fast

---

26. Ps 89:15-17   27. Rm 12:1   28. Ezk 4:16

and receive help, lower themselves and increase in excellence. Therefore, anyone who fasts from all foods and avoids all evil things and does all good things, his fast is perfectly evident. Moreover, if he eats bread and water only, he will do even better. If he eats bread by weight (c.825) and drinks water by measure, so that not even dry bread and cold water will satisfy, he will excel all the more and be made pure. And if he sprinkles ashes upon bread and eats as it is written, 'I have eaten ashes like my bread',[29] while lowering himself before all people and greeting all people, with these things he greatly breaks down his body, his spirit is strengthened by our Lord [who] will have mercy upon him and save him.

If he fasts from fancy clothes and from all he possesses and empties himself and becomes celibate and is without anxiety, his mind residing in our Lord all the time, night and day, our Lord will immediately save him and perfect him. For on account of great amounts of food and fancy clothes people bear [the burden of] anxiety and suffocate, and ceasing from [involvement with] God, are without fruits.

6.   Therefore, as there are different [kinds of] fasts with respect to these foods, so also those people who are incapable of these fasts of which I have spoken and are married, when they loosen the bonds of iniquity and cut off the chains of deceit, and set the oppressed free,[30] they will genuinely fast, as it is written, 'This fast is preferred by God in which a person avoids evil things and eats (c.828) food rather than fasting from food and doing evil things'. If a person avoids evil things, gives alms, redeems the afflicted, and gives relief to the needy, he will steadily progress in his fast [even] when he eats and drinks well and when he dresses nicely and possesses wealth. He is an Upright one [even] while married.

29. Ps 102:9   30. Is 58:6

For fasting and prayer restrain a person from evil things and encourage him to do good things. Therefore, whoever surpasses all these evil things, and empties himself and becomes celibate, and fasts these [kinds of] fasts of which I have spoken above, fasts to the world[31] and is able to pray and keep the commandments of our Lord. Our Lord gives him the power to live according to his great and acceptable and perfect will.[32]

7.   Just as there are many kinds of fasts, so there are many kinds of pleasures that annul many fasts. Just as one who is overpowered by many foods and many wines eats gluttonously and drinks intemperately, lives extravagantly and is lascivious, and is guilty; so one who exerts his own will through his anger lives extravagantly and is guilty. Whoever exerts his own will through adultery and fancy clothes (c.829) and is adorned for the desire of his flesh, lives extravagantly and is guilty. Revelers are not able to know the truth, [for] they are not free men, but even if they do something virtuous while they are [involved] in pleasures, they are greatly inferior and indeed are scarcely like the servants in the country of our Lord, and not like those who are free or the children and the heirs.[33]

Whoever steals or takes advantage, plunders or cheats, lives extravagantly and is guilty. With arrogance, licentiousness, and enmity, with song and game, speech and laughter, and by evil customs, a person will live extravagantly and be judged. By magic, murder, and falsehood, a person will live extravagantly and die. By divinations, oracles, incantations, by everything evil, and by every vain and hateful word, a person will live extravagantly and be guilty and be accused. If he does not repent and avoid these things, he will be found guilty and judged. But if he restrains himself from all these and fasts and lowers himself, he will triumph and rescue himself [from judgment]. (c.832)

31. Gospel of Thomas 27   33. Cf. Lk 15:13-17
32. Rm 12:2

8.   God is not in need of our fasts, nor is he harmed by our pleasures. But, since God knows that by these fasts we are turned around toward our house of life, and by means of them, moreover, we defeat evil, [God] commands us to fast earnestly, for our Lord knows that by pleasures and debauchery, sin will be strengthened against us at all times and Satan will corrupt us. On account of this our Lord warns us of pleasures and debauchery, for by them all evil deeds come to pass, but by fasts and prayers and afflictions all good things happen.[34] Because our Lord commands us, 'Be constant in prayer',[35] [it is] not by our prayer that our Lord will become great, but in order that we might pray and make supplication and ask our Lord to have mercy on us, guard and give us our virtuous requests, save us from all our sufferings, and rescue us from temptations, as he had said, 'Pray so that you do not enter into temptation'.[36] But by your grace and your compassion, save and deliver us from evil. Praise be to our savior and to our redeemer, forever and ever, Amen. (c.833)

9.   Not by nature are these foods unclean, nor because they enter the mouth of a person is one made unclean, but the body, living extravagantly and luxuriously, tenders to the mouth something that will defile it. A person bears the heaviness of food and it becomes in him an occasion for sin and [sin] causes him to sleep from the truth, eat gluttonously, drink intemperately, and grow fat from pleasures and to resist and forget our Lord and his commandments, as it is written, 'Israel grew fat and resisted, and forgot the Mighty One who had saved them'.[37]

Because of this our Lord commands, 'Take care lest your hearts become weighed down with food and drunkenness and thought of wealth,[38] and forgetting the truth and falling asleep from righteousness, you turn away from

34. Acts of Thomas 144:8   37. Dt 32:15
35. Lk 18:1; Col 4:2   38. Lk 21:34
36. Mt 26:41

my commandments and become guilty'. 'Pay attention and take care, because you do not know when the thief will come.[39] Your enemy Satan is awake and roars like a lion, seeking to swallow you alive.'[40]

It is not that ornate clothes are unclean, but those who wear them, [for] their eyes are lifted up and their heart is relieved [from anxiety], and transgressing the Law and breaking the commandments, they will be guilty on the day of our Lord [who] gives life to all. Because of this, our Lord said, 'This kind of Satan and sin will not (c.836) come out except through fasts and afflictions and love and through good works'.[41]

For the kind of days during which a person fasts [is not like] the kind of days during which he eats, and a person cannot return to prayer and lowliness, except by fasting. One does not exalt himself and become mighty except by the debauchery of food and of ornate clothes. For when the body is healthy through food, sin is strengthened in this way against the body and the soul by all sorts of evils and a person will be completely overcome. But when the body is sick through fasts and afflictions, in this way the soul is mighty in spirit and prayer.

10.   Therefore, just as there are many fasts and pleasures, so there are many kinds of humiliations that will defeat sin: greet this one, worship that one, honor another, and stand before this one. Call this one 'my brother' and 'my sister', and these 'my father' and 'my mother', and these 'my son' and 'my daughter'. Teach this one and love that one and delight in another. Follow this one and admonish that one and visit this one and sit with that one. Keep company with this one and greet that one and be greeted by that other one. Give relief to one and be afraid of another because he is evil. If you are able, honor him so that he

39. Mt 24:42; Lk 12:39
40. 1 P 5:8
41. Mt 17:21

will be regretful (c.837) and not treat [someone else] badly. Let your lowliness be evident to everyone by its right measure, so that you will know to which one you should owe each one of these acts of lowliness and to whom [is owed] two of them and to whom three and four, and to whom you should owe all of them, to him who brings you to Perfection and to perfect food, as it is written, 'Let your lowliness be evident to all people.[42] And know what you owe every person:'[43] to whom a greeting, to whom love and compassion, and to whom fear and honor. Do not owe a person anything except to love one another. May the Lord of peace be with you from God our Father and from our Lord Jesus Christ.[44]

11.   Moreover, in this way, my brothers, let us recognize that there are many harsh [people], as in the case of one [who] quarrels or strikes or persecutes, becoming even harder and being condemned.[45] In this way whenever someone hates another person, when he is angry or envious, enraged, haughty, or loathes a sinful person, and does not rebuke his [own] mind nor feel sorry for him—because we ourselves are sinners—and when he falls among rumor-mongers, if a person does not watch himself with regard to these and similar things, (c.840) he will indeed be harsh and sin.

Everyone is afraid [of him] and flees from him as from a vicious lion; [likewise:] when he observes [with envy] the honor of his neighbor; when he holds on to a grudge in his heart; when he rebels against the teaching; when he disdains the true word and cheats the truth; when he judges [someone] on account of these futile and transitory [things]; when he believes a report from afar even though he has neither seen nor examined it; when he proclaims a fact that is not truthful and fair to a person, and when he rebukes without righteousness and chastises without com-

---

42. Ph 4:5
43. Rm 13:7
44. Rm 15:33; Ph 1:2
45. Hermes, *Similitudes*, VI, 5, 5

passion; when he strikes secretly and speaks untruthfully;
when he is unjust and haughty; when he has an evil eye;
when he lies and does not keep his word; when he possesses something and does not relieve one who is needy of
it; when he is abusive and his mouth is full of filthy speech;
when he does not share honor with one who is deserving;
when he speaks about virtuous things with hateful words
or mocks the righteous ones or blasphemes the good; when
he attacks [someone] and brings forth and spitefully alleges
[rumors that] no one believes; when he hates strangers and
defrauds laborers; when he reveals the secret of his neighbor; [and] when he hates a person or reveals his secret.

By all these [things] and the rest, (c.841) which are
like them, a person will be condemned and hated and considered an abomination, and he will sin and be rejected by
God and by human beings.

But whoever defeats evil and rises above all these things
will live spiritually with our Lord and do all good things
and be compassionate upon all people, good and bad. By
his abundant love he will not forget anyone in order to call
him and turn him back to the house of life. Blessed is one
who acts this way, for he will be with our Lord.

12.   Concerning what the Spirit said in Isaiah—'This is
not a fast so that a person may bow his neck like a hook
and lower himself with sackcloth and ashes, but this is a
fast that I have chosen so that you may break the bonds of
iniquity and cut the burdens of deceit'.[46] Scripture did not
say that this fast is not virtuous. For the Lord did not completely reject sackcloth and ashes nor whoever bows his
neck like a hook in hunger and thirst, in poverty, renunciation, and solitariness; but the Lord reviled through Isaiah
the liars who inwardly were full of wiles and robbery and
spoils between their teeth and oppressed (c.844) free people

46. Is 58:5-6

with slavery, and 'they devour the houses of orphans and widows',[47] and do everything evil. The ashes and sackcloth under their feet lowered them falsely and they fasted from bread falsely so that they might show off to people. They humbled their bodies and disfigured their faces[48] and prayed in the market places in the sight of people so that they might be seen to be righteous ones,[49] while laboring secretly at wickedness.

Therefore, the Lord reviled these false people who fraudulently fasted and lowered themselves falsely, and said, 'I will not accept a deceitful lowliness and a false fast. It would be better for a person to eat and drink and wear white [clothes] than to do evil things while fasting and wearing sackcloth and causing everyone to wail through the evil things he does.'

13. But as for the rest, anyone who [desires to] transcend all these evil things and pursue good things, the Lord desires that he fast and lower himself, wear sackcloth and eat ashes and pray at all hours until he is redeemed by our Lord and triumphs in all [his] battles and refreshes himself. By this we should realize that the Lord reviled the false ones in Isaiah: see the prophets (c.845) and the apostles who lowered themselves, [how] they wore the skins of lambs and goats and put on sackcloth, and ate by weight and drank by measure[50] and ate ashes as it is written.[51] The Lord rejoiced over them and did not revile them, but said good things about them and made them great.

In this same way, the Lord delights today in whoever chooses the portion of solitariness and loves celibacy and desires to make his heart pure and see the Lord in his glory, and become perfect and dwell in him so that they might judge his body,[52] as Paul has said, and be humbled and

---

47. Mk 12:40; Mt 23:14
48. Mt 6:16
49. Mt 6:5
50. Ezk 4:10-11
51. Ps 102:9
52. 1 Co 9:27

make his body die, and fast constantly and pray and empty himself and become celibate and take up his cross and journey with the sufferings of our Savior. And if not, he is not able to be worthy of him and become Perfect and attain the portion that comes to the saints in light.

14. But as for the rest, everyone will find [reward] in the way that he labors and [the Lord] will reward every person according to his works and he will not deal unfairly with anyone who gives a cup of water or a morsel of bread.[53] No person [who] fasts discerningly even one hour, and missing the time of the meal prays and then eats, will be rejected.

When is a person so poor that he cannot afford a cup of water and morsel of bread, nor afford the washing (c.848) of feet nor the bandaging of [the wounds] of the sick nor hosting strangers [for the night], [if] he has a house? No one is too poor to [be able to give] compliments and a loving greeting, unless he wishes to become an evil one. But God, who sees the diligence of those who wish to make the weary live despite their poverty and are afflicted in order to keep his commandments, will treat them well with these visible things, and will give them these things that are promised, but not visible.[54]

15. A spiteful word may be spoken about someone, yet whether false or true, the speakers of these vain words shall have to give an answer on the day of judgment and they will [have to] give an excuse for them, [both] they and those who confirm them or repeat them after their speakers without having actually seen them nor really touched them. Because of this, the righteous ones should watch themselves so that not even when they have seen [something happen] should they speak, lest they pit one person against

53. Mt 10:42
54. Heb 6:1

another, in order that on the day of judgment and refutation they will not thereby be held captive. 'By your words you shall be justified and by your words you shall be condemned.'[55] And 'You will give a response to them on the day of judgment.'[56] Because of this (c.849) everyone who fears the judgment to come will guard himself from these things lest he be guilty and flee from many sins.

For if nothing that happens in the kingdom escapes this earthly king and his scribes, how much more is nothing done by people forgotten by that heavenly king and that spiritual scribe so that he may refute them about everything in an orderly fashion, saying the following, 'What did "so and so" say in "such and such" place? Come give an answer.' And if he says, 'I heard from "so and so",' no one will accept [it] from him. But [someone will say], 'Give some proof of the word. Why did you confirm and proclaim it while you had not seen it?'

16. It is also said in Isaiah, 'This is my rest; comfort the weary'.[57] See how the almsgivers comfort the weary, and [so] comfort the Lord, and [then the Lord] comforts them on his great day. In this world [the Lord] does not desert them, because David said, 'I have not seen the righteous one who was abandoned, nor even his seed who lacked bread'.[58]

Therefore, it is not because of this that the solitaries will be prohibited from meat and wine, but they shall strive hard not to be filled with dry bread and water, because in this way a person may be kept pure and become light and be glorified through fasting and prayer and the sufferings (c.852) of the body and through its scourging. If a person does not die during his life from the dangers of this world, or from harmful pleasures, or from murderous lusts, or from having placed on his head condemnatory things, he

55. Mt 12:37
56. Mt 12:36
57. Is 28:12
58. Ps 37:25

is not able to be with our Lord when he departs from his body, as Paul said,[59] and as our Lord said, 'My way is narrow and difficult'.[60] 'Whoever loves me will lose his soul on account of me',[61] that is, he will prohibit from [his soul] all physical comforts of its dissolute desire, and 'Whoever loses his soul with sufferings shall find it',[62] and 'His heart shall rejoice in me, says the Lord, and no one shall take away his joy'.[63] Because of this the Spirit spoke through the mouth of David, 'Toil in the world and you will live forever and not see corruption.'[64]

Therefore, why does he command us to labor and toil in this visible work? For we were not commanded to hew stones and make bricks and build buildings that will fall down or disappear tomorrow, nor even to acquire wealth and bury treasures in the earth because they exist only for a little while:[65] either we die and our riches remain in the earth, or they perish and leave us on the earth. (c.853)

17.   My brothers, everyone who does not labor in the service of truth will fall by spiteful desires and be worn out; if not, look, he will work the hoe all the days of [his] life. But if ceasing from the labor of truth he does not labor on the land, he will fall heavily by the lusts that kill at all times and be condemned. But because of this the Spirit said, 'Labor forever';[66] that is, as long as you are in this world, toil and run and make supplication with fasting and prayer, with vigil and petition, with asceticism, lowliness and love, with celibacy, poverty and patience, with sufferings, truth and knowledge, so that you may live forever and ever.·

18.   Let us realize, my brothers, and see how we are dead from righteousness and live by sin, and are healthy in the matter of transitory labor but sick in the labor that does not

59. 2 Co 5:8   63. Jn 16:22
60. Mt 7:14   64. Ps 49:8
61. Mt 16:25   65. Mt 16:19
62. Mt 10:39   66. Ps 49:8

pass away. As we labor carelessly in [the latter] and labor in transitory things with all our strength, our bodies are dead from the truth, love, and (c.856) celibacy, and live through the falsehood of error. For it was right that we should die from falsehood and lusts and live for truth and love and celibacy. Everyone who associates our body with sin and becomes its companion, because [our body] has tasted death from the beginning through the transgression of the commandment of our father Adam,[67] and strayed from truth and died from good things and lived by bad things, only through great labor will [our body] not die from evil things and live and be established in good things.

19. So now let us be joined to our Lord and let us fast and pray until he roots out[68] from us the old person, the outer and the inner.[69] May the grace of our Lord Jesus Christ be with all people that they may live, Amen.

Also concerning our despisers and our enemies, may [Jesus'] mercy be upon them, and may he forgive us all our sins. Moreover, may his grace abound especially over our friends, and may they reign by the hand of Christ. Amen.

Those who read [this book] and work diligently and learn and do and teach through our Lord Jesus Christ, remember me in prayer in the name of Jesus Christ. That is, the name that the Trinity desired so that through it the diseases and wounds of Adam and of his children will be healed and their spots will be made white and their sins will be cured. That is to say, the Tree of Life of the Garden of Eden (c.857) by which people are saved from death, this Tree being the Life-giving Spirit, as Paul has said. 'At this name of Jesus every knee shall bow and by it every tongue, which is in heaven or on earth, shall praise.'[70]

In this way it is appropriate for us to say in our petition, 'Our Lord Jesus, save us from the evil one and make

---

67. Gospel of Thomas, 1, 18, 19   69. Ep 4:22
68. Literally, 'perfects'—*gāmar*   70. Ph 2:10
(participle).

us according to your will. Our Father who is in heaven, blessed is Jesus Christ. Save us from temptations and make us according to your acceptable and perfect will.' Since Paul knew that without this name our road would not ascend to the top, he commanded us, 'Everything we do in word and in deeds, do in the name of our Lord Jesus Christ'.[71] Keep his words and you will triumph over the evil one and [Jesus] will save you.

The end of the twenty-ninth *Mēmrā*, which is on the discipline of the body.

---

71. Col 3:17

Mēmrā Thirty

ON THE
COMMANDMENTS OF FAITH AND
THE LOVE OF THE SOLITARIES

Summary: The second longest *mēmrā* begins by distinguishing between the commandments and disciples of faith and love—the latter being intermediary between the Upright and the Perfect. A summary of the standards of Perfection is given. The author concludes the work with a strong affirmation of the ministry and salvation of the Upright, Zacchaeus being the model.
(c.860)

1.   [This *mēmrā* is] concerning the commandments of faith and of love, as well as the way of life of the solitaries, [showing] how a person might know how to pursue love and ascend to Perfection.

The Savior will come to whoever wishes to become a solitary and pursue solely the commandments of love, for the commandments of love are distinguished from those of faith, which is inferior to love. Because the commandments of faith educate all children and sick ones, and appeal to those who do not know God, [faith] commands and reminds them that they should be fleeing from the company of evil people, until they are educated and are strengthened (c.861) and can distinguish one utterance from another—which is the greater and which is the lesser, which is hateful and which is virtuous. [Faith] assists them in this way, even if they [have to] isolate themselves for a brief time from cruel and evil people. It is better for them to be isolated from boastful, troublesome, and debauched people, [along with] harlots, adulterers, and covetous ones, than to be led away through their innocence and ignorance by their evil teaching and completely perish.

For this reason faith isolates its disciples from every brother who behaves wickedly, or from one who has something impure in him, until they grow up and are strong and securely established. Then they will become disciples of universal love, which is superior to faith, for [love] teaches its disciples something superior to faith, but is not useful to its disciples. Because faith commands its disciples, 'Distance [yourselves] from being with evil men and from every brother who behaves wickedly',[1] [faith] knows that its disciples are young and do not as yet understand how to distinguish which are the commandments of faith and which are those of love. As a person ascends from love to Perfection, in order that they may not be troubled and perish, [faith] establishes for them a temporary law until (c.864) they have strength and are filled with knowledge; [faith] will then commit them to love in order to instruct them [in] Perfection, and make them acquire that great, acceptable, and perfect mind of Christ.

2.   The commandments of love are more lowly than those of faith; they are all [things] to all [people].[2] But the commandments of faith are harder than those of love; they flee from being with evil ones. They were made [almost] as the opposite to one another. Faith and love [are both] educators of the young. Faith says to its disciples, 'Do not eat with adulterers, or with any brother who behaves wickedly'.[3]

1. 2 Th 3:6   3. 1 Co 5:11; 2 Th 3:6
2. 1 Co 9:22

Love [on the other hand] teaches its disciples since it knows they have the strength,

> I am sending you as lambs among wolves[4] so that you might be good ones among evil ones in order to convert them. Be innocent like doves and cunning like snakes,[5] so that you may be all [things] with all [people][6] and know how to speak with everyone in order to give vegetables to the sick and milk to the infants, and [the minor] commandments to the Upright and solid food to the Perfect and the strong, so that you may take on the illness of the sick.[7] Bless whoever curses you and love whoever hates you, and pray for whoever persecutes you[8] and deals harshly with you. Have in your mind to become (c.865) like lambs for the slaughter, just as it is written, 'Because of you, our Lord, we die everyday and have become like sheep for the slaughter'.[9]

Faith, which knows love, teaches its disciples as if it does not know [faith]. Because love knows where its disciples are going, they will help the sinners and evil ones. If they enter the house of licentious ones they will greatly chasten them, and [if they enter the house of] sinners they will greatly justify them, and [if they enter the house of] adulterers they will actually sanctify them. [Even] if they do not help them, the disciples of love will not fall from their truth. [Love] commands them, 'Consider everyone as better than yourself';[10] while knowing in your mind that you are better than he, as you enter [the home of] everyone and teach everyone.

4. Mt 10:16
5. Mt 10:16
6. 1 Co 9:22
7. Rm 15:1
8. Mt 5:44
9. Ps 44:23
10. Ph 2:3

Lower yourself from the commandments of love and teach a young mind the commandments of faith, which are lower than love. Once you have taught him how to walk resolutely in faith, go [back] up to Perfection and consider him better than you, and place him in front of you and greet and bow down to him, since you are inferior to him.

3. Perfection is tied to love(c.868) because through love its building rises and is completed and perfected, and through [love, Perfection] grows and is glorified. Also [Perfection] teaches the disciples of love something better and greater, and raises them up to be perfect in Christ, as Paul said.[11] But the Perfect one loves and is perfected knowing everything, as it is written, 'A man in the Spirit judges everything, but he is not judged by anyone'.[12] Because he is exalted and great, and because he has loved this one, he knows everything necessary for him to know.

Therefore, this person who has loved and is perfected, is able to build up the church because he knows with whom it is necessary to speak the commandments of faith so that he might be preserved and saved through them; and with whom it is necessary to speak the commandments of love so that he might profit through them, and to whomever it is right to teach the ministry of Perfection so that he might become great through it. For just as solid food is dangerous for an infant a day old, so milk is harmful to whoever has been weaned from the breasts and has tasted solid food.

It is said in the prophet, 'To whom shall he teach knowledge and to whom shall he explain the message? To him who has been weaned from milk or to one who has [just] been drawn away from the breasts'.[13] That is, the people who love all the minor commandments, which are milk and inferior knowledge. (c.869) They do not wish to

11. Col 1:28   12. 1 Co 2:15   13. Is 28:9

move up to the major commandments, which are solid food and complete knowledge. Because of this, no one is able to discern the whole will of God, which is acceptable and perfect, because through it a person could know the whole truth of the new world and live with the dwellers of that city of saints, which is the higher Jerusalem, [and live] with our Lord forever and ever.

4.   Therefore, the disciples of faith confront the disciples of love, ignorantly persecuting them, [while] the disciples of love endure, as it is written, 'Love endures all things and bears all things'.[14]

The disciples of faith also endure the heretics, are persecuted by the idolaters—because they are their opponents—and, being killed, become martyrs. They are known as martyrs of faith and as [martyrs] of love. The martyrs of faith are persecuted and killed by idolaters and pagans, because they resolutely confront them for their evil doctrine, tearing down their altars and enduring wherever they are persecuted in order not to become vain idolaters in the land of the Lord our God, (c.872) but [in order to] 'Serve only the Lord God who made heaven and earth and all which is in them'.[15] Because of this excellent zeal, they are killed while not loving their murderers and their persecutors, condemning them while they are indeed dying on account of our Lord. There are some who have sins and are forgiven, because they die for the sake of our Lord lest they renounce him. And there are those who do not have sins who are not yet perfected, since they do not love their murderers nor pray for them. Therefore, in that [the martyrs of faith] do not repay them the evil things that they do to them, [even] if they could, because of this the martyrs who do not have sins are better than these martyrs who do have sins.

14. 1 Co 13:7   15. Ac 14:15

The Book of Steps

However, the martyrs of love are persecuted and killed by the members of the household of faith. Since they teach the idolaters with lowliness, they do not kill them but rejoice over them. But. since the members of the household of faith believe that they have understood the whole truth through faith, when a person of love speaks something that is hidden from them, they are stirred up against him and kill him, [saying,] 'Why do you teach something that is not proclaimed in the whole church?' They do not (c.873) understand that if a person does not love as our Lord and his apostles loved, he will not understand the whole truth, and 'vainly he will be puffed up in the mind of his flesh',[16] as said Paul.

But the martyrs of love who imitate Stephen and the apostles teach that love is not jealous[17] nor does it persecute, and it does not hate, nor does it get angry, but sincerely loves and honors everyone. Faith does not command its disciples to kill the evil ones, but to flee from their presence and to expel [the evil ones] from their midst. Therefore, these who kill do not become the disciples of faith, but are disciples of Satan.

5.   My brothers, when one or another of us hears a word difficult for him to obey, let us imitate Gamaliel. If something we hear is pleasant for us, [excellent]; if not, let us keep that person away from us and not kill him and die ourselves for his murder. But, let us speak as Gamaliel did to the people in the *Acts of the Twelve Apostles,* 'Leave these people [alone], for if this undertaking is from deception it will destroy [itself] and its doers; but if it is from God, there is no one [who will be able] to destroy or render it void'.[18] (c.876)

Let us be careful.[19] When the persecution of these martyrs of faith and of these martyrs of love is equal, and

---

16. Col 2:18
17. 1 Co 13:4
18. Ac 5:38-39

19. Literally, 'let us be with ourselves'.

the murder of both is the same, these martyrs of love are much greater, not only than those martyrs who hate and despise their killers and persecutors, but also [greater] than those martyrs who do not hate their killers and persecutors, but do not love or pray for them nor condemn them. For when these martyrs of love were being killed, they prayed for their murderers and persecutors and blessed them with their love, just as our Lord and his apostles had done, [and] they will become very great and be glorified with our Lord.

6. These martyrs of faith were [also] killed for the sake of our Lord, some of them hating their murderers and persecutors and some not hating them, but not loving them [either]. All of them died on account of the name of our Lord without renouncing him and due to this their faults were forgiven and our Lord rewarded them for their good deeds. They were not able to become as great as these martyrs of love and Perfection, even if they did not have any sins, because they did not understand (c.877) love and Perfection like them. [Still, the martyrs of faith] on this side of them are virtuous. But our Lord exalted above everyone these martyrs of love and of Perfection who were killed while being perfect and they were glorified with him, just as they had suffered with him.[20]

If there are some who loved and were perfected, but [their enemies] did not kill them, they are Perfect ones just the same as these martyrs who were killed, because they also suffered and endured evil things, although no one assailed and killed them—just as [in the case of] some of the Twelve apostles who died by their own natural death and escaped, no one killed them. Perhaps they were greater than those who were killed, just as we know that John, that disciple whom Jesus loved more,[21] was greater. It is written that he died by a natural death and no one killed him. So

20. Rm 8:17   21. Jn 21:28

then, is [John] not as great as these apostles who were killed?

7.　　Between the disciples of love and these disciples who minister in Perfection there is peace. When they speak with one another they do not contend about anything, because love does not (c.880) contend with its teachers, but they speak their words persuasively. If the disciples of love are able to receive the ministry of Perfection [good], and if not, they depart in peace from one another, because love rules over both sides.

The knowledge of the Perfect ones is rich. [The Perfect ones] are greater than the disciples of love—these who have not as yet attained Perfection—for [the disciples of love] will not have yet actually reached the ministry of Perfection. When the time comes that they will be able to attain it by the power of love that teaches them, they will receive Perfection without dispute, be initiated in [Perfection], grow great through it, and be glorified through the grace of our Lord who redeems them from the death that dwells in their body, which is hidden sin, and from a veil, which is the hidden darkness, the hosts of the enemy which stands between them and our Lord.

But if the disciples of love do not attain and receive the ministry of Perfection, their love will not be enriched quite yet and they will remain deficient of the power of universal love. If they wish to love more, and possess the power of love and its knowledge, they must attain the ministry of Perfection, receiving it and being perfected through it. (c.881)

8.　　The disciple of faith flees from the company of evil people and sinners, because [faith] teaches him to do this. So long as his knowledge is immature, murderous sin resides within him, for he does not yet know that he ought to love the evil ones and lower himself before them. But love does not allow the disciple of love—[who] while recognizing [who are] the evil ones and the proud, the haughty, the boastful, and the sinners more than anyone [does]—to make distinctions among them, saying to them, 'I will not be mixed up with you; I will not speak [with you]', though he will strongly rebuke and admonish [them].

If there are some who despise and beat, persecute and kill him, he is unable wherever he sees transgression and turmoil not to rebuke and admonish, set in order, teach, and coax patiently. But after he teaches and rebukes, he thinks little of himself and impoverishes his spirit, and regarding those who are inferior to him as greater than he, bows down to them and grows in the lowliness of our Lord.

The disciple of faith, because his soul is not yet able to teach and rebuke and is impatient, says the following, 'Why should I bother teaching someone and being despised?' The disciples of love despise themselves, saying that they are impious while they are righteous, in order to love the impious and honor them (c.884) and in order to love their enemies and pray for them. They are despised in [their] lowliness of mind so that they might be fools for the sake of Christ[22] and consider evil ones better than themselves. They become good servants through their love for everyone, and love and honor the evil ones as they would the good ones, just as our Lord became a good servant of the many, of the good and of the evil through his love, and suffered their insult and honored and prayed for them.

9. With cunning the disciples of love know the bad from the good, in order not to lead them astray and to reward them good things instead of bad. As long as a person does not lead you astray from the road of our Lord and from his love, be gentle as a dove[23] with everyone while you are enriching many through the knowledge of the passions of our Lord and of his crucifixion. But when a person seeks to steer you away from the love of our Lord and from his passions, be cunning like a serpent[24] and do not err and

22. 1 Co 4:10   23. Mt 10:16   24. Mt 10:16

do not make the many err with you.

The disciples of faith discern the evil ones from among the good and make [the evil ones] leave, saying to them, 'Get out, you tares, doers of evil deeds, from among the wheat. Far be it from us that we should associate with you or pray with you, or that (c.885) you should stand with us in worship or come near us.'

10.   Listen to me, o members of the household of faith, and I will instruct you how you can grow great pleasantly until [you attain] the peace and the bread and the water and the garment and the washing of feet. Do not say that 'so and so is worthy' and 'so and so is not worthy', but when you see someone hungry or thirsty or naked or oppressed, whether he is evil or good, greet him earnestly and be justified through him. Until [you attain] the teaching and the [complete] education of the mind, do not say that the teaching of 'so and so' and of another is the same, until you truly examine many [teachings]. Is the knowledge of all the sons of the church equal? Do all the sons of the church teach according to the will of our Lord? Is the education of everyone the same?

Be careful until your knowledge is great enough and you know the whole truth as it is, until you break the power of sin and until you are experienced and know everything. Distinguish one teacher from another and one educator from another until you know the way of our Lord and travel directly on it. Do not give your attention to everyone so long as you are young, because everyone will sow in you (c.888) his seed and you will be confused with many seeds. Because of this, the first law reminds, 'Be careful, do not put on a garment made of different materials';[25] that is, be careful, do not accept all teachings because the seed of every person is not the same.

25. Lv 19:19

11.   There is one who sows wheat and is a good teacher. There is another who sows barley and is lacking in his knowledge. Then there are the rest [who sow] other [kinds of] grains that do not even enter the barns. For, our king stores the good wheat in his storehouses of light.[26] There are some who sow tares and some who sow thorns, that is, some who teach falsehood and some who stray and make those who listen to him stray.

Therefore, if you give food and clothing to the evil and the good and greet them, nothing will harm you, but great righteousness will be yours because our Lord will reward you in heaven. But if you give your attention and consort with evil ones as long as your mind is young, you will err easily and your destruction will happen quickly. On account of this, our Lord said, 'Do not throw something holy to the dogs, nor pearls before swine, lest they trample them with their feet and turn around and tear you away from your teaching,.[27] Look, see (c.889) how our Lord called the earth which does not know itself, 'a race of dogs and swine', which means a person who on account of transitory possessions will make for himself many lords[28] — [that is,] many doctrines or many counselors—and destroy his soul because he did not let it out to the good plowman,[29] who is the true teacher.

12.   Therefore, one should not have to trust everyone, but his peace should be extended to everyone, as it is written, 'Peace to those who are far away and to those who are near',[30] says the Lord, to whom everything belongs. But listen to me, members of the household of faith, and do not walk contrarily: when a person teaches you to greet the good along with the evil, and give them food and clothing, do not become involved with the evil ones and learn their

26. Mt 13:30
27. Mt 7:6
28. Gospel of Philip 119

29. Gospel of Philip 115
30. Is 57:19

evil deeds and risk dying through their ways of life. Moreover, whenever someone says to you, 'Do not associate with
evil people and do not learn their doctrine until you understand which is the truth', then, when whoever is concerned
about you tells you, 'Guard against evil ones', do not go
and become their enemies, persecutors, and evil ones and
do not become evil ones yourselves. But, if you are able on
your own part, greet every person (c.892) 'and especially
the members of the household of faith'.[31] For no one has
the right to despise anyone who is human, nor to scorn
him, nor to deny him anything he asks, if there is something for which he asks, and there shall be no anxiety or
distress on account of this request. For it is said, 'It is not
that you should become a relief to others and a burden to
yourself, but you should be in a state of balance in this
world'.[32]

13.   Live this way, my sons, and see who is reliable and
straight, rational and orderly, loving and patient, and teaches
the truth. Keep close to him and cleave to him. May your
foot tread on his doorstep everyday until you understand
the truth and thoroughly learn the way of our Lord and his
steps. But as long as you are young, you are not authorized to be all [things] with all [people] and to walk with
everyone. That is, until you grow up you should not associate with licentious men and women, but with whomever
admonishes you and holds you back from evil things, and
teaches you [how] to become people who give honor and
[are] not insolent ones, just as our Lord teaches you by his
spirit and grace to become sheep among wolves and good
ones among the evil.[33] You have the right to speak humbly
(c.893) about yourself, 'We are wicked', while you are righteous. But you do not have the right to call someone else
'wicked', whether he is wicked or righteous.

31. Ga 6:10
32. 2 Co 8:13
33. Mt 10:16

Therefore, when our Lord taught, he taught with discernment and offered each one the food that aided his illness, like a wise physician who knows which food is good and helpful to the sick person, lest he eat something not suitable for him and disease afflict him; in the same way, the Perfect one teaches everyone with discernment. He gives milk to one whose mind is young; that is, something that is easier for him to digest. He gives vegetables to one whose conscience is ill; that is, something that is appropriate to his conscience. 'With the sick I was sick so that I might gain the sick.[34] And with those who had no law, I became as a lawless man, while my heart is in the law of Christ, in order that I might also gain those who are without the law.[35] And to those who had reached Perfection, I gave them solid food.'

14. The teacher has the right to say to one of his disciples, 'Go among the tax-collectors and sinners and adulterers and among the wicked and heathens', because he knows he is a good swimmer and is able to cross over (c.896) the Euphrates while it is stormy and the sea while it is troubled. He commands his other disciple, who knows that he is not able to cross over the Lesser Zaba,[36] 'You should not talk with such and such a person, and you [should not] go to such and such place. Beware of the tax-collectors and of the sinners and adulterers, and of all who are licentious and talk idly and live wickedly.[37] Do not be involved with the cursers or the greedy or the gluttons or the idol worshipers.'[38]

With one disciple he speaks love and health and simplicity;[39] and with the other disciple he speaks illness and division and caution because he knows that this is necessary for him, as our Lord said to his disciples while they were immature, 'Do not travel on the road of the Gen-

---

34. 1 Co 9:22
35. 1 Co 9:21
36. The Lesser or Little Zab

River is a branch of the Tigris River in present-day northeast Iraq.

37. 1 Co 6:9; 2 Th 3:6
38. 1 Co 5:11
39. Mt 10:16

tiles'.[40] But after they had received the spirit of the Paraclete, he said to them, 'Go among the Gentiles and be good people among the evil, and eat whatever they place before you',[41] just as [Jesus] went among the tax-collectors and harlots and sinners.[42]

He commands others, 'Inquire who is worthy and go with him'.[43] He commanded [yet] another group of his disciples to love those who hate them and pray for them.[44] He commands others, 'Whoever does not obey you, consider him to be like the tax-collectors and pagans'.[45] (c.897) While to others he said, 'Blessed are the peacemakers, for they shall be called the children of God'.[46] He said to others, 'Whoever does not say to you, 'I repent', do not forgive him'.[47] Paul commanded his disciples, 'Do not eat bread with adulterers, nor associate with evil people'.[48] [Paul] commanded others, 'Take up the illness of the sick and consider everyone as better than yourselves'.[49]

15.   Why is a person not able to make peace with everyone? First, if his love has not grown, he will not abandon the law of sin to make peace with everyone. [Second, if] his mind is weak, he is not able to make peace with everyone, lest on the pretext of peace he becomes involved with evil ones and is destroyed, or he is continually in the company of wayward ones and perishes. Moreover, he commands others, 'Work and then you may eat'.[50] He commands still others, 'Be like ones dead to the world, and seek and think of what is above and not of what is on the earth'.[51] There were many other commandments that our Lord·and his disciples commanded and they were different from each other.

40. Mt 10:5
41. Lk 10:8
42. Mt 9:10, 11:19; Mk 2:16
43. Mt 10:11
44. Mt 5:44
45. Mt 18:17

46. Mt 5:9
47. Mt 18:15
48. 1 Co 5:11
49. Ph 2:3
50. 2 Th 3:12
51. Col 3:1

16.   Look above, everything is explained by us, how even
the prophets somewhere [in Scripture] said (c.900) to their
disciples, 'Sacrifice to the Lord bulls and sheep and goats'.[52]
But to others they commanded, 'The Lord does not desire
sacrifices[53] and [God] does not eat the flesh of calves nor
drink the blood of goats,[54] nor even does he accept whole
burnt-offerings. The sacrifices of God are a lowly spirit and
he loves a sincere heart'.[55] In [another] place they said, 'He
requires a cheek for a cheek.'[56]

   And in [another] place they said, 'Blessed is whoever
carried your burden in his youth. And he sat by himself
and was silent because he received upon himself your burden and placed his mouth in the dust and [offered] his cheek
to whoever would strike him and filled his life with reproach.'[57] In [another] place they said, 'Whoever approaches
a dead [body] becomes impure'.[58] However, in [another]
place, 'They bore the bones of Joseph on their shoulders
and were not contaminated'.[59] In [another] place, they
brought back the dead to life, the sons of widows, and were
not made impure.[60]

   In [another] place, 'Keep the Sabbath'.[61] Yet in [an-
other] place they broke the Sabbath and the precepts of the
Law, and entered among the impure, because the Law was
not established for the just and the upright, for the good
and the virtuous; they established the good law for themselves, also for whomever hears them. (c.901)

   For this reason the Law does not have authority over
them to judge them, because they do the will of our Lord
more than when it was written in the Law.[62] The Law was
intended for other sinners in order to have authority over
them. They said to them, 'If you transgress, you will die',

52. Lv 1:2
53. Jr 6:20
54. Ps 50:13
55. Ps 51:17
56. Ex 21:24
57. Lm 3:27-30

58. Nb 19:11
59. Ex 13:19
60. 1 K 17:21-24; 2 K 4:24
61. Lv 19:3
62. Rm 2:14

because they knew that since they do not have the good law in their hearts, it is appropriate for them to be constrained under the law, and if they are not constrained in this way, the murderous sin hidden in their heart would kill them.

17. There are commandments that each person is permitted to use. There are other commandments that the majority of the world is not permitted to use. But these people, who have our Lord in them and are full of his spirit and purified from sin, walk as our Lord himself shows them. The law forcefully compels these [other] people, who were not as yet filled by our Lord [for] sin [still] resides in them, lest they have authority over everything. For, unless they are filled by our Lord and are emptied of sin, they can not find the strength for everything.

18. The wise and experienced disciples, who (c.904) are students of heavenly wisdom and desire to seriously learn, seek out the true teachers who imitate our Lord and his apostles who are his disciples because they imitate him through their love, their lowliness, their poverty, and their asceticism. When they find teachers who are like this, they do not transgress against the word of their fathers who are their teachers, just as Timothy obeyed Paul even as far as [the matter of] the cup of wine about which he wrote to him in a letter, because he knew that he should not drink without his command.

[Paul] wrote to him, 'Drink a little wine for your occasional ailments and for your stomach'.[63] Because he knew that his body was worn out and that it had died from sin as it is written, 'If Christ is within you, the body is dead on account of sin; but the spirit is alive on account of righteousness'.[64] Because he knew that as long as sin resided in his body, he [needed to] guard his soul from foods and

63. 1 Tm 5:23　　　　　　　64. Rm 8:10

from wine. When [Timothy] had defeated sin [Paul] wrote him, 'Take a little emollient because your body has died'. Therefore, we who have become disciples (c.905) [only] yesterday, sin [still] residing in us, and our body [still] alive with transient desires—for these swallow up the soul and the body—we learn that Paul wrote to Timothy to drink wine on account of his ailments. But when we also acquire ailments from [too] much fasting and our knees grow weak from asceticism,[65] and our body is dead from sin as the body of Timothy died from evil thoughts, then may we drink a little, as it is written, on account of our illnesses.

19. We discover, moreover, that our Lord commanded his disciples, 'Whenever you enter a Gentile home, eat whatever they place before you and do not ask [about it]'.[66] To whom did our Lord say [this]? [He spoke] to these disciples who had received the spirit, the Paraclete, and were perfected and filled with the spirit until it poured forth from them upon others, and their hearts were purified from sin and they were full of the grace and righteousness of our Lord Jesus Christ. When we have been purified from sin and are filled with grace and righteousness like them, let us eat whatever is placed before us, a little as is appropriate, and not ask [about it]. For in this way it is written, 'The apostles ate vegetables and salt and olives (c. 908) and fasted continually'.

In this way, our Lord wrote and commanded them, 'Be careful not to weigh down your hearts with fleshy food and with drinking of wine and with the anxiety of habitation and with thought of this transitory wealth'.[67] But we sit [like] children whose bodies are alive with sin and observe old men, whose bodies have grown old, who drink a drop of wine on account of their ailments. And we say, 'We will drink like "so and so"; and what is the difference between "so and so" and me who eats and drinks, enters among the evil ones or speaks to and teaches women [who knows] how many times? Because you observe him today eating or drinking or being able to speak with everyone, be aware that while you were sucking milk by night and by day, he was truly fasting and praying day and night, and he struggled with and crucified his body from all desires. He came to a good old age,[68] as David had said, 'There will be a good end for Upright people'.[69]

20. Let us rebuke our soul and say to it, 'When you have become like "so and so" and you have fasted as he had fasted, and you have died from lusts and evil thoughts, and you have gained a good name up to the age (c.909) that "so and so" attained, then I will allow you to eat and drink with grace and order'.

Not even for those who are older and are troubled still, knowing in their soul that sin resides in them and the power of sin is still strong in them and [sin] leads them to things that are not right, is it not right to reject foods or not to speak with [just] anyone, until they subdue their bodies and obey them as Paul said, 'I subdue and subjugate my body lest I, who have proclaimed to others, will myself be rejected'.[70] But they will grow strong in their old age, fasting, becoming lowly, keeping vigil, and guarding their soul as long as sin is young in them. Also, when they have triumphed, they will be chaste and walk in the ways of asceticism on account of their lowliness, while not needing [to be so], in order to become an example to their disciples by their deeds as well as by their words, in the model of our Lord, for that is virtuous. They will become a good example to those who follow them. For the apostles also behaved in this way, so that when they died from sin, they fasted continually, kept vigil, prayed, and 'laid up good treasures (c.912) for their children',[71] as it is written.

68. Gn 15:15   70. 1 Co 9:27
69. Ps 37:39   71. 2 Co 12:14

21.   Love, because it has conquered death, is not ashamed to admonish every person and say the following to its disciples, 'The Jews ask for signs and the Gentiles seek wisdom; but we proclaim Jesus Christ crucified, and imitate him',[72] when he becomes the servant of his disciples, thinking less of himself than his creation.

One should not be like these Jews for whom the lowliness of Christ became a stumbling-block and were forever asking for signs like those lacking in faith, nor like those Gentiles who seek wisdom and elegant speech, and seek to speak to our Lord with great rhetoric and with excellent praises. Because they did not imitate the lowliness [of Christ], the passions of our Lord became for them his scornful contemptibility and they were ashamed of his lowliness, saying, 'This is contemptible'. But [our Lord] said, 'Whoever is ashamed of me and of my lowliness, my deeds, my poverty, and my asceticism, I will also be ashamed of him on that great day when I will be revealed in my glory'.[73] Woe to him who shall be ashamed of our Lord. How much he will be ashamed on that great day of our Lord.

Those who are like this are not able to endure[74] the cross (c.913) of Christ. [That is,] neither the Jews who ask for signs, nor the Gentiles who seek wisdom, which is empty of the passion, love, and lowliness of our Lord, can find the heavenly wisdom that is completely full of the passion, love, and lowliness of our Lord. But there come to the Jews people of knowledge and love, in which Perfection and lowliness ascends, by which that whole building of the heavenly house is completed, but because [these persons]·do not make signs, they become a stumbling block for those who are lacking in faith. Therefore, let us not be ashamed of the passions of our Lord, [nor be ashamed] of his lowliness and of his need, as Paul wrote, 'Do not be ashamed of the lowliness of Christ, nor even of us who are his prisoners,[75] but observe Jesus who became the first fruits and the

72. 1 Co 1:22-23
73. Lk 9:26

74. Literally, 'to be persecuted by the cross'.
75. 2 Tm 1:8

head and perfecter of your faith,[76] and imitate him'. Whoever says, 'I love Jesus', must walk according to his commandments.

22.   There are the commandments that our Lord and his apostles established for the people to keep in order to be saved. However, it is not like this: 'A person should love evil people or whomever has faults (c.916) even if a few', because the hearers [of these commandments] were not capable of the power of love that loves and pacifies all things, which prays for its persecutors and for its murderers. But, 'Love good people and whoever is better than you', for the sake of education of the mind so that they might learn from better [people] whatever is right for them. As long as they do not persecute and kill the evil ones, shall they not become great?

[But] as long as they do not love and pray for everyone and for their persecutors and murderers, they have abandoned the first law, which contains the commandments our Lord and the prophets had established. For [these commandments], not only held people back from love like these of the New Testament, but commanded [them] to do evil to the evil ones. In certain places [the prophets] even actually murdered because in this way it was better for their hearers, as it is written (c.917) above concerning these judgments by which no one is saved, but through them his torment became a little easier.

23.   Our Lord has been called, 'the first born of creation'.[77] It was not about these first creatures [that] the apostle spoke, but about these creatures who were created anew through the son of God.[78] The apostle said that they were made perfect through the son of God who became their firstborn. Some were creatures from the beginning and others were those who were made new through our Lord Jesus.

76. Heb 12:2   77. Col 1:15   78. 2 Co 5:17

That is to say, he is the creator of the first things and the one who makes the last things new. Everything came to be through him and through him they were created,[79] as it is written, 'Without him not even one thing came to be'.[80]

24.   'For our Lord was and is from the time his Father is, from everlasting and forever and ever, without limit.'[81] For no one among human beings was perfected until our Lord was perfected before them—while he had no need [to be] except to teach them how they should become perfect. Because of this, he is called 'the first born of the Perfect ones';[82] that is, (c.920) the first Perfect one. Because people fell short of the Perfection through which God created Adam and [fell short of] the purity of heart that belonged to Adam while he had not yet sinned, and [fell short of] the holiness in which he was created in the image of the angels, on account of this, the apostle witnesses, saying, 'In Jesus everything is made new again'.[83] Therefore, our Lord came and was perfected while not needing to be, and was sanctified while not needing to be, and purified his heart just like one who was not pure. He gave a demonstration to people so that they might imitate him and be perfected. He became the first born of Perfection in heaven and on earth. Amen.

25.   That great and acceptable and perfect will of our Lord[84] is this: all people should maintain their virginity and empty themselves and sanctify their hearts from all hateful thoughts of sin, and imitate our Lord, lifting up his cross and following him[85] and becoming perfect through his

79. Col 1:16
80. Jn 1:3
81. A free rendering of the Nicene definition of the co-existence of Christ and God, perhaps in the style of Jn 8:58.
82. Col 1:15
83. 2 Co 5:17
84. Rm 12:2
85. Mt 10:38

universal love that makes peace with all, as he had said,
'Whoever does not leave everything he has and everything
he possesses on the earth and [leave] his father and his
mother, his brothers and his sisters, his sons, and his family, and rise above (c.921) sexuality, is not worthy of me'.[86]

Truly, my brothers, whoever does not act this way is
not worthy to be glorified with our Lord. Because our Lord
had seen that all people fall short of this Perfection, which
is only acquired through strenuous effort, since this door
is very narrow,[87] a person is able to enter through it only
with tremendous effort, and except for the few who compel themselves through lowliness and patience, no one can
attain this portion of Perfection. In order that the whole
world not be afraid of this effort, and fall short through
fear and perish, our Lord compassionately lowered himself and gave other lesser commandments [that] were not
very difficult and inferior to that major commandment.
People are able to perform them while they are in their
homes with their wealth and their wives and children, and
[still] be saved.

26. But there is another commandment that is inferior to
the first one: 'Dwell with your father and your mother and
honor them; do not kill; do not commit adultery; do not
steal; do not bear false witness; do not desire and take anything that belongs to your neighbor;[88] and whatever you
hate that people do (c.924) to you, do not do to them.[89]
Love the Lord your God with all your heart and with all
your strength and with all your soul and with all your
mind;[90] and love your neighbor as yourself.'[91] Fast and
pray in right measure[92] and you will have eternal life, [even]
while you have your wealth and are in your house with

---

86. Mt 10:37, 19:29; Lk 14:26
87. Mt 7:14
88. Ex 20:12-17; Dt 5:16-22
89. Tb 4:16; Didache 1:2

90. Dt 6:5; Mt 22:37
91. Mt 22:39
92. Literally, 'fast your stations and
pray at your times'.

your wife and children. But if you desire to reach that great and perfect portion, 'Imitate me and be glorified with me; leave everything and take up your cross and follow me; but if not, you are not worthy of me'.[93]

27. Understand from this that people are saved if they do as they were commanded—[following] that precept that is lower than that perfect and superior precept, [even] while they are married and possessing wealth. [This is clear] by that demonstration when our Lord entered the house of Zacchaeus, a sinner and an extortioner and doer of evil things, and, admonishing him made him a disciple with these commandments, which are inferior to Perfection.

[Jesus] did not say to him, 'Unless you leave your wife and your house and your children and empty yourself from everything you own, you will not be saved'. Look, the response of Zacchaeus makes it clear that our Lord admonished him in such a way that he need not empty himself, because he knew that he could not reach the power of that great portion. (c.925) Zacchaeus said, 'Everyone whom I have cheated I will repay four-fold, and half of my wealth only I will give to the poor'.[94] See, while he did not say to our Lord, 'I will abandon everything I have', our Lord did say the following to him, 'Today salvation has come into this house'.[95] Zacchaeus shall be called a son of Abraham, he who when he promised to repay their lords what he had extorted had said, 'Half of my wealth only I will give'.[96] But whoever gives to the poor half of his wealth while not defrauding anyone, look, is he not greater than Zacchaeus, who was called righteous? When he gave two portions of his wealth, look, does not he grow greater still? Whoever gives all he possesses to the poor and the strangers, look, is [that person] not better and greater?

93. Mt 10:38; Lk 14:27
94. Lk 19:8
95. Lk 19:9
96. Lk 19:9

28.   Therefore, let no one say that whoever does not empty everything he has and follow our Lord is not saved. If people then desire to become sons of Abraham while being wealthy, as Zacchaeus had become, they will grow in abundance and receive whatever is better in the kingdom, as our Lord said to the Jews, 'But if you had been sons of Abraham, you would have done the deeds of Abraham,[97] and you would become the sons of Abraham through the deeds of Abraham, while you are with your wives and your children and your wealth (c.928) as when Abraham was with his wife and children, with his servants and all of his possession'.

[Abraham] did not treat anyone badly and he removed from them many evil things. He did good things with his wealth for all the people who were in need and encountered him. He walked among them and treated well [equally] the good [people] and the evil, those who treated him badly, and those who treated him well. With these he became an heir in heaven and an excellent example for all the generations after him so that they might imitate him. Because of this he became great and was glorified and called the ruler of the feast[98] so that all the Upright and the righteous might be comforted in the bosom of his righteousness.[99]

29.   You see that whoever wishes to imitate [the example][100] and hope of Abraham will be called by the righteousness of Abraham. For it is written in this way in [the Psalms of] David about people who love visible gain and property and marriage and children, yet wish to become Upright ones while keeping their possessions and be saved on the day of our Lord [for] eternal life. The prophet said the following, 'O Lord, who shall dwell in your tent and who shall dwell on your holy mountain,[101] among those who have property and visible possessions'. The Lord said to him, 'Who-

97. Jn 8:39
98. Mt 8:11
99. Lk 16:23

100. *Hawreh* ('the example of . . .')
missing in Ms R.
101. Ps 15:1

ever walks blamelessly and does (c.929) righteousness by means of his wealth and does not plan to do evil to anyone, neither in his heart nor with his tongue, and does not receive a bribe against anyone who is human, and does not harm anyone, neither the evil ones nor even the good ones, and neither the guilty nor the innocent'.[102]

But he will speak truthfully as [if] before God and dwell among the people who assail him [by] their judgments and their quarrels, and rejecting with his eyes those who provoke God with their evil deeds,[103] lest observing them he imitate their provocative deeds. He loves and honors those who fear the Lord[104] and comforts them by means of his possessions, listening to everyone who is afflicted and in need, hearing their words and receiving them, and providing an apologia for his deeds. He does not deceive concerning whatever they desire through him, and he does not lend his silver with interest,[105] but lends to the poor and takes from them [only] what he loans with his principle and not with interest. He gives to those who have nothing on account of God who commanded him, 'Give, and you will have righteousness in heaven,[106] and our Lord will reward you when this world and all in it has passed away'. He does not take a bribe against the innocent in order not to pervert justice on an innocent one and have him die by judgment on the day of our Lord.

Whoever (c. 932) does these things and endeavors to pray and fast in right measure[107] will not be troubled on that day of Judgment. Whoever acts this way will dwell in

102. Ps 15:2-5
103. Ps 15:2-5
104. Ps 15:2-5
105. Ps 15:5
106. Mt 6:1
107. Literally, 'through prayer according to his times, and then with the fast of his stations'.

my tent and reside on my holy mountain that is the comfort to come for the Upright, says the Lord Omnipotent, who seeks and judges and kills the evil ones, yet saves and forgives everyone who listens to him and does the will of our Lord, for to save the penitent or to kill the wicked is his prerogative.

The end of the thirtieth *Mēmrā*.

So are finished in this book the above thirty *mēmrē*, which are about the ways of Perfection and about the discernment of the commandments of our Lord that were set down by the blessed one who did not make known his name.

Bibliography

TEXT

Liber Graduum. Edited, translated, and introduced by Michael Kmosko (*Patrologia Syriaca* 3: Paris, 1926). Latin translation and introduction. Greek documents on Messalian controversy.

MODERN TRANSLATIONS.
Preface & Mēmrē 1-4, 6:
Parmentier, Martien F. G. *Liber Graduum: The Book of Grades* (Utrecht: Dutch Interchurch Aid, 1984).

Mēmrē 12 and 18:
Brock, Sebastian P. *The Syriac Fathers on Prayer and the Spiritual Life* (Cistercian Studies 101; Kalamazoo, Michigan: Cistercian Publications, 1987) 42-61.

Mēmrā 12:
Murray, Robert. *Symbols of Church and Kingdom* (Cambridge: Cambridge University Press, 1975) 264-268.

Mēmrā 14:
Wickham, Lionel. 'Teachings About God and Christ in the *Liber Graduum*', in *Logos: Festschrift für Luise Abramowski zum 8. Juli 1993* ed. H.C. Brennecke, E.L. Grasmück, C. Markschies (Berlin, New York: Walter de Gruyter, 1993) *Beihefte zur Zeitschrift für die Neutestamentliche Wissenschaft* 67 (1993) 496-498.

Mēmrē 1-30:
(English translation from Kmosko's Latin translation): translator unknown. Pusey House Library, Oxford (catalogue 63.50.c9) Photocopy of typescript. Preface omitted.

Arabic translation: *Kitab al Maraki,* translated by Fr Francis Baysari (Beirut, Lebanon: Paulist Press, 1989).

STUDIES

Abou-Zayd, Shafiq. *Ihidayutha: A Study of the Life of Singleness in the Syrian Orient. From Ignatius of Antioch to Chalcedon 451 A.D.* (Oxford,1993).

_____. 'Violence and Killing in the Liber Graduum,' *Aram* 11-12 (1999-2000) 451-465.

Aveta, Michela. 'Ad instar angelorum: Per un'analisi storico-religiosa dell'antropologia del Liber Graduum,' *Cristianesimo nella storia* 8 (1987) 481-500.

Bäss, Paul. 'Der Liber Graduum, ein messalianisches Büch?' in W. Voigt, ed. *XVII Deutscher Orientalistentag* (Wiesbaden, 1969, II) 368-374.

Baker, Aelred. 'Fasting to the World,' *Journal of Biblical Literature* 84 (1965) 291-294.

_____. 'The Gospel of Thomas and the Syriac Liber Graduum,' *New Testament Studies* 12 (1965/1966) 49-55.

_____. 'The Significance of the New Testament of the Syriac Liber Graduum,' *Studia Evangelica 5, Texte und Untersüchungen* 103 (Berlin, 1968) 171-175.

_____. 'Early Syrian Asceticism,' *Downside Review* 88 (1970) 393-409.

Bassari, F. 'Liber Graduum,' in *Patrimoine Syriaque V* (Antelias, 1998) 61-68.

Baumstark, Anton. *Geschichte der syrischen Literatur mit Ausschlus der christlich palästinischen Text* (Bonn, 1922) 165.

Bianco, M. G. 'Liber Graduum,' *Dizionario patristico e di antichità cristiane* (Il Casale Monferrato, 1984) 1944-1945.

Beggiani, S. J. *Introduction to Eastern Christian Spirituality: The Syriac Tradition* (University of Scranton Press,1991) 29-34.

Bettiolo, Paolo. 'Confessare Dio in perfetta spogliazione. La via del discernimento dei commandamenti nel Liber Graduum,' *Cristianesimo nella Storia* 19 (1998) 631-651.

Böhlig, Alexander. 'Zur Rhetorik im Liber Graduum,' *Orientalia Christiana Analecta* 229 (1987) 297-305.

Brown, Peter. *The Body and Society: Men, Women, and Sexual Renunciation in Early Christianity* (Columbia University Press: New York, 1988) cf. 334-337.

Caner, Daniel. *Wandering, Begging Monks: Spiritual Authority and the Promotion of Monasticism in Late Antiquity* (The Transformation of the Classical Heritage 33: Berkeley: University of California Press, 2002), esp. 106-112, 153-156.

Colless, Brian. 'The Book of Degrees and Adelphios of Edessa,' unpublished paper presented at the VIII Symposium Syriacum in Sydney, Australia, August 2000.

Corbett, John. 'They Do Not Take Wives or Build, or Work the Ground: Ascetic Life in the Early Syriac Christian Tradition,' Paper presented at Canadian Society for Syriac Studies public lecture, University of Toronto, January 22, 2003; *Canadian Journal of Syriac Studies* 3 (2003) 3-20.

Davids, A. J. M. 'Von der Anonymität zur Pseudonymität. Der Liber Graduum und das Corpus Macarianum,' in W. Voigt, ed. *XVII Deutscher Orientalistentag* (Wiesbaden, 1969, II) 375-379.

Desprez, Vincent. 'L'ascétisme mésopotamien au IVe siècle: III. Le 'Livre des degrés',' *La Lettre de Ligugé* 262 (1992) 16-29.

Dolabany, Filoksinos Yohanna. *Catalogue of Syriac Manuscripts in St. Mark's Monastery (Dairo DMor Marqos)* (Sidawi Printing House: Damascus, 1994) 377-380.

Doran, Robert. 'The Agraphon at Liber Graduum 3.3,' *CBQ* 63 (2001) 298-303.

Fitschen, Klaus. *Messalianismus und Antimessalianismus: Ein Beispiel ostkirchlicher Ketzergeschichte.* (Forschungen zur Kirchen- und Dogmengeschichte 71; Göttingen: Vandenhoeck und Ruprecht, 1998) cf. 108-119 re Liber Graduum.

Golitzin, Alexander. 'Recovering the 'Glory of Adam', 'Divine Light' Traditions in the Dead Sea Scrolls and the Christian Ascetical Literature of the Fourth-Century Syro-Mesopotamia,' Paper given at the International

Conference on the Dead Sea Scrolls, St. Andrews, Scotland, June 28, 2001. *http://www.marquette.edu/maqom/ Recovering*

Gribomont, Jean. 'Les homélies ascétiques de Philoxène de Mabboug et l'écho du messalianisme,' *Orient Syrien* 2 (1957) 419-432.

_____. 'Le Monachisme au IVe s. en Asie Mineure: de Gangres au Messalianisme,' (*Studia Patristica 2; Texte und Untersuchungen* 64; Berlin, 1957) 400-415.

_____. 'Liber Graduum,' *Dizionario degli Istituti di Perfezione* 5 (Rome, 1978) 641-642.

_____. 'Monasticism and Asceticism: Eastern Christianity,' in *Christian Spirituality: Origins to the Twelfth Century* (ed. B. McGinn, J. Meyendorff, J.Leclercq) (Routledge & Kegan Paul: London, 1986) 102.

Guillaumont, Antoine. 'Nêsteuein ton kosmon P. Oxy. 1, verso 1.5-6,' *Bulletin de l'Institut Français d'archéologie orientale* 61 (1962) 15-23.

_____. 'Les 'arrhes de l'Esprit' dans le Livre des degrés,' *Mémorial Mgr Gabriel Khouri-Sarkis*, (Louvain, 1969) 107-113.

_____. 'Christianismes orientaux,' *Annuaire de l'École de Hautes Études* 76 (1968/69), 77 (1969/70), 78 (1970/ 71) 180-183, 286-290, 262-266.

_____. 'Situation et signification du Liber Graduum dans la spiritualité syriaque,' *Symposium Syriacum 1972; Orientalia Christiana Analecta* 197 (1974) 311-322.

_____. 'Liber Graduum,' *Dictionnaire de Spiritualité* 9

(Paris, 1976) 749-754.

_____. 'Les 'Spirituels' et leur Rapports avec l'institution ecclésiastique dans le christianisme oriental des premiers siècles,' *Annuaire du College de France 1984-1985* (Paris, 1985) 491-497. Also in *Études sur le Spiritualité de l'Orient Chrétien* (Spiritualité Orientale 66; Abbaye de Bellefontaine, 1996) 179-187.

Harb, Paul. 'Le rôle exercé par Philoxène de Mabbûg sur l'évolution de la morale dans l'église syrienne,' *Parole de l'Orient* 1 (1970) 27-48.

Hausherr, Irenée. 'Quanam aetate prodierit Liber Graduum,' *Orientalia Christiana Periodica* 1 (1935) 495-502.

_____. 'L'erreur fondamentale et la logique du Messalianisme,' *Orientalia Christiana Periodica* 1 (1935) 328-360 [= *Études de spiritualité orientale, Orientlia Christiana Analecta* 183 (Rome, 1969) 64-96].

_____. 'Le Messalianisme,' *Atti del XIX Congresso Internazionale degli Orienta listi* (Rome, 1938) 634-636.

Juhl, Diana. *Die Askese im Liber Graduum und bei Afrahat: eine vergleichende Studie zur frühsyrisch Frömmigkeit (Orientalia Biblica et Christiana* 9; Wiesbaden: Otto Harrasowitz, 1996).

Kemmer, A. *Charisma maximum. Untersuchung zu Cassians Vollkommenheitslehre und seiner Stellung zum Messalianismus* (Lšwen, 1938) cf. 52-91 re Liber Graduum.

Kitchen, Robert A. *The Just and the Perfect in the Ascetical Homilies of Philoxenus of Mabbug and the Liber*

Graduum. M.A. dissertation, Catholic University of America, 1978.

_____ . 'The Gattung of the Liber Graduum: Towards a Sociology of Asceticism,' *Orientalia Christiana Analecta* 229 (1987) 173-182.

_____ . 'Conflict on the Stairway to Heaven: The Anonymity of Perfection in the Syriac *Liber Graduum,*' *Orientalia Christian Analecta* 256 (1998) 211-220.

_____ . 'Becoming Perfect: The Maturing of Asceticism in the Syriac Book of Steps,' *Canadian Journal of Syriac Studies* 2 (2002) 30-45.

_____ . 'Syriac Additions to Anderson: The Garden of Eden in the Book of Steps and Philoxenus of Mabbug,' *Hugoye: Journal of Syriac Studies* 6.1 (2003).

Kmosko, Michael. 'Praefatio' in *Liber Graduum, Patrologia Syriaca* 3 (Paris, 1926) i-cccvii.

Kowalski, Aleksander. 'Il sangue nel Liber Graduum,' in F. Vattioni (ed.), *Atti della Settimana Sangue e Antropologia nella letteratura cristiana* (Roma, 26 novembre-4 dicembre 1982) (Rome, 1983) III, 1193-1205.

_____ . *Perfezione e giustizia di Adamo nel Liber Graduum* (*Orientalia Christiana Analecta* 232; Rome, 1989).

_____ . 'Die Gebete im Liber Graduum,' *Orientalia Christiana Periodica* 55 (1989) 273-282.

_____ . 'Adam i Ewa jako dzieci w egzegezie syryjskiej,' *Roczniki Teologiczno-Kanoniczne* 30 (1983) fasc. 1, 117-122.

Lane, D. J. 'The Book of Grades, or Steps,' *The Harp* 14 (2001) 81-88.

Louf, A. 'Une ancienne exégèse de Phil. 2,6 dans le Ketaba deMasqata (Livre des degrés),' *Studiorum Paulinorum Congressus Internationalis Catholicus, Analecta Biblica* 17-18 (Rome, 1963) II, 523-533.

Martikainen, J. *Gerechtigkeit und Güte Gottes. Studien zur Theologie von Ephraem dem Syrer und Philoxenos von Mabbug,* (Wiesbaden, 1981) cf. 22-29 re *Liber Graduum.*

_____. 'Das Böse in den Schriften des Syrers Ephraem, in Stufenbuch und in Corpus Macarianum,' in W. Strothmann (ed.), *Makarios-Symposium über das Böse* (Wiesbaden, 1983) 36-46.

Mirkis, Yousif. *Le Liber Graduum. Livre des Montées,* I-II. Translation, notes, commentary and studies. Doctoral dissertation: Strasbourg, 1979.

Murray, Robert. *Symbols of Church and Kingdom: A Study in Early Syriac Tradition* (Cambridge, 1975) especially 34-36, 263-269.

Nagel, Paul. 'Die 'Martyrer des Glaubens' und die 'Martyrer der Liebe' im syrische Liber Graduum' in B. Kohler (ed.), *Religion und Wahrheit. Religiongeschichtliche Studien. Festschrift für Gernot Wiessner* (Wiesbaden, 1998) 127-142.

_____. 'Die sichtbare und die unsichtbare Kirche im syrischen 'Buch der Stufen' (*Liber Graduum*),' *Stimme der Orthodoxie* 3 (1996) (Festschrift Konrad Onasch) 40-42.

Ortiz de Urbina, I. *Patrologia Syriaca* (Rome, 1965, 2nd edition) 89-91.

Parsons, Fiona J. *The Nature of the Gospel Quotations in the Syriac Liber Graduum* Doctoral dissertation: University of Birmingham, 1969.

Persic, Allessio. 'La Chiesa di Siria e i 'gradi' della vita cristiana,' *Per foramen acus: Il cristienesimo antico di fronte alla pericope evangelica del 'giovane ricco'* ed. B. Maggioni & L. F. Pizzolato (*Studia Patristica Mediolanensia* 14; Milan: Vita e Pensiero, 1986) 208-263.

Ratcliff, Robert A. *Steps Along the Way of Perfection: The Liber Graduum and Early Syrian Monasticism* Doctoral dissertation: Emory University, 1988.

Roux, Renato. *Cristo esempio di umilta' da imitare. Sulla cristologia del Liber Graduum*, M.A. dissertation, Institutum Patristicum Augustinianum, Rome, 1993.

_____. 'The doctrine of the imitation of Christ in the Liber Graduum: Between Exegetical Theory and Soteriology,' *Studia Patristica* 30 (1997) 259-264.

Rücker, A. 'Die Zitate aus dem Matthäusevangelium im syrischen Buche der Stufen,' *Biblische Zeitschrift* 20 (1932) 342-354.

Stewart, OSB, Columba. *'Working the Earth of the Heart': The Messalian Controversy in History, Texts, and Language to AD 431* (Oxford, 1991).

Strothmann, Werner. 'Jesus-Sirach-Zitate bei Afrahat, Ephraem und in Liber Graduum,' in *A Tribute to Arthur Vööbus* R. Fischer (ed.) (Chicago, 1977) 153-158.

Terzoli, R. *Il tema della beatitudine nei Padri siri. Presente e futuro della salvezza* (Brescia, 1972) 149-177 re *Liber Graduum*.

Vööbus, Arthur. 'Liber Graduum: Some Aspects of its Significance for the History of Early Syrian Asceticism,' in *Charisteria Iohanni Kopp octogenario oblata (Papers of the Estonian Theological Society in Exile* 7; Stockholm, 1954) 108-128.

_____. *History of Asceticism in the Syrian Orient*, I (*Corpus Scriptorum Christianorum Orientalium* 184/Subsidia 14; Louvain, 1958) 178-184, 190-197.

_____. *History of Asceticism in the Syrian Orient*, III (*Corpus Scriptorum Christianorum Orientalium* 500/Subsidia 81; Louvain, 1988) 1-18.

Westerhoff, M. 'Zur Paulus-Rezeption im Liber Graduum: der Apostel als Vorbild,' in M.Tamcke ed, *Syriaca: Zu Geschichte Theologie Liturgie und Gegenwartslage der syrischen Kirchen (Studien z.Or. Kirchengeschichte* 17, 2002), 253-9.

Wickham, Lionel. 'Teachings About God and Christ in the Liber Graduum,' in *Logos: Festschrift für Luise Abramowski zum 8. Juli 1993* ed. H.C. Brennecke, E.L. Grasmück, C. Markschies (Berlin, New York: Walter de Gruyter, 1993) *Beiheft zur Zeitschrift für die neutestamentliche Wissenschaft* 67 (1993) 496-498.

_____. 'The "*Liber Graduum*" Revisited,' *Symposium Syriacum 6th*: Cambridge 1992; *Orientalis Christiana Analecta* 247 (1994) 177-187.

GENERAL WORKS ON SYRIAC CHRISTIANITY

Beggiani, S. J. *Early Syriac Theology with Special Reference to the Maronite Tradition* (Lanham, New York, 1983).

_____.*Introduction to Eastern Christian Spirituality: The Syriac Tradition* (University of Scranton Press,1991).

Bondi, Roberta C. 'The Spirituality of Syriac-speaking Christians,' in *Christian Spirituality I* (New York: 1986) 152-161.

Brock, Sebastian P. 'Early Syrian Asceticism,' *Numen* 20 (1973) 1-19.

_____. *Spirituality in the Syriac Tradition*, Moran Etho Series 2, (Kottyam, India: St. Ephrem Ecumenical Research Institute,1989).

Edwards, Jr., O. C. 'Extreme Asceticism in Early Syriac Christianity,' in *Worship Points the Way: A Celebration of the Life & Work of Massey Hamilton Shepherd, Jr.*, ed. Malcolm C. Burson (New York: The Seabury Press, 1981) 200-213.

Harvey, Susan Ashbrook. 'Creation and Asceticism: Syriac Christian Thought' in *Christian Thought: A Brief History*, ed. Adrian Hastings, Alistair Mason, and Hugh Pyper (Oxford: Oxford University Press, 2002) 33-37.

Moffatt, Samuel H. *A History of Christianity in Asia*, vol. I (Harper San Francisco, 1992)

Murray, s.j., Robert. 'The Features of the Earliest Christian Asceticism,' in *Christian Spirituality: Essays in honor of Gordon Rupp*, ed. Peter Brooks, (SCM Press: London, 1975) 65-77.

_____ . 'The Characteristics of Earliest Syriac Christianity,' in *East of Byzantium*, ed. N. Garsoian, T.W. Mathews, R.W. Thomson, (Washington, D.C.: Dumbarton Oaks, 1980.

Old, Hughes Oliphant. 'The Syriac Church' in *The Reading and Preaching of the Scriptures in the Worship of the Christian Church, volume 2: The Patristic Age* (Grand Rapids, Michigan: William B. Eerdmans, 1998) 247-295.

Scripture References
to Liber Graduum

Index to Proper Names
and Places